CAREER OPPORTUNITIES IN LAW ENFORCEMENT, SECURITY, AND PROTECTIVE SERVICES

CAREER OPPORTUNITIES IN LAW ENFORCEMENT, SECURITY, AND PROTECTIVE SERVICES

SUSAN ECHAORE-McDAVID

Facts On File, Inc.

CAREER OPPORTUNITIES IN LAW ENFORCEMENT, SECURITY, AND PROTECTIVE SERVICES

Checkmark Books
An imprint of Facts On File, Inc.
11 Penn Plaza
New York NY 10001

Library of Congress Cataloging-in-Publication Data

Echaore-McDavid, Susan.
    Career opportunities in law enforcement, security, and protective
services / by Susan Echaore-McDavid.
        p.   cm.
    Includes bibliographical references.
    ISBN 0-8160-3955-0.—ISBN 0-8160-3956-9 (alk. paper)
    1. Law enforcement—Vocational guidance—United States.
2. Police—Vocational guidance—United States. 3. Private security,
services—Vocational guidance—United States. 4. Safety engineers—
Vocational guidance—United States. I. Title.
HV8143.M2   1999
363.2′023′73—dc21   99-20619

Checkmark Books are available at special discounts when purchased in bulk quantities for businesses, associations, institutions or sales promotions. Please call our Special Sales Department in New York at (212) 967-8800 or (800) 322-8755.

You can find Facts On File on the World Wide Web at http://www.factsonfile.com

Text layout by Grace M. Ferrara
Cover design by Nora Wertz

Printed in the United States of America

VB FOF 10 9 8 7 6 5 4 3 2
    (pbk) 10 9 8 7 6 5 4 3 2 1

This book is printed on acid-free paper.

To Richard McDavid
and to
Frances D. Echaore
—two wonderful people who give me
lots and lots
of inspiration, joy, and love!

CONTENTS

ACKNOWLEDGMENTS

I am very grateful and thankful to all the individuals and organizations who provided me with information via the telephone, mail, and the Internet. In particular, I would like to thank the following: American Academy of Forensic Sciences; American Industrial Hygiene Association; American Society for Industrial Security; Charlottesville-Albemarle Rescue Squad, Inc.

Sgt. Jack Adkins, Bomb Squad Commander, Big Ben Bomb Squad, Tallahassee Police Department; Alex Arends, Crime Prevention Association of Michigan; David Arndt, Education Assistant, International Association of Fire Fighters; Patrick Barker, WALMART Investigation Task Force; Jon Berryhill, Berryhill Computer Forensics.

Jeanne Choy-Allen, Special Agent, Drug Enforcement Administration; Diane L. Cowan, Certified Legal Investigator; Jamey Crandall, Personnel Administrator, Nebraska Game and Parks; Leroy Dal Porto, Special-Agent-in-Charge, San Francisco Field Office, Secret Service; Joseph N. Dassaro, VP, Local 1613-San Diego, National Border Patrol Council; Dr. Edmund R. Donoghue, Chief Medical Examiner of Cook County, Illinois; Jerry Elder, VP, Airline Dispatchers Federation.

Rodney Eldridge, Loss Prevention Training Specialist, TJ Maxx; Tammy Empson, American Public Works Association; Janet Fox, Special Agent, Federal Bureau of Investigation; Amy Geffen, Director of Professional Development, Risk and Insurance Management Society; Ed German, Special Agent, United States Army Criminal Investigation Laboratory.

Robert Heard, President, California Association of Polygraph Examiners; Lt. Tom Honan, Charleston County Sheriff's Office, South Carolina; Morgan Hurley, Technical Director, Society of Fire Protection Engineers; Rhonda A. Jackson, Building Officials and Code Administrators International; M.E. Kabay, Ph.D., CISSP, Director of Education, ICSA, Inc.; Ken Kerle, Managing Editor, American Jail Association; Jim King, International Association of Personal Protection Agents; Chris Krall, CIRSA, Inc.; Robert E. Kramer, Investigator, Cedar Falls Police Department, Iowa; Mike Lane, Corporate Investigative Services; Donald C. Lhotka, CSP (Ret.), American Society of Safety Engineers.

Sgt. Steve Lindley, Anderson County Sheriff's Office, South Carolina; Ning Ludovico, U.S. Postal Inspection Service; Doug McDavid, Consultant, IBM Global Services; Mary McKendree, Manager, Assessment and Continuing Education, American Society of Clinical Pathologists; Gary Martin, North American Wildlife Enforcement Officers Association; Sgt. Jonathan B. Mills, Calistoga Police Department, California; Ron Morris, President, Sheffield School of Aeronautics; Jeff Obrecht, Information Officer, Services Division, Wyoming Game and Fish Department; Captain Ken R. Pence, Metro Nashville Police.

Detective Carl Rackley and Bubba, Cedar Park Police Department, Williamson County, Texas; Joseph Remigio, Special Agent, Deputy U.S. Marshal; Selwyn Russell, SIGMOD, Association for Computing Machinery; Glenn Sanders, Illinois Conservation Police; WCO John G. Smith, Pennsylvania Game Commission; Anthony W. Stoll, Master Indiana Conservation Officer, Indiana Conservation Officers Organization, VP.

Ralph Thomas, Director, National Association of Investigative Specialists, Inc.; Jim Watson, National Secretary, North American Police Work Dog Association; Emily Will, Questioned Documents Expert; Steve Wolin, Society of Fire Protection Engineers; Dawn Wright, Air Traffic Controller, Otis ANGB (Air National Guard Base), Massachusetts; Sgt. Brian Wunderlich, Douglas Co. Sheriff's Office, Castle Rock, Colorado.

Without the presence of the Internet, I doubt that I could have done this book. So, I must also give my thanks to all those dedicated webmasters who created and maintain the web sites—for all the police departments, sheriff's offices, fire departments, professional associations, organizations, institutions, federal agencies, universities, companies, libraries, etc.—that I have visited.

Finally, this book could not have been completed without the support and confidence of my husband, Richard McDavid, and my editor, James Chambers.

Thank you!

HOW TO USE THIS BOOK

So you're interested in a career in law enforcement, security, fire protection, or other protective service field. That's wonderful! This book—*Career Opportunities in Law Enforcement, Security, and Protective Services*—was written for you. It's also written for those of you who are already in protective services and want to explore other career possibilities. Further, this book is for those of you who just want to learn more about the many different protective service occupations that are available. Perhaps after reading some, or all, of the job profiles, you'll find a protective service field that's right for you.

Protective service jobs are often portrayed in the movies, TV shows, books, and media as exciting, intriguing, and yes, even dangerous. But how much of what you see or read is fictitious, and how much is real? What is a job—as a police officer, for example—really like? What requirements do you need to be eligible for a job? What are your chances of getting a job? What kind of career can you have? Those are some of the questions that are answered in this book. In fact, you'll learn about 79 protective service jobs in the areas of law enforcement, forensic investigations, corrections, security, private investigations, computer security, fire protection, emergency services, compliance inspections, code enforcement, occupational safety and health, and aviation safety.

Sources of Information

The information for *Career Opportunities in Law Enforcement, Security, and Protective Services* comes from many different sources. They include:

- books about the different professions
- professional textbooks, handbooks, and manuals
- articles from general newspapers and magazines as well as professional journals and other professional periodicals
- brochures, pamphlets, and other written materials from professional associations, federal agencies, professional firms, and other organizations
- questionnaires answered by professional individuals as well as organizations
- interviews with professionals about general information such as computer security, police work, and private investigation
- interviews with professionals about their particular areas such as canine handling, wildlife conservation, polygraph examination, SWAT, forensic computer investigation, loss control, and aircraft dispatching

In addition, the Internet proved a valuable reference source. Through the Internet, hundreds of web sites of law enforcement agencies, fire departments, federal agencies, professional associations, security firms, and other related organizations and businesses were visited to research the many different professions described in this book.

How This Book Is Organized

Career Opportunities in Law Enforcement, Security, and Protective Services is especially designed to be accessible to the reader. The 79 jobs are divided into twelve sections. A section may have between four to twelve job profiles, and the profiles are between two to three pages long. Each profile follows the same format so that you can read the job profiles or sections in any order you prefer.

The first two sections of the book describe police and special agent jobs that can be found in local, state, and federal law enforcement agencies. The third section describes jobs that are part of crime scene investigations and forensic labs. Sections four through six discuss occupations in the security industry—private investigations, physical security, security management, and computer security. In section seven, several professions in corrections are described, and section eight discusses jobs that provide emergency services to the public. Sections nine and ten detail occupations as compliance inspectors and code enforcers. And sections eleven and twelve cover occupations that specifically address safety and security issues and measures in the workplace or in the air.

The Job Profiles

Each job profile gives you basic information about one of 79 protective service careers. Each entry starts with *Career Profile,* a summary of a job's major duties, salary, job outlook, and promotion possibilities. In addition, this section provides a brief description of requirements that are needed to be eligible for a job. *Career Ladder* is a visual presentation of a typical career path, showing what positions lead to and stem from the job being profiled.

The rest of the job profile is a narrative description that is divided into the following sections:

- *Position Description* details a job's major responsibilities and working conditions; with some positions, duties may vary depending on the type of employers.

- *Salaries* presents a general idea of the kind of wages that workers may earn. Salary information comes from the U.S. Bureau of Labor Statistics or from salary surveys done by professional associations or other recognized organizations.
- *Employment Prospects* describes employers and the job outlook for today as well as for the future. Much of the job outlook information can be attributed to the U.S. Bureau of Labor Statistics.
- *Advancement Prospects* discusses promotional opportunities, and whenever possible, alternative career paths.
- *Special Requirements* is a section that usually appears with occupations mostly found in government agencies. This section describes job qualifications and selection processes that individuals must meet.
- *Education and Training* describes educational training prerequisites needed to apply for a job, as well as training programs that recruits must successfully complete.
- *Experience and Skills* discusses the minimum experience requirements for a job, as well as employability and job skills that employers look for in candidates.
- *Unions/Associations* gives the names of national and, sometimes, international professional organizations that have branch offices throughout the country.
- *Tips for Entry* presents advice for finding jobs; suggestions for enhancing your employability and chances for promotions; and ways to find out more information on the Internet.

The Appendixes

At the end of the book are ten appendixes that provide additional information about the various professions described in *Career Opportunities in Law Enforcement, Security, and Protective Services.* You can learn about some colleges and universities as well as vocational and technical schools that provide educational training for some of the professions. You can also find names and contact information of professional associations and other organizations that can provide general information about a career, field, or industry. In addition, you can find names of books, professional periodicals, and Internet web sites that can give you further information and insight about the occupations that interest you.

This Book Is Yours

Career Opportunities in Law Enforcement, Security, and Protective Services is your reference book. Use it to read about jobs you have often wondered about. Use it to learn about protective services that you never knew existed. Use it to start your search for the career of your dreams.

Good luck!

Susan Echaore-McDavid

INTRODUCTION

Think of jobs you would find in protective services. What are some of them?

More than likely, you thought of Police Officers, FBI Special Agents, Security Guards, Bodyguards, and Firefighters, and perhaps, Lifeguards, Police Detectives, Correctional Officers, Secret Service Special Agents, Store Detectives, and Park Rangers. Those are jobs we most commonly think of as protective service occupations—and ones that will be described in this book.

But protective services cover a wide variety of areas including law enforcement, forensic investigations, private investigations, physical security, security management, computer security, corrections, fire protection, emergency services, compliance inspections, code enforcement, workplace safety, and aviation safety. Thus, there are many other protective service jobs that we don't normally consider. For example, the following are also protective service jobs, which will be described in this book, too: Airport Police Officers, Crime Prevention Specialists, Crime Scene Technicians, Firearms/Toolmarks Examiners, Polygraph Examiners, Financial Investigators, Background Investigators, Locksmiths, Fire Protection Engineers, Security Consultants, Bailiffs, Probation Officers, Emergency Medical Technicians, Public Safety Dispatchers, Food Safety Inspectors, Environmental Health Officers, Immigration Inspectors, Plan Reviewers, Plumbing Inspectors, Industrial Hygienists, and Air Traffic Controllers.

Protective service professionals work for government agencies, private businesses and companies, and nonprofit organizations. Some enforce laws, codes, standards, rules, or regulations as part of their jobs. Some conduct investigations into criminal activities, workplace accidents, or other matters. Other professionals develop or manage security or safety plans. Others guard individuals, property, premises, or other assets. Still other professionals provide rescue services in emergency situations; or monitor events, security procedures, or other types of situations to make sure everything is safe and secure. They perform many other duties and tasks that vary from job to job; but essentially all protective service professionals do this: in some manner, they provide for the safety and security of people, communities, organizations, businesses, and companies.

Those who enter the various protective service fields usually have high ethical and moral standards along with strong commitments to protect the general welfare of people and businesses. They generally are leaders who have positive attitudes and enjoy helping people. Typically they are reliable, self-motivated individuals who can work with little or no supervision, yet have the ability to work well with others. Protective service professionals are analytical, flexible, and can manage multiple tasks and issues. Most are faced with making decisions that may affect the safety and well-being of their lives and/or others. Furthermore, protective service professionals willingly take on the stress that comes with enforcing laws or regulations, inspecting sites for violations, monitoring potential problems, helping people in trouble, issuing citations for violations, taking criminals into custody, or any of the other more dangerous duties that they perform.

Those who choose to work in protective service fields are brave souls.

Job Outlook

Job opportunities, in general, are good in the protective service industry. According to the U.S. Department of Labor, this industry will grow 34%—faster than average—between 1994 and 2005. Job opportunities will more than likely continue growing at such a pace, and in some fields increase, beyond 2005 due to the growing concern over crime, the need for stronger security measures, and adherence to federal regulations and standards.

The fastest growing area is private security, which has seen a creation of many new jobs in the last few years to handle computer crime and workplace security. The American Society for Industrial Security estimates that by 2000, the American private sector will have spent more than $100 billion in security measures for their homes, businesses, and companies.

Job opportunities in law enforcement and fire protection agencies vary from area to area, depending on the availability of funds to create additional positions. Competition, however, is tough for law enforcement and fire protection jobs. Although these are demanding and stressful jobs, turnover rates are low due to job security and potential career development in these areas.

Job Requirements

Minimum education and experience requirements vary with the different jobs as well as with the different employers. Professionals in the various protective service fields encourage young people to get life experiences and college educations before applying. In fact, to stay competitive with other job seekers and to enhance chances for promotions, college education is necessary.

As you read the different job descriptions in this book, you may notice that certain employability skills—communication, reading, writing, teamwork, and people skills—are emphasized again and again. Those skills are highly important to success in protective service careers. In addition, learning basic computer skills would be to your advantage as most, if not all, professionals use computers for routine tasks, such as report writing, record keeping, and searching databases.

The Selection Process

Years ago, to get a job you merely had to complete a job application and pass one or more job interviews. Usually, you learned whether you got a job in a day or two, or within one or two weeks. These days, the selection process is more complex and can be rather long. In addition to job applications and oral interviews, applicants may also need to pass job-related aptitude and skills tests; medical examination; screening for drug use; psychological review; and polygraph examinations. Most employers also complete background investigations that may include looking into current and past employment, financial, criminal, driving, and other relevant records.

For law enforcement positions, particularly with federal agencies, the selection process can take several months, and sometimes up to a year. Individuals who pass an agency's selection process are usually placed on an eligibility list. As positions or training sessions become available, the agency then recruits individuals from its eligibility list.

Professional Certification

Many security, safety, and compliance professionals obtain voluntary certifications (such as Certified Protection Professional, Certified Legal Investigator, Certified Safety Professional) to enhance their employability and promotional chances. Many employers and clients see professional certification as a demonstration of experience and credibility. In order to be eligible for professional certifications, individuals must have several years of acceptable work experience, complete certified training, and pass rigid written and/or oral professional examinations.

Using the Internet

The Internet has become a valuable tool for career development and job hunting. Hundreds of law enforcement agencies, fire departments, federal agencies, professional associations, private companies, and professionals have web sites on the Internet that allow you to learn about their different departments, services, and activities. Many web sites also list career information and job opportunities; some even let you apply for jobs on-line.

Many web sites also provide a web page of links that can point readers to other relevant web sites on the Internet. Some web sites allow you to download job applications, job descriptions, brochures, tables, and even work manuals to your computer for you to read at your leisure when you're off the Internet.

In addition, you can find articles on the Internet about issues, techniques, and other matters written by professionals in the different fields. You can learn about prospective employers, and find their names, addresses, and phone numbers. Furthermore, you can network with professionals throughout the country by way of the Internet, as many web sites provide names with their e-mail addresses whom you can contact for further information. To get started, see Appendix VIII, which lists relevant web sites.

(Note: Web site addresses change from time to time. If you come across an address that no longer works, you may be able to find a new address by entering the name of the organization in a search engine.)

One Final Note

Keep in mind that *Career Opportunities in Law Enforcement, Security, and Protective Services* introduces you to 79 protective service occupations. The references mentioned throughout the book and in the appendixes can help you further research careers in which you are interested. In addition, you can learn whether an occupation is right for you by:

- reading professional journals, magazines, and other periodicals
- reading books about the profession
- visiting relevant web sites on the Internet
- talking with professionals
- attending professional conferences or meetings
- taking courses related to the profession
- volunteering, if possible, in an actual workplace (for example, a police department if you are interested in going into law enforcement or security work)
- obtaining internships in related businesses, agencies, or other organizations
- obtaining part-time or seasonal entry-level positions such as security guards, store detectives, lifeguards, or park rangers

Should you decide to pursue a career, you'll find that you already have some knowledge of the field, possibly some experience, and perhaps the beginning of a valuable network with professionals who can help you with the next steps—getting further education, training, and work.

Good luck!

POLICE WORK

POLICE OFFICER

CAREER PROFILE

Duties: Enforce laws; preserve peace; protect life and property; investigate crime; apprehend lawbreakers; provide community service

Alternative Title: Patrol Officer

Salary Range: $19,200 to $64,500

Employment Prospects: Good

Advancement Prospects: Excellent
Prerequisites:

Special Requirements—Must be a U.S. citizen; have a driver's license; meet department qualifications; pass the selection process

Education—High school diploma; police academy training, field training

Experience—No experience necessary

Special Skills—Interpersonal and communication skills; reading, writing, observation, and problem-solving skills; self-management skills

CAREER LADDER

```
┌─────────────────────────────────────┐
│  Special Assignments, Police Detective, │
│        or Police Sergeant           │
└─────────────────────────────────────┘

┌─────────────────────────────────────┐
│          Police Officer             │
└─────────────────────────────────────┘

┌─────────────────────────────────────┐
│       Police Officer Trainee        │
└─────────────────────────────────────┘
```

Position Description

Police Officers work for city or municipal police departments. Their job is to enforce laws; preserve peace; protect life and property; investigate crime; apprehend lawbreakers; and provide community service. The basic unit of all police departments is the uniformed Police Officer who performs patrol duty within the jurisdiction of the police department. These officers are assigned beats, or areas, in which they patrol regularly to make sure that people and businesses are safe. Working alone or with partners, Police Officers patrol their beat in police cars or on foot, keeping in contact with their headquarters by two-way radios.

Police Officers must be familiar with the daily routines of people and businesses on their beats. As they do their rounds, they watch for suspicious activities, investigate potential trouble and, if necessary, call their headquarters for assistance. Police Officers have the authority to stop people and question them about their actions. In addition, they have the power to arrest people who are committing crimes or are suspected of committing crimes. They may also arrest people who are public nuisances, such as drunk persons who are bothering others.

Police Officers also enforce traffic laws on their beats. For instance, they look for motorists who drive over speed limits or run through red traffic lights and stop signs. Violators stopped by an Officer are either issued warnings or citations.

As part of their rounds, Police Officers must also be alert to public hazards such as fallen electrical wires, missing traffic signs, potholes, and spilled chemicals. They report such hazards to the proper authorities; and, if necessary, block off streets and direct traffic around the danger. When an accident, fire, or other emergency occurs, Police Officers must take immediate control of the scene. They make sure people are safe and unharmed, provide first aid, and summon emergency medical help. In addition, they block off the scene from traffic and crowds.

Throughout their work shift, Police Officers receive dispatches from headquarters to investigate trouble or provide immediate help to individuals and businesses. For example, a Police Officer might be called on to respond to the following situations: a patient is missing from a nursing home; a person is attempting to commit suicide; a fight has broken out at a shopping center; traffic lights are out at an intersection; a resident complains about noisy neighbors; a grocery store is being robbed; people are living in an abandoned building.

Police Officers keep a daily field notebook on their activities as well as complete accurate accidents and incidents reports. Report-writing is an essential duty for all Police Officers as their reports are permanent public records that can be used as evidence in trials.

Police Officers fulfill other duties as they are needed. For example, they might:

- escort citizens
- guard visiting dignitaries
- guard prisoners
- direct traffic around parades, fairs, and other special events
- assist in crowd control at public demonstrations
- operate radar equipment to catch speeding violators
- investigate serious traffic accidents
- assist in criminal investigations, such as doing surveillance or undercover work
- collect and process evidence at crime scenes
- testify at court trials
- present crime prevention workshops
- perform office duty

Police Officers work a rotating shift that includes nights, weekends, and holidays. They are on call 24 hours a day, every day of the year.

Salaries

Salaries vary from department to department. In 1996, the annual salary for police officers ranged from as low as $19,200 to as high as $64,500. Police officers with supervisory duties typically earn more than those with non-supervisory duties. Also, Police Officers who work in metropolitan areas—such as New York, Miami, Chicago, Dallas, Los Angeles, and Seattle—generally receive higher wages. In some departments, Police Officers receive additional pay for special unit assignments. In addition to their base salary, Police Officers also receive compensation for working overtime—hours worked beyond their regular work shift—as well as for working weekends, holidays, and late night shifts. Most Police Officers receive uniform allowances.

Employment Prospects

Job opportunities are expected to grow as fast as all other jobs until 2006. Most openings will be created to replace officers who retire, resign, or are promoted to higher positions. The creation of additional positions in a police department will depend on its budget. Applicants can expect to face a long and highly competitive selection process for any police job.

Advancement Prospects

Police Officers can develop satisfying and diverse law enforcement careers. After serving two to three years of patrol

duty, Police Officers can apply for special units, such as bike patrol, bomb squad, SWAT, crime prevention, and traffic enforcement. Special unit duties are in addition to Police Officers' regular duties. Police Officers may apply for different special units throughout their careers. Some Police Officers are part of two or more special units at the same time.

In addition, Police Officers might choose to pursue a career in police investigations. They become eligible to take the competitive detective exam in their department after completing two or three years of patrol duty. Officers interested in supervisory or administrative duties can seek promotions as sergeants, lieutenants, and captains. They must have additional experience and education as well as pass competitive exams and reviews.

Another path for Police Officers is to work in the private security field or with other law enforcement agencies such as a Sheriff's Department, state police, U.S. Border Patrol, and U.S. Secret Service.

Special Requirements

Most departments require applicants to be U.S. citizens and have a valid driver's license. Applicants must have no criminal records. They must meet certain vision, weight, and height requirements. Age, residency, and other specific qualifications vary from department to department.

Applicants must pass every step of a selection process that includes any or all of the following: job application, written exam, panel interview, medical examination, physical aptitude or agility test, background investigation, psychological review, polygraph examination, and drug testing.

Education and Training

Applicants must have a high school diploma or general equivalency diploma. Many departments also require applicants to have a minimum number of college credits with courses in police science or other related study. Some police departments require applicants to have either an associate's or bachelor's degree.

Police Officer trainees complete 12 to 14 weeks of training at a police academy where they study law, investigative procedures, self-defense, use of firearms, and other basic law enforcement skills. After their academy training, trainees are assigned to patrol duty under the supervision of field-training officers.

Experience and Skills

No law enforcement experience is necessary to apply for a trainee position. Departments look for applicants who are mature, intelligent, and honest. Applicants should have a strong commitment to serving their community. They should be in excellent physical condition and have experience handling stressful situations.

Applicants need strong interpersonal and communication skills for the job as well as good reading, writing, observational, and problem-solving skills. In addition, they need self-management skills, such as the ability to get to work on time, follow directions, take initiative, work safely, and stay calm while working under pressure.

Unions/Associations

Many Police Officers belong to local and state police associations that provide professional services and programs such as training, networking, and union representation. Many also belong to national groups such as the American Federation of Police, Fraternal Order of Police, International Association of Women Police, and International Union of Police Associations.

Tips for Entry

1. Gain experience by joining the Police Explorers or Police Reserves, or do volunteer work with a police department.

2. Earn an associate's or bachelor's degree in police science or other related field as more and more police departments are making a college degree a requirement.

3. Call a police department or city personnel office to learn about current and upcoming job openings.

4. Many police departments have web sites on the Internet, giving information about their organization as well as job opportunities. Enter the phrase *police department* in a search engine to get a list of web pages.

POLICE DETECTIVE

CAREER PROFILE

Duties: Investigate criminal cases; apprehend criminals; testify in court

Alternative Titles: Police Investigator, Police Inspector

Salary Range: $19,200 to $64,500

Employment Prospects: Good

Advancement Prospects: Excellent
Prerequisites:
Special Requirements—Pass competitive exam and oral review
Education—Academic study and field training
Experience—One to five years of police duty
Special Skills—Interpersonal and teamwork skills; communication and interviewing skills; report-writing and critical thinking skills; organizational and self-management skills

CAREER LADDER

```
┌─────────────────────────────────┐
│         Police Sergeant         │
└─────────────────────────────────┘

┌─────────────────────────────────┐
│         Police Detective        │
└─────────────────────────────────┘

┌─────────────────────────────────┐
│          Police Officer         │
└─────────────────────────────────┘
```

Position Description

Police Detectives are plainclothes police officers who conduct criminal investigations. They are responsible for identifying suspects as well as finding proof that links them to crimes in order to arrest and prosecute them in court. Robbery, burglary, vandalism, theft, assault, murder, suicide, stalking, domestic violence, fraud, forgery, arson, vice, narcotics, gangs, and terrorism are some of the many types of crime that Police Detectives may investigate.

Police Detectives usually begin each case by gathering information to help them decide upon an effective plan of investigation. They carefully examine a crime scene, writing thorough notes as well as drawing well-detailed sketches. (Some Police Detectives also photograph the crime scene.) They search for physical evidence including bullets, weapons, tools of entry, bloodstains, fibers, hair, and fingerprints. Police Detectives might collect and process the physical evidence or direct other officers in performing these tasks. Police Detectives interview victims, witnesses, and suspects, and other people who may have knowledge of the crime in question. In addition, they assess crime lab reports, medical examiner reports, and other pertinent police reports. They review written statements of interviews conducted by themselves or other officers.

Using such information, Police Detectives develop leads on suspects, conduct more interviews, gather additional facts, and examine police records for possible suspects. When suspects are identified, Police Detectives then must prove that the suspects had the motives, means, and opportunity to commit the crimes. Police Detectives look for evidence that links the suspects to the victims, physical evidence, or the crime scene. They re-read reports and records. They may interview additional witnesses and often return to talk with persons they have previously interviewed. In addition, Police Detectives may do surveillance or stake-outs on suspects, and with the proper warrants, they might search suspects' property. Once sufficient evidence is gathered, Police Detectives arrest suspects or order their arrest.

With every case, Police Detectives keep accurate and proper documentation of their activities, as their reports may be used in court trials. Police Detectives obtain signed written statements from witnesses, victims, and suspects. They keep well-detailed field notes and progress reports. They prepare comprehensive summaries that include all documentary, testimonial, and physical evidence. Police Detectives may assist prosecutors in preparing for court trials. If necessary, Police Detectives gather more facts to strengthen a case, and in some cases, testify in court about their findings.

Depending on the size and need of a police department, Police Detectives might specialize in one or more types of criminal cases. They might handle cases alone, with a partner, or as part of a crime investigation unit. A case may take several days, weeks, months, or years to solve. Some cases remain unsolved.

Detectives are assigned an eight-hour shift, but put in many hours of overtime to solve their cases. They are on call 24 hours a day, seven days a week.

Salaries

Salaries vary from department to department. In 1996, the annual salary for Police Detectives ranged from as low as $19,200 to as high as $64,500. Police Detectives who work in metropolitan areas—such as New York, Miami, Chicago, Dallas, Los Angeles, and Seattle—generally receive higher wages. Also, Police Detectives with supervisory duties typically earn more than those with non-supervisory duties. In some departments, Police Detectives receive additional pay for special unit assignments such as SWAT, canine unit, and bomb squad.

In addition to their base salary, Police Detectives also receive compensation for working overtime—hours worked beyond their regular work shift—as well as for working weekends, holidays, and late shifts.

Employment Prospects

Job opportunities for Police Detectives are expected to grow as fast as all other jobs until 2006. However, qualified Detective candidates often outnumber the positions that open up in a department. Most openings will be created to replace Police Detectives who retire, resign, or who are promoted to higher positions. The creation of additional positions within any police department depends on its budget.

Opportunities are usually better with large police departments or police departments in metropolitan areas.

Advancement Prospects

Police Detectives may continue to apply for special unit details such as SWAT, bomb squad, and aviation unit. (Special detail duties are in addition to their detective duties.) In large police departments, Police Detectives can apply for special investigation detail such as intelligence or computer crime. Those interested in supervisory or administrative duties can seek promotions as sergeants, lieutenants, and captains. They must have additional experience and education as well as pass competitive exams and reviews.

Other career paths for Police Detectives are found in state and federal law enforcement agencies in such positions as Special Agents and other investigative specialists. Police Detectives might also consider working in the private sector as private investigators.

Special Requirements

Along with meeting their department's educational and experience requirements, police officers must pass a competitive detective exam and panel review. Successful candidates are placed on a Police Detective eligibility list according to their scores and are offered jobs as positions become available.

Education and Training

Newly hired Police Detectives complete a probation period in which they receive field training as well as academic investigative training at a police academy, college, or their police department. Those who go into specialized investigative areas, such as arson and homicide, receive additional training.

Experience and Skills

Depending on the police department, Police Detective candidates may be required to have completed one to five years of patrol duty.

Police Detectives work with other law enforcement personnel and interview many different people, so it is important that candidates work well as part of a team as well as possess good communication, interviewing and interpersonal skills. They must also write clear, professional reports, demonstrate critical thinking skills and be well-organized.

Police Detectives should be curious, open-minded, fair, unbiased, patient, confident, logical, and perceptive.

Unions/Associations

Many Police Detectives join different professional organizations for the opportunity to network with peers and to obtain training, continuing education, current research, and other professional services and support. Most continue their membership with the unions and police organizations that they joined as police officers. In addition, Detectives might join professional groups such as the International Homicide Investigators Association, International Narcotics Interdiction Association, and International Association of Crime Analysts.

Tips for Entry

1. Take criminal justice, law, computer science, logic, forensic science, and other classes that can enhance and improve investigative skills and knowledge.
2. Keep up with new and improved forensic techniques.
3. Contact a police department's criminal divisions commander or personnel office to find out the specific qualifications for a Police Detective.
4. You can read about the criminal investigation units of some police departments on the Internet. Enter the phrase *police criminal investigation units* in a search engine to get a list of web pages.

DEPUTY SHERIFF

CAREER PROFILE

Duties: Perform patrol duty; conduct investigations; act as officers of local courts; perform jail duty

Salary Range: $15,900 to $48,400

Employment Prospects: Fair

Advancement Prospects: Good

Prerequisites:

Special Requirements—Must be a U.S. citizen; have a driver's license; meet department qualifications; pass the selection process

Education—High school diploma; academy training, field training

Experience—One to two years of law enforcement experience preferred

Special Skills—Problem-solving, memory, and observational skills; communication, reading, writing, and interpersonal skills

CAREER LADDER

```
┌─────────────────────────────────┐
│     Deputy Sheriff Sergeant     │
└─────────────────────────────────┘

┌─────────────────────────────────┐
│        Deputy Sheriff           │
└─────────────────────────────────┘

┌─────────────────────────────────┐
│      Deputy Sheriff Trainee     │
└─────────────────────────────────┘
```

Position Description

Deputy Sheriffs are uniformed law enforcement officers who represent county governments, and enforce county and state laws and ordinances. As members of a Sheriff's Office, Deputy Sheriffs might perform a variety of assignments in a number of areas—patrol, criminal investigations, court security, and jail (or corrections). Their jurisdiction covers all the cities, rural areas, and unincorporated cities and towns within the county. But they mostly focus on rural and unincorporated areas and cities without a municipal police department.

Driving marked sheriff's vehicles, Deputy Sheriffs perform patrol duty within their assigned areas. They usually work alone, using two-way radios to keep in contact with their headquarters. While making their rounds, Deputy Sheriffs investigate suspicious activities, report public hazards, enforce traffic laws, and provide community service. They respond to dispatches to investigate trouble or provide immediate assistance. They issue warnings and citations to violators and arrest lawbreakers.

A Deputy Sheriff's investigative duties differ in every sheriff's department. In small departments, Deputy Sheriffs generally conduct complete criminal investigations. In larger departments, they usually perform crime scene investigations only. They might also assist in joint investigations with federal, state, and local law enforcement officers.

As officers of the court, Deputy Sheriffs serve and execute subpoenas, court orders, summonses, and other court documents. They may also collect fees, such as property taxes, that citizens owe the county. During trials, Deputy Sheriffs provide court security by patroling the grounds, keeping order in the courtrooms, and guarding the jury and judge. They also guard the inmates who are on trial and escort them between jail and the courtroom.

Some sheriff's departments are in charge of local jails. In those departments, Deputy Sheriffs may be assigned to various duties. They may book inmates and take custody of their possessions, supervise or guard inmates, and even transport inmates to hospitals, courts, and other locations. They also may maintain records such as fingerprint files.

Deputy Sheriffs are responsible for keeping accurate, detailed field logs on all of their activities as well as writing reports. Their logs and reports are permanent public records and can be submitted as evidence in court trials.

Deputy Sheriffs perform other duties as they are required. They might:

- testify in court
- do surveillance and undercover work
- collect and process physical evidence
- teach crime prevention workshops to the public or other government agencies

- teach classes on dangerous drugs, crime scene investigations, and other departmental functions to other staff members
- perform office duty

Deputy Sheriffs work rotating shifts that include nights, weekends, and holidays. They are on call 24 hours a day, every day of the year.

Salaries

Salaries vary from department to department. Deputy Sheriffs in metropolitan areas generally earn higher wages. In 1996, most Deputy Sheriffs earned an annual salary between $15,900 and $48,400. In addition to their basic salary, Deputy Sheriffs receive compensation for overtime hours.

Employment Prospects

Job opportunities for Deputy Sheriffs are expected to grow as fast as all other occupations until 2006. However, the competition for Deputy Sheriff positions is high. Most positions become available as Deputies retire, resign, or are promoted to higher offices.

Advancement Prospects

Supervisory and managerial positions are available in sheriff's departments. Deputy Sheriffs can rise through the ranks of sergeant, lieutenant, captain, chief deputy, and assistant sheriff. In most counties, the sheriff is elected by the voters.

In most sheriff departments, Deputy Sheriffs can apply for specialized assignments such as canine patrol, marine patrol, criminal investigation, crime scene investigation, and airport security.

Special Requirements

Most departments require applicants to be U.S. citizens and have a valid driver's license. Applicants must have no criminal records. They must meet certain vision, weight, and height requirements. Age, residency, and other specific qualifications vary from department to department.

Applicants must pass every step of a selection process that includes any or all of the following: job application, written exam, panel interview, medical examination, physical aptitude or agility test, background investigation, psychological review, polygraph examination, and drug testing.

Education and Training

Sheriff's departments require a high school diploma or general equivalency diploma. Some departments require an associate's degree or a minimum of 60 credits in police science or other related study from an accredited college.

Most departments require Deputy Sheriff trainees to complete 12 to 14 weeks of training at a law enforcement academy. The trainees study such subjects as law, local and state ordinances, court proceedings, investigative procedures, self-defense, use of firearms, and jail security. After their academy training, trainees perform routine duties under the supervision of field training officers.

Experience and Skills

Many sheriff's departments prefer Deputy Sheriff candidates to have one to two years of law enforcement experience. They choose candidates who are in good physical condition and able to make wise decisions in stressful situations. In addition, they look for the following skills: problem-solving, memory, observational, interpersonal, communication, reading, and writing.

Successful candidates show that they are professional, self-motivated, dependable, and have strong moral character. They project authority as well as fairness and tolerance.

Unions/Associations

Many Deputy Sheriffs join at least one professional organization for the opportunity to network with peers, as well as to obtain training, continuing education, and other professional services and support. Two national organizations to which Deputy Sheriffs might belong are the National Sheriffs' Association and American Deputy Sheriffs' Association. In addition, Deputy Sheriffs might belong to sheriff unions and associations in their region or state.

Tips for Entry

1. Become a Deputy Sheriff volunteer to get valuable law enforcement experience within the sheriff's department.
2. Contact a Sheriff's Office or county personnel office to learn about job announcements.
3. Obtain military experience, college training, or work experience in law enforcement or related fields to enhance your chances of finding law enforcement jobs.
4. Many sheriff's departments have web sites on the Internet, giving information about their organization as well as job opportunities. Enter the phrase *sheriff's department* in a search engine to get a list of web pages.

STATE TROOPER

CAREER PROFILE

Duties: Enforce criminal and traffic laws; preserve peace; protect life and property; apprehend lawbreakers; provide community service

Alternate Title: Highway Patrol Officer

Salary Range: $15,900 to $48,400

Employment Prospects: Good

Advancement Prospects: Good
Prerequisites:

Special Requirements—Must be a U.S. citizen; be between 21 and 29 years old; have a driver's license; meet department qualifications; pass the selection process

Education or Training—High school diploma; academy training; field training

Experience—No law enforcement experience is needed

Special Skills—Interpersonal and communication skills; reading, writing, observational, and problem-solving skills; self-management skills

CAREER LADDER

```
┌─────────────────────────────┐
│   State Trooper Sergeant     │
└─────────────────────────────┘

┌─────────────────────────────┐
│      State Trooper           │
└─────────────────────────────┘

┌─────────────────────────────┐
│   State Trooper Trainee      │
└─────────────────────────────┘
```

Position Description

State Troopers are law enforcement officers for state police departments. They are responsible for enforcing criminal and traffic laws, preserving the peace, protecting lives and property, apprehending lawbreakers, and providing community service. In some states, the state police department is known as the highway patrol department. Some states have two separate divisions for police enforcement and traffic enforcement.

State Troopers are uniformed officers who patrol their assigned area in marked state police cars. They work alone, communicating with their headquarters on two-way radios. Their major responsibilities are enforcing traffic laws and managing traffic on a state's freeways, highways, turnpikes, roads, and streets. They monitor the traffic in all types of weather. They issue warnings or citations to motorists who are breaking speed limits or other traffic laws as well as motorists who are endangering lives by tailgating, weaving through traffic, or other reckless driving. If necessary, State Troopers arrest violators and escort them to headquarters for detainment.

When automobile accidents or other emergency situations occur, State Troopers take command of the scene. They make sure people are safe and unharmed. They provide first aid and summon ambulances, tow trucks, and other appropriate assistance. They block off the scene and direct traffic around it.

As part of their traffic duty, State Troopers also help motorists. They might give motorists directions to their destinations as well as information about nearby restaurants, gas stations, and lodging. They might make calls to tow truck companies for motorists with car trouble.

In rural and unincorporated areas that do not have a police department or sheriff's department, State Troopers perform patrol duties. They safeguard buildings and property, investigate suspicious activities, report public hazards, enforce traffic laws, provide community service, interrogate suspects, and arrest lawbreakers. In addition, State Troopers respond to dispatches from headquarters to investigate trouble or provide immediate assistance.

Many State Troopers also take turns performing station duty. They do routine desk work, such as preparing reports or correspondence and making entries into station records. They send and receive radio messages. They answer questions from the public about road conditions, weather conditions, directions, or other subjects.

State Troopers are also assigned special duties from time to time. For example, they might:

- manage traffic during parades and special events
- escort visiting dignitaries, military convoys, and funeral processions on highways and freeways
- patrol areas that were devastated by fires, bombings, floods, earthquakes or other man-made or natural disasters
- check weights of commercial vehicles
- present workshops on highway safety, crime prevention, and other topics to the public
- conduct drivers' examinations
- perform desk duty
- conduct auto theft investigations
- execute search and arrest warrants

State Troopers are on call 24 hours a day, seven days a week. They work rotating shifts that include nights, weekends, and holidays.

Salaries

In 1996, annual salaries for State Troopers ranged between $15,900 and $48,400. They are paid overtime pay in addition to their basic salary.

Employment Prospects

Every state but Hawaii has a state police department. Job opportunities for State Trooper positions are expected to grow as fast as all other occupations until 2006. However, the number of available jobs differs each year and differs from state to state. Applicants can expect to face a long and highly competitive selection process for any State Trooper job.

Advancement Prospects

State Trooper trainees are assigned anywhere in their state. Upon completing their probation period, they usually can request a transfer to other parts of a state. They are also eligible to apply for special assignments such as canine patrol, motorcycle patrol, air support detail, and auto theft investigations.

Opportunities for supervisory and management positions are available. State Troopers can become sergeants, lieutenants, captains, and majors. Promotions are based on job performance and education, and in some states, high scores on competitive exams.

Special Requirements

All states require that applicants be U.S. citizens who are between 21 and 29 years old. They must have a valid driver's license, no criminal record, and meet certain weight, height, and residency requirements.

Applicants must pass every step of a selection process that includes any or all of the following: job application, written exam, panel interview, medical examination, physical aptitude or agility test, background investigation, psychological review, polygraph examination, and drug testing.

Education and Training

State police departments require a high school diploma or a general equivalency diploma. Some departments require an associate's degree or a minimum of 60 credits in police science, law, or other related field from an accredited college.

State Trooper Trainees complete four to six months of law enforcement academy training. The curriculum includes basic law, motor vehicle codes, vehicle patrol, investigation skills, use of firearms, advanced driving skills, first aid, and self defense. After their academy training, trainees perform routine duties under the supervision of field training officers or senior officers.

Experience and Skills

Previous law enforcement experience is not necessary for a trainee position. Applicants do need to be in excellent physical condition and should have experience handling stressful situations.

Applicants need good interpersonal and communication skills for the job along with good reading, writing, observational, and problem-solving skills. In addition, they need self-management skills—such as the ability to get to work on time, follow directions, take initiative, work safely, and stay calm while working under pressure.

Unions/Associations

State Troopers belong to their state police and highway patrol association. They might also belong to national law enforcement organizations such as the Fraternal Order of Police. In addition, they might belong to regional associations made up of local and state law enforcement officers. Professional associations provide State Troopers the chance to network with peers and participate in professional services such as training and continuing education programs.

Tips for Entry

1. Obtain some law enforcement experience, such as volunteer work with a police department, to enhance your chances in the highly competitive selection process for State Trooper positions.

2. Find out if your state has a State Trooper cadet program for high school graduates. Cadets are paid to perform civilian duties. When they reach the appropriate age, they may apply for available State Trooper trainee positions.

3. Many state police departments have web sites on the Internet, giving information about their organization as well as job opportunities. Enter the phrase *state police department* or *state highway patrol* in a search engine to get a list of web pages.

CONSERVATION OFFICER

CAREER PROFILE

Duties: Enforce state game and fishing laws; perform patrol duty; promote wildlife preservation; teach hunting and boating safety workshops

Alternate Titles: Fish and Wildlife Officer, Game Warden, Conservation Police Officer

Salary Range: $18,000 to $59,000

Employment Prospects: Limited

Advancement Prospects: Fair
  Prerequisites:
  Special Requirements—Must be a U.S. citizen; be at least 21 years old; have a driver's license; no criminal record; meet department qualifications; pass the selection process
  Education—Requirements differ with each state; academy training, field training
  Experience—Law enforcement experience or natural resource conservation experience is desirable
  Special Skills—Interpersonal, writing, and public speaking skills; outdoor skills; organizational and self-management skills

CAREER LADDER

```
┌─────────────────────────────────────┐
│  Supervising Conservation Officer    │
└─────────────────────────────────────┘

┌─────────────────────────────────────┐
│      Conservation Officer            │
└─────────────────────────────────────┘

┌─────────────────────────────────────┐
│   Conservation Officer Trainee       │
└─────────────────────────────────────┘
```

Position Description

Conservation Officers work for state wildlife or natural resource conservation departments. They are responsible for law enforcement and public safety of state-owned parks, recreation areas, fish and wildlife areas, and other state properties. They are commissioned as police officers, but most Conservation Officers are allowed to make felony arrests only in emergency situations. Many Conservation Officers enforce boating laws and regulations. Some Conservation Officers enforce state environmental laws and regulations. Others enforce certain federal wildlife laws and regulations.

Conservation Officers are uniformed officers who are required to live within their assigned area, which may cover several counties. They perform patrol duty alone, working in all kinds of weather and terrain. They patrol by foot, four-wheel-drive trucks, motorboats, canoes, and any other type of vehicle that gets them where they need to go.

As part of their patrol duty, they might:

- issue hunting licenses
- check hunting and fishing licenses
- issue warnings or citations for violations
- investigate reports of illegal hunting and fishing
- inspect game farms and other commercial operations
- arrest lawbreakers
- respond to public complaints about deer, wildcats, and other wildlife that come into urban areas

Another major duty is educating the public about wildlife preservation as well as hunting and boating safety. Conservation Officers give workshops and presentations to schools, sports clubs, and other civic groups on topics such as the safe use of firearms and wildlife conservation.

Conservation Officers perform other duties as required. They may prepare incident reports for use in court as well as testify in trials. They may assist in putting out forest fires, or participate in rescue and search operations for missing persons. They also may assist other law enforcement agents with criminal investigations.

Accurate report-writing is essential to the job. They keep a daily log of their activities, wildlife observations, and arrest information and complete all necessary reports.

Many officers work out of their homes. They are on call 24 hours a day, seven days a week.

Salaries

According to a survey by *International Game Warden,* the annual salary for Conservation Officers in 1997 ranged from $18,000 to $59,000. Most Conservation Officers receive compensation for overtime hours as well as a uniform allowance. Officers who work from their homes may receive a monthly allowance for office expenses.

Employment Prospects

All 50 states have a fish and game department. It may be known as the fish and wildlife department, natural resources division, conservation police, or other names.

Job opportunities for Conservation Officers are limited. Some departments recruit in one-or two-year cycles, while other states have continuous recruitment. Usually positions become available when Conservation Officers have retired, resigned, or been promoted. The competition for jobs is tough. For example, a department might receive hundreds of applications for a few openings.

Advancement Prospects

Promotions in rank are based on experience, job performance, and competitive examination scores. However promotional opportunities for supervisory and management positions are limited.

Conservation Officers might pursue other career paths. With further experience and education, they can become training officers, special wildlife investigators, canine handlers, resource specialists, and forensic examiners.

Special Requirements

Applicants must be U.S. citizens who are at least 21 years old and have no criminal record. They must meet certain vision, weight, and height requirements. In addition, they must have a valid driver's license. Residency and other specific requirements vary from department to department.

Applicants must pass every step of a selection process that includes any or all of the following: job application, written exam, panel interview, medical examination, physical aptitude or agility test, background investigation, psychological review, polygraph examination, and drug testing.

Education and Training

Education requirements vary from state to state. Some states require only a high school diploma or general equivalency diploma. Other states require an associate's or a bachelor's degree—preferably in natural resources conservation, biological sciences, criminal justice, or another related field.

Trainees complete one to six months of police academy training by studying a basic wildlife law enforcement curriculum. After their academy training, trainees are assigned to field training officers and begin performing routine patrol duty. Trainees serve a probation period, which varies from department to department. Upon passing their probation, they officially become Conservation Officers.

Experience and Skills

Many departments choose candidates who have some experience and knowledge in law enforcement and natural resource conservation. They also look for candidates who have good interpersonal, writing, and public speaking skills along with good organizational and self-management skills. In addition, candidates must show that they have outdoor skills (such as hunting, fishing, hiking, and boating) as well as outdoor survival skills (such as reading maps, using a compass, and wilderness first aid).

Unions/Associations

Many Conservation Officers are members of fish and wildlife associations in their states or regions. Many also belong to the North American Wildlife Enforcement Officers Association.

Tips for Entry

1. Talk with conservation officers and professional associations to find out about job opportunities.
2. Obtain field experience with fish and wildlife agencies by volunteering, getting an internship, or doing seasonal work.
3. Earn a college degree in natural resources, police science, or other related field to improve your chances of being hired.
4. Many state fish and wildlife departments have web sites on the Internet, giving information about their organization as well as job opportunities. Enter the phrase *fish and wildlife department* (or *division*) or *game and fish department* in a search engine to get a list of web pages.

DEPUTY U.S. MARSHAL

CAREER PROFILE

Duties: Fugitive investigations; personal and witness security; asset seizure; court security; prisoner transportation and custody

Salary Range: $25,000 to $49,000

Employment Prospects: Limited

Advancement Prospects: Good
Prerequisites:

Special Requirements—Must be a U.S. citizen; be between 21 and 37 years old; be in excellent physical condition; agree to specific conditions; pass the selection process

Education or Training—Bachelor's degree; academy training, field training

Experience—Three years relevant work experience

Special Skills—Interpersonal skills; foreign language skills; problem-solving, communication, and writing skills

CAREER LADDER

```
┌─────────────────────────────────┐
│   Specialist or Supervisory Deputy │
│          U.S. Marshal            │
└─────────────────────────────────┘

┌─────────────────────────────────┐
│        Deputy U.S. Marshal       │
└─────────────────────────────────┘

┌─────────────────────────────────┐
│     Deputy U.S. Marshal Trainee  │
└─────────────────────────────────┘
```

Position Description

Deputy U.S. Marshals work for the United States Marshals Service, a law enforcement agency affiliated with the Department of Justice. These federal law enforcement agents have two major roles: they provide protective services for the federal government, and they act as officers of the federal courts.

Throughout their careers, Deputy U.S. Marshals are assigned to several types of duties. One common duty is conducting fugitive investigations. These cases involve prisoners who have escaped from federal prison as well as parolees (of federal prisons) who have violated their parole, probation, or other conditions of release. Some cases involve tracking fugitives from other countries who may be in the United States.

Another assignment is personal and witness security. Deputy U.S. Marshals protect important federal witnesses who will testify in serious cases such as those involving organized crime and terrorism. The Deputy U.S. Marshals move witnesses and their families to safe locations; and, if necessary, provide changes of identity for them.

Deputy U.S. Marshals also perform asset seizure. In federal drug and criminal cases, they seize all proceeds made from the sale of illegal drugs or other criminal activity. They are responsible for managing and disposing of millions of dollars of assets and forfeited properties such as cash, jewelry, vehicles, banks, hotels, and retail businesses.

As officers of the federal courts, Deputy U.S. Marshals provide court security. They guard federal judges and juries. They plan for and set up security systems in federal court buildings for important court cases. In addition, they serve court summonses and complaints.

The transport of federal prisoners is another type of duty. Deputy U.S. Marshals are responsible for delivering federal prisoners to prisons, courts, hospitals, and other institutions. They are also responsible for escorting foreign fugitives back to the appropriate nations.

Deputy U.S. Marshals perform other duties as required. In some cases, they are dispatched to assist at man-made and natural disaster catastrophes.

In addition to working a 40-hour week, Deputy U.S. Marshals put in many long and irregular overtime hours.

Salaries

Deputy U.S. Marshals receive a salary based on a pay schedule called *General Schedule*. The pay schedule starts at the GS-1 grade and goes up to the GS-15 grade, with each grade having 10 steps. After the GS-15 grade, salary is based on the Senior Executive Service schedule.

Depending on their education and experience, Deputy U.S. Marshals begin at the GS-5 or GS-7 grade. In 1999, annual salaries for new Deputy U.S. Marshals who were appointed at the GS-5 grade ranged between $25,000 and $32,000. The annual salaries for those who were appointed at GS-7 grade ranged between $29,000 and $37,000. They can progress up to the GS-11 grade (between $38,000 and $49,000 or more per year) within a few years depending on their job performance. Salaries are generally higher for Deputy U.S. Marshals who live in metropolitan areas where the cost of living is higher. In addition, Deputy U.S. Marshals qualify for overtime pay called "availability pay"—an extra amount that equals 25% of their salary.

Employment Prospects

The U.S. Marshals Service has field offices throughout the United States, Puerto Rico, Guam, and the Virgin Islands. Applicants may apply during open recruitment drives. The service expects the next recruitment drive to take place in the year 2002, but it may be earlier or later depending on the agency's needs.

Advancement Prospects

New Deputy U.S. Marshals are on probation for one year. They must complete three years of service at their first assigned field office before they can request a transfer to another field office. After three years, they also become eligible to apply for special key operations duty.

After serving five to seven years, Deputy U.S. Marshals are eligible to become supervisors, academy instructors, and specialists (such as court security inspectors).

Special Requirements

Applicants must be U.S. citizens who are between 21 and 37 years old. They must be in excellent physical shape and meet specific conditions such as having a driver's license at the time of appointment.

Applicants must pass each step of the agency's selection process: job application, written test, oral interview, medical exam, physical agility exam, drug test, and background check. Successful applicants are placed on an eligibility list and are offered jobs as positions become available. The wait can last anywhere from eight months to three years.

Deputy U.S. Marshals must retire when they turn 57 years old.

Education and Training

For the GS-5 grade, applicants need at least a bachelor's degree with a 3.0 GPA or higher in their majors. For the GS-7 grade, applicants must have completed graduate work in law, police science, or other field related to law enforcement.

Deputy U.S. Marshal trainees complete an intensive 16-week training program at the U.S. Marshals Service Training School in Glynco, Georgia, which includes criminal investigation training. Upon graduation, trainees are assigned to a field office in the United States. They begin performing routine duties under the supervision of a field-training officer.

Experience and Skills

Applicants need three years of paid or non-paid work experience that shows they have the leadership to be Deputy U.S. Marshals. Previous jobs, for example, may have been in law enforcement, security, classroom teaching, management, and sales.

The U.S. Marshals Service wants candidates who have the ability to meet and deal with many different types of people. Candidates who are fluent in a foreign language have an advantage. In addition, the agency chooses candidates who show that they have strong problem-solving, writing, and communication skills.

Unions/Associations

Deputy U.S. Marshals might belong to the Federal Law Enforcement Officers Association, a professional organization for all federal law enforcement agents. This group offers professional support, services, and networking opportunities.

Tips for Entry

1. College students might apply for the U.S. Marshals Service Centralized Student Career Experience Program, a college work-study program.
2. For current recruitment information, contact a U.S. Marshals Service field office. You might find a listing in your local telephone book under *U.S. Government.*
3. To learn more about the U.S. Marshals Service, visit its web site on the Internet. Its web address is *http://www.usdoj.gov/marshals.*

FBI SPECIAL AGENT

CAREER PROFILE

Duties: Enforce over 260 federal laws; conduct criminal investigations

Salary Range: $35,000 to $70,000

Employment Prospects: Limited

Advancement Prospects: Good

Prerequisites:

Special Requirements—Must be a U.S. citizen; be between 23 to 37 years old; agree to specific conditions; pass the selection process

Education or Training—Bachelor's degree; academy training, field training

Experience—Three years of work experience, which may be waived if one is a law school or accounting graduate, or fluent in a foreign language

Special Skills—teamwork and interpersonal skills; communication and writing skills; deductive and problem-solving skills

CAREER LADDER

```
┌─────────────────────────────────┐
│     Senior FBI Special Agent     │
└─────────────────────────────────┘

┌─────────────────────────────────┐
│        FBI Special Agent         │
└─────────────────────────────────┘

┌─────────────────────────────────┐
│     FBI Special Agent Trainee    │
└─────────────────────────────────┘
```

Position Description

Special Agents for the Federal Bureau of Investigation (FBI) are criminal investigators for the federal government. As part of the U.S. Department of Justice, the FBI Special Agents conduct investigations in over 200 types of federal crime. Their investigations are divided into seven programs:

- applicant matters—background investigations of federal applicants, appointees, and candidates
- civil rights violations
- counterterrorism, such as sabotage and bombings
- foreign counterterrorism, such as espionage
- organized crime/drugs
- violent crimes and major offenders
- white collar crime, such as bank fraud, environmental crimes, and health care fraud

With every case, FBI Special Agents analyze the charges and determine the laws that have been violated. They identify the issues that must be addressed and determine the types of evidence they must find. Their primary activity is gathering accurate information to link suspects to their crimes. When they have sufficient evidence in a case, they present it to a U.S. Attorney or Department of Justice official who decides what action should be taken. If suspects are prosecuted, the Special Agents must prepare to testify in court about their findings.

Due to the nature of their investigations, FBI Special Agents have the authority to gather confidential information about persons, businesses, and groups. With the proper court documents, Special Agents collect credit reports, bank statements, police records, personnel files, medical records, business correspondence, and other confidential files.

Along with gathering paper information, FBI Special Agents interview witnesses, victims, and any person who they believe can help them with their cases. They interrogate possible suspects and develop informants. They may also perform surveillance and undercover work.

FBI Special Agents carry firearms, but have limited powers to arrest criminals. They may only arrest persons who are committing federal offenses in their presence. If Special Agents have reasonable grounds to believe that someone is committing a felony, they may arrest that person.

FBI Special Agents also work with other law enforcement agencies in joint investigations and in formal task forces. For example, FBI Special Agents and local and state authorities might work together on a kidnapping case.

FBI Special Agents can be reassigned to any FBI office in the United States and throughout the world at any time in their career. They are on call 24 hours a day.

Salaries

FBI Special Agents receive a salary based on a pay schedule called *General Schedule*. The pay schedule starts at the GS-1 grade and goes up to the GS-15 grade, with each grade having 10 steps. After the GS-15 grade, salary is based on the Senior Executive Service schedule.

FBI Special Agents enter service at GS-10 grade. In 1999, the salary for new FBI Special Agents was in the $35,000 to $46,000 range. In field assignments, FBI Special Agents can advance to the GS-13 grade (between $54,000 and $70,000 or more per year). FBI Special Agents typically receive higher salary in parts of the United States (such as New York, Chicago, San Francisco, or Boston) that have a higher cost of living. In addition, FBI Special Agents qualify for overtime pay called "availability pay"—an extra amount that equals 25% of their salary.

Employment Prospects

The Federal Bureau of Investigation has 55 field offices in the United States and one field office in Puerto Rico. It also has legal attaché offices throughout the world. In 1998, the FBI completed an intensive recruitment drive and plans to hire new agents based upon need. Most openings become available when Special Agents retire, resign, or are promoted to higher positions. The creation of additional Special Agent positions depends on legislation passed by Congress.

Advancement Prospects

Throughout their careers, FBI Special Agents can advance to supervisory and administrative positions. After serving five years, they may become Senior Special Agents, who head investigation teams. They also qualify for additional training for special assignments.

Special Requirements

Applicants must be U.S. citizens or citizens of the Northern Mariana Islands who are between 23 and 37 years old. They must meet physical standards and agree to specific conditions such as having a valid driver's license at the time of their appointment. They must also qualify under one of four entrance programs—law, accounting, language, or diversified.

In addition, applicants must pass every step of the agency's selection process, which includes the following: application, written exam, oral interview, medical examination, background investigation, polygraph examination, and drug test.

Successful applicants are placed on an eligibility list, and are offered positions as they become available.

FBI Special Agents must retire when they turn 57 years old.

Education and Training

Applicants must have bachelor's degrees, preferably in law, accounting, computer science, criminal justice, or other area in which the FBI can use expertise and knowledge.

FBI recruitees complete 15 weeks of intensive training at the FBI Academy in Quantico, Virginia. Courses include law, organized crime, informant development, forensic science, computer skills, firearm skills, ethics, behavioral science, physical training, and defensive tactics. Upon graduation from the academy, new Special Agents are assigned to a field office, working under the supervision of a field training officer.

Experience and Skills

Applicants need three years of work experience that shows they are capable of performing as FBI Special Agents. The agency may waive this requirement for accounting and law school graduates, as they have skills and knowledge critical to the job. The agency may also waive the requirements for those who are fluent in a foreign language that the agency needs.

The FBI looks for dedicated candidates with high moral integrity. The candidates must show that they have good teamwork and interpersonal skills as well as good communication and writing skills. Candidates must also demonstrate that they have a strong ability for deduction and problem solving. Furthermore, candidates must be in excellent physical condition.

Unions/Associations

FBI Special Agents might belong to the Federal Law Enforcement Officers Association, a professional organization for all federal law enforcement agents. It offers networking opportunities and professional support and service programs.

Tips for Entry

1. Learn how to use computers, as computer skills are rapidly becoming essential in law enforcement careers.
2. The FBI hires its personnel directly. Special Agent recruitment is done through the FBI's 56 field offices. For current information, contact an FBI field district office. You might find a listing in your local telephone book under *U.S. Government.*
3. To learn more about the FBI, visit its web site on the Internet. Its web address is *http://www.fbi.gov.*

DEA SPECIAL AGENT

CAREER PROFILE

Duties: Enforce federal drug laws and regulations; conduct criminal investigations

Salary Range: $29,000 to $59,000

Employment Prospects: Good

Advancement Prospects: Good

Prerequisites:

Special Requirements—Must be a U.S. citizen; be between 21 to 36 years old; agree to specific conditions; pass the selection process

Education or Training—Bachelor's degree; academy training, field training

Experience—one year relevant work experience

Special Skills—Teamwork, interpersonal, communication, and problem-solving skills

CAREER LADDER

Senior DEA Special Agent

DEA Special Agent

DEA Special Agent Trainee

Position Description

Special Agents of the Drug Enforcement Agency (DEA) investigate major violators of federal drug laws and regulations. As part of the Department of Justice, DEA Special Agents conduct investigations on individuals and groups who are suspected of growing, manufacturing, or distributing controlled substances in the United States. They gather sufficient proof to link suspects to their crimes in order for federal attorneys to prosecute the suspects in court.

DEA investigations are complex and dangerous. Some are joint investigations with other law enforcement agencies. As part of their investigative duties, DEA Special Agents analyze the charges and the appropriate laws that are violated. They identify principal suspects and the issues that must be addressed. They identify the types of evidence they must find, such as the assets earned from drug trafficking.

Gathering information is their primary activity. Special Agents conduct interviews and interrogations. They collect and process evidence. They develop confidential sources. In addition, they may perform surveillance and undercover work, sometimes becoming part of the drug world.

DEA Special Agents prepare necessary affidavits for search warrants and execute search warrants. They confiscate illegal narcotics and drug-making equipment and supplies. They also confiscate drug money, vehicles, jewelry, property and any other profits that suspects made from selling drugs. DEA Special Agents have limited arresting powers, however,

and they may only arrest persons who are committing a federal offense in their presence. If Special Agents have reasonable grounds to believe that someone is committing a felony, they may arrest that person.

As part of their duties, DEA Special Agents keep accurate and proper documentation on their cases. They write clear, highly detailed technical reports that can lead to the conviction of criminals. In addition, Special Agents give sworn testimony in court trials.

DEA Special Agents travel frequently in their work, often at short notice. At any time in their career, they may be reassigned to any DEA post in the United States or in foreign countries.

Salaries

DEA Special Agents receive a salary based on a pay schedule called *General Schedule.* The pay schedule starts as the GS-1 grade and goes up to the GS-15 grade, with each grade having 10 steps. After the GS-15 grade, salary is based on the Senior Executive Service schedule.

Depending on their education and experience, entry-level DEA Special Agents start at the GS-7 grade or GS-9 grade. In 1999, annual salaries for new DEA Special Agents who were appointed at the GS-7 grade ranged between $29,000 and $37,000. The annual salaries for those who were appointed at the GS-9 grade ranged between $32,000 and $42,000. Usually within three years, DEA Special Agents can progress up to the GS-12 grade (between $45,000 and $59,000 or more per year). Salaries are typically higher for DEA Special Agents who live in metropolitan areas—such as Chicago, New York, or San Francisco—where the cost of living is higher. In addition, they qualify for overtime pay called "availability pay"—an extra amount that equals 25% of their salary.

Employment Prospects

The Drug Enforcement Administration has offices throughout the United States and in 41 foreign countries. Between 1997 and 2003, the DEA plans to hire an additional 2,000 to 3,000 Special Agents. Applicants should expect to face a long and highly competitive selection process.

Advancement Prospects

Throughout their careers, DEA Special Agents can advance to supervisory and administrative positions. After serving five to seven years, they may be promoted to Senior Special Agents. In addition, they are eligible to apply for overseas assignments.

Special Requirements

Applicants must be U.S. citizens who are between 21 and 36 years old. They must meet certain conditions such as having a valid driver's license at the time of their appointments.

In addition, applicants must pass every step of the agency's selection process, which includes the following: application, written exam, panel interview, medical examination, physical aptitude test, background investigation, polygraph examination, drug test, and psychological review. Successful applicants are placed on an eligibility list, and are offered positions as they become available, which can take up to a year.

DEA Special Agents must retire when they turn 55 years old.

Education and Training

Applicants must have bachelor's degrees, preferably in business, criminal justice, or accounting. To enter at the GS-9 grade, applicants must have master's degrees or two years of postgraduate education.

DEA Special Agent trainees complete 16 weeks of specialized training at the FBI Academy in Quantico, Virginia. The program includes academic, tactical, practical, firearms, and legal instruction. Upon completion of their training program, new DEA Special Agents are assigned to a field office, working under the supervision of field training officers.

Experience and Skills

Applicants need one year of work experience that shows they can perform duties as a DEA Special Agent. The agency is particularly interested in applicants with experience in law enforcement, accounting, computers, aviation, and the military.

The DEA looks for compassionate and incorruptible candidates who are willing to work with different types of people and to share work responsibilities. In addition, candidates must show that they have good communication skills and problem-solving skills.

Unions/Associations

DEA Special Agents might belong to the Federal Law Enforcement Officers Association, a professional organization for all federal law enforcement officers. They might also join the National Drug Enforcement Officers Association. These organizations provide opportunities for networking as well as offer professional support and services.

Tips for Entry

1. Computer skills and a foreign language fluency are two areas that can enhance your chances for a law enforcement position.
2. Call 1-800-DEA-4288 for the latest information about Special Agent openings or contact a DEA field office. You might find a listing in your local telephone book under *U.S. Government*.
3. To learn more about DEA, visit its web site on the Internet. Its web address is *http://www.usdoj.gov/dea*.

BORDER PATROL AGENT

CAREER PROFILE

Duties: Detect and prevent undocumented aliens from entering the United States; detect and prevent drug smuggling into the United States

Salary Range: $25,000 to $59,000

Employment Prospects: Good

Advancement Prospects: Good
  Prerequisites:

  Special Requirements—Must be a U.S. citizen; be between 18 and 37 years old; agree to certain conditions; pass the selection process

  Education—Bachelor's degree (without work experience); academy training, field training

  Experience—one year general work experience (without college degree)

  Special Skills—Spanish fluency or the ability to learn a foreign language; physical fitness; interpersonal, problem-solving, and decision-making skills

CAREER LADDER

```
┌─────────────────────────────────┐
│   Senior Border Patrol Agent    │
└─────────────────────────────────┘

┌─────────────────────────────────┐
│      Border Patrol Agent        │
└─────────────────────────────────┘

┌─────────────────────────────────┐
│     Border Patrol Trainee       │
└─────────────────────────────────┘
```

Position Description

Border Patrol Agents work for the United States Border Patrol, a law enforcement agency of the U.S. Immigration and Naturalization Service (INS). They have two major responsibilities. They detect and prevent:

- undocumented aliens from entering the United States illegally
- the smuggling of drugs along the United States borders and land ports of entry

As part of their job, Border Patrol Agents carry firearms and operate a variety of vehicles including four-wheel, all-terrain vehicles. The majority of the Border Patrol Agents work along the United States and Mexico border. Part of their duty is to be able to speak Spanish fluently (many new Border Patrol Agents learn the language during their academy training).

Line watch is the basic activity for Border Patrol Agents. This work can be dangerous and hard. They usually work alone in remote areas, such as deserts and mountains, without any backup. They often work at night, in bad weather, and on rough terrain. They might perform surveillance from a hidden position; respond to electronic sensor alarms and use infrared scopes; or follow tracks, marks, and other physical evidence.

In addition, they may be involved in high-speed chases and armed encounters.

Border Patrol Agents are also assigned to checkpoint stations along the borders where they complete traffic and transportation checks. Some Border Patrol Agents are assigned to interior stations such as in Dallas, San Francisco, and New York. They observe traffic on highways and roads, keeping a watch for vehicles that may be smuggling illegal aliens. The Border Patrol Agents also patrol cities and agricultural areas for illegal aliens who may be living there. In addition, they check ranches and farms for illegal aliens who may be working there.

Border Patrol Agents are assigned a rotating shift, but they often work long and irregular overtime hours. It is not unusual for Border Patrol Agents to be involved in operations that keep them away from home for more than a month.

Salaries

Border Patrol Agents receive a salary based on a pay schedule called *General Schedule.* The pay schedule starts at the GS-1 grade and goes up to the GS-15 grade, with each grade having 10 steps. After the GS-15 grade, salary is based on the Senior Executive Service schedule.

Depending on their education and experience, they begin at the GS-5 or GS-7 grade. In 1999, annual salaries for new Border Patrol Agents who were appointed at the GS-5 grade ranged between $25,000 and $32,000. Salaries for those who were appointed at the GS-7 grade ranged between $29,000 and $37,000. Border Patrol Agents can progress up to the GS-12 grade (between $45,000 and $59,000 or more per year) while performing field assignments. Agents can expect higher pay if they live in parts of the United States (such as New York, San Diego, Miami) where the cost of living is higher. Along with receiving extra compensation for working nights, Sundays, and holidays, Border Patrol Agents qualify for overtime pay called "availability pay"—an extra amount that equals 25% of their salary.

Employment Prospects

The Border Patrol has 145 stations along the Mexican and Canadian borders, the sea border along the Gulf of Mexico and the Florida coast, and throughout the interior of the United States. Some stations are also in the Commonwealth of Puerto Rico.

Job opportunities with the Border Patrol are expected to increase about as fast as all other occupations through 2006. From time to time, Congress passes legislation for additional Border Patrol Agents. But applicants can expect to face a long and highly competitive selection process.

Advancement Prospects

After passing their probation period, Border Patrol Agents may apply for special units such as horse patrol, bike patrol, canine detail, and tactical detail. Those who pursue supervisory and administrative positions can seek promotions to senior border patrol agents, supervisory border patrol agents, patrol agents-in-charge, and watch commanders. Interested Border Patrol Agents can also apply for investigator positions with INS Criminal Investigations.

Many Border Patrol Agents go on to work with other law enforcement agencies such as police departments, sheriff's departments, the Federal Bureau of Investigation, Drug Enforcement Agency, and U.S. Secret Service.

Special Requirements

Applicants must be United States citizens who are between the ages of 18 and 37. In addition, they must agree to certain conditions such as learning Spanish and accepting appointments on or near the Mexican border.

They must pass a written exam that tests general aptitude and the ability to learn a foreign language (a candidate already fluent in Spanish takes a Spanish aptitude test instead). Applicants must also pass a panel interview, a medical exam, a drug test, and a background check. This selection process can take several months.

Successful applicants are placed on an eligibility list, and offered jobs as training sessions become available at the Border Patrol Academy. The waiting period can range anywhere from a few weeks to almost a year.

Border Patrol Agents must retire when they turn 57 years old.

Education and Training

Applicants without any work experience can qualify at the GS-5 grade with a bachelor's degree. They can qualify at the GS-7 grade if they have completed one year of graduate work in law, police science, criminal justice, or another related field.

Border Patrol Trainees attend 19 weeks of physical and academic training at either the Federal Law Enforcement Training Center in Glynco, Georgia, or the Immigration and Naturalization Service (INS) facility in Charleston, South Carolina. Among the subjects the trainees study are immigration and naturalization law, border patrol duties, use of firearms, and Spanish.

Upon graduation from the academy, trainees are assigned to a post on or near the Mexican border. They perform patrol duties under the supervision of a field training officer. They are tested for Spanish fluency after six months and ten months. If they do not pass by the ten-month test, their probationary period ends, and they must leave the job.

Experience and Skills

Applicants who have no college degrees can qualify at the GS-5 grade with one year of general work experience. They can qualify at the GS-7 grade with one year of law enforcement experience.

The U.S. Border Patrol looks for applicants who are fluent in Spanish or have the ability to learn the language. It chooses applicants who show they have the stamina and strength to perform duties under harsh environmental conditions. Applicants also show that they have interpersonal skills, problem-solving abilities, and decision-making skills.

Unions/Associations

The National Border Patrol Council is the union for Border Patrol Agents. In addition, Border Patrol Agents might belong to the Federal Law Enforcement Officers Association, which offers professional support and service programs and networking opportunities.

Tips for Entry

1. Take Spanish classes in high school and college to improve your chances of getting a Border Patrol job.
2. Applicants can complete all required examinations at one time with a special process called expedited hiring. It is scheduled throughout the year in various cities. Applicants must arrange and pay for their travel to an expedited hiring session.
3. To learn more about the U.S. Border Patrol, including recruitment information, visit its web site on the Internet. Its address is *http://www.ins.usdoj.gov/borderpatrol/default.htm.*

SECRET SERVICE SPECIAL AGENT

CAREER PROFILE

Duties: Protect U.S. president and other officials; investigate counterfeiting and financial crime

Salary Range: $25,000 to $59,000

Employment Prospects: Limited

Advancement Prospects: Good
Prerequisites:

Special Requirements—Must be a U.S. citizen; be between 21 and 37 years old; have excellent health; pass the selection process

Education or Training—Bachelor's degree (without experience); academy training, field training

Experience—Three years of law enforcement or criminal investigation experience (without a college degree)

Special Skills—Teamwork and interpersonal skills; foreign language skills desired; problem-solving, writing, and communication skills

CAREER LADDER

```
┌─────────────────────────────────────────┐
│   Senior Secret Service Special Agent    │
└─────────────────────────────────────────┘

┌─────────────────────────────────────────┐
│      Secret Service Special Agent        │
└─────────────────────────────────────────┘

┌─────────────────────────────────────────┐
│   Secret Service Special Agent Trainee   │
└─────────────────────────────────────────┘
```

Position Description

Secret Service Special Agents are part of the U.S. Secret Service, which is part of the Department of Treasury. These Special Agents have two major responsibilities. The more familiar duty is that of protecting the U.S. president and other important officials. The other duty is conducting counterfeiting and financial crime investigations.

As part of the protective detail, Secret Service Special Agents protect the president, vice president, and their families. They protect former presidents, their spouses, and their children who are sixteen or younger. In the last few months of a presidential campaign, Special Agents protect all major presidential and vice presidential candidates and their spouses. In addition they protect heads of foreign countries or governments and their spouses who visit the United States. Also, official United States representatives on special missions to foreign countries are protected by the Secret Service Special Agents.

The U.S. Secret Service refers to an individual that it protects as a *protectee*. When a protectee plans to visit a city or other locale, Secret Service Special Agents organize and arrange security measures as well as gather information about individuals and groups who may be threats or risks to their protectee. Secret Service Special Agents also plan travel itineraries and arrange the modes of transportation.

Secret Service Special Agents on advance teams inspect the locations that their protectees will visit. There they create security perimeters and determine what equipment and staff is needed to safeguard their protectee. They also make necessary arrangements with local authorities for security measures such as police escorts or special police patrols. In addition, they investigate threats made against their protectees.

As part of the investigative detail, the Secret Service Special Agents investigate the counterfeiting of U.S. currency in the United States or other countries. They also have the authority to investigate forgery, theft, and trafficking of government identification, government checks, bonds, and other financial certificates. Major financial crime, such as credit card fraud, computer fraud, automatic teller machine fraud, and cellular telephone fraud, is also the responsibility of Secret Service Special Agents.

Information that is gathered on a case is presented to a U.S. Attorney or other appropriate official who decides what action should be taken. If suspects are prosecuted, the Secret Service Special Agents may testify in court about their findings.

Secret Service Special Agents carry firearms, but have limited powers to arrest criminals. They may only arrest persons who are committing a federal offense in their presence. If Special Agents have sufficient facts to believe that someone is committing a felony, they can arrest that person.

They work a regular 40-hour week, but put in many long, irregular hours of overtime. Throughout their careers, Secret Service Special Agents may be reassigned to any Secret Service office in the United States or in other countries.

Salaries

Secret Service Special Agents receive a salary based on a pay schedule called *General Schedule.* The pay schedule starts at the GS-1 grade and goes up to the GS-15 grade, with each grade having 10 steps. After the GS-15 grade, salary is based on the Senior Executive Service schedule.

Depending on their education and experience, they begin at the GS-5 or GS-7 grade. In 1998, annual salaries for new Secret Service Special Agents who were appointed at the GS-5 grade ranged between $25,000 and $32,000. Those who were appointed at the GS-7 grade received between $29,000 and $37,000. They can progress up to the GS-12 grade (between $45,000 and $59,000 or more per year) while performing field assignments. Those who live in metropolitan areas (such as New York, Chicago, Baltimore, or Los Angeles) where the cost of living is higher can expect higher pay. In addition, Secret Service Special Agents qualify for overtime pay called "availability pay"—an extra amount that equals 25% of their salary.

Employment Prospects

The U.S. Secret Service has over 125 field offices throughout the United States and in some foreign countries. The agency is always interested in qualified applicants, but job opportunities are limited. The attrition rate is low, and most openings become available when Secret Service Special Agents retire, resign, or are promoted to higher positions.

Advancement Prospects

Throughout their careers, Secret Service Special Agents are rotated in tours of duty to gain knowledge, skills, and experience in all areas. Those with the desire and ability to assume supervisory and administrative responsibilities compete for available positions. Upon reaching the GS-12 grade, they may be promoted to Senior Secret Service Special Agent.

Special Requirements

Applicants must be U.S. citizens who are between 21 and 37 years old and are in excellent physical condition. In addition, applicants must pass every step of the agency's selection process, which includes the following: application, written exam, panel interview, medical examination, background investigation, drug test, and polygraph examination. Successful applicants are placed on an eligibility list, and are offered positions as they become available, which may take up to one year or longer.

Secret Service Special Agents must retire when they turn 57 years old.

Education and Training

A bachelor's degree, without relevant work experience, qualifies an applicant at the GS-5 level. An additional year of graduate work in law enforcement, criminal justice, or other related field qualifies an applicant at the GS-7 level.

Secret Service Special Agent trainees undergo nine weeks of criminal investigative training at the Federal Law Enforcement Training Center in Glynco, Georgia. This is followed by 11 weeks of training at the Secret Service Training Academy in Beltsville, Maryland. They learn specific Secret Service policies, procedures, and basic knowledge. In addition, they receive firearms training, control tactics, water survival skills and physical fitness training. Upon completion of academy training, they are assigned to a field office, and under the supervision of a field-training officer, begin performing routine tasks.

Experience and Skills

Applicants who have no college degree can qualify at the GS-5 grade with three years of criminal investigative or law enforcement work experience. Applicants with a bachelor's degree and one year of criminal investigative or law enforcement experience can qualify at the GS-7 level.

The Secret Service looks for candidates who are team players and have good interpersonal skills. It especially wants candidates who are fluent in a foreign language. In addition, the agency chooses candidates who show that they have strong problem-solving, writing, and communication skills.

Unions/Associations

Secret Service Special Agents might join the Federal Law Enforcement Officers Association, a professional organization that offers networking opportunities and professional service and support programs.

Tips for Entry

1. To apply for a Special Agent position, contact a Secret Service field office. You might find a listing in your local telephone book under *U.S. Government.*
2. The Secret Service participates in the Cooperative Education Program, in which qualified college students are part of a two-year work-study program in selected fields of study. Also available are Secret Service Special Agent co-op positions, which are limited to the Washington D.C. area. Contact a Secret Service office for more information.
3. To learn more about the United States Secret Service, visit its web site on the Internet. Its web address is *http://www.treas.gov/usss/index.htm.*

SPECIAL POLICE UNITS

BIKE PATROL OFFICER

CAREER PROFILE

Duties: Perform patrol duties by bicycle

Alternate Titles: Police Cyclist, Bicycle Officer

Salary Range: $40,000 to $56,000

Employment Prospects: Fair

Advancement Prospects: Limited
Prerequisites:
Education—Certified police bicycle training
Experience—Two to three years experience of patrol duty
Special Skills—Bicycle skills; excellent physical condition; interpersonal and communication skills

CAREER LADDER

```
┌─────────────────────────────────────┐
│  Police Cyclist Instructor or Bike Patrol │
│           Unit Commander            │
└─────────────────────────────────────┘

┌─────────────────────────────────────┐
│         Bike Patrol Officer         │
└─────────────────────────────────────┘

┌─────────────────────────────────────┐
│           Police Officer            │
└─────────────────────────────────────┘
```

Position Description

Bike Patrol Officers perform patrol duties on mountain bicycles. They are part of a police department's bicycle patrol unit, a special detail for which police officers may volunteer.

Police bicycles are equipped with necessary gear such as two-way radios, first aid supplies, report forms, and bicycle maintenance kits. Unlike their peers in police vehicles, Bike Patrol Officers have the advantage of being unseen and unheard by criminals. Their patrol duties, however, are similar. Bike Patrol Officers:

- preserve the peace
- respond to calls for service
- enforce traffic laws
- keep an eye out for public hazards
- watch for suspicious criminal activities
- investigate crime
- apprehend lawbreakers
- keep detailed field logs and write police reports

Bike Patrol Officers patrol residential areas, downtown areas, shopping centers, campuses, parks, jogging trails, and bike trails. Their beats include congested areas and areas with special terrain that are inaccessible to patrol vehicles. Due to their mobility, they patrol parades, marathons, festivals, and other special events. Besides their patrol duties,

Bike Patrol Officers also conduct bicycle safety workshops for children.

Bike Patrol Officers ride alone or in pairs. Many officers ride their bicycles for their entire work shift. Some officers attach their bicycles to their patrol car and put them in use for part of their shift or for specific areas of their beat. Bike Patrol Officers pedal normally between 15 to 25 miles every day in almost any weather, except for extreme conditions.

In large bike patrol units, Bike Patrol Officers work rotating shifts. In smaller units, Bike Patrol Officers are assigned to work shifts when criminal activity is known to be most prevalent. Like other Police Officers, Bike Patrol Officers are on call 24 hours a day, seven days a week.

Salaries

Bike Patrol Officers are paid according to their rank and level in their police department. Depending on their agency, officers might earn additional compensation for performing bike patrol duty. The Bureau of Labor Statistics (of the U.S. Department of Labor) reported in its 1996 "Occupational Compensation Survey" that many police officers who performed one or more special police duties, such as bike patrol, earned a salary between $40,924 and $56,160 per year (or between $787 and $1,080 per week). That did not include compensation for working overtime, holidays, weekends, and late-night shifts.

Employment Prospects

Many police departments—as well as some county, state, and federal law enforcement agencies—have bike patrol units. In 1998, there were more than 3,000 bike patrol units. This is expected to grow to 5,000 units by the year 2000. The creation or expansion of bike patrol units for any police department is dependent on its budget. Many police departments have been able to start units with the support and financial assistance of their communities.

Advancement Prospects

Police officers have the opportunity to develop a career according to their personal interests and ambitions. Volunteering for special police units such as bike patrol broadens their experience and may serve as a stepping stone in their careers. In addition to tackling special assignments, many officers pursue promotions to detective, sergeant, lieutenant, and so on. Depending on the police department, officers with administrative and managerial duties may be limited in their capacity to volunteer for special police units.

Many departments require that Bike Patrol Officers commit to a two-year assignment. Supervisory and administrative positions within the bike patrol detail are limited to unit commanders. Becoming certified police cyclist instructors is another career path for Bike Patrol Officers.

Education and Training

Once selected to work the bike patrol detail, officers complete a certified police bike training course. They learn bicycle patrol procedures, pursuit tactics, traffic enforcement, bicycle maintenance, bicycle safety, and other basic tactical bicycle riding skills.

Experience and Skills

Police officers must complete two to three years of patrol duty before they are eligible to apply for a Bike Patrol Officer position.

Candidates must have some bicycle skills and be in excellent physical condition. They must have the strength and stamina to pedal a bicycle with 20 pounds of gear for several hours over different types of terrain, and sometimes at top speed. Being in closer contact to the community, Bike Patrol Officer candidates must have excellent interpersonal and communication skills.

Unions/Associations

The International Police Mountain Bike Association (a division of the League of American Bicyclists) and the Law Enforcement Bicycle Association are two organizations specifically for Bike Patrol Officers. Both groups offer professional resources, services, networking opportunities, training, and certification.

Tips for Entry

1. As a police officer, let the bike patrol unit commander know of your interest, especially before you are eligible or before an opening is available.
2. Ride a bicycle regularly to build up and maintain physical stamina and endurance.
3. Get the community involved in starting or expanding a bike patrol unit. Many bike patrol units were started with community involvement, such as raising funds for buying bicycles and equipment.
4. Learn more about different law enforcement bike patrol units on the Internet. Enter the phrase *bike patrol unit* in a search engine to get a list of web sites.

K-9 HANDLER

CAREER PROFILE

Duties: Search for suspects and evidence at a crime scene with a trained police dog

Alternate Title: K-9 (Canine) Officer

Salary Range: $40,000 to $56,000

Employment Prospects: Fair

Advancement Prospects: Limited
   Prerequisites:
   Education—Certified police canine training
   Experience—Two to three years of patrol duty
   Special Skills—Able to handle and train dogs

CAREER LADDER

```
┌─────────────────────────────────────┐
│  K-9 Trainer or K-9 Unit Commander   │
└─────────────────────────────────────┘

┌─────────────────────────────────────┐
│            K-9 Handler               │
└─────────────────────────────────────┘

┌─────────────────────────────────────┐
│           Police Officer             │
└─────────────────────────────────────┘
```

Position Description

K9 Handlers (or Canine Handlers) search for suspects and physical evidence with trained police dogs as their partners. Together, K9 Handlers and their dogs are known as K9 teams. They are part of a police department's K9 unit, a special detail for which police officers may volunteer. Police officers perform canine duty in addition to their regular patrol, detective, or administrative duty.

Canine teams are either trained for general patrol purposes or for specific purposes such as locating narcotics. They are called out to crime scenes when their specially trained support is needed. The teams are used for tracking criminals in rural, suburban, or urban settings. In addition, they are used to search buildings for suspects, evidence, drugs, or explosives.

Patrol officers are usually assigned to heavy crime areas, using their dogs as backups in dangerous situations. Their dogs also chase and apprehend criminals. In addition, many police departments use their K9 teams for search and rescue missions. The K9 teams help locate missing or lost persons. They also search for survivors and victims in man-made or natural disasters.

K9 Handlers are responsible for the well-being and safety of their dogs. They feed, water, groom, and exercise their dogs daily. They make sure their dogs get any necessary shots. And they train their dogs weekly, if not daily, on their tracking, obedience, aggression, and control skills. Most K9 Handlers keep their dogs at home with them.

K9 Handlers must have complete control over their dogs at all times. They decide in what situations to use their dogs, making sure there is no risk present for either themselves or their partners. For example, before having their dogs search a crime scene, K9 Handlers first inspect the area for hazards such as broken glass, harmful substances, and other dogs.

In departments with a large canine unit, K9 teams are assigned to any work shift. With small canine units, K9 teams are assigned an afternoon or midnight shift when there is more criminal activity. K9 Handlers and their partners are on call 24 hours a day, every day of the year.

Salaries

K9 Handlers earn a salary commensurate with their rank and level in their police department. Depending on their agency, officers might earn additional compensation for performing canine duty. Most officers receive compensation for taking care of city-owned dogs in their homes.

The Bureau of Labor Statistics (of the U.S. Department of Labor) reported in its 1996 "Occupational Compensation Survey" that many police officers who performed one or more special police duties, such as canine duty, earned a salary between $40,924 and $56,160 per year (or between $787 and $1,080 per week). That did not include compensation for working overtime, holidays, weekends, and late-night shifts.

Employment Prospects

The police dog has become one of the fastest crime prevention tools in law enforcement. Besides police departments, other law enforcement agencies also have K9 units—such as sheriff's departments, state police departments, fish and wildlife divisions, the U.S. Border Patrol, and Drug Enforcement Administration.

Opportunities for K9 Handlers are available, but the competition is keen as the jobs are popular and the turnover rate is low. The creation or expansion of K9 units depends on a police department's budget.

Advancement Prospects

Police officers have the opportunity to carve out a career in accordance with their personal interests and ambitions. Volunteering for special police units such as canine duty broadens their experience and may serve as a stepping stone in their careers. Along with working special assignments, many officers pursue promotion to detective, sergeant, lieutenant, and so on. Depending on the police department, officers with administrative and managerial duties may be limited in their capacity to volunteer for special police units.

Many departments require that officers commit to a minimum number of years to canine duty due to the cost and time required for training. Supervisory and administrative positions within the canine detail are limited to unit commanders. Becoming certified police canine trainers is another career path for K9 Handlers.

Education and Training

Police officers selected to be K9 Handlers are provided 14 weeks of training at an accredited police canine training school. The curriculum includes basics on dog temperaments and abilities, principles of dog training, training drills, dog maintenance and nutrition, and tracking skills. Those officers who will handle single-purpose dogs, such as for detecting narcotics, train for additional weeks.

Some departments require that K9 teams be recertified once or twice a year.

Experience and Skills

After serving on their force for two or three years and meeting specific departmental requirements, police officers can apply for canine duty. Police departments look for officers who show job stability and are mature, even-tempered, patient, and self-disciplined.

K9 Handler candidates should enjoy being around dogs for long periods of time and must be perceptive to how dogs react with their environment. Most important, they should have the ability to train dogs. They should be physically fit in order to keep up with their dogs. And they should be willing to speak and praise their dogs in soft, and sometimes baby-like, tones in public.

Unions/Associations

The North American Police Work Dog Association and the United States Police Canine Association are two national organizations to which many K9 Handlers belong. Both groups provide professional support services and networking as well as offer continuing education classes and certified training programs. In addition, K9 Handlers might belong to state and local law enforcement canine associations.

Tips for Entry

1. Get lots of experience being around, caring for, and training dogs.
2. As a police officer, let the K9 unit commander know of your interest, especially before you are eligible or before an opening is available.
3. Learn more about different law enforcement K9 units on the Internet. Enter the phrase *K9 unit* in a search engine to get a list of web sites.

OBSERVER

CAREER PROFILE

Duties: Perform patrol and tactical assistance from police aircraft

Alternate Titles: Flight Officer or Tactical Flight Officer

Salary Range: $40,000 to $56,000

Employment Prospects: Fair

Advancement Prospects: Limited
Prerequisites:
Education—In-house training
Experience—Three to five years of police work; knowledge of aircraft and Federal Airway regulations; knowledge of geography
Special Skills—Observational, communication, and organizational skills; decision-making skills

CAREER LADDER

```
┌─────────────────────────────────────────┐
│  Pilot or Air Support Unit Commander     │
└─────────────────────────────────────────┘

┌─────────────────────────────────────────┐
│               Observer                   │
└─────────────────────────────────────────┘

┌─────────────────────────────────────────┐
│            Police Officer                │
└─────────────────────────────────────────┘
```

Position Description

Observers provide patrol and tactical assistance from the air to support ground police operations. They are part of a police department's air support unit, a special detail for which police officers may volunteer. Police officers perform air support duty in addition to their regular patrol, detective, or administrative duty.

The flight crews are made up of pilots and one or more Observers. The crews fly in either helicopters or small fixed-wing planes. They perform patrol duty as well as assist in tactical ground operations in which, for example, the crews might help search for fleeing criminals, pursue high-speed drivers, or contain crime scenes. Flight crews perform other missions as well. They might perform surveillance work, recover stolen vehicles, transport prisoners, protect dignitaries, locate missing persons, assist in putting out fires, or assess the damage and danger in man-made and natural disasters.

In the air, Observers are watchful of the activity on the ground and relay their observations to police ground units. For example, Observers might inform ground units where fleeing suspects are hiding in bushes along a river. Observers operate specialized equipment from the police aircraft. They look through high-powered binoculars. They use high-powered searchlights and operate thermal imaging devices that detect the "heat signatures" of persons and objects. They also work with public address systems, video surveillance equipment, and tracking systems. In addition, Observers manage all police radio communications.

Observers assist the pilots by keeping watch on flight instruments and gauges. They look for wires, towers, and other air traffic. At the end of each flight, most Observers complete the flight log.

Air support duty may be part-time or full-time duty, depending on the police department. Part-time officers are assigned to work a few hours each week in the air support unit. The rest of their time is spent performing their regular duty as patrol officers, detectives, or administrators. Most departments rotate their aviation crew on an on-call schedule for nights and weekends.

Salaries

Observers earn a salary according to their rank and level in their police department. Depending on their agency, they might earn additional compensation for performing air support duty. In its 1996 "Occupational Compensation Survey," the Bureau of Labor Statistics (of the U.S. Department of Labor) reported that many police officers who performed one or more special police duties such as air support duty, earned a salary between $40,924 to $56,160 per year (or between $787 to $1,080 per week). That did not include compensation for working overtime, holidays, weekends, and late night shifts.

Employment Prospects

Besides police departments, air support units can be found in county, state, and federal law enforcement agencies. Job opportunities for Observers generally are more available in large police departments. In the next few years, opportunities may also become available in smaller departments because local law enforcement agencies may obtain surplus military helicopters for free from the federal government.

Advancement Prospects

Police officers have the ability to develop a career commensurate with their personal interests and ambitions. Volunteering for special police units such as air support duty broadens their experience and serves as a stepping stone in their careers. In addition to working special assignments, many officers pursue promotions to detective, sergeant, lieutenant, and so on. Depending on the police department, officers with administrative and managerial duties may be limited in their opportunities to volunteer for special police units.

Many departments require that officers commit to a minimum number of years for air support duty. Supervisory and administrative positions within the air support detail are limited to unit commanders. Becoming pilots in the air support unit is another career path for Observers.

Education and Training

At most departments, Observers receive in-house training. They learn the geographical layout of their jurisdiction, cockpit resource management, use of specialized equipment, search techniques, and basic aircraft operation. Some agencies teach Observers basic aircraft maneuvers in case of emergencies.

Depending on the department, Observers participate in monthly in-service training.

Experience and Skills

Generally police officers need three to five years of police duty before they are eligible to apply for an Observer position. Police departments look for mature and responsible candidates who have knowledge of aircraft, Federal Airway Regulations, and geography. In addition, candidates should have strong observational, communication, and organizational skills. Furthermore, they should be able to size up stressful situations quickly and make sensible decisions.

Unions/Associations

Many Observers belong to Airborne Law Enforcement Association, a national organization that offers professional support, networking, and educational programs to all law enforcement officers who are involved in air-support duty. Many Observers also belong to the Law Enforcement Thermographers' Association, an international law enforcement group involved in promoting the use of thermal imaging in law enforcement operations. This group offers professional networking, training, and certification.

Tips for Entry

1. Young people might join the Law Enforcement Explorers and/or Civil Air Patrol to gain experience in both aviation and law enforcement.

2. Take college courses or earn a degree in Aerospace Engineering.

3. As a police officer, let the air support unit commander know of your interest, especially before you are eligible or before an opening is available.

4. Learn more about different law enforcement air support units on the Internet. Enter the phrase *police air support unit* or *police aviation unit* in a search engine to get a list of web sites.

BOMB TECHNICIAN

CAREER PROFILE

Duties: Neutralize and dispose of bombs and other explosive devices

Salary Range: $40,000 to $56,000

Employment Prospects: Fair

Advancement Prospects: Limited
Prerequisites:
Education—FBI training for Bomb Technicians
Experience—Five years of police work
Special Skills—Concentration and problem-solving skills; mechanical, electrical, or electronic skills

CAREER LADDER

```
┌─────────────────────────────────────────┐
│  Specialist or Bomb Squad Commander      │
└─────────────────────────────────────────┘

┌─────────────────────────────────────────┐
│           Bomb Technician                 │
└─────────────────────────────────────────┘

┌─────────────────────────────────────────┐
│           Patrol Officer                  │
└─────────────────────────────────────────┘
```

Position Description

Bomb Technicians safely neutralize and dispose of explosive devices—such as bombs, dynamite, incendiary devices, ammunition, military ordnance, firecrackers, and pipe bombs and other improvised devices. Bomb Technicians are part of a police department's bomb squad or Explosive Ordnance Disposal (EOD) unit. This is a special detail for which police officers may volunteer. Police officers perform bomb squad duty in addition to their regular patrol, detective, or administrative duty.

Working in teams of two or more, Bomb Technicians investigate situations where explosive devices are or may be present. They are called out to homes, business offices and buildings, factories, colleges, schools, airports, sports arenas, parking lots, grassy fields, and other locations. They also examine vehicles, buses, and airplanes. Executing great care and precision, Bomb Technicians examine explosive devices as well as hoax devices (objects or packages made to look like explosives). They render safe, remove, and dispose of all explosives that they find.

Bomb Technicians wear protective suits while working. They use hand tools, X-ray machines, remote-controlled robots, and other equipment. To defuse bombs, they might use counter-explosives or water cannons called disrupters.

Besides disarming explosive devices, Bomb Technicians perform other duties.

They:

- investigate "post blast" crime scenes where explosive devices may have been used

- assist in special operations such as providing support to tactical teams
- perform bomb sweeps to secure locations or areas where dignitaries will visit
- present bomb threat awareness and safety programs to public and private groups
- develop evacuation and search plans for government agencies and private companies

Bomb Technicians are available for duty 24 hours a day, seven days a week. In large bomb squad units, Bomb Technicians are rotated on an on-call schedule.

Salaries

Bomb Technicians are paid according to their rank and level in their police department. Many officers also earn additional compensation for performing bomb squad duty. In its 1996 "Occupational Compensation Survey," the Bureau of Labor Statistics (of the U.S. Department of Labor) reported that many police officers who performed one or more special police duties, such as bomb squad duty, earned a salary between $40,924 to $56,160 per year (or between $787 to $1,080 per week). That did not include compensation for working overtime, holidays, weekends, and late-night shifts.

Employment Prospects

Along with police departments, bomb squad units can be found in county, state, and federal law enforcement agencies. Some bomb squad units are formed using officers from different law enforcement agencies in an area or region.

With the increase in reported bombing incidents in recent years, more and more police departments are seeing the need for establishing highly trained bomb squad units.

Advancement Prospects

Police officers have the ability to develop a career commensurate with their personal interests and ambitions. Volunteering for service in special police units, such as bomb squad duty broadens their experience and may serve as a stepping stone in their careers. In addition, to taking on special assignments, many officers pursue promotions to detective, sergeant, lieutenant, and so on. Depending on the police department, officers with administrative and managerial duties may be limited in their capacity to volunteer for special police units.

Many departments require that officers commit to a certain number of years for bomb squad duty. Supervisory and administrative positions within the bomb squad detail are limited to unit commanders. Becoming a specialist in robotics, render safe procedures, or other technical area is another career path for Bomb Technicians.

Education and Training

Selected officers complete FBI training for Bomb Technicians at the Hazardous Devices School in Huntsville, Alabama. The training lasts about 28 days. They learn basic procedures for handling hazardous explosive devices including the FBI's Render Safe and Disposal procedures for Improvised Explosive Devices.

Experience and Skills

To be considered for a Bomb Technician position, police officers need at least five years of full-time experience. They may be patrol officers, detectives, or administrators. Police departments look for candidates who are in excellent physical condition with exceptional eyesight and hearing. Candidates should be long on patience and have steady nerves. And they should have good concentration and decision-making skills. In addition, candidates should have mechanical, electrical, or electronic skills.

Unions/Associations

Bomb Technicians might join the International Association of Bomb Technicians and Investigators, an organization that provides professional support, networking, and education.

Tips for Entry

1. As a police officer, let the bomb squad commander know of your interest, especially before you are eligible or before an opening is available.
2. Get a background in mechanical, electronic, or electrical engineering.
3. Learn more about different law enforcement bomb squads on the Internet. Enter the phrase *police bomb squad* or *bomb squad unit* in a search engine to get a list of web sites.

SWAT SNIPER

CAREER PROFILE

Duties: Provide disciplined, accurate marksmanship in high-risk operations

Alternate Title: Marksman

Salary Range: $40,000 to $56,000

Employment Prospects: Fair

Advancement Prospects: Limited
  Prerequisites:
  Education—Certified sniper training
  Experience—Be a SWAT team member
  Special Skills—Marksmanship skills and camouflaging skills; concentration skills

CAREER LADDER

```
┌─────────────────────────────────┐
│   SWAT Instructor or SWAT Unit   │
│           Commander              │
└─────────────────────────────────┘

┌─────────────────────────────────┐
│          SWAT Sniper             │
└─────────────────────────────────┘

┌─────────────────────────────────┐
│        SWAT Team Member          │
└─────────────────────────────────┘
```

Position Description

SWAT Snipers are specially trained police officers with sharpshooting expertise. They are part of a police department's tactical operations detail usually called the Special Weapons and Tactics (SWAT) unit. This is a special detail for which police officers may volunteer. Police officers perform SWAT duty in addition to their regular patrol, detective, or administrative duty.

SWAT units provide weapon and fire support in high-risk operations. They are called to assist in situations where:

- heavily armed suspects have barricaded themselves to resist arrest
- armed suspects have taken hostages
- suspects are shooting at others from hidden or faraway locations
- warrants are being executed to suspects who may be heavily armed

In addition, SWAT units are called out to help other law enforcement agencies. They might assist in drug arrrests, protection of visiting dignitaries, riot suppression, and other special circumstances.

In a SWAT call-out, SWAT Snipers work together with SWAT observers, forming two-member sniper teams. Sniper teams locate the best positions for SWAT Snipers to take accurate aim on the suspects. Using camouflage and concealment techniques, sniper teams might scale high walls and fences, climb trees, run across wide open spaces, crawl on the ground, or creep through brush and grassy fields. Sniper teams keep in contact with the command post by two-way radios at all times. The observers are in charge of communication and relay information back and forth between the sniper teams and the command post.

Upon reaching an advantageous location, SWAT Snipers calculate distance, elevation, wind, and other factors to find the best firing position to aim at a suspect. When SWAT Snipers have settled comfortably into favorable firing positions, the observers notify the command post. SWAT Snipers stay in their positions, ready to fire when they receive the order from the command post.

According to the National Tactical Officers Association, most SWAT call-outs end in peaceful resolutions without any shots ever being fired.

SWAT team members are on call 24 hours a day, seven days a week. In large SWAT units, members may be rotated on an on-call schedule.

Salaries

SWAT Snipers are paid according to their rank and level in their police department. Most also receive additional compensation for performing SWAT duty. In its 1996 "Occupational Compensation Survey," the Bureau of Labor Statistics (of the U.S. Department of Labor) reported that many police officers who performed one or more special police duties, such as SWAT duty, earned a salary between $40,924 and $56,160 per year (or between $787 and $1,080 per week).

SPECIAL POLICE UNITS 33

That did not include compensation for working overtime, holidays, weekends, and late night shifts.

Employment Prospects

Besides police departments, many county, state, and federal law enforcement agencies also have SWAT units or tactical details. The expansion or creation of SWAT units depends on the region or an agency's need for tactical details. In recent years, more smaller police departments have been forming SWAT units.

Advancement Prospects

Police officers have the ability to develop a career commensurate with their personal interests and ambitions. Volunteering for special police units such as SWAT broadens their experience and may serve as a stepping stone in their careers. In addition to taking on special assignments, many officers pursue promotions to detective, sergeant, lieutenant, and so on. Depending on the police department, officers with administrative and managerial duties may be limited in their capacity to volunteer for special police units.

Many departments require that officers commit to a minimum number of years for SWAT duty. Supervisory and administrative positions within the SWAT detail are limited to unit commanders. Becoming certified SWAT instructors is another career path for SWAT Snipers.

Education and Training

SWAT Snipers must pass intensive certified training. Most, if not all, departments require that Snipers be tested once or twice a year to ensure that they are retaining their high marksmanship skills. SWAT Snipers are required to train monthly, practicing in different lighting and weather conditions as well as shooting from different positions. They also practice shooting in special situations, such as shooting through glass.

In addition, Snipers must train with the whole SWAT unit monthly. Furthermore, SWAT units must attend a week-long training session every year. Many departments also require SWAT members to pass a physical training test once or twice a year.

Experience and Skills

SWAT team members who have passed their probation period are eligible to apply for SWAT Sniper positions. Successful candidates have excellent shooting and camouflaging skills. They are in outstanding physical condition, plus they have the ability to concentrate for long periods of time.

Unions/Associations

Many SWAT Snipers belong to a state or regional professional SWAT association. Some also join two national professional groups: the American Special Operations Sniper Association and the National Tactical Officers Association. Both organizations offer the opportunity for networking as well as provide professional training, education programs, and other services.

Tips for Entry

1. As a SWAT candidate, let the unit commander know of your interest in becoming a SWAT Sniper.
2. Learn a form of martial arts, such as Tae Kwon Do or Karate. Many SWAT commanders have found the discipline of martial arts to be a valuable asset for performing SWAT duties.
3. Learn more about different SWAT units on the Internet. Enter the phrase *SWAT unit* in a search engine to get a list of web sites.

CRIME PREVENTION SPECIALIST

CAREER PROFILE

Duties: Provide crime prevention and awareness programs to the community

Alternate Title: Crime Prevention Officer

Salary Range: $40,000 to $56,000

Employment Prospects: Fair

Advancement Prospects: Limited
Prerequisites:
Education—A college degree; certified training
Experience—Two to five years of law enforcement experience; knowledge and experience with crime prevention or community relations programs
Special Skills—Program development and organizational skills; public speaking and teaching skills; interpersonal skills

CAREER LADDER

```
┌─────────────────────────────────────┐
│   Crime Prevention Unit Commander    │
└─────────────────────────────────────┘

┌─────────────────────────────────────┐
│      Crime Prevention Officer        │
└─────────────────────────────────────┘

┌─────────────────────────────────────┐
│           Police Officer             │
└─────────────────────────────────────┘
```

Position Description

Crime Prevention Officers provide crime prevention and awareness programs to the community. They are part of a police department's crime prevention unit, a special detail for which police officers may volunteer. The position may be full time or part time. Part-time officers perform crime prevention duty in addition to their regular patrol, detective, or administrative duty.

Crime Prevention Officers develop and organize many different crime prevention programs, such as neighborhood watch groups, tenant patrols, business watch groups, property identification programs, child safety programs, senior citizen safety programs, and driving safety programs. To create effective programs, they work directly with the community—individuals, businesses, churches, schools, nonprofit groups, and other government agencies and law enforcement agencies.

Most Crime Prevention Officers provide crime prevention and safety instruction, covering topics such as robbery, drugs in the workplace, rape prevention, child safety, bicycle safety, and security techniques. They conduct workshops for resident groups, businesses, schools, civic groups, and social organizations about crime prevention and personal safety. Some Crime Prevention Officers teach other officers about crime prevention techniques. Some Crime Prevention Officers also train volunteers and reserves to present workshops and seminars.

Other duties for Crime Prevention Officers vary from department to department. Crime Prevention Officers might:

- provide security inspections for businesses and residences
- provide escort services to banks
- check residences while owners are away
- provide victim assistance to local support agencies
- develop crime prevention materials such as brochures, public service announcements, and training worksheets
- compile crime statistics and perform other research tasks
- design crime prevention programs and procedures for other government agencies

Crime Prevention Officers normally work a regular work shift. They also put in additional overtime hours—including nights, weekends, and holidays—to provide the many different crime prevention programs to the community.

Salaries

Crime Prevention Specialists' salaries range according to the rank and level they hold in their police department. Depending on their agency, they might earn additional compensation for performing crime prevention duty. In its 1996

"Occupational Compensation Survey," the Bureau of Labor Statistics (of the U.S. Department of Labor) reported that many police officers who performed one or more special police duties, such as crime prevention duty, earned a salary between $40,924 and $56,160 per year (or between $787 and $1,080 per week). That did not include compensation for working overtime, holidays, weekends, and late-night shifts.

Employment Prospects

Along with police departments, many sheriff's departments and state police agencies have crime prevention units. Some agencies hire qualified civilians as Crime Prevention Specialists.

Community participation in crime prevention has increased in recent years. More and more departments are starting crime prevention units, and those with established units are adding more Crime Prevention Officers.

Advancement Prospects

Police officers have the opportunity to develop a career according to their personal interests and ambitions. Volunteering for special police units, such as for crime prevention, broadens their experience and may further their careers. In addition to taking on assignments, many officers pursue promotions to detective, sergeant, lieutenant, and so on. Depending on the police department, officers with administrative and managerial duties may be limited in their capacity to volunteer for special police units.

Many departments require that officers commit a minimum number of years to crime prevention on duty. Supervisory and administrative positions within the crime prevention detail are limited to unit commanders.

Another career path for Crime Prevention Officers is to work in the private sector for crime prevention businesses or nonprofit crime prevention agencies. Some former Crime Prevention Officers become consultants or start their own business providing crime prevention services.

Education and Training

Education requirements differ with every police department. Many police departments prefer candidates who have associate's or bachelor's degrees. They especially prefer applicants who have completed courses in communication, journalism, and education.

Training requirements also vary in each police department. Generally, police officers complete certified training programs before performing their duties as Crime Prevention Officers.

Experience and Skills

Experience requirements depend on the complexity of the Crime Prevention Officer's duties in an agency. Depending on the department, applicants need two to five years of law enforcement experience. They should also have experience with crime prevention or community relations programs. In addition, they should have the ability to plan and manage projects as well as have public speaking and teaching skills.

People skills are also very important for the job. Crime Prevention Officers must be able to gain trust, respect, and cooperation from the community. They interact with children, adults, elderly, business people, professionals, and persons from many different backgrounds.

Unions/Associations

Crime Prevention Specialists might belong to local and state crime prevention councils and associations that offer professional support, networking, training, educational programs, and other services. Many also belong to professional organizations such as the International Society of Crime Prevention Practitioners and American Society for Industrial Security.

Tips for Entry

1. Volunteer in Neighborhood Watch and other crime prevention programs.
2. As a police officer, let the crime prevention unit commander know of your interest, especially before you are eligible or before an opening is available.
3. Get experience developing, planning, and organizing programs by helping out with school, church, social, and other group functions.
4. Learn more about crime prevention on the Internet. Enter the phrase *crime prevention* in a search engine to get a list of web sites.

FORENSIC INVESTIGATIONS

CRIME SCENE TECHNICIAN

CAREER PROFILE

Duties: Collect and process physical evidence from crime scenes

Alternate Titles: Crime Scene Examiner, Crime Scene Investigator

Salary Range: $40,000 to $56,000

Employment Prospects: Fair

Advancement Prospects: Limited
Prerequisites:
Education—Requirements vary with the different departments

Experience—One to three years of police work with fingerprinting and crime scene experience; photography and photo processing experience

Special Skills—Communication, writing, interpersonal, and teamwork skills

CAREER LADDER

```
┌─────────────────────────────────┐
│   Crime Scene Unit Commander    │
└─────────────────────────────────┘

┌─────────────────────────────────┐
│    Crime Scene Technician       │
└─────────────────────────────────┘

┌─────────────────────────────────┐
│        Police Officer           │
└─────────────────────────────────┘
```

Position Description

Crime Scene Technicians collect and process physical evidence from crime scenes. They are part of a police department's crime scene unit, a special detail for which police officers may volunteer. The positions may be part time or full time. Part-time officers perform crime scene duty in addition to their regular patrol, detective, or administrative duty.

Their first task at any crime scene is to learn about the crime. Crime Scene Technicians talk with police officers and detectives to get the facts: what kind of crime took place, what happened, who was involved, and so on. With this information, Crime Scene Technicians plan their search for physical evidence that may link suspects to their crimes. If it will not destroy potential evidence, Crime Scene Technicians walk through the crime scene following the apparent path of the crime.

Crime Scene Technicians carefully document the crime scene. They write well-detailed notes as well as draw clear sketches of the scene. In addition, they take rolls and rolls of photographs. Some Crime Scene Technicians also videotape the crime scene.

Using special equipment and techniques, Crime Scene Technicians search thoroughly for all items that may relate to a crime. They look for physical clues, such as bullets, weapons, tools, drugs, papers, clothing, shoe prints, fingerprints, palm prints, and tire impressions. They also examine the area for trace evidence such as body fluids, hair, blood, tool marks, paint chips, glass fragments, and fibers.

Crime Scene Technicians follow certain procedures for collecting different types of evidence. They make sure that all evidence is noted, sketched, and photographed before being placed in proper containers. The containers are labeled accurately with their origins, the date and time when they were collected, and other necessary information. Crime Scene Technicians keep a precise inventory of everything that is collected. The whole process of collecting physical evidence may take several hours, and sometimes may take several days, to complete. The Crime Scene Technicians submit the collected physical evidence to crime labs for further processing.

Besides crime scenes, Crime Scene Technicians might collect physical evidence at autopsies. Crime Scene Technicians also gather evidence at non-crime scenes such as suicides and serious car accidents.

Their other duties vary, depending on their department. Many Crime Scene Technicians process and develop film as well as maintain photographic equipment. Some may take fingerprints of living and deceased persons. Some may maintain files of fingerprints, photographic evidence, and other crime scene data. Others may maintain crime scene equipment.

Crime Scene Technicians work in any type of environment, indoors and outdoors. They often stand, bend, kneel, or crouch in awkward positions. They are on call 24 hours a day, seven days a week. In large crime scene units, they may be rotated on an on-call schedule.

Salaries

Police Crime Scene Technicians earn a salary commensurate with their rank and level in their department. Depending on the agency they work for, they might earn additional compensation for performing crime scene duty. In its 1996 "Occupational Compensation Survey," the Bureau of Labor Statistics (of the U.S. Department of Labor) reported that many police officers who performed one or more special police duties, such as crime scene duty, earned a salary between $40,924 and $56,160 per year (or between $787 and $1,080 per week). That did not include compensation for working overtime, holidays, weekends, and late-night shifts.

Employment Prospects

Most police departments have crime scene units as do sheriff's departments, state police departments, and federal law enforcement agencies. Job opportunities generally become available when Crime Scene Technicians retire, resign, or are promoted to higher positions. The best job opportunities are in large police departments or in areas with high crime activity.

Advancement Prospects

Police officers have the opportunity to develop a career in accordance with their personal interests and ambitions. Volunteering for special police units work such as crime scene duty broadens their experience and furthers their careers. In addition to volunteering for special assignments, many officers pursue promotions to detective, sergeant, lieutenant, and so on. Depending on the police department, officers with adminstrative and managerial duties may be limited in their capacity to volunteer for special police units.

Many departments require that officers commit to a minimum number of years for crime scene duty. Supervisory and administrative positions within the crime scene detail are limited to unit commanders. Another path for Crime Scene Technicians is to obtain additional education and become trace evidence examiners, firearms/toolmarks examiners, or other forensic scientists who work in crime labs. Some Crime Scene Technicians become private consultants in crime scene reconstruction and investigation.

Education and Training

Many departments require an associate's degree in police science or other related field. Some departments accept applicants with a high school diploma or general equivalency diploma if they have completed a minimum of 60 semester units in science, law enforcement, and other related fields.

Many agencies require that new Crime Scene Technicians complete certified training in crime scene investigations.

Experience and Skills

Police officers need one to three years of police duty before they are eligible to apply for crime scene duty. They must have experience in fingerprinting and the handling of physical evidence. They also need one to three years experience in photography and photo processing and development. Some agencies allow applicants to substitute graduation from a certified professional school of photography for experience.

Applicants need good communication skills and interpersonal skills to establish and maintain working relationships with other employees. They also need good writing skills to compose accurate reports and correspondence. In addition, they must be able to work with little or no supervision, and be able to pay close attention to details.

Unions/Associations

Crime Scene Technicians might belong to state or regional organizations that are for professionals involved in crime scene investigations in their areas. At the national and international levels, Crime Scene Technicians might join the International Association for Identification or the Association of Crime Scene Reconstruction. Joining professional organizations gives officers the opportunity to network with peers and obtain professional support and services, such as certified training, continuing education, research resources, and job referrals.

Tips for Entry

1. College students might sign up for internships or do volunteer work with crime scene divisions.
2. Learn basic photography skills as well as how to process and develop both black-and-white and color films.
3. As a police officer, let the crime scene unit commander know of your interest, especially before you are eligible or before an opening is available.
4. Learn more about Crime Scene Technicians and crime scene investigations on the Internet. Enter the phrase *crime scene technician* or *crime scene investigations* in a search engine to get a list of web sites.

LATENT PRINT EXAMINER

CAREER PROFILE

Duties: Identify latent print evidence that is found at crime scenes

Alternate Title: Latent Print Analyst

Salary Range: $14,000 to $70,000 or more

Employment Prospects: Excellent

Advancement Prospects: Limited
Prerequisites:
Special Requirements—Pass a selection process
Education—Bachelor's degree in physical science, forensic science, police science, or related field
Experience—One to five years experience in crime scene investigation, fingerprinting, and latent print analysis; expert witness experience preferred
Special Skills—Memory and communication skills

CAREER LADDER

```
┌─────────────────────────────────┐
│       Unit Supervisor           │
└─────────────────────────────────┘

┌─────────────────────────────────┐
│    Latent Print Examiner        │
└─────────────────────────────────┘

┌─────────────────────────────────┐
│  Latent Print Examiner Trainee  │
└─────────────────────────────────┘
```

Position Description

Latent Print Examiners are forensic scientists who assist in criminal investigations. They work in law enforcement forensic labs, or crime labs. Their expertise is to analyze latent prints, or fingerprints, and establish their positive identity. Because everyone has a unique set of fingerprints, it is possible to link suspects to crime scenes by any prints that they leave behind.

Physical evidence is submitted to Latent Print Examiners to process for latent prints and to preserve or record for future comparisons. They do this in several ways. By using special chemicals, they can lift the latent prints from the surface of objects. They can take photographs of the latent prints. Or they can convert the latent prints into digital images and store them on a computer or other electronic media.

Latent Print Examiners compare the latent prints evidence with known fingerprints of suspects, victims, and other persons. A positive identification is made when the small ridge details are clearly the same in both the prints evidence and the known prints.

Often Latent Print Examiners use a computer to find matching prints. They first categorize a set of latent prints by its type of fingerprint pattern. With that information, they can then perform a computer database search through millions of latent print files. Within minutes, the Latent Print Examiners

have a list of possible matches on their computer monitor. They then compare each file to make a positive identification of the unknown prints taken from the evidence.

As part of their investigations, Latent Print Examiners write reports of their findings and conclusions. They also testify in court as an expert witness on their conclusions and about latent print methods and procedures.

Depending on the crime lab, Latent Print Examiners perform other duties. They might organize and maintain latent print files, logs, and records. They might train identification technicians and other personnel. They might also take finger, palm, and foot prints from crime suspects, victims, and dead bodies.

Latent Print Examiners mostly work in a semi-dark area in order to more easily view small latent prints. They use chemical sprays, but the health risk is minimal if proper procedures are followed. On occasion, they are called out to crime scenes to help locate, collect, and process latent print evidence including palm prints and footprints. They might also assist in collecting other physical evidence such as impressions of shoe prints, tire tracks, and tool marks.

They work a regular 40-hour week, but are on call 24 hours a day, seven days a week. In large crime labs, Latent Print Examiners may be rotated on an on-call schedule.

Salaries

Salaries vary widely from $14,000 to over $70,000. The federal government usually pays the highest salaries followed by agencies in large states and metropolitan cities.

Employment Prospects

Latent Print Examiners work in government crime labs at the local, state, and federal levels. Currently there is a shortage of Latent Print Examiners and opportunities are expected to be good for several years. Additional positions may be created with the availability of computer fingerprint database systems to police departments. Having access to these systems allows police to process evidence from burglary and other property crime scenes.

Advancement Prospects

Supervisory and management opportunities in crime labs are limited to a few positions—unit supervisors, assistant lab directors, and lab directors. Many Latent Print Examiners pursue career growth by way of salary increases and complexity of new assignments. Some examiners become private fingerprint consultants.

Special Requirements

As prospective employees of government agencies, applicants must pass a selection process that includes any of the following steps: written exam, panel interview, medical exam, drug test, and background check. In addition, some agencies require that Latent Print Examiners by U.S. citizens.

Education and Training

Many agencies require a bachelor's degree in physical science, forensic science, police science, or another related field. Most agencies require Latent Print Examiners to be certified by the FBI, the International Association of Identification, or another recognized organization.

Experience and Skills

Depending on their education, Latent Print Examiner candidates need one to five years of experience in crime scene investigation, fingerprinting, and latent print analysis. Many agencies prefer that candidates have some experience testifying in court as an expert witness.

Candidates need excellent memory skills as well as writing and communication skills. They should also be self-disciplined and be able to work with little or no supervision.

Unions/Associations

Latent Print Examiners might belong to the International Association for Identification, the oldest and largest professional forensic organization. It offers certified training in latent print examination, networking opportunities, and other professional resources and services.

Tips for Entry

1. Take chemistry, biology, and computer imaging courses in high school or college to gain useful knowledge and skills for work in latent print examination.
2. Contact crime labs directly to learn about current job opportunities as well as jobs that may become available soon.
3. Gain useful work experience as fingerprint technicians for police departments or other law enforcement agencies.
4. Learn more about Latent Print Examiners on the Internet. Enter the phrase *latent print examiner* or *latent print examination* in a search engine to get a list of web sites. For information on crime labs, or forensic labs, enter the phrase *forensic lab*.

FORENSIC CHEMIST

CAREER PROFILE

Duties: Perform chemical analysis on physical evidence

Salary Range: $21,000 to $65,000

Employment Prospects: Good

Advancement Prospects: Limited
Prerequisites:
Special Requirements—Pass a selection process
Education—Bachelor's degree in chemistry
Experience—Knowledge of chemical principles, theories, and laboratory work
Special Skills—Computer and technical writing skills; self-management skills

CAREER LADDER

```
┌─────────────────────────┐
│     Unit Supervisor     │
└─────────────────────────┘

┌─────────────────────────┐
│     Forensic Chemist    │
└─────────────────────────┘

┌─────────────────────────┐
│     College Student     │
└─────────────────────────┘
```

Position Description

Forensic Chemists are forensic scientists who assist in criminal investigations. They work in law enforcement forensic labs, or crime labs. Their expertise is to use chemical analysis and scientific principles to examine physical evidence. For example, a Forensic Chemist might analyze the content of fire debris for an arson investigation.

Before testing any evidence, Forensic Chemists need to know the type of criminal offense from which the evidence was obtained, what needs to be known about the evidence, and the chemical and physical properties of the substances involved. Forensic Chemists use this information to determine what specific data they need to obtain and the best approach, methods, and procedures to use.

Forensic Chemists perform several different tests to positively detect and identify a substance. Afterward, they evaluate and interpret the results. They make sure that all necessary data has been obtained, and they draw conclusions about their findings. They prepare reports, describing the results of the analyses and their conclusions. If necessary, they testify in court as expert witnesses on their findings.

Some Forensic Chemists work in chemistry labs that do specific investigative work. For example, in drug chemistry labs, Forensic Chemists analyze controlled substances in drug cases.

In all chemistry labs, Forensic Chemists do research. They are constantly developing new and better analytical and testing methods for forensic investigations.

Forensic Chemists work a regular 40-hour week. They are on call 24 hours a day. In large crime labs, Forensic Chemists are rotated on an on-call schedule. They work mostly in the chemistry lab, but from time to time, they are called out to a crime scene to help locate and collect physical evidence.

Salaries

The salary for Forensic Chemists varies, depending on their experience, education, and job responsibilities, as well as the size and location of the crime lab they work for. Generally, Forensic Chemists who have advanced degrees can expect higher wages. Also, they can usually earn more working for larger crime labs or for labs in metropolitan areas such as New York City and Los Angeles.

Listed below are examples of salary ranges for Forensic Chemists at four law enforcement agencies:

- $25,512 to $55,464 at the Ventura County Sheriff's Department (California)
- $32,738 to $49,400 at the Anne Arundel County Police Department (Maryland)
- $21,000 to $59,000 at the U.S. Drug Enforcement Administration
- $33,560 to $63,436 at the U.S. Bureau of Alcohol, Tobacco, and Firearms

According to a 1998 survey of its members by the American Chemical Society, the median annual salary for chemists with a bachelor's degree working for analytical service laboratories (such as crime labs) is $39,200. The median annual salary for those chemists with a Ph.D. degree is about $65,000.

Employment Prospects

Most Forensic Chemists are employed by government crime labs at the local, state, and federal levels. Job opportunities for Forensic Chemists are good and expected to grow in the next few years due to rising crime and increased use of advanced technology to analyze smaller size samples of physical evidence.

Advancement Prospects

Supervisory and management opportunities in crime labs are limited to a few positions—unit supervisors, assistant lab directors, and lab directors. Many Forensic Chemists pursue career growth by way of salary increases and complexity of new assignments.

Another career path for Forensic Chemists is to become an expert in an area such as trace evidence analysis or drug analysis. Some Forensic Chemists become private consultants.

Special Requirements

As prospective employees of government agencies, applicants must pass a selection process that includes any of the following steps: written exam, panel interview, medical exam, drug test, and background check. In addition, some agencies require that Forensic Chemists be U.S. citizens.

Education and Training

Entry-level applicants need a bachelor's degree in chemistry. Some agencies accept applicants who have a bachelor's degree in a life science or other physical science if they have a required number of hours in chemistry.

Most crime labs require Forensic Chemists to be certified by either the state in which they will work or the American Board of Criminalistics.

Experience and Skills

Previous crime lab work is not needed for entry-level positions. However, crime labs hire candidates who have knowledge of chemical principles, theories, practices, and laboratory work. Candidates should also have computer and technical writing skills. In addition, they must have self-management skills—such as the ability to get to work on time, follow directions, take initiative, work safely, and stay calm while working under pressure.

Unions/Associations

Forensic Chemists belong to regional and state professional associations for forensic scientists or criminalists which offer networking opportunities, training and educational programs, and other professional services. Many also belong to the American Academy of Forensic Sciences, an international organization that promotes education and high professional standards in forensic science.

Tips for Entry

1. Take as many science and math courses as possible in high school.
2. Earn a bachelor's degree in chemistry, forensic science, or other physical and life science that includes chemistry courses. If possible, gain experience at crime labs as an intern or volunteer.
3. Contact professional associations such as the American Academy of Forensic Sciences to learn about job openings.
4. Learn more about Forensic Chemists on the Internet. Enter the phrase *forensic chemist* in a search engine to get a list of web sites. For information on crime labs, or forensic labs, enter the phrase *forensic lab.*

TRACE EVIDENCE EXAMINER

CAREER PROFILE

Duties: Analyze and identify small particles of physical evidence

Alternate Titles: Trace Evidence Analyst, Trace Evidence Specialist

Salary Range: Approximately $26,000 to $71,000, but varies from agency to agency

Employment Prospects: Good

Advancement Prospects: Limited
Prerequisites:
Special Requirements—Pass a selection process
Education—Bachelor's degree in chemistry
Experience—One to three years of crime lab or related experience; expert witness experience
Special Skills—Public speaking and technical writing skills; concentration skills

CAREER LADDER

```
┌─────────────────────────────────────┐
│          Unit Supervisor            │
└─────────────────────────────────────┘

┌─────────────────────────────────────┐
│      Trace Evidence Examiner        │
└─────────────────────────────────────┘

┌─────────────────────────────────────┐
│  Criminalist I or Forensic Scientist I  │
└─────────────────────────────────────┘
```

Position Description

Trace Evidence Examiners are forensic scientists who assist in criminal investigations. They work in law enforcement forensic labs, or crime labs. Their expertise is analyzing small particles of physical evidence, or trace evidence, from a crime scene or a victim's body. For example, they might examine hair, tissue, saliva, blood, body fluids, fibers, soil, glass, plastic, metal, fire debris, explosives, or paint chips. Their findings help establish facts in criminal investigations.

Using various techniques and methods, Trace Evidence Examiners may be able to identify the contents or composition of trace evidence and their origins. These forensic scientists work on the principle that when two objects have come together, each object will leave particles on the other. With computers, microscopes, and instruments, Trace Evidence Examiners compare the composition, color, shade, and makeup of unknown particles with known ones. For example, cat hair is collected as evidence at a crime scene. Detectives want to know if that cat hair matches a certain cat. A Trace Evidence Examiner would examine a known sample of the cat hair alongside the cat hair evidence.

After performing complex chemical and physical analyses, Trace Evidence Examiners interpret test results and draw conclusions. They prepare written reports of their findings

and conclusions. And, when requested, they testify in court as expert witnesses about their findings and conclusions.

Trace Evidence Examiners also conduct research in developing new and better analytical and testing methods for forensic investigations. In some crime labs, Trace Evidence Examiners analyze other evidence such as fingerprints, footwear, tire impressions, and track impressions. They might also examine vehicle speedometers, headlamps, and taillights.

From time to time, Trace Evidence Examiners leave the crime lab to assist at crime scenes, locating and collecting physical evidence. They work a regular 40-hour week, but are on call 24 hours a day. Those working in large crime labs may be rotated on an on-call schedule.

Salaries

Salaries depend on the size and location of a crime lab, as well as the experience, education, and job responsibilities of Trace Evidence Examiners. Generally, examiners earn more working for larger crime labs or for labs in metropolitan areas such as New York City and Los Angeles. In addition, earnings are higher for those who perform supervisory duties.

Listed below are examples of salary ranges for Trace Evidence Examiners at three law enforcement agencies:

- $28,116 to $58,752 at the California (State) Department of Justice
- $37,797 to $58,546 at the Arizona (State) Department of Public Safety
- $25,897 to $71,017 at the FBI Laboratory Division, Washington, D.C.

Employment Prospects

Most Trace Evidence Examiners are employed by government crime labs at the local, state, and federal levels. Job opportunities for Trace Evidence Examiners are good and are expected to increase in the next few years. The advancement of technology to analyze smaller samples of physical evidence should create further demand for Trace Evidence Examiners.

Advancement Prospects

Supervisory and management opportunities in crime labs are limited to a few positions—unit supervisors, assistant lab directors, and lab directors. Many Trace Evidence Examiners pursue career growth by way of salary increases and complexity of new assignments. Some examiners become private consultants.

Special Requirements

As prospective employees of government agencies, applicants must pass a selection process that includes any of the following steps: written exam, panel interview, medical exam, drug test, and background check. In addition, some agencies require that Trace Evidence Examiners be U.S. citizens.

Education and Training

Entry-level applicants need a bachelor's degree in chemistry. Some agencies accept applicants who have a bachelor's degree in a life science or other physical science if they have a required number of hours in chemistry.

Most agencies require that Trace Evidence Examiners have completed certified training by the American Board of Criminalistics or from another recognized program.

Experience and Skills

Depending on the crime lab, an applicant needs one to three years of crime lab or related work experience in addition to experience testifying in court as an expert witness. Some crime labs accept an equivalent combination of experience, training, and education that provides the required knowledge, skills, and abilities for the job. In addition, applicants must have excellent public speaking skills and technical writing skills.

Due to the nature of their job, Trace Evidence Examiners must have the ability to concentrate for long hours on small details.

Unions/Associations

Trace Evidence Examiners might belong to the American Academy of Forensic Sciences and the International Association for Identification. Some Trace Evidence Examiners belong to regional and state forensic science associations. Joining professional organizations gives officers the opportunity to network with peers and obtain professional support and services, such as certified training, continuing education programs, current research findings, and job listings.

Tips for Entry

1. Take police science, criminal justice, law, or other courses related to law enforcement to gain valuable skills and knowledge for a career in the crime lab.

2. Learn about job openings on the Internet. Many law enforcement agencies, professional associations, and forensic science organizations post job opportunities on their web sites.

3. Learn more about Trace Evidence Examiners and trace evidence examination on the Internet. Enter the phrase *trace evidence analyst* or *trace evidence examiner* in a search engine to get a list of web sites. For information on crime labs, or forensic labs, enter the phrase *forensic lab*.

FIREARMS/TOOLMARKS EXAMINER

CAREER PROFILE

Duties: Determine whether firearms and tools left at crime scenes were used in crimes

Alternate Title: Firearms/Toolmarks Specialist

Salary Range: Approximately $26,000 to $71,000, but varies from agency to agency

Employment Prospects: Good

Advancement Prospects: Limited
  Prerequisites:
  Special Requirements—Pass a selection process
  Education—Minimum high school diploma, but varies with each agency
  Experience—Three to five years in firearms and toolmarks examinations; expert witness experience
  Special Skills—Public speaking and technical writing skills; concentration skills

CAREER LADDER

```
┌─────────────────────────────────────┐
│          Unit Supervisor            │
└─────────────────────────────────────┘

┌─────────────────────────────────────┐
│     Firearms/Toolmarks Examiner     │
└─────────────────────────────────────┘

┌─────────────────────────────────────┐
│  Firearms/Toolmarks Examiner Trainee │
└─────────────────────────────────────┘
```

Position Description

Firearms/Toolmarks Examiners are forensic scientists who assist in criminal investigations. They work in law enforcement forensic labs, or crime labs. Their expertise covers two areas of physical evidence—firearms and toolmarks. They determine if firearms and tools found at a crime scene were used in the crime, based on the fact that all firearms and tools produce their own unique markings. For example, two screwdrivers may be identical in size, shape, and makeup, but each makes individual markings.

As firearms experts, Firearms/Toolmarks Examiners can make a positive match between a specific gun and recovered bullets. Every firearm has microscopic markings that are unique to itself. When it is fired, its markings are transferred to the fired bullets or other ammunition. Thus, the Firearms/Toolmarks Examiners test fire a gun in question, and then compare the test bullets with those in evidence under a special microscope that allows them to see the bullets side by side. If the markings are the same on both bullets, the Firearms/Toolmarks Examiners have proof that the bullets in evidence came from the gun in question.

On occasion, Firearms/Toolmarks Examiners may be asked to determine the path bullets may have taken and re-create possible crime scene scenarios. They may also be asked to estimate the distance from which a gun was shot by examining the gunpowder residue on clothing or around wounds.

As toolmarks experts, they can determine if tools and tool marks recovered from a crime scene match. The Firearms/Toolmarks Examiners compare test tool marks made by the tools in question with the tool markings in evidence. For example, if a crowbar found at a crime scene is suspected of being used to pry open a door, the crowbar and a piece of the door frame with markings on it are brought to the crime lab. A Firearms/Toolmarks Examiner makes test marks with the crowbar and then compares them with the markings on the door frame. If the markings match, the Firearms/Toolmarks Examiner has proof that the markings on the door frame were made by the crowbar.

After making their analyses and evaluations, Firearms/Toolmarks Examiners draw conclusions and prepare necessary reports. They may be called upon to testify as expert witnesses in court about their findings and conclusions.

Other duties may include establishing new or better policies and procedures for their crime lab. Some Examiners also perform other forensic examinations such as those involving footwear, tire impressions, metal, and plastics.

Firearms/Toolmarks Examiners work mostly in the crime lab. Sometimes, they are called out to examine crime scenes to help locate and collect physical evidence. They work a

40-hour week; but are on call 24 hours a day, seven days a week. In large crime labs, they may be rotated on an on-call schedule.

Salaries

Salaries depend on the size and location of a crime lab, as well as the experience, education, and job duties of Firearms/Toolmarks Examiners. Generally, examiners earn more working for larger crime labs or for labs in metropolitan areas such as New York City and Los Angeles. In addition, earnings are higher for those who perform supervisory duties.

Listed below are examples of salary ranges for Firearms/Toolmarks Examiners at three law enforcement agencies:

- $37,797 to $58,546 at the Arizona (State) Department of Public Safety
- $34,902 to $50,544 at the Ohio State Attorney General Office
- $25,897 to $71,017 at the FBI Laboratory Division, Washington, D.C.

Employment Prospects

Most Firearms/Toolmarks Examiners are employed by government crime labs at the county, state, and federal levels. Job opportunities are good and expected to grow in the next few years due to the increase in crime. However the number of job openings at a specific crime lab will depend upon that law enforcement agency's budget.

Advancement Prospects

Supervisory and management opportunities in crime labs are limited to a few positions—unit supervisors, assistant lab directors, and lab directors. Many Firearms/Toolmarks Examiners pursue career growth by way of salary increases and complexity of new assignments. Some examiners become private consultants.

Special Requirements

As prospective employees of government agencies, applicants must pass a selection process that includes any of the following steps: written exam, panel interview, medical exam, drug test, and background check. In addition, some agencies require that Firearms/Toolmarks Examiners be U.S. citizens.

Education and Training

Education requirements vary with each agency. Applicants need at least a high school diploma or general equivalency diploma. Some agencies do not require a bachelor's degree but prefer that candidates have one. Other agencies require a bachelor's degree in physical, natural, or forensic science. Most agencies require that Firearms/Toolmarks Examiners have completed certified training by the American Board of Criminalistics or from another recognized program.

Experience and Skills

Depending on the crime lab, applicants need three to five years of experience in firearms and toolmark examination and evidence identification techniques. They also must have experience testifying in court as expert witnesses. In addition, applicants must have excellent public speaking skills and technical writing skills. Due to the nature of the job, Firearms/Toolmarks Examiners must have the ability to concentrate for long hours on small details.

Unions/Associations

The Association of Firearm and Toolmark Examiners is a professional organization specifically for Firearms/Toolmarks Examiners. Firearms/Toolmarks Examiners might also belong to the International Association for Identification. Many Firearms/Toolmarks Examiners are members of regional and state professional forensic scientist associations. Joining professional organizations affords officers the opportunity to network with peers and obtain professional support and services, such as certified training, continuing education programs, current research findings, and job listings.

Tips for Entry

1. Join professional associations as many crime labs prefer to hire applicants with professional affiliations.
2. Go to professional conventions and network with other forensic scientists. You may be able to learn about upcoming job openings at various crime labs.
3. Learn more about Firearms/Toolmarks Examiners on the Internet. Enter the phrase *firearms/toolmarks* in a search engine to get a list of web sites. For information on crime labs, or forensic labs, enter the phrase *forensic lab*.

QUESTIONED DOCUMENT EXAMINER

CAREER PROFILE

Duties: Determine if documents are authentic or forgeries; identify types of inks, papers, writing instruments, and business machines

Alternate Titles: Questioned Documents Specialist, Forensic Document Examiner

Salary Range: Approximately $21,000 to $53,000, but varies from agency to agency

Employment Prospects: Good

Advancement Prospects: Limited
  Prerequisites:
  Special Requirements—Pass a selection process
  Education—Bachelor's degree preferred
  Experience—Knowledge of computer, photography, microscopy, and job-related examination techniques
  Special Skills—Writing, communication, and observational skills

CAREER LADDER

Unit Supervisor

Questioned Document Examiner

Questioned Document Trainee

Position Description

Questioned Document Examiners are forensic scientists who assist in criminal investigations. They work in law enforcement forensic labs, or crime labs. Their expertise is analyzing documents such as checks, currency, vouchers, invoices, contracts, certificates, business correspondence, passports, wills, notes, and personal letters. They determine facts about documents that may help establish a link between suspects and crime scenes. For example, they can analyze documents and determine:

- if documents are real or counterfeit
- if handwriting or signatures are authentic or forgeries
- if any changes have been made to documents
- what words and sentences have been erased or crossed out

Questioned Document Examiners are also trained to identify the types of inks and papers that are used for a document. They can determine the type of writing instrument or typewriter, printer, copy machine, or other business machine that produced a document.

As part of their job, Questioned Document Examiners obtain authentic handwriting samples and other documents to make comparisons with the physical evidence. They use various microscopes, magnifiers, measuring devices, and special instruments. They write and submit reports of their findings and conclusions. They also testify in court as expert witnesses on their findings and conclusions.

Questioned Document Examiners work mostly in the crime lab. Occasionally, they are called out to crime scenes to help locate and collect physical evidence. They work a regular 40 hours a week, but are on call 24 hours a day, every day of the year. In large crime labs, they may be rotated on an on-call schedule.

Salaries

Salaries depend on the size and location of a crime lab as well as the experience, education, and job responsibilities of Questioned Document Examiners. Generally, examiners earn more working for larger crime labs or for labs in metropolitan areas such as New York City and Los Angeles. In addition, earnings are higher for those who perform supervisory duties.

Listed below are examples of salary ranges for Questioned Document Examiners at three law enforcement agencies:

- $27,552 to $35,064 at the Washington State Patrol Crime Lab
- $21,421 to $42,198 at the IRS General Inspector Forensic Science Laboratory

- $22,208 to $52,927 at the FBI Laboratory Division, Washington, D.C.

Employment Prospects

Most Questioned Document Examiners are employed by government crime labs at the local, state, and federal levels. Job opportunities are good and are expected to grow in the next few years due to the increase in crime. However the number of job openings at a crime lab will depend upon its budget.

Advancement Prospects

Supervisory and management opportunities in crime labs are limited to a few positions—unit supervisors, assistant lab directors, and lab directors. Many Questioned Document Examiners pursue career growth by way of salary increases and complexity of new assignments. Some examiners become private consultants.

Special Requirements

As prospective employees of government agencies, applicants must pass a selection process that includes any of the following steps: written exam, panel interview, medical exam, drug test, and background check. In addition, some agencies require that Questioned Document Examiners be U.S. citizens.

Education and Training

Many agencies require Questioned Document Examiners to have a bachelor's degree, preferably in forensic science, criminal justice, chemistry, or other related field. In addition, they must complete an apprenticeship with either a crime lab or a certified private Questioned Document Examiner. The apprenticeship is usually two years long.

Experience and Skills

Requirements for Questioned Document Trainee positions vary from agency to agency. Many agencies prefer trainees who have at least one year's work experience in a crime scene unit, forensic science lab, or other related field. Trainees should have a working knowledge of computers, photography, and microscopy as well as examination techniques that are related to the job. They also need excellent writing and communication skills along with excellent powers of observation.

Unions/Associations

Questioned Document Examiners might belong to one or two national associations: the American Society of Questioned Document Examiners or the National Association of Document Examiners. Both organizations offer networking opportunities, research and education programs, referral services, and other professional services and support.

Tips for Entry

1. Earn a bachelor's degree as more and more agencies are making that a requirement for Questioned Document Examiners.
2. Contact certified private Questioned Document Examiners about apprenticeship opportunities.
3. Learn more about Questioned Document Examiners on the Internet. Enter the phrase *questioned documents* in a search engine to get a list of web sites. For information on crime labs, or forensic labs, enter the phrase *forensic lab*.

FORENSIC PATHOLOGIST

<table>
<tr><td>

CAREER PROFILE

Duties: Perform autopsies to determine the cause and manner of a person's death

Alternate Title: Medical Examiner

Salary Range: $50,000 to $200,000 or more

Employment Prospects: Good

Advancement Prospects: Good
  Prerequisites:
  Education—Bachelor's degree; medical school degree; residency training
  Experience—Residency in forensic pathology
  Special Skills—Interpretive and analytical skills; communication and interpersonal skills

</td><td>

CAREER LADDER

```
┌─────────────────────────────────────┐
│   Deputy Chief Medical Examiner      │
└─────────────────────────────────────┘


┌─────────────────────────────────────┐
│ Forensic Pathologist (Medical Examiner) │
└─────────────────────────────────────┘


┌─────────────────────────────────────┐
│   Resident in Forensic Pathology     │
└─────────────────────────────────────┘
```

</td></tr>
</table>

Position Description

Forensic Pathologists are medical doctors who work for state and county medical examiner systems. More commonly known as *Medical Examiners,* they have been trained to perform autopsies in medicolegal death investigations. They investigate the deaths of persons who have died suddenly, unexpectedly, or violently.

Through their autopsies, Forensic Pathologists attempt to answer questions such as time of death; whether the manner of death was natural, accidental, suicidal, or homicidal; the cause of death; what type of instrument may have been used if the death was the result of injury; and whether the death occurred where the body was found as well as if the body was moved after death.

Forensic Pathologists are most often called out to crime scenes or other locations to do brief, preliminary examinations of dead bodies before they are moved. They also gather information about a death, such as what the person was doing at the time he or she died. They also obtain information about the person's medical history.

At the laboratory, Forensic Pathologists do a thorough external and internal examination of the body. They perform various laboratory tests. They take X rays. They remove tissue, fluids, and organs for microscopic, chemical, and toxicological studies. They also look for medical evidence on and inside the body, properly documenting, collecting, and processing any evidence such as bullets, hair, fibers, fingernail clippings, blood, and body fluids. All evidence is forwarded to forensic specialists, such as trace evidence examiners, for identification and analysis. If the identity of a body is unknown, Forensic Pathologists obtain help from other forensic specialists. For example, a forensic odontologist may be able to determine an identity by investigating dental records.

Forensic Pathologists evaluate the autopsy and lab results with the case history and draw a conclusion as to the cause and manner of death. They prepare comprehensive reports of their findings and conclusions, and may testify in court as expert witnesses. When natural deaths have been determined, Forensic Pathologists might meet with the family of the deceased to discuss the circumstances and cause of death.

Besides medicolegal investigations, Forensic Pathologists do research for publication in scientific journals. They also design protocol and standards for specialized death investigations such as infant deaths.

Forensic Pathologists work 40 hours a week but are on call 24 hours a day, every day of the year. In large medical examiner offices, Forensic Pathologists may be rotated on an on-call schedule.

Salaries

Forensic Pathologists receive an annual salary that ranges from $50,000 per year for Forensic Pathology residents up to $200,000 per year for some chief medical examiners.

Employment Prospects

Job opportunities are good at the present time and are expected to grow into the next decade. Forensic Pathologists are mostly hired by county and state government medical examiner offices. Some may find jobs with medical schools, military services, and the federal government. A few may find jobs with private groups or hospitals that perform forensic autopsies on a contractual basis.

Advancement Prospects

After completing a residency in forensic pathology, these specialist doctors are usually hired as either assistant or associate medical examiners. Those seeking supervisory responsibilities become deputy chief medical examiners. The top positions in medical examiner systems are chief medical examiners.

Because there are so few Forensic Pathologists, advancement opportunities are good. However, many Forensic Pathologists change locations in order to move up to higher positions. Some may leave small offices at high ranks to work at lower ranks at larger offices in order to perform more interesting or challenging cases. Some Forensic Pathologists become private consultants.

Education and Training

Forensic Pathologists must complete at least 13 years of study before they are qualified to enter the field. They need four-year college and medical school degrees. This is followed with four to five years of residency training, first in pathology in a hospital, and then in forensic pathology, usually in a medical examiner's office.

Experience and Skills

In addition to their technical training, Forensic Pathologists must have strong interpretive and analytical skills for medicolegal investigations. They also need excellent communication and interpersonal skills.

Unions/Associations

Different professional organizations that Forensic Pathologists might belong to are the National Association of Medical Examiners, the American Society of Clinical Pathologists, the American Medical Association, and the American Academy of Forensic Sciences. Joining professional organizations gives Forensic Pathologists the opportunity to network with peers and obtain professional support and services, such as certified training, continuing education programs, current research findings, and job listings.

Tips for Entry

1. Obtain the best training possible in anatomic and/or clinical pathology.
2. While you are waiting to get into a medical school, become a medical technologist and work in a medical examiner office's crime lab for exposure to the field.
3. Contact the Accreditation Council for Graduate Medical Education to get information about forensic pathology residency programs. The address is 515 North State Street, Suite 2000, Chicago, IL 60610-4322. The telephone number is (312) 464-4920.
4. Learn more about forensic pathology investigations on the Internet. Enter the phrase *forensic pathology* or *medical examiner* in any search engine to get a list of web sites.

POLYGRAPH EXAMINER

CAREER PROFILE

Duties: Determine if people are being truthful or deceptive about issues in criminal investigations

Alternate Titles: Polygraphist, Forensic Psychophysiologist

Salary Range: $40,000 to $56,000

Employment Prospects: Good

Advancement Prospects: Limited
Prerequisites:
Education—College degree is preferred
Experience—Five years of investigative experience in law enforcement
Special Skills—Interviewing, organizational, communication, and interpersonal skills

CAREER LADDER

```
┌─────────────────────────────────┐
│   Polygraph Unit Commander      │
└─────────────────────────────────┘

┌─────────────────────────────────┐
│     Polygraph Examiner          │
└─────────────────────────────────┘

┌─────────────────────────────────┐
│   Polygraph Examiner Intern     │
└─────────────────────────────────┘
```

Position Description

Police Polygraph Examiners assist in criminal investigations by providing another investigative tool. They are part of the polygraph detail in a detective bureau for which police officers may volunteer. They perform authorized polygraph examinations on suspects, victims, witnesses, and informants to determine if they are being truthful about specific issues under investigation. Polygraph Examiners operate a polygraph instrument, which is more commonly known as a lie detector machine. It measures a person's pulse, blood pressure, breathing, and sweat gland activity as that person is asked a set of questions pertaining to a criminal case. Polygraph Examiners review the polygraph results and determine if the person is being truthful or deceptive.

(Research by the Department of Defense, Johns Hopkins University, and other respected organizations has shown that polygraph examinations performed by experienced Polygraph Examiners are valid and credible, achieving a 90% to 95% accuracy rate in determining whether someone is being truthful or deceptive.)

In order to help them with their investigations, police investigators may request that witnesses and suspects be tested. They might use polygraph results, for example, to help them determine investigative leads, confirm allegations that cannot be disproved by other evidence, or establish probable cause to seek a search warrant. All authorized polygraph examinations are voluntary and they follow state laws and department policies.

The polygraph examination may be about one or more issues that are under investigation. Polygraph Examiners develop a series of nine or ten questions for each issue. So if a polygraph exam is about two issues—such as two robberies—a Polygraph Examiner develops one series of questions for each issue.

Before administering a polygraph test, Polygraph Examiners get background information about the case and the person, or subject, they will be testing. They talk with investigators and other sources. They review the case file along with all other pertinent documents and records. Upon reviewing all available information, Polygraph Examiners develop the questions to ask the subject.

The structured polygraph examination is conducted in a room free of distractions. The test has two stages and takes about two to three hours. The first stage is the pretest interview. Polygraph Examiners explain the testing process, how the polygraph works, and the subject's legal rights. They discuss the issue under investigation. They also review the series of questions that the subject will be asked about that issue. The Polygraph Examiners also confirm that the subject understands the proceedings.

The second stage is the in-test. Attachments are placed on the subject to monitor physiological responses during the exam. The subject is asked the series of questions. It is repeated a second, and sometimes, a third time. The questions do not change. If an additional issue needs to be addressed, a second series of questions is then developed.

Polygraph Examiners interpret the polygraph charts and determine one of three conclusions: the subject answered the questions truthfully; the subject did not answer the questions truthfully; or the test results were inconclusive. For inconclusive results, Polygraph Examiners decide whether to conduct another examination. They then write and submit reports on their findings and conclusions, and may testify in court as expert witnesses. (Currently, polygraph results are admissible as evidence at trials in only some federal circuits and in about 20 states.)

Polygraph Examiners also maintain and protect polygraph files and records. Many Polygraph Examiners also perform polygraph examinations on job applicants for law enforcement positions.

Police Polygraph Examiners are on call 24 hours a day, seven days a week.

Salaries

Police Polygraph Examiners are compensated according to their rank and level in their police department. Many officers also earn additional income from performing polygraph duty. In its 1996 "Occupational Compensation Survey," the Bureau of Labor Statistics (of the U.S. Department of Labor) reported that many police officers who performed one or more special police duties, such as polygraph duty, earned a salary between $40,924 and $56,160 per year (or between $787 and $1,080 per week). That did not include compensation for working overtime, holidays, weekends, and late night shifts.

Employment Prospects

In addition to police departments, Polygraph Examiners work in county, state, and federal law enforcement agencies. In some law enforcement agencies, Polygraph Examiners are civilians rather than law enforcement officers. Polygraph Examiners also work for lawyers, courts, private detective agencies, and security agencies. Some Polygraph Examiners are self-employed or run their own polygraph services.

The need for Polygraph Examiners has increased in the last few years and is expected to continue into the millennium. This is partly because polygraph examination has become part of the selection process for many jobs in government and private businesses.

Advancement Prospects

Police officers have the chance to develop a career in keeping with their personal interests and ambitions. Volunteering for special police units such as polygraph units broadens their experience and may provide a stepping stone in their career advancement. In addition to taking on special assignments, many officers pursue promotions to detective, sergeant, lieutenant, and so on. Depending on the police department, officers with administrative and managerial duties may be limited in their opportunity to volunteer for special police units.

Many departments require that officers commit to a minimum number of years for the assignment. Supervisory and administrative positions within the polygraph detail are limited to unit commanders. Many retired Police Polygraph Examiners start their own business and contract with law enforcement agencies to do polygraph examinations.

Education and Training

Most law enforcement agencies prefer candidates with associate's or bachelor's degrees in criminal justice, law, police science, or other related fields. Candidates must complete a certified training program and field training with a senior Polygraph Examiner.

Many states require that Polygraph Examiners have a license. Qualifications for a license differ in each state. Generally, Polygraph Examiners need a bachelor's degree and certification from an accredited polygraph school. In addition, they must complete an internship and pass their state's licensing exam.

Experience and Skills

Applicants should have at least five years of experience in all levels of investigation. It is important that they have excellent interviewing, organizational, and communication skills. They must be able to relate well with many different people. They must also have the ability to be impartial, calm, and levelheaded.

Unions/Associations

The American Polygraph Association and the American Association of Police Polygraphists are two professional organizations specifically for Polygraph Examiners. Both associations have a certification program recognized by law enforcement agencies.

Police polygraph examiners might also be members of professional state polygraph associations. Joining professional organizations gives officers the opportunity to network with peers and obtain professional support and services, such as certified training, continuing education programs, current research findings, and job listings.

Tips for Entry

1. If you are planning to enroll in a polygraph school, make sure it is recognized by professional associations and law enforcement agencies.
2. Keep up with the current polygraph training and technology as well as relevant legislation.

3. As a police officer, let the polygraph unit commander know of your interest, especially before you are eligible or before an opening is available.

4. Learn more about polygraph examinations on the Internet. Enter the phrase *polygraph examination* in a search engine to get a list of web sites.

PRIVATE INVESTIGATIONS

PRIVATE INVESTIGATOR

CAREER PROFILE	CAREER LADDER

Duties: Conduct investigations and provide protection for clients

Alternate Title: Private Detective

Salary Range: $5,000 to $80,000

Employment Prospects: Good

Advancement Prospects: Limited

Prerequisites:

Special Requirements—Private investigator's license, in most states

Education—High school diploma

Experience—Requirements differ with each agency

Special Skills—Problem-solving, organizational, and self-management skills; interpersonal communication, and writing skills; computer and research skills

```
┌─────────────────────────────────────┐
│          Manager or Owner            │
└─────────────────────────────────────┘

┌─────────────────────────────────────┐
│        Private Investigator          │
└─────────────────────────────────────┘

┌─────────────────────────────────────┐
│     Private Investigator Trainee     │
└─────────────────────────────────────┘
```

Position Description

Private Investigators perform specific investigative or protection services for their clients. They are hired by individuals, attorneys, businesses, corporations, and organizations for services that include:

- locating missing persons, assets (such as cash and property), documents, or information
- performing background checks—that is, verifying that information about individuals, businesses, or groups is true (Example: A Private Investigator might verify information on job applications for employers.)
- verifying information on insurance claims
- determining if a theft, fraud, or other criminal activity has occurred
- gathering evidence for criminal or civil trials
- performing surveillance or undercover work in order to gather information about the activities of a person, group, or business (Example: A Private Investigator might pose as a worker in a warehouse to discover who may be stealing merchandise.)
- protecting clients or their property from theft, robbery, personal harm, or other danger

Many Private Investigators provide almost any kind of investigative or protective service that clients want. Other Private Investigators specialize in a few areas such as background investigations, arson investigations, surveillance work, or personal protection services.

When conducting investigations, Private Investigators perform any number of tasks. They search for information on computer databases and public records such as courthouse records. They review documents, computer files, and other materials that clients give them. They examine scenes where a crime, accident, suicide, or other incident took place. They interview people, sometimes traveling to other cities and states. They may perform surveillance and undercover work. They may file complaints with police and other law enforcement agencies. Furthermore, they may testify in court about their investigations.

With every case, Private Investigators maintain accurate, well-detailed notes. They provide verbal or written progress reports to their clients as well as submit a comprehensive summary of their investigation.

Private Investigators who have their own agency oversee daily business operations. For example, they may do accounts, invoice clients, and pay bills and salaries. They may supervise both investigative and support staffs. They may maintain file systems and do routine office work.

Their jobs involve constant travel and meeting new people. They work long and irregular hours, including nights, weekends, and holidays.

Salaries

Most Private Investigators earn between $5,000 and $80,000 a year. In 1996, the average salary for Private Investigators was $37,800, according to a study by Abbott, Langer & Associates. Their earnings depend on factors such as experience, abilities, number of cases, and case fees. (Fees typically range between $35 and $150 an hour.) Private Investigators who live in metropolitan areas usually earn higher incomes. Most Private Investigators receive reimbursement for expenses, and may sometimes be provided with company vehicles.

Employment Prospects

Private Investigators work for private detective agencies or have their own agencies. The job opportunities for Private Investigators are expected to grow as fast as the average of all other occupations through 2006. Additional jobs with private agencies should be created due to the turnover rate among staff workers.

Job competition is expected to be high since many law enforcement officers and military personnel retire early and begin second careers as Private Investigators.

Advancement Prospects

Supervisory and management positions are limited to case managers. Thus, many Private Investigators pursue career growth by way of wage or fee increases and complexity of new assignments. The goal for some Private Investigators is to start their own agencies.

Special Requirements

Depending on where they are located, Private Investigators must hold either a state or local private investigator's license to practice. License requirements, which include age, education, and experience qualifications, vary from state to state or city to city. In addition, Private Investigators may be required by their state or city to complete certified training programs from recognized organizations. (For information about private investigator licensing in your state, contact your state department of licensing, state attorney general, state police, or state department of public safety.)

Private Investigator trainees are covered by the licenses of the Private Investigators under whom they work.

Education and Training

Education requirements for entry-level Private Investigators vary from agency to agency. However, more and more agencies are hiring applicants who have associate's or bachelor's degrees in any field. Entry-level Private Investigators receive on-the-job training, performing basic tasks such as searching for information on computer databases.

Experience and Skills

Some agencies prefer hiring entry-level Private Investigators who have law enforcement or military experience, especially with investigative experiences. Some agencies are willing to hire individuals with little or no investigative work experience. Agencies look for objective, honest, and curious applicants who show strong problem-solving and organizational skills. Applicants also show that they have good self-management skills—the ability to get to work on time, follow directions, take initiative, work safely, stay calm while working under pressure, and so on.

In addition, applicants should have good interpersonal skills, communication skills, and writing skills. Also highly desirable are applicants with computer and research skills.

Unions/Associations

Besides professional associations within their state or region, Private Investigators might belong to the National Association of Investigative Specialists, an organization that offers professional resources, networking, and training programs.

Tips for Entry

1. Contact local private investigators about part-time or full-time trainee positions.
2. Take speech, psychology, English, history, sociology, business law, and physical education courses in high school or college to obtain valuable knowledge and skills for this field.
3. Contact your local or state police department, state public safety department, or state licensing division to learn about licensing requirements for private investigators.
4. A good source on the Internet to learn about the private investigation field is the National Association of Investigative Specialists web site. Its web address is: *http://www.pimall.com/nais/home.html.*

BACKGROUND INVESTIGATOR

CAREER PROFILE

Duties: Verify that the information individuals and businesses state about themselves is true

Salary Range: $5,000 to $80,000

Employment Prospects: Good

Advancement Prospects: Limited
Prerequisites:
Special Requirements—Private investigator's license, in most states
Education—High school diploma
Experience—Requirements vary with the different agencies
Special Skills—Computer skills; research and interviewing skills; communication and writing skills; organizational and self-management skills.

CAREER LADDER

```
┌─────────────────────────────────────┐
│         Manager or Owner            │
└─────────────────────────────────────┘

┌─────────────────────────────────────┐
│      Background Investigator         │
└─────────────────────────────────────┘

┌─────────────────────────────────────┐
│   Background Investigator Trainee    │
└─────────────────────────────────────┘
```

Position Description

Background Investigators specialize in verifying information for clients who include individuals, nonprofit groups, businesses, corporations, and government agencies. Their investigations help clients decide whether to:

- hire people for jobs
- marry people or become personally involved with people
- contribute money to organizations
- give loans to individuals or companies
- do business with companies or individuals
- buy or sell companies
- invest money in companies

For an investigation on an individual, Background Investigators might verify personal facts about him or her such as social security number, vital statistics, and family history as well as current and past residential addresses. They also might collect facts about a person's employment history, education history, professional licenses, group memberships, and military service. In addition, they investigate an individual's driving record, financial history, medical history, and criminal record. In some cases they might verify information about property ownership, lawsuits, and insurance claims such as worker's compensation.

A background check on a business or company might consist of verifying information about its operations—for example, how long it has been in existence, what products it makes or sells, how many employees it has, and who its executive and management officers are. Background Investigators might check licenses, certificates, and public filing information such as Occupational Safety and Health Administration records. In addition, they might verify facts about the business's or company's financial history, including credit reports.

Background Investigators perform their information searches in several ways. They search many different computer databases that are available on the Internet and from information services, industry sources, and government offices. Sometimes they visit libraries, schools, courthouses and other institutions to research public records, directories, yearbooks, and other sources. Background Investigators also interview people who can verify information. They talk with personnel departments, bank managers, landlords, teachers, professors, school counselors, job counselors, medical personnel, neighbors, friends, relatives, and others. These interviews may be conducted by phone or in person.

Background Investigators work a 40-hour week, but may work extra hours to complete rush requests.

Salaries

Background Investigators earn between $5,000 and $80,000 a year. Their earnings depend on their experience, abilities, number of cases, and case fees. (Fees range from

$20 to $200 or more per service, depending on the type of background check that is performed.) Background Investigators who live in metropolitan areas usually earn higher incomes.

Employment Prospects

Background Investigators work for private detective agencies or own their own firms. The job opportunities for the private investigation field are expected to grow as fast as the average of all other occupations through 2006.

Advancement Prospects

Supervisory and management positions are limited to case managers. So, many Background Investigators pursue career growth by way of wage or fee increases and complexity of new assignments. The goal for some Background Investigators is to start their own agencies.

Special Requirements

Most Background Investigators need either a state or local private investigator's license to practice. License requirements, which include age, education, and experience qualifications, vary from state to state or city to city. In addition, Background Investigators may be required by their state or city to complete certified training programs from recognized organizations. (For information about private investigator licensing in your state, contact your state licensing department, state attorney general, state police, or state department of public safety.)

Background Investigator trainees are covered by their employers' licenses.

Education and Training

Most agencies require trainees to have a high school or general equivalency diploma. Many agencies, however, are hiring trainees who have associate's or bachelor's degrees in any field.

Experience and Skills

Small agencies are willing to hire applicants with little or no investigative work experience. Applicants should have strong computer skills as well as the ability to do research and interview people. They also need excellent communication and writing skills along with organizational and self-management skills.

Unions/Associations

Background Investigators might belong to the National Association of Investigative Specialists, a group that offers professional resources, networking, and training programs.

Tips for Entry

1. Take investigative courses through community colleges and adult education programs.
2. Some detective agencies hire trainees for part-time work. Call up agencies in your area to find out if they are currently hiring or planning to hire soon.
3. Get an idea of the different services that Background Investigators offer clients. Read about some detective agencies on the Internet. Enter the phrase *background investigations* in a search engine to get a list of web sites.

ARSON INVESTIGATOR

CAREER PROFILE

Duties: Investigate fires that may have been started on purpose for money or other reasons; provide expert witness testimony

Alternate Title: Fire Investigator

Salary Range: $5,000 to $80,000

Employment Prospects: Good

Advancement Prospects: Limited
   Prerequisites:
   Special Requirements—Private investigator's license, in most states
   Education—College work and certified training desirable
   Experience—Three years of firefighting experience
   Special Skills—Communication and presentation skills; report-writing skills; computer skills

CAREER LADDER

```
┌─────────────────────────────┐
│      Manager or Owner        │
└─────────────────────────────┘

┌─────────────────────────────┐
│     Arson Investigator       │
└─────────────────────────────┘

┌─────────────────────────────┐
│        Firefighter           │
└─────────────────────────────┘
```

Position Description

Private Arson Investigators are hired by attorneys and insurance companies to investigate fires in which properties may have been burned down on purpose so that owners can get money from their insurance companies for the loss of property. Their cases include suspicious burning of homes, apartment buildings, office buildings, churches, schools, hotels, stores, factories, automobiles, boats, and aircraft.

With every investigation, Arson Investigators gather evidence in the form of documents, witnesses, and physical proof to substantiate that a fire was arson. They carefully examine fire scenes to determine where a fire began and how it was started; they look for signs such as burn patterns and physical evidence that show the fire was set intentionally. They also keep an open mind to the possibility that a fire may have started naturally or by accident.

Arson Investigators document all fire scenes. They write well-detailed notes about their observations. They make clear diagrams of the burnt structure and physical evidence of arson. They take photographs of the scene and may make videotapes of it. In addition, they review police and fire marshal reports. Throughout their investigation, they may exchange information with police officers and fire marshals who are also investigating the case.

Interviewing people for pertinent information is an essential part of an arson investigation. Arson Investigators interview police and firefighters who were at the fire scene as well as people who witnessed the fire. In addition, the investigators interview the owners and occupants of the property to learn more about them. They also interview neighbors, friends, relatives, bank managers, and any other persons who may have knowledge about the fire, the property, the owners, and the occupants.

Furthermore, Arson Investigators do background checks on the scorched property and its owners. They examine insurance policies, and learn pertinent facts about the structure such as its age, its purpose, what kind of fire alarm systems it had, and who had access to the building. They do intensive background checks on suspects, including owners and occupants.

Arson Investigators complete and submit well-detailed reports, which include witness statements, documents, photographs, and physical evidence. In addition, Arson Investigators may testify in court as expert witnesses about their findings and their expertise in arson investigations. More than any other witness, the Arson Investigator can influence the outcome of an arson trial by his or her testimony.

Arson Investigators often work evenings and weekends in order to interview people when they are most available.

Salaries

Earnings for self-employed Arson Investigators depend on factors such as experience, abilities, number of cases, and case fees. (Fees typically range between $35 and $150 an hour.) Most Arson Investigators earn between $5,000 and $80,000 a year. In 1996, the average salary for private investigators, including Arson Investigators, was $37,800, according to a study by Abbott, Langer & Associates. Arson Investigators who live in metropolitan areas usually earn higher incomes. Most Arson Investigators receive reimbursement for expenses, and may sometimes be provided with company vehicles.

Employment Prospects

Most private Arson Investigators work for detective agencies. Some Arson Investigators have their own agencies. Job opportunities for private investigators, including Arson Investigators, are expected to grow as fast as the average of all other occupations through 2006.

Advancement Prospects

Supervisory and management positions are limited to case managers. So, many Arson Investigators pursue career growth by way of wage or fee increases and complexity of new assignments. The goal for some Arson Investigators is to start their own agencies.

Special Requirements

Most Arson Investigators need either a state or local private investigator's license to practice. License requirements, which include age, education, and experience qualifications, vary from state to state or city to city. In addition, Arson Investigators may be required by their state or city to complete certified training programs from recognized organizations. (For information about private investigator licensing in your state, contact your state licensing department, state attorney general, state police, or state department of public safety.)

Arson Investigator trainees are covered by their employers' licenses.

Education and Training

Many agencies desire applicants who have a college degree in fire science, criminal justice, or other related field. They also prefer applicants who have taken courses in fire protection engineering and fire investigation. In addition, Arson Investigator trainees must complete certified training programs from recognized organizations such as the International Association of Arson Investigators.

Experience and Skills

Arson Investigator trainees should have three years of firefighting experience plus a strong background in the chemistry of fire. In recent years, more and more agencies are hiring applicants who have backgrounds in fire protection engineering.

Skills especially needed by Arson Investigators are related to communication, presentation, and report-writing. Computer skills are also necessary since computer modeling is becoming more common to the profession.

Unions/Associations

Many Arson Investigators belong to the International Association of Arson Investigators, a professional organization that offers seminars and certification programs as well as resources and networking. Arson Investigators might also belong to regional, state, and national professional associations for private investigators and firefighters. Joining professional organizations gives investigators the opportunity to network with peers and obtain certified training, continuing education, professional resources, job listings, and other professional services and support.

Tips for Entry

1. Take business courses. Having an understanding of business is valuable in arson investigations.
2. Learn about job openings from professional associations and at professional conventions.
3. Keep a competitive edge in your field by taking relevant classes and training programs from colleges and professional organizations.
4. Get an idea of the different services that private Arson Investigators provide. Read about some detective agencies on the Internet. Enter the phrase *fire investigations* or *arson investigations* in a search engine to get a list of web sites.

INSURANCE CLAIMS INVESTIGATOR

CAREER PROFILE

Duties: Verify that the information on insurance claims are true for insurance companies

Alternate Title: Insurance Investigator

Salary Range: $17,000 to $31,000

Employment Prospects: Good

Advancement Prospects: Limited

Prerequisites:

Special Requirements—Private investigator's license, in most states

Education—High school diploma, but college degree is preferred

Experience—Requirements vary with the different agencies

Special Skills—Organizational and self-management skills; analytical and observational skills; research, interviewing, communication, and writing skills

CAREER LADDER

```
┌─────────────────────────────────────┐
│          Manager or Owner           │
└─────────────────────────────────────┘

┌─────────────────────────────────────┐
│    Insurance Claims Investigator    │
└─────────────────────────────────────┘

┌─────────────────────────────────────┐
│ Insurance Claims Investigator Trainee │
└─────────────────────────────────────┘
```

Position Description

Insurance Claims Investigators are hired by insurance companies to look into claims submitted by their clients for losses that are covered by the insurance companies. Insurance claims can range from a few hundred dollars to millions of dollars. The Insurance Claims Investigator verifies that the information on the insurance claims is true.

There are many different types of claims to which Insurance Claims Investigators might be assigned. They might investigate claims for:

- damaged, wrecked, or stolen vehicles
- damaged, lost, or stolen computers, jewelry, or other insured valuables
- damaged or destroyed homes
- medical and hospital costs
- loss of income due to injuries or illnesses
- injuries, illnesses, or deaths resulting from using a company's products or a business's services
- deaths or disappearances of insured persons

Most Insurance Claims Investigators begin an investigation by reviewing the insurance claim and the client's insurance policy in order to plan their investigation. As part of their investigations, they consider the possibility of fraud.

Most investigations involve a lot of travel and meeting many different people. Insurance Claims Investigators visit police departments, fire departments, courthouses, public health offices, medical offices, and other places to get copies of documents related to the claim. These documents include medical records, traffic reports, police investigation reports, fire reports, and death certificates.

Insurance Claims Investigators also examine the insured property as well as the scene where the loss, injury, or death took place. They look for evidence that backs up the information on an insurance claim in addition to possible evidence of fraud. They write well-detailed notes about their observations. They take photographs and draw clear sketches. Some Claims Insurance Investigators may make videotapes.

In addition, Insurance Claims Investigators interview the claimant, witnesses, doctors, police, and other people who have information about the incident. Those interviewed sign a formal statement written by themselves or by the Insurance Claims Investigators. Many Insurance Claims Investigators may also tape-record interview sessions with the permission of those interviewed.

Throughout an investigation, Insurance Claims Investigators maintain a proper and accurate case file that includes notes, documents, photographs, sketches, and formal statements. Upon completion of the investigation, they write a summary report and submit it and the case file to the insurance company.

Insurance Claims Investigators usually set their own work schedule, working nights and weekends in order to interview people when they are available.

Salaries

Salaries vary with the different agencies. In 1996, the annual salary for most Insurance Claims Investigators was between $17,680 and $30,680. Insurance Claims Investigators who live in metropolitan areas usually earn higher incomes. Most Insurance Claims Investigators receive reimbursement for expenses.

Employment Prospects

Insurance Claims Investigators are employed by insurance companies and private investigation agencies. Some Insurance Claims Investigators have their own agencies. The National Association of Investigative Specialists reports that insurance claims investigation is one of the fastest growing areas in private investigation.

Advancement Prospects

Supervisory and management positions are limited to case managers. Many Insurance Claims Investigators pursue career growth by way of wage or fee increases and complexity of new assignments. The goal for some Insurance Claims Investigators is to start their own agencies.

Special Requirements

Depending on their location, Insurance Claims Investigators must hold either a state or local private investigator's license to practice. License requirements, which include age, education, and experience qualifications, vary from state to state or city to city. In addition, Insurance Claims Investigators may be required by their state or city to complete certified private investigator training programs from recognized organizations. (For information about private investigator licensing in your state, contact your state licensing department, state attorney general, state police, or state department of public safety.)

Insurance Claims Investigator trainees are covered by the licenses of the investigators under whom they work.

Education and Training

The minimum education requirement is a high school or general equivalency diploma. Many employers prefer hiring trainees with bachelor's degrees in business administration or liberal arts.

Experience and Skills

Some employers hire recent college graduates with no prior investigative work experience. Others prefer applicants who have experience in law enforcement or private investigations. Employers choose candidates who have a general knowledge of the insurance industry. In addition, candidates show that they have organizational and self-management skills as well as strong analytical and observational skills. They also show that they have the abilities to do research, conduct interviews, and write accurate statements and reports.

Unions/Associations

Two professional groups for Insurance Claims Investigators are the International Association of Special Investigation Units and the National Society of Professional Insurance Investigators. Both organizations offer networking opportunities and professional support and services such as training and education programs.

Tips for Entry

1. Many insurance companies recruit on college campuses. Find out if any insurance companies may be attending job fairs at the colleges in your area.

2. Learn how to use computers and word processing programs. In addition, learn basic photography and videotaping skills—valuable skills to have in the private investigation field.

3. On the Internet, you can learn about the types of services some private investigators offer in insurance claims investigations. Enter the phrase *insurance claims investigations* in a search engine to get a list of web sites.

LEGAL INVESTIGATOR

CAREER PROFILE

Duties: Gather evidence for attorneys who are preparing for criminal or civil trials

Salary Range: $15,000 to $35,000

Employment Prospects: Good

Advancement Prospects: Limited
Prerequisites:
  Special Requirements—Private investigator's license, in most states
  Education—Some college education is preferred
  Experience—Requirements vary with the different agencies
  Special Skills—Interpersonal skills; problem-solving, organizational, communication, writing, and self-management skills

CAREER LADDER

```
┌─────────────────────────────┐
│     Manager or Owner,        │
│  Legal Investigation Service │
└─────────────────────────────┘

┌─────────────────────────────┐
│     Legal Investigator       │
└─────────────────────────────┘

┌─────────────────────────────┐
│    Assistant Investigator    │
└─────────────────────────────┘
```

Position Description

Private Legal Investigators are hired by attorneys to help them prepare cases for court trials. They gather documentary, testimonial, and physical evidence that allows attorneys to put together a sound and logical case.

Legal Investigators might conduct investigations for criminal or civil trials. In criminal trials, private Legal Investigators usually work for lawyers of the defendant—the person who is accused of committing a crime. They work for lawyers of either party in civil trials—the defendant (the one who is being sued), or the plaintiff (the one who is suing).

Legal Investigators perform similar tasks when investigating for either criminal or civil cases. One task is gathering and reviewing documents that are pertinent to a case. For example, in a lawsuit that involves injuries from a car accident, a Legal Investigator might obtain insurance policies, claims applications, and investigators' reports; police accident reports and traffic citations; medical and hospital records; and driving records of both drivers in the accident.

Another important task is locating persons who may be potential witnesses for the attorneys. For example, a Legal Investigator working on a case in which the attorney's client is accused of embezzling thousands of dollars from his employer would look for co-workers, neighbors, and other persons willing to testify on behalf of the client. In addition, Legal Investigators also look for expert witnesses, such as physicians, forensic scientists, forensic accountants, and other private investigators, who may be able to develop evidence for the lawyers.

Legal Investigators also examine the locations where injuries or crimes occurred. They carefully document the scenes. They write well-detailed notes about their observations. They make clear sketches. They take photographs of the scene and may make videotapes of it. In addition they look for physical evidence that may help the lawyers' cases.

Other duties that Legal Investigators might perform are:

- serving subpoenas
- preparing exhibits for the trial
- testifying in court

Legal Investigators might work nights, weekends, and holidays in order to complete their investigations.

Salaries

Entry-level Legal Investigators earn between $15,000 and $18,000 while experienced Legal Investigators earn between $20,000 and $35,000. Legal Investigators who live in metropolitan areas usually earn higher incomes. Most Legal Investigators receive reimbursement for expenses, and may sometimes be provided with company vehicles.

Employment Prospects

Legal Investigators work directly for attorneys and law firms, or work on a contractual basis as part of a detective agency. Job opportunities in the private investigation field are expected to grow as fast as the average of all other occupations through 2006.

Advancement Prospects

Supervisory and management positions are limited to case managers. Many Legal Investigators pursue career growth by way of wage or fee increases and complexity of new assignments. The goal for some Legal Investigators is to start their own agencies.

Some private Legal Investigators take positions, such as a Federal Public Defender Office Investigator, in government agencies.

Special Requirements

Most Legal Investigators need either a state or local private investigator's license to practice. License requirements, which include age, education, and experience qualifications, vary from state to state or city to city. In addition, Legal Investigators may be required by their state or city to complete certified private investigator training programs from recognized organizations. (For information about private investigator licensing in your state, contact your state licensing department, state attorney general, state police, or state department of public safety.)

Legal Investigator trainees are covered by their employers' licenses.

Education and Training

Requirements vary with each law firm and detective agency. Many law firms require Legal Investigators on their staffs to have at least an associate's degree in any field. Some employers prefer applicants who have taken courses in criminal justice, law enforcement, business administration, or journalism.

Every agency and law firm has its own way of conducting investigations. So all newly hired Legal Investigators, experienced or inexperienced, receive extensive training on the job.

Experience and Skills

Many employers prefer hiring trainees who have law enforcement, journalism, or business management backgrounds. Some employers are willing to hire inexperienced applicants who have a desire to learn, are not easily convinced, and genuinely like to work with people. The applicants also show that they have strong problem-solving and organizational skills along with communication and writing skills. In addition, applicants must have excellent self-management skills as they will often work alone and with little supervision on the job.

Unions/Associations

Legal Investigators might belong to the National Association of Legal Investigators and the National Association of Investigative Specialists. Joining professional organizations gives investigators the opportunity to network with peers and obtain certified training, continuing education, professional resources, job listings, and other professional services and support.

Tips for Entry

1. Take courses in criminal justice, law, and paralegal studies to enhance your qualifications for trainee positions.
2. Network with attorneys and Legal Investigators in your area to learn about career resources and job opportunities. Some businesses offer summer internships to college students, giving them the chance to work with experienced Legal Investigators.
3. Get an idea of the different services that Legal Investigators offer clients. Read about some detective agencies on the Internet. Enter the phrase *legal investigations* or *legal investigator* in a search engine to get a list of web sites.

FINANCIAL INVESTIGATOR

CAREER PROFILE

Duties: Investigate or protect financial matters for businesses, companies, organizations, and individuals; provide expert witness testimony

Alternate Titles: Finance Detective, Fraud Investigator

Salary Range: $5,000 to $80,000

Employment Prospects: Good

Advancement Prospects: Limited
  Prerequisites:
  Special Requirements—Private investigator's license, in most states
  Education—Bachelor's degree in accounting
  Experience—Requirements vary with each agency
  Special Skills—Problem-solving, communication, interpersonal, and computer skills

CAREER LADDER

```
┌─────────────────────────────────┐
│      Manager or Owner           │
└─────────────────────────────────┘

┌─────────────────────────────────┐
│     Financial Investigator      │
└─────────────────────────────────┘

┌─────────────────────────────────┐
│  Financial Investigator Trainee │
└─────────────────────────────────┘
```

Position Description

Financial Investigators are private detectives who specialize in the field of finance. They are hired by businesses, companies, and organizations to investigate or protect various financial matters. With a strong background in forensic accounting (investigative accounting), much of a Financial Investigator's work involves examining financial statements, inventory records, and other business records and correspondence.

Financial Investigators offer several different services. They develop financial profiles on companies and individuals with whom clients are thinking about doing business. They perform background checks on potential executive officers and business partners for clients. They investigate companies or businesses that clients may want to buy or sell. They gather financial information about competitors.

Financial Investigators also do asset investigations. They locate missing or stolen assets that a company or individual owns. For example, a Financial Investigator might recover thousands of dollars worth of missing shipments for a company. Another Financial Investigator might uncover hundreds of thousands of dollars of missing money hidden in various bank accounts of his client's former employees. And still another Financial Investigator might track how a client's stolen stocks had been converted by the client's broker to buy a home in another state.

Financial Investigators also conduct investigations that involve fraud, theft, embezzlement, scams, or other criminal activity. For example, they might do undercover work to determine if employees are stealing office equipment or if vendors are defrauding a company by delivering fewer products to the company.

In much of their work, Financial Investigators audit financial records. In addition, they develop financial models to reconstruct financial statements and to forecast a company's financial status for the future. Other tasks include searching for information on computer databases. They interview employees, executives, bank personnel, and other people pertinent to their cases. On occasion, they may do surveillance and undercover work. In addition, they may provide testimony in court as an expert witness on their investigations and on financial matters.

Financial Investigators generally work a 40-hour week, but may work longer when it is needed.

Salaries

Earnings for Financial Investigators depend on factors such as experience, abilities, number of cases, and case fees. (Fees typically range between $35 and $150 an hour). Most Financial Investigators earn between $5,000 and $80,000 a year. In 1996, the average salary for private investigators, including Financial Investigators, was $37,800, according to a study by Abbott, Langer & Associates. Financial Investigators who live in metropolitan areas usually earn higher incomes. Most Financial Investigators receive reimbursement for expenses.

Employment Prospects

Financial Investigators work for detective agencies or have their own agencies. Job opportunities in the private detective field are expected to grow as fast as the average of all other occupations through 2006. In addition, the increase in white collar crimes should place a demand for more Financial Investigators.

Advancement Prospects

Supervisory and management positions are limited to case managers. Many Financial Investigators pursue career growth by way of wage or fee increases and complexity of new assignments. The goal for some Financial Investigators is to start their own agencies.

Special Requirements

Depending on location, Financial Investigators must hold a state or local private investigator's license in order to practice. License requirements, which include age, education, and experience qualifications, vary from state to state or city to city. In addition, Financial Investigators may be required by their state or city to complete certified private investigator training programs from recognized organizations. (For information about private investigator licensing in your state, contact your state licensing authority, state attorney general, state police, or state department of public safety.)

Financial Investigator trainees are covered by employers' licences.

Education and Training

There are no specific educational requirements in this field, but most Financial Investigators have a bachelor's degree in accounting. Financial Investigators are trained on the job.

Experience and Skills

Some agencies are willing to hire recent accounting graduates as trainees. Other agencies prefer trainees who have some experience as forensic accountants and as expert witnesses in court.

Along with basic accounting skills, Financial Investigator trainees should possess common business sense and be creative thinkers. Problem-solving skills, communication skills, interpersonal skills, and computer proficiency are also needed.

Unions/Associations

Financial Investigators might belong to different professional groups that represent their different areas of expertise: National Association of Investigative Specialists, Association of Certified Fraud Examiners, International Association of Financial Crime Investigators, and American Institute of Certified Public Accountants. Joining professional organizations gives investigators an opportunity to network with peers and obtain certified training, continuing education, professional resources, job listings, and other professional services and support.

Tips for Entry

1. To keep a competitive edge in this field, obtain professional certification such as becoming a Certified Public Accountant and Certified Fraud Examiner.

2. As an accountant, specialize in forensic accounting, a specialized field of accounting in which accounting skills and investigative methods are combined. You can find forensic accountant jobs with accounting firms as well as with detective agencies.

3. Learn about job openings from professional organizations in addition to attending professional conventions and meetings.

4. On the Internet, you can learn about the types of services some Financial Investigators offer clients. Enter the phrase *financial investigator* or *financial investigations* in a search engine to get a list of web sites.

STORE DETECTIVE

CAREER PROFILE

Duties: Protect retail business's cash, stock, and other assets; detect and apprehend shoplifters; other duties vary from store to store

Alternate Title: Loss Prevention Specialist

Salary Range: $11,000 to $25,000

Employment Prospects: Excellent

Advancement Prospects: Good

Prerequisites:

Education—High school diploma

Experience—Requirements vary from store to store

Special Skills—Self-management skills; observation, writing, and communication skills; interpersonal and teamwork skills

CAREER LADDER

```
┌─────────────────────────────┐
│   Senior Store Detective    │
└─────────────────────────────┘

┌─────────────────────────────┐
│       Store Detective       │
└─────────────────────────────┘

┌─────────────────────────────┐
│   Store Detective Trainee   │
└─────────────────────────────┘
```

Position Description

Store Detectives are responsible for protecting a store's assets—cash, merchandise, and property. As part of a store's loss prevention department, they watch out for suspicious activity among shoppers, store employees, vendors, and delivery people.

Duties vary for Store Detectives from store to store. In all stores, their primary job is to detect and apprehend shoplifters. Store detectives do not have the authority to arrest; but they can question suspects and hold them in custody until law enforcement officers arrive at the store.

Depending on the store, Store Detectives either help or conduct investigations. They might work on external investigations that involve trouble with customers such as shoplifting, credit card fraud, and refund scams. In addition, they might work on internal investigations that involve losses or theft committed by employees, vendors, and delivery people.

Some Store Detectives perform audits to make sure that employees are following the store's policies and procedures. Some Store Detectives are also responsible for periodic safety inspections. This is to make sure that a store's safety program is effective and follows government laws.

In many stores, Store Detectives conduct various training programs for store employees. Some workshops cover loss prevention topics such as how to handle theft, fraud, and potentially dangerous situations. Other workshops cover employee safety concerns such as avoiding injuries and reporting safety hazards.

Other duties that Store Detectives may perform are:

- maintain and test physical security equipment such as locks, security alarms, and fire alarms
- help open and close the store
- prepare loss prevention and security reports
- file complaints with the police
- testify in court about apprehensions or investigations in which they took part

Store Detectives work either full time or part time for stores. They work on rotating schedules that include late shifts, weekends, and holidays. Store Detectives who work for corporate chain stores might work a rotation of several stores.

Salaries

Salaries depend on several factors, including level of experience and education, job duties, and employer's size, location, and financial status. Entry-level Store Detectives generally earn an annual salary between $11,440 and $20,800 (or between $5.50 and $10 per hour). Annual salaries for Senior Store Detectives normally range from $15,600 to $24,960 (between $7.50 and $12 per hour). In 1996, the average salary for Store Detectives was about $19,100, according to a study by Abbott, Langer & Associates.

Employment Prospects

Store Detectives work for department stores, corporate chain stores, and shopping malls. They are also employed by security agencies that provide contractual services to retail businesses. Retail employers are in constant need for full-time and part-time Store Detectives, especially for entry-level positions. The number of jobs may increase as retail loss prevention is a fast-growing field.

Advancement Prospects

Store Detectives can advance to senior, or lead, Store Detectives and loss prevention managers who may manage one store, several stores, or several districts. The highest position in the retail loss prevention field is director or vice president, depending on the retail company. Other career options for Store Detectives are becoming loss prevention trainers or loss prevention investigators.

Advancement depends upon an employee's ambition, skills, commitment to a company's ideals, and a willingness to relocate, particularly for district and regional loss prevention positions.

Education and Training

Store Detectives need a high school or general equivalency diploma. However, more and more retail stores are hiring applicants with associate's and bachelor's degrees.

Store Detectives usually complete an in-store training program that covers safety, auditing, investigative methods, and interviewing and interrogation techniques.

In some parts of the country, Store Detectives are required to be trained in state certified security courses or through police officer training centers.

Experience and Skills

Experience requirements for Store Detective differ with every retail business. Many stores are willing to hire applicants with little or no experience who show honesty, dependability, and a willingness to learn. In addition, stores hire candidates who can think fast on their feet and are not afraid of being confrontational.

Candidates also show that they have the organizational and self-management skills needed to work alone with little supervision. Stores also look for good observational skills, writing skills, communication skills, interpersonal skills, and teamwork skills.

Unions/Associations

Store Detectives might belong to state and regional security associations. In addition, they might belong to the National Association of Investigative Specialists. Joining professional organizations gives investigators the opportunity to network with peers and obtain certified training, continuing education, professional resources, job listings, and other professional services and support.

Tips for Entry

1. Stores hire Store Detectives for temporary part-time and full-time positions for the Christmas holiday shopping season. Begin applying for these positions in September and October.
2. Research potential retail employers and find a company that is committed to career development and training of its employees.
3. Get a job as a sales worker, stock clerk, office worker, or other position in a retail store. This experience is valuable for understanding the role of Store Detectives and retail loss prevention professionals.
4. You can learn about job openings for Store Detective on the Internet. On web sites that offer job databases, such as "Career Mosaic," enter the phrase *store detective, loss prevention specialist,* or *retail investigator.*

PERSONAL PROTECTION SPECIALIST

CAREER PROFILE

Duties: Protect clients from danger and invasion of privacy

Alternate Titles: Bodyguard, Executive Protection Agent

Salary Range: $100 to $500 a day

Employment Prospects: Good

Advancement Prospects: Limited
  Prerequisites:
  Special Requirements—Private investigator's license, in most states
  Education—High school diploma
  Experience—Security or law enforcement experience preferred
  Special Skills—Protective driving skills; self-defense and firearms skills; observation, planning, decision-making, and interpersonal skills

CAREER LADDER

```
┌─────────────────────────────┐
│      Manager or Owner        │
└─────────────────────────────┘

┌─────────────────────────────┐
│   Personal Protection Agent  │
└─────────────────────────────┘

┌─────────────────────────────┐
│  Personal Protection Trainee │
└─────────────────────────────┘
```

Position Description

Personal Protection Specialists, or bodyguards, protect their clients from physical harm, kidnapping threats, and invasion of privacy. Their clients are individuals who need to safeguard their security, such as entertainers, sport figures, diplomats, government officials, business executives, military officials, threatened families, victims of stalkers, and high-risk witnesses.

Personal Protection Specialists provide a safe place in which their clients can live, work, play, and travel. They guard clients in their homes and workplaces. They escort clients to work, appointments, speaking engagements, stores, restaurants, and other locations. They accompany clients on trips to other cities and countries.

At all times, Personal Protection Specialists are on the alert for potential trouble. They are constantly observing people and keeping track of activity around their clients. They are watchful for suspicious persons as well as packages that may be bombs.

In order to prevent dangerous situations, Personal Protection Specialists plan out security in advance. They choose suitable cars and plan the safest driving routes. They inspect clients' homes and set up necessary security systems, including closed circuit television systems. They make sure they have adequate access to their clients' offices.

In confrontational situations, Personal Protection Specialists act quickly to divert attackers and act as shields for their clients. They may use deadly force on attackers if that is the only way to preserve the life of their clients.

Before starting an assignment, Personal Protection Specialists and clients agree on their non-security duties. These duties might include chauffeuring and planning travel arrangements for clients. Personal Protection Specialists make sure the clients understand that they are not personal servants or valets.

Personal Protection Specialists might be hired to protect a client for several days, months, or years. Most Personal Protection Specialists do not perform 24-hour duty. They are normally assigned to a work shift that may include nights, weekends, and holidays.

Salaries

Personal Protection Specialists are usually paid by assignment. They earn between $100 to $500 a day, depending on the assignment and their experience.

Employment Prospects

Most Personal Protection Specialists work for detective agencies. Some have their own agencies. Job opportunities in the private detective field are expected to grow as fast as all other occupations in the United States through the year 2006. An increased demand for Personal Protection Specialists may be expected due to the increasing concern over kidnapping threats, bomb threats, and other criminal danger.

Job competition is expected to be high since many law enforcement officers and military personnel retire early and begin second careers as Personal Protection Specialists.

Advancement Prospects

Supervisory and management positions are limited to case managers. Many Personal Protection Specialists pursue career growth by way of wage or fee increases and complexity of new assignments. The goal for some Personal Protection Specialists is to become independent contractors or head their own agencies.

Special Requirements

Depending on where they are located, Personal Protection Specialists must hold a state or local private investigator's license in order to practice. License requirements, which include age, education, and experience qualifications, vary from state to state or city to city. In addition, Personal Protection Specialists may be required by their state or city to complete certified private investigator training programs from recognized organizations. (For information about private investigator licensing in your state, contact your state licensing department, state attorney general, state police, or state department of public safety.)

Personal Protection Specialists trainees are covered by their employers' licenses.

Education and Training

Most agencies require applicants to have only a high school or general equivalency diploma. Many Personal Protection Specialists, however, have college degrees. Some agencies also require Personal Protection Specialists to complete certified training programs.

Experience and Skills

Agencies look for mature and disciplined applicants who are at least 21 years old and are in excellent physical condition. Most Personal Protection Specialists are in their 30s, 40s, and 50s and were formerly law enforcement agents or military personnel.

Applicants should have general knowledge of security technology and prevention measures. They should have experience in protective driving, unarmed defense, and firearms. They need strong observational and planning skills along with the ability to quickly assess situations and make decisions. They must be personable, being able to gain the trust of their clients.

Unions/Associations

Personal Protection Specialists might belong to regional and state private investigators or security associations. Many belong to the International Association of Personal Protection Specialists. Joining professional organizations gives Personal Protection Specialists the opportunity to network with peers and obtain certified training, continuing education, professional resources, job listings, and other professional services and support.

Tips for Entry

1. Enroll in a personal protection school that is recognized by detective agencies and professional associations.
2. Maintain a regular physical fitness program to stay in top physical and mental shape.
3. To learn more about the field and job opportunities, contact professional associations.
4. You can learn more about Personal Protection Specialists on the Internet. Enter the phrase *personal protection specialist, executive protection agent,* or *bodyguard* in a search engine to get a list of web sites.

PHYSICAL SECURITY

LOCKSMITH

CAREER PROFILE

Duties: Install and repair mechanical locks; make keys; open locks and safes when keys are lost or missing; may install and repair electronic security systems

Salary Range: $9,000 to $50,000

Employment Prospects: Good

Advancement Prospects: Limited
Prerequisites:
Special Requirements—Locksmith license in many states and cities
Education—High school diploma; apprenticeship
Experience—Some knowledge of locksmithing as well as electricity and electronics
Special Skills—Math, reading, and writing skills; communication and interpersonal skills; self-management skills

CAREER LADDER

```
┌─────────────────────────────────────────┐
│  Manager or Owner, Locksmith Business    │
└─────────────────────────────────────────┘

┌─────────────────────────────────────────┐
│              Locksmith                   │
└─────────────────────────────────────────┘

┌─────────────────────────────────────────┐
│         Locksmith Apprentice             │
└─────────────────────────────────────────┘
```

Position Description

Locksmiths install and repair mechanical locks, deadbolts, and other locking devices for residents, businesses, industries, and institutions. They help safeguard the security of homes, safes, vehicles, apartment complexes, schools, stores, office buildings, corporate complexes, warehouses, laboratories, factories, refineries, and many other types of facilities.

Traditionally, Locksmiths own shops or work for other Locksmiths. Along with lock installations and repairs, Locksmiths offer other services. Some Locksmiths install and service electronic security systems for vehicles, homes, and businesses. These systems include burglar alarms, smoke detectors, electronic access control systems (such as electronic card-operated locks), and closed circuit television systems. Most Locksmiths make duplicates of original keys for customers. They also make replacements for lost keys by inserting key blanks into locks to get impressions of the lock tumblers. In addition, they make master keys that open different locks. For example, a Locksmith might make a master key for a hotel that opens several hotel rooms.

Many Locksmiths offer a service to design and maintain security systems for commercial, industrial, and institutional customers. Locksmiths might rekey all the door locks in a facility—that is, changing locks completely for a new set of original keys. They might make different sets of master keys.

They might install access control systems or other security systems.

Another service is responding to emergency calls from people who have lost or forgotten their keys and have locked themselves out of their vehicles, homes, or businesses. Locksmiths use lockpicks or key impressions to open locks; when necessary, they use other methods to force locks to open or break. Most Locksmiths offer emergency services 24 hours a day.

Some Locksmiths specialize in safes. They might sell different types of safes to customers, such as money, jewelry, and gun safes. They might install and service safes. They might open safes when combinations are lost by safecracking, or listening for the contact points when turning the wheels. When that fails, drilling holes into the locks might be necessary.

Besides locksmith shops, Locksmiths work for corporations, universities, and other institutions as part of their security forces. They are usually known as in-house or institutional Locksmiths. Institutional Locksmiths are responsible for maintaining mechanical locks and electronic devices, such as padlocks, furniture locks, computer security locking devices, and access control systems. As part of their job, they learn and stay up-to-date with government safety codes, ordinances, and laws as well as their facilities' internal security procedures.

Locksmiths use different types of tools and equipment. These include files, screwdrivers, tweezers, electric drills, soldering equipment, key-cutting machines, and special tools such as lock picks.

Locksmiths work alone, but often work around other people. Depending on the jobs, they work indoors or outdoors, day or night, in any type of weather. Institutional Locksmiths work a 40-hour week, occasionally working overtime to complete jobs. Traditional Locksmiths work between 35 to 60 hours a week.

Salaries

Earnings depend on a Locksmith's level of experience and work skills as well as the size and location of an employer. Typically, Locksmiths earn higher wages in metropolitan areas such as Chicago, San Francisco, and New York City. The annual salary for entry-level Locksmiths is between $9,360 and $13,000 (or between $180 and $250 per week). The annual salary for experienced Locksmiths, on staff, is between $11,700 and $26,000 (or between $225 and $500 per week). Self-employed Locksmiths typically earn annual incomes between $12,000 and $50,000.

Employment Prospects

Locksmiths have their own shops or work for other locksmiths. Institutional Locksmiths are hired by universities, colleges, corporations, government agencies, and other institutions.

Experienced Locksmiths are expected to be in constant demand due to the great concern for adequate security to deter crime. The best opportunities will continue to be for Locksmiths who are licensed to install and maintain electronic security systems. Competition is keen for trainee positions as many locksmith shops have small staffs and prefer to hire experienced Locksmiths.

Advancement Prospects

Supervisory and management positions are limited in both retail and institutional fields. Many Locksmiths pursue career growth by earning higher incomes or specializing in particular skills such as safecracking and installing electronic security systems. The goal for some Locksmiths is to start their own shop.

Special Requirements

Many states and cities require Locksmiths to have locksmithing licenses. Requirements differ with each state and city. The process generally involves being fingerprinted and having their fingerprints on file with local authorities; passing a police background check; and passing a state examination on basic locksmithing skills and knowledge. Many states and cities also require that Locksmiths be bonded or have a specific amount of insurance coverage.

Locksmiths may also need to get additional licensing if they install electronic security devices.

Some employers require candidates to have a valid driver's license.

Education and Training

Locksmithing is an apprenticeship trade in which trainees work with experienced Locksmiths while mastering basic skills on the job. Some apprentices participate in on-the-job programs that offer both classroom and practical training. Apprenticeships last from three months to four years, depending on the area of specialty and level of expertise that is required.

Many employers prefer trainees to have a high school or general equivalency diploma.

Experience and Skills

Employers prefer to hire trainees who have some knowledge of the locksmithing trade along with knowledge of electricity and electronics. They look for applicants who have adequate math, reading, and writing skills as well as good communication and interpersonal skills. In addition, employers choose candidates who have strong self-management skills—the ability to get to work on time, follow directions, take initiative, work safely, and stay calm while working under pressure, and so on.

Unions/Associations

Many Locksmiths are members of state and regional locksmith associations. Many also belong to the Associated Locksmiths of America, a national group that offers a professional certification program. Institutional Locksmiths might join the Institutional Locksmiths Association. Joining professional organizations gives Locksmiths the opportunity to network with peers and obtain professional support and services such as certified training, continuing education, and job listings.

Tips for Entry

1. Talk directly with Locksmiths in your area about their requirements and opportunities for apprenticeships with them.
2. To prepare for a Locksmith career while in high school, take courses in mathematics, mechanical drawing, metalworking, basic electronics, physics, English, and business education.
3. Taking courses in a locksmithing school or program can provide a basic knowledge of the trade and may shorten the length of time spent as an apprentice. Enroll in a locksmithing school or program that is recognized by professional Locksmiths and Locksmith

associations. Contact Locksmiths in your area for recommendations.

4. On the Internet, you can learn about the types of services some Locksmiths offer. Enter the phrase *Locksmiths* in a search engine to get a list of web sites.

ALARM INSTALLER

CAREER PROFILE

Duties: Install electronic security and fire alarm systems in residences and businesses; may inspect, repair, and service systems

Alternate Titles: Burglar Alarm Installer, Fire Alarm Installer, Protective Signal Installer, Alarm Service Technician, Alarm Systems Agent, Security Technician

Salary Range: $24,000 to $53,000

Employment Prospects: Good

Advancement Prospects: Limited
Prerequisites:

Special Requirements—Alarm systems license in many states and cities

Education—High school diploma; on-the-job training

Experience—Knowledge of electricity and electronics; use of hand tools and power tools

Special Skills—Reading skills; communication, interpersonal, and self-management skills

CAREER LADDER

```
┌─────────────────────────────┐
│  Alarm Installer Supervisor │
└─────────────────────────────┘

┌─────────────────────────────┐
│       Alarm Installer       │
└─────────────────────────────┘

┌─────────────────────────────┐
│   Alarm Installer Trainee   │
└─────────────────────────────┘
```

Position Description

Alarm Installers put in and repair electronic security and fire alarm systems in vehicles, homes and businesses. The different types of systems they might install are:

- burglar alarms
- fire alarms
- special alarms, such as smoke detectors
- alarm systems to protect metal containers such as safes and files
- alarm monitoring systems, which transmit signals to a police station, security firm's central station, or other location upon sensing intrusion, break-ins, or fire on the premises
- intercom systems
- surveillance systems such as closed-circuit televisions
- access control systems (such as electronic card-operated locks)

Before installing any security system in a building, Alarm Installers look at building blueprints and electrical layouts to determine where wires, sensors, switches, and various parts of a system will be placed. Alarm Installers also read the oper-

ations manuals and manufacturer's specifications for the systems they are installing.

An installation involves putting in the necessary electronic equipment such as wire, conduits, motion sensors, horns, lights, and control panels throughout the building. The Alarm Installer also programs the systems according to the manufacturer's specifications and then tests the systems to make sure they are working properly.

Many Alarm Installers perform regular inspection checks on security systems to make sure the systems are working properly. They tighten loose connections as well as repair or replace defective parts and wiring. They test electrical circuits and sensors, making any necessary adjustments. Detailed records are kept on every alarm system.

Alarm Installers use different hand tools, power tools, and other equipment for their work; for example, they use wire cutters, wire strippers, screwdrivers, electric drills, soldering irons, voltmeters, and ohmmeters. As part of their duties, Alarm Installers keep detailed records of each installation or service job they perform.

Their work is performed both indoors and outdoors. They often need to climb ladders, crawl into small spaces, stoop over, and kneel or crouch on the ground to do their work. They usually carry equipment that weighs 25 to 50 pounds.

Alarm Installers work 40 hours a week, which may include Saturdays and evenings. They may be rotated on an on-call schedule for emergency repair work. Large companies have three work shifts, in which case Alarm Installers might be assigned a permanent shift or be rotated.

Salaries

Most Alarm Installers are paid hourly wages. In 1996, the average annual salary for electricians, including Alarm Installers, was between $24,336 and $52,936 (or between $468 and $814 per week). Salaries are typically higher in metropolitan areas and in large cities.

Employment Prospects

Most Alarm Installers work for security alarm companies. Job opportunities are readily available and should increase in the future because of the growing concern for adequate security to deter crime.

Advancement Prospects

Supervisory and management positions are limited. In large companies, most managers have bachelor's degrees. Many Alarm Installers pursue career growth by way of wage increases. The goal for some Alarm Installers is to start their own companies.

Special Requirements

Many states and cities require Alarm Installers to have licenses for installing security systems. Requirements differ with each state and city. The process generally involves being fingerprinted and passing a police background check. Trainees are usually required to have their fingerprints and other identification registered with local authorities. In some states, applicants must pass an alarm installer examination. Some states also require Alarm Installers to complete a certified training program that includes basic alarm system electronics.

Many employers require Alarm Installers to have a valid driver's license.

Education and Training

Many employers prefer to hire applicants who have a high school or general equivalency diploma. In addition, they seek applicants who have completed basic electricity and electronic courses in high school, community colleges, or vocational schools.

Trainees receive on-the-job training, learning their employers' specific installation procedures.

Experience and Skills

Trainee applicants do not need prior work experience, but they should have knowledge of electricity and electronics. They should be able to read schematic diagrams and follow operation manuals. In addition, they should know how to safely operate many of the hand tools and power tools that are used on the job.

Applicants also should have good communication and interpersonal skills along with self-management skills. In addition, applicants should be in good health and physically fit.

Unions/Associations

Many Alarm Installers belong to the National Burglar and Fire Alarm Association, which offers professional training and certification.

Tips for Entry

1. Apply directly to companies for trainee positions. To find out what companies are in your area, look in the yellow pages of your telephone book under *Burglar Alarm Systems, Fire Alarm Systems,* and *Automobile Alarm and Security Systems.*

2. Take mathematics, electricity, electronics, mechanical drawing, science, and shop courses in high school to obtain valuable knowledge and skills for this field.

3. On the Internet, you can learn about the types of services some security alarm companies offer customers. Enter the phrase *security alarms* in a search engine to get a list of web sites.

FIRE PROTECTION ENGINEER

CAREER PROFILE

Duties: Design building features to reduce the risk of fire damage; design, install, and maintain fire detection and fire suppression systems; analyze fire hazards to determine the degree of fire risk in a facility; conduct research projects

Salary Range: $40,000 to $60,000 or more

Employment Prospects: Excellent

Advancement Prospects: Good
  Prerequisites:
  Special Requirements—State Professional Engineer license for Fire Protection Engineers in the design field
  Education—Bachelor's degree in engineering
  Experience—Requirements vary from employer to employer
  Special Skills—Computer skills; interpersonal and communication skills

CAREER LADDER

Senior or Lead Fire Protection Engineer

Fire Protection Engineer

Fire Protection Engineer Trainee

Project Description

Fire Protection Engineers are engineers who specialize in limiting the destruction of fire on lives and property. They create comprehensive fire safety plans for high-rise residence and office buildings, shopping center complexes, hospitals, schools, libraries, museums, parking garages, warehouses, factories, oil refineries, airports, and other various kinds of facilities. Their employers include government agencies, insurance companies, private corporations, architect firms, and engineering firms.

Fire Protection Engineers work in several different areas. Some Fire Protection Engineers help plan the design of buildings to reduce the risk of fire damage, working with building owners, architects, other engineers (such as civil and electrical engineers), and fire marshals. For example, Fire Protection Engineers recommend materials and structures that are more fire resistant. They design features that can act as fire barriers, such as windows constructed to block the spread of fire between buildings. They plan emergency lighting systems as well as plan where fire escapes, fire stairs, and fire exits should go.

Some Fire Protection Engineers design various fire safety systems for employers or clients. They configure alarm and detector systems that upon detecting heat, smoke, or flames trigger off warning signals. They also design fire suppression systems, such as automatic sprinkler systems, that extinguish fires using water, foam, dry chemical, or other agents. In addition, they plan out adequate water supply systems for a facility.

Along with installing fire safety systems, Fire Protection Engineers maintain them. They perform routine inspections and tests on the different fire safety systems to make sure they are in working order as well as provide preventive maintenance on those systems.

Some Fire Protection Engineers analyze fire hazards to determine the risk of fire losses in a facility. They test and evaluate existing fire safety systems and survey all potential fire hazards in the facility. In addition, they recommend how to prevent the fire losses.

Some Fire Protection Engineers work on research projects for government agencies, universities, professional organizations, standards testing facilities, or corporations. Examples of research projects are:

- developing new fire suppression methods
- analyzing the behavior of fire in various materials, such as construction materials, children's clothing, or fire fighting gear
- estimating the time it takes occupants to safely clear burning rooms

- determining fire risk in consumer products, such as appliances, clothing, furniture, and computers

As part of their professional duty, Fire Protection Engineers stay up-to-date with the constantly changing developments in fire research and technologies. In addition, Fire Protection Engineers also are responsible for knowing current governmental fire codes and standards.

Most Fire Protection Engineers normally work a 40-hour week. Occasionally, they work overtime, under considerable stress, to meet deadlines.

Salaries

Starting salaries for Fire Protection Engineers are generally higher than engineers in other disciplines. According to the Society of Fire Protection Engineers, the median salary for entry-level fire protection engineers is over $40,000 per year. Depending on location and employers, Fire Protection Engineers can earn annual salaries of $60,000 or more.

Employment Prospects

Fire Protection Engineers are hired by insurance companies, private corporations, government agencies, and engineering firms. Job opportunities typically exceed the number of Fire Protection Engineer graduates each year. The demand is expected to continue into the next millennium, especially with the need to handle fire protection problems involving high-rise buildings, new chemical hazards, and the use of plastics.

Advancement Prospects

Fire Protection Engineers can pursue several paths in their field. Supervisory and management positions are readily available. Fire Protection Engineers can seek promotions to senior and team leader positions, assistant project managers, and managers. Some Fire Protection Engineers start their own consulting businesses. Other career paths in Fire Protection Engineering lead to such positions as university professors, fire investigators, and sales representatives for the various fire safety systems.

Special Requirements

In all 50 states and the District of Columbia, Fire Protection Engineers in the design field are required to have a Professional Engineer (PE) license. Licensing requirements generally require: a bachelor's degree in engineering (from an engineering program recognized by the Accreditation Board of Engineering and Technology); four to five years of relevant work experience; and passing a state engineering examination.

Education and Training

Entry-level Fire Protection Engineers need a bachelor's degree in engineering or fire protection engineering. Newly hired Fire Protection Engineers receive on-the-job training.

Experience and Skills

Many employers hire newly graduated engineering students for entry-level positions. Applicants must have fundamental knowledge of the nature and characteristics of fire and fire combustion. They must also be computer literate. In addition, they must have excellent communication and interpersonal skills in order to interact with the many different people they will work with on a project.

Unions/Associations

Among the professional associations that Fire Protection Engineers might belong to are Society of Fire Protection Engineers, National Fire Protection Association, and National Society of Professional Engineers. Joining professional organizations gives Fire Protection Engineers the opportunity for networking with peers and obtaining professional support and services such as certified training, continuing education, current research findings, and job listings.

Tips for Entry

1. To begin preparing for a career in fire protection engineering, take these courses in high school: math, chemistry, physics, English, and computer science (if offered).

2. As an engineering student, do internships with fire protection employers. Not only will you get valuable work experience but also a chance to decide if fire protection engineering is a field you want to pursue.

3. Join professional organizations such as the Society of Fire Protection Engineers to keep up to date with valuable information and resources in the constantly changing field as well as learn about available job openings.

4. Many Fire Protection Engineer consultants have web sites on the Internet. To read about some firms, enter the phrase *Fire Protection Engineer* or *Fire Protection Engineering* in a search engine to get a list of web sites. For more general information about Fire Protection Engineers, visit one of these web sites: Worcester Polytechnic Institute (http://www.wpi.edu/Academics/Depts/Fire/) or Society of Fire Protection Engineers (*http://www.sfpe.org*).

SECURITY GUARD

CAREER PROFILE

Duties: Protect property, assets, information, employees, tenants, and visitors from criminal activity, fire, and other danger; enforce employer's policies, security procedures, and safety plans

Alternate Title: Security Officer

Salary Range: $10,000 to $25,000

Employment Prospects: Excellent

Advancement Prospects: Good
Prerequisites:
Special Requirements—Security Guard license in many states and cities; pass a selection process
Education—High school diploma preferred
Experience—No experience is necessary
Special Skills—Interpersonal and communication skills; reading, writing, observational, and self-management skills

CAREER LADDER

```
┌─────────────────────────────────┐
│   Security Guard Supervisor     │
└─────────────────────────────────┘

┌─────────────────────────────────┐
│        Security Guard           │
└─────────────────────────────────┘

┌─────────────────────────────────┐
│     Security Guard Trainee      │
└─────────────────────────────────┘
```

Position Description

Security Guards are hired to protect their employer's building, grounds, assets, employees, tenants, and visitors against criminal activity, accidents, fires, and natural disasters. Furthermore, Security Guards enforce their employers' policies, rules, and regulations for maintaining order and safety on the premises. Banks, office complexes, government buildings, data processing centers, restaurants, malls, airports, museums, libraries, universities, hospitals, laboratories, factories, and refineries are some facilities where Security Guards work. Security guards also work temporary assignments, such as at concerts, sports games, conferences, weddings, and construction sites.

Security Guards are assigned to guard posts that may be gatehouses, building lobbies, or reception areas along with sensitive and dangerous locations in the facilities. Most Security Guards are unarmed. They carry two-way radios to communicate with other guards and command posts. Some Security Guards monitor surroundings on closed-circuit televisions.

From their guard posts, Security Guards are watchful for suspicious persons, packages, and activities. They make sure unauthorized persons do not enter restricted areas. Security Guards might check for employee and vendor identification. They might inspect vehicles and packages as well as monitor

deliveries. In addition, they might screen visitors for weapons, explosives, and other contraband. They may call employees to verify visitors' appointments and have visitors sign in and sign out on visitor registers. Security Guards may also escort visitors to their destinations with the facilities.

Some Security Guards answer questions for visitors and employees as part of their duty. Some Security Guards direct traffic on the premises and issue parking permits. Security Guards also respond to emergency situations such as providing first aid and sounding appropriate security and fire alarms.

Security Guards also perform patrol duty, making regular rounds in their assigned areas. They check for safety problems such as blocked fire exits. They may inspect fire protection equipment to make sure they are working properly. They are on alert for unusual sounds or odors (such as gas) and any hazardous conditions. At night, Security Guards check gates, entrances, doors, windows, and vents to ensure that they are locked and secure against break-ins.

In some states, Security Guards can obtain certification as special police officers that gives them the authority to make some arrests while on duty. Security Guards may make citizen's arrests if persons are committing crimes in front of them or they have reasonable grounds to believe that persons have committed crimes. Security Guards can interview suspicious persons and suspects to determine facts and, if warranted, detain persons while investigating the situation or until police arrive. Security Guards may only use force to control attackers if they are using force to create bodily harm or are using deadly force.

Keeping a record of their daily activities is part of Security Guards' job. They include reports of employee violations, accidents, unauthorized persons, criminal incidents, safety problems, and hazardous or dangerous conditions. In some facilities, Security Guards enter their information into computers.

Security guards work part time or full time. They work a rotating shift that includes nights, weekends, and holidays.

Salaries

Salaries for Security Guards depend on several factors, including level of experience and education; job duties (such as being armed or unarmed); and type, size, location, and budget of an employer. Security Guards with little or no experience may earn as low as the federal minimum wage to as high as $12 per hour. In 1996, most full-time Security Guards earned an annual income between $10,300 and $25,100. Security Guards can expect to receive higher salaries (in the mid-$20,000s or more) working for employers such as mining firms, utilities, and state and local governments. Lower salaries can be expected working for employers such as nonprofit organizations, museums, security services, and transportation services.

Typically, Security Guards with higher education and/or certified training can earn higher wages. In addition, armed Security Guards usually earn more than unarmed Security Guards. Furthermore, wages are typically higher in the largest cities and lower in smaller cities and rural areas.

Employment Prospects

Security Guards are hired by companies, institutions, and government agencies as well as security guard agencies that provide contractual services. The Security Guard field is expected to provide the greatest number of job openings for the economy through 2006 due to the high turnover rate and the growing concern about crime and terrorism. The greatest job growth will be with contract security guard agencies.

Applicants can expect keen competition for the higher paying and more responsible Security Guard positions as many retired law enforcement officers and military personnel begin second careers in security.

Advancement Prospects

Security Guards in small companies pursue advancement through salary increases because of limited opportunities. Those working for large companies can pursue supervisory and managerial positions along with higher wages; however, employers usually prefer Security Guards who have bache-

lor's degrees (in any field) for managerial positions and advanced degrees for administrative positions.

Other career paths for Security Guards are becoming law enforcement officers, corrections officers, private investigators, and personal protection agents.

Special Requirements

Most states and many cities require Security Guards to have licenses. Licensing requirements vary with the different states and cities. For example, some states require trainees to complete certified training in order to get licenses.

Every employer has its own set of requirements and conditions for employment, such as being a minimum age and having a driver's license. Employers usually do not hire applicants who have criminal records. In addition, many employers have a screening process in which applicants must pass every step. It may include any or all of the following: job application, written exam, interview, medical exam, background investigation, psychological review, polygraph examination, and drug testing.

Education and Training

Most employers prefer applicants who have at least a high school or general equivalency diploma.

All employers have some kind of on-the-job training program, covering their rules and regulations, security procedures, first aid, fire rescue, and other basic skills. Many security guard firms include both classroom instruction and field training. Armed Security Guards complete a more intense training program that covers areas such as the use of firearms and the laws pertaining to their use.

Experience and Skills

Many employers hire applicants without any experience for entry-level Security Guard positions, but applicants should have some experience handling emergencies and other stressful situations. Applicants should be in good health, physically fit, and emotionally stable. They should have adequate interpersonal skills and communication skills along with good reading, writing, and observational skills. In addition, applicants should show that they have strong self-management skills—such as the ability to get to work on time, follow directions, take initiative, work safely, and stay calm while working under pressure.

Unions/Associations

Many Security Guards belong to the International Foundation of Protective Officers, a professional association that offers networking, support, and training programs.

Tips for Entry

1. Apply directly to companies, government agencies, institutions, and security guard agencies for jobs.

2. Read the job want ads in local newspapers, particularly the Sunday edition, for notices about Security Guard openings.

3. On the Internet, you can learn about the different protective services that some security firms offer clients.

Enter the phrase *security guard services* or *security guard company* in a search engine to get a list of web sites.

SECURITY SUPERVISOR

CAREER PROFILE

Duties: Oversee the daily activities of the guard operations; complete all necessary reports and record-keeping; may perform guard post or patrol duties

Salary Range: Approximately $25,000 to $35,000

Employment Prospects: Excellent

Advancement Prospects: Good
Prerequisites:
Special Requirements—Security Guard license in many states and cities; pass a selection process
Education—High school diploma preferred
Experience—Six months to two years experience in guard work
Special Skills—Leadership skills; interpersonal skills; communication, writing, and record-keeping skills

CAREER LADDER

```
┌─────────────────────────────┐
│      Security Manager       │
└─────────────────────────────┘

┌─────────────────────────────┐
│     Security Supervisor      │
└─────────────────────────────┘

┌─────────────────────────────┐
│       Security Guard        │
└─────────────────────────────┘
```

Position Description

Security Supervisors directly oversee the activities of the security guard staff on a day-to-day basis. Staffs vary, depending on the size of the facilities, but Security Supervisors may supervise as few as two or as many as 25 or more guards. Their job is to make sure that security guards understand and enforce the policies, security procedures, and emergency plans of their employers against criminal activity, accidents, fires, and natural disaster.

All work shifts have Security Supervisors. Their responsibilities vary from employer to employer. Most Security Supervisors draw up work schedules and make guard post or patrol assignments. They also perform regular inspections of security and fire safety equipment to make sure they are in working order. Many perform investigations of security and safety problems such as theft or employee accident. Some may perform regular guard duties.

Security Supervisors also train and retrain their staff regarding employers' rules, protective procedures, first aid, fire safety, and other pertinent security matters. In addition, Security Supervisors regularly evaluate the job performance of each staff member, usually completing and signing performance appraisals. When staff members are performing poorly, Security Supervisors recommend disciplinary actions to their superiors. And if staff members must be disciplined (such as being docked pay for tardiness), Security Supervisors are responsible for handling the appropriate discipline.

They meet regularly with security management, giving updates on daily operations, reporting any problems or potential trouble spots, and requesting any necessary equipment or personnel changes. From time to time, Security Supervisors might suggest ways to improve procedures or modify existing policies to provide better protection. Furthermore, Security Supervisors may take part in the selection process for new staff members and make recommendations.

Security Supervisors prepare various administrative reports, such as payroll, overtime, and part-time reports. They also write business correspondence and reports such as monthly theft reports.

Security guard firms have either on-site or field supervisors, or both. Field Security Supervisors are usually responsible for security crews at one or more locations. They visit locations on a rotating basis, often performing unscheduled and unannounced spot inspections to make sure the security guards are performing their jobs satisfactorily.

In-house Security Supervisors work 40 hours a week. Security Supervisors work part time or full time for security guards firms.

Salaries

Salaries for Security Supervisors vary with different employers, and generally are higher in urban areas. Typically, supervisors with more experience and education can earn higher wages. The American Society for Industrial Security reports the average annual salary for Security Supervisors who oversee a staff of 25 or more security guards is $31,494. The average annual salary for Security Supervisors who oversee a staff of six or fewer is about $25,195.

Employment Prospects

Security Supervisors are hired by companies, institutions, and government agencies as well as by security guard agencies who provide contractual services. Job opportunities within all levels of the security industry, including Security Supervisors, are available and should continue to grow through 2006. The security industry is continually growing due to the increased concern of workplace violence, theft, terrorism, and white-collar crime.

Advancement Prospects

Security Supervisors can pursue management and administrative positions, such as security directors, security managers, security chiefs, and vice presidents or presidents of security. Many employers prefer that managerial and administrative officers have a college degree in any field. Security Supervisors choose to go into law enforcement, become security specialists, or head their own security guard agencies.

Special Requirements

In most states and many cities, Security Supervisors must be licensed. Licensing requirements vary with the different states and cities. Furthermore, applicants must pass an employer's screening process, which may include any or all of the following: job application, written exam, interview, medical exam, background investigation, psychological review, polygraph examination, and drug testing.

Education and Training

Employers usually hire applicants who have a high school or general equivalency diploma; many prefer applicants with some college background.

Security Supervisors receive on-the-job training. Type and length of training varies with the different employers.

Experience and Skills

Applicants generally need six months to two years experience in guard work. Employers look for candidates who have leadership and interpersonal skills. In addition, they should have excellent communication and writing skills as well as the ability to maintain schedules, payroll reports, and other routine records.

Unions/Associations

Security Supervisors might belong to the International Foundation for Protection Officers or the American Society for Industrial Security, two organizations that promote professional standards in the security industry. Both organizations offer certified training programs, continuing education, research resources, and the opportunity to network with peers.

Tips for Entry

1. Apply directly to security guard firms for jobs. To find out what companies are in your area, look in the yellow pages of your telephone book under *Security Guard* and *Patrol Services.*

2. To improve your chances for supervisory and management positions in security, take courses in law, police science, security, business management, and personnel. Courses in computer science, communications, electronics, and information technology are also valuable for a career in security.

3. Enhance your employability by obtaining certification, such as *Certified Protection Professional* (CPP), from recognized organizations.

4. On the Internet, you can learn about the different protective services that some security firms offer clients. Enter the phrase *security guard services* or *security guard company* in a search engine to get a list of web sites.

SECURITY MANAGER

CAREER PROFILE

Duties: Be responsible for the day-to-day physical security operations that safeguard their employers' buildings, grounds, assets, employees, tenants, and visitors

Salary Range: Approximately $40,000 to $65,000

Employment Prospects: Excellent

Advancement Prospects: Good
Prerequisites:
Education—Bachelor's degree; CPP (*Certified Protection Professional*) certification preferred
Experience—Requirement varies with the different employers
Special Skills—Planning, organizational, personnel management, and supervisory skills; communication, writing and interpersonal skills

CAREER LADDER

```
┌─────────────────────────────┐
│      Security Director       │
└─────────────────────────────┘

┌─────────────────────────────┐
│      Security Manager        │
└─────────────────────────────┘

┌─────────────────────────────┐
│     Security Supervisor      │
└─────────────────────────────┘
```

Position Description

Security Managers are in charge of the day-to-day physical security operations that safeguard their employers' buildings, grounds, assets, employees, tenants, and visitors. They make sure that the security force, security systems, fire safety systems, security procedures, and safety plans are in effect against criminal activity, accidents, fires, and natural disasters.

Security Managers oversee the whole security guard force. They organize the security force so that there are adequate guard posts and patrols to cover the grounds and buildings, particularly sensitive and dangerous areas, as well as sufficient staff for 24-hour coverage. They delegate responsibilities to supervisors and maintain close communication with them.

They make sure security controls are in place to keep unauthorized persons—visitors as well as employees—out of restricted areas and to prevent criminal activity in shipping, warehousing, cash handling, and other sensitive areas. When security problems arise, such as theft or hazardous conditions, Security Managers oversee the investigations. And if law enforcement and fire agencies are involved, Security Managers are the liaisons for their employers.

Security Managers make regular reviews of the security procedures and safety plans to ensure their effectiveness. That involves inspecting the condition of security barriers, protective equipment, communication systems, and so on. They also audit security controls as well as review the performance,

appearance, and competence of the security guards. Depending on their employers, Security Managers have the authority to make policy changes or advise their employers (or immediate supervisors) of the need for appropriate changes.

Furthermore, Security Managers are responsible for allocating funds for staff salaries, security equipment, and other operational costs within the established department budget. They hire and fire security personnel as well as make recommendations for promotions. Security Managers also handle any grievance matters that any security personnel have. In addition, Security Managers develop security training programs as well as establish staff evaluation procedures and oversee disciplinary actions. They may also develop security and safety education programs for all the employees.

Security Managers also have duties that are particular to their specialty area. For example, some duties that a Security Manager for a university has are managing contract guard services, overseeing campus escort operations, and controlling parking systems.

Security Managers sometimes work beyond their 40-hour week. They are on call 24 hours a day to attend to emergencies.

Salaries

Salaries vary according to type and size of employer as well as the job duties and individuals' experiences. According to an American Society for Industrial Security survey, the average yearly salary for Security Managers, without authority to make policies, is $45,537. According to a 1998 salary survey of *Access Control & Security Systems Integration* magazine readers, most Security Managers earned between $40,000 and $65,000 per year.

Wages are generally higher in metropolitan areas and most highly populated cities. In addition, individuals with college degrees, particularly graduate degrees, typically make more than do those who have some college background but without a college degree.

Employment Prospects

Security Managers are hired by companies, institutions, and government agencies as well as security guard agencies. Security is one of the fastest growing fields worldwide, and job opportunities for Security Managers are expected to increase favorably through 2006.

Advancement Prospects

Depending on their employers, Security Managers can advance to district managers, regional managers, security chiefs, security directors, vice presidents, and presidents of security.

Another career path is to become self-employed Security Consultants, who offer security management services or other specific security expertise to companies, institutions, and government agencies.

Education and Training

Most employers require Security Managers to have at least a bachelor's degree, and many prefer candidates with advanced degrees such as a master's in business administration. More and more employers are also hiring candidates who have *Certified Protection Professional* (CPP) certification.

Experience and Skills

Depending on the type and size of the employers as well as job duties, applicants generally need three to five years expe-

rience in security or law enforcement. In addition, applicants should have general knowledge and background in the specialty area in which they would be working, such as lodging security or corporate security.

Employers look for candidates who have planning and organizational skills as well as personnel management and supervisory skills. They should also be able to work with budgets, write reports, give presentations, and interact with subordinates, upper management, department managers, vendors, and others. In addition, candidates need skills that are particular to their specialty area. For example, Security Managers for hotels and resorts must know how to give first aid and CPR (Cardiac Pulmonary Resuscitation).

Unions/Associations

Security Managers might belong to the American Society for Industrial Security, which promotes professional standards in the security industry and offers networking opportunities, certified training programs, continuing education, and other professional services and support.

Tips for Entry

1. Network with other professionals to learn about job openings that are currently available or will be available soon.
2. Stay current with the latest security trends, issues, and concerns, particularly in your area of specialty (such as healthcare security, computer security, or utilities security).
3. Courses in security, computer science, business management, law, police science, personnel, and information management can provide you with valuable knowledge and skills for a career in security.
4. To learn more about the security field, visit the American Society for Industrial Security web site on the Internet. Its web address is *http://www.asisonline.org*.

COMPUTER SECURITY

DATA SECURITY SPECIALIST

CAREER PROFILE

Duties: Safeguard information assets from theft, damage, and destruction; administer policies that control access to computer data files

Alternate Title: Data Security Administrator

Salary Range: $20,000 to $75,000

Employment Prospects: Excellent

Advancement Prospects: Good
Prerequisites:
Education—Varies from employer to employer
Experience—Previous work experience in data security or information systems
Special Skills—Writing and communication skills, interpersonal skills, teamwork skills

CAREER LADDER

```
┌─────────────────────────────────┐
│   Senior Data Security Specialist │
└─────────────────────────────────┘

┌─────────────────────────────────┐
│      Data Security Specialist     │
└─────────────────────────────────┘

┌─────────────────────────────────┐
│   Data Security Specialist Traine │
└─────────────────────────────────┘
```

Position Description

Data Security Specialists are responsible for protecting the valuable information that is stored and managed on computer-based information systems in banks, schools, hospitals, companies, and other institutions. For example, some information assets that a department store might hold in computer systems are store accounts, inventory records, bills, invoices, and employee information. So, working alone and in teams, Data Security Specialists safeguard data from theft, tampering, and unauthorized access by employees as well as by outside crackers—criminals who manage to enter computer files by trial and error methods. Data Security Specialists also protect data from virus corruption, systems failures, and natural disasters.

One of their main responsibilities is maintaining the confidentiality of the various databases in an institution's computer systems. They make sure that employees have access only to computer files and applications for which they have authorization. For example, a personnel worker might have access to employee files but not to executive files.

Data Security Specialists maintain the authorization and authentication systems. They assign passwords, log-on identifications, smart cards, and other forms of identification to employees for the particular databases, applications, and computers that they are allowed to access for their jobs. They help users when they have access problems. They reassign passwords and other identification when users forget or lose

them. When necessary, Data Security Specialists remove names of employees from the authorization and authentication systems as well as add names of new employees. In addition, they report any problems or potential trouble to their supervisors.

Another major responsibility is maintaining the integrity of the databases. Data Security Specialists monitor access and transaction logs to check for possible security violations and break-ins. They regularly check the different software for viruses, trojan horses, and worms. And from time to time, they use hacker's techniques to get into the security systems to find their flaws and weaknesses. As critical problems and potential trouble spots are found, the Data Security Specialists report them to their supervisors.

Other duties that Data Security Specialists usually perform are:

- gather information for risk assessment surveys
- help develop security policies
- work with programmers and other security personnel to improve methods or procedures that strengthen security measures
- advise employees on ways to practice preventative security measures
- keep up to date with security software revisions
- make recommendations for new security software

Data Security Specialists work 40 hours a week; they work overtime during emergencies. Many Data Security Specialists are on call for emergencies 24 hours a day.

Salaries

Salaries vary from employer to employer and depend on job duties and work experience. According to a 1998 survey by *Information Security* magazine, the annual salary for most experienced computer security professionals, including Data Security Specialists, is between $50,000 and $75,000. Entry-level and less experienced professionals earn between $20,000 and $50,000 per year. In general, professionals earn the most money working for large companies (with 5,000 or more employees) and small companies (with less than 100 employees). In addition those working in the computer/data processing, finance, and insurance fields receive higher wages.

Employment Prospects

Data Security Specialists work for banks, insurance companies, government agencies, universities, data processing centers, hospitals, and many other institutions. In addition, they work for data security or information security consulting firms who do contractual work for various institutions.

Computer jobs, including Data Security Specialists, are expected to be the fastest growing occupations through the year 2006. Most job openings for Data Security Specialists will become available to replace workers who move into higher positions or other occupations or retire. As more and more institutions turn to computer-based information systems and do business using computers, the demand for Data Security Specialists will most likely increase.

Advancement Prospects

There are different paths that Data Security Specialists can take. They can pursue supervisory and managerial positions in Data Security by becoming team leaders, project managers, data security managers, and, eventually, information security officers.

Another path is to get into other areas of information systems security such as network security analysis, security software development, or computer forensic work. In addition, Data Security Specialists might become self-employed consultants or start their own data security consulting firms.

Education and Training

Most employers prefer applicants with a bachelor's degree, particularly in computer science, management information systems, or other related majors. Many employers hire applicants with a high school diploma, general equivalency diploma, or some college background with the required number of years of experience in data security.

Experience and Skills

Requirements vary with the different employers, and depend on the complexity of job responsibilities that entry-level Data Security Specialists perform. In general, applicants should have background in programming, systems analysis, and telecommunications along with one to four years of work experience in data security or information systems. Applicants need a broad knowledge of computers and computer networks, and should have knowledge in the operating systems that prospective employers use. Having knowledge in networking systems is desirable.

In addition, applicants should have strong writing and communication skills as they must be able to explain technical terms and procedures in language that is understood by everyone. Applicants also need good interpersonal skills as well as good teamwork skills.

Unions/Associations

Two professional groups that Data Security Specialists might join are ICSA, Inc. (formerly known as International Computer Security Association) and Information Systems Security Association. Joining such organizations gives Data Security Specialists the opportunity for networking with peers and obtaining professional support and services, such as certified training, continuing education, technical information, and job listings.

Tips for Entry

1. Talk with data security professionals about the current security needs and hiring requirements of their employers. Some places where you can make contacts are professional computer security associations, university or college computer departments, and data security consulting firms.

2. If there is a particular industry such as manufacturing, banking, or healthcare in which you are interested in working, become familiar with that industry. Take college courses that may be useful for working in the industry as well as obtain paid or voluntary experience.

3. Research the companies for which you are interested in working before you apply or interview for a job. Learn about what they do, their assets, what their computer security is like, and their commitment to employee career development.

4. Get an idea of the type of work involved in data security by looking at web sites of data security consulting firms on the Internet. In a search engine, enter the phrase *data security consulting firms*. To learn more about computer security, or information systems security, in general, enter the phrase *computer security*.

INFORMATION SYSTEMS SECURITY (INFOSEC) SPECIALIST

CAREER PROFILE

Duties: Implement information systems security policies and procedures; evaluate computer security systems for their effectiveness; identify security weaknesses and help develop ways to reduce the risks of unauthorized entry, theft, or damage.

Alternate Title: Computer Security Specialist

Salary Range: $20,000 to $100,000 or more

Employment Prospects: Excellent

Advancement Prospects: Good
Prerequisites:
Education—Bachelor's degree preferred
Experience—Three to five years of work in computer security
Special Skills—Writing, communication, analytical, and presentation skills; interpersonal and teamwork skills

CAREER LADDER

```
┌─────────────────────────────────┐
│     Senior Infosec Specialist   │
└─────────────────────────────────┘

┌─────────────────────────────────┐
│        Infosec Specialist       │
└─────────────────────────────────┘

┌─────────────────────────────────┐
│    Infosec Specialist Trainee   │
└─────────────────────────────────┘
```

Position Description

Information Systems Security (Infosec) Specialists work for companies, government agencies, and other institutions. Their job is to safeguard information assets and the computer-based information system from theft, tampering, accidental erasures, system failures, virus corruption, natural disasters, and so on. Information systems are made up of computer hardware, software, and databases. Networks in which computers are connected through telecommunications are also part of information systems: local area networks (LANs) connect computers to each other within an institution; wide area networks (WANs) connect an institution's computers to computers outside the institution; and internetworks, such as the Internet, connect an institution's computers to many different networks at the same time. In addition, computer-based information systems include the procedures for running the various systems and the people who input, process, and output information.

Infosec Specialists are constantly evaluating all aspects of their employers' information systems, particularly with network security, to identify flaws within the systems that are security threats. For example, they might use hacker's techniques—trial and error—to find ways to get through their own firewalls that are built to prevent unauthorized access from outside the company (such as through the Internet). Or they might examine computer logs and log files to check for possible break-ins by crackers (criminal hackers who have gained unauthorized access).

Infosec Specialists work with other security personnel to find solutions to security problems or issues. For example, in a corporate retail store, Infosec Specialists might work on the problem of finding the best encryption methods to send and receive sensitive data over the Internet. In addition, Infosec Specialists help develop plans and security measures to reduce security risks. In many infosec divisions, the Infosec Specialists are responsible for implementing new security procedures once they are approved.

Other duties Infosec Specialists may perform are:

- be responsible for data security
- write security manuals for the various networks and stand-alone computer systems as well as update manuals when needed
- install new security software and updates, making sure they are compatible with security measures
- talk with users who have violated security policies

COMPUTER SECURITY   93

Infosec Specialists work 40 hours a week. On occasion, they may work evenings and weekends to finish projects or to resolve emergency situations. In large computer installations, Infosec Specialists work on different shifts.

Salaries

Due to the shortage of information security professionals, salaries for very experienced Infosec Specialists can rise up to $100,000 and more. According to a 1998 survey by *Information Security* magazine, the annual salary for most entry-level and less experienced professionals is between $20,000 and $50,000 per year and between $50,000 and $75,000 for most experienced Infosec Specialists. Professionals working for large companies (5,000 or more employees) and small companies (less than 100 employees) generally earn the most in addition to those working in the computer/data processing, finance, and insurance fields.

Employment Prospects

Infosec Specialists work for banks, insurance companies, government agencies, universities, data processing centers, hospitals, and many other institutions. In addition, they work for information security or data security consulting firms that do contractual work for various institutions.

Informational systems security jobs are in great demand due to the growth of institutions conducting business over wide access networks and internetworks. In 1998, the number of infosec job opportunities was greater than the number of experienced candidates, particularly for higher-level positions such as Infosec Specialists.

Advancement Prospects

Infosec Specialists can advance to senior and lead positions, which include supervisory duties, as well as to managerial positions. The highest position is infosec manager or information security officer. In addition, Infosec Specialists might become self-employed consultants or start their own consulting firms.

Education and Training

Most employers hire applicants with bachelor's degrees, preferably in computer science or a major that is related to their industry. For example, a bank might hire an experienced applicant who has a degree in accounting. In 1998, due to the shortage of computer security professionals, many applicants who had no degrees or college backgrounds were hired because they had the technical skills. However, as more and more individuals enter the infosec field, employers will more likely consider applicants with college degrees.

Experience and Skills

Depending on the job duties, applicants need between three and five years work of infosec experience. In addition, they must have experience in the specific technologies, such as operating systems, networking systems, firewalls, and Internet architecture, that are used by prospective employers.

Furthermore, applicants should have excellent writing, communication, analytical, and presentation skills. They should have good interpersonal skills and teamwork skills, as they will work with many different people, including infosec staff, users, and vendors.

Unions/Associations

Infosec Specialists might belong to ICSA, Inc. (formerly known as International Computer Security Association) and Information Systems Security Association. Many professionals also belong to SIGMOD, or Special Interest Group on Management of Data, part of the Association for Computing Machinery. Joining such organizations gives Infosec Specialists the opportunity for networking with peers and obtaining professional support and services such as certified training, continuing education, technical information, and job listings.

Tips for Entry

1. To learn about job openings in computer security, contact college and university placement centers, and professional associations. Also apply directly to companies and institutions for which you would like to work.

2. While in college, participate in internship or co-op programs, working in the information security divisions of companies or other institutions.

3. Consider joining the military to begin a career in information systems security. According to M.E. Kabay, Director of Education at ICSA, Inc., many security professionals started their careers in the military, volunteering or applying for training in military intelligence and military police as well as becoming part of system and network operations or management.

4. You can learn more about the Infosec field on the Internet. In a search engine, enter the phrase *infosec, computer security,* or *information systems security.* You will get a list of web sites that include consulting firms, infosec products, and professional organizations.

INFORMATION SYSTEMS SECURITY (INFOSEC) MANAGER

CAREER PROFILE

Duties: Plan, execute, and oversee the security of the computer-based information systems in companies, government agencies, and other institutions

Alternate Titles: Director of Information Security, Chief Security Officer

Salary Range: $50,000 to $100,000

Employment Prospects: Excellent

Advancement Prospects: Limited
Prerequisites:
Education—Bachelor's degree preferred
Experience—Five to ten years of Infosec experience; experience in security management, project management, and application development
Special Skills—Writing, communication, and interpersonal skills; organizational, project management, and supervisory skills

CAREER LADDER

```
┌─────────────────────────────────┐
│           Consultant            │
└─────────────────────────────────┘

┌─────────────────────────────────┐
│         Infosec Manager         │
└─────────────────────────────────┘

┌─────────────────────────────────┐
│   Infosec Specialist or other   │
│       Infosec Profession        │
└─────────────────────────────────┘
```

Position Description

Information Systems Security (Infosec) Managers are responsible for the overall computer security operations for companies, government agencies, and other institutions. Their job is to develop and administer security policies that safeguard their employers' computer-based information systems 24 hours a day.

An institution's information systems include its information assets—various databases about organizational accounts, inventory, customer accounts and employee records. These systems also include all computer hardware and software as well as communication networks that connect computers to each other within the company (local access networks or LANs), to computers outside the company (wide access networks or WANs), and to networks such as the Internet. So, Infosec Managers make sure that their staff protects every part of these information systems from loss or damage.

Infosec Managers manage all aspects of computer security, such as:

- physical security and fire safety measures for the computer systems

- emergency plans for recovering data in case of power failures, fires, or natural disasters
- authorization and authentication systems to make sure that access to computer files or software programs are given only to authorized personnel who have the proper identification
- selection, testing, and installation of new security software and hardware
- the detection, reporting, and investigation of security violations by employees as well as security breaches by crackers (criminals who use trial and error, or hacking, techniques to gain access into databases)
- training programs that teach employees the safe and proper use of computer systems

To keep tabs on the different security areas, Infosec Managers meet regularly with staff managers and team leaders. Infosec Managers also review audits, risk management surveys, and other reports to check on the continuing effectiveness of the various security measures. Upon finding weaknesses or potential trouble, Infosec Managers direct staff members to find solutions and develop new security procedures.

Infosec Managers are the liaisons for the infosec departments. They meet with user departments, such as data processing, to discuss the security needs or issues that those departments may have. In addition, Infosec Managers are the liaisons between their employers and law enforcement agencies.

Infosec Managers also handle routine administrative tasks. For example: they manage departmental budgets; negotiate contracts with vendors and consulting firms; hire and fire infosec staff members as well as suggest that staff members earn promotions or salary raises; handle personnel grievances or complaints; and develop staff training programs.

Infosec Managers work a regular 40-hour week, but often put in many overtime hours to complete responsibilities or handle emergencies.

Salaries

Salaries vary with different employers and also depend on the size and type of the employer, region, or job responsibilities. In 1998, most Infosec Managers received an annual salary between $50,000 and $100,000.

Employment Prospects

Infosec Managers work in many industries, such as banking, insurance, education, and manufacturing. In 1998, the number of job opportunities outnumbered available candidates. The shortage of experienced security professionals, especially for higher level positions such as Infosec Managers, is expected to continue into the future.

Advancement Prospects

Infosec Managers are generally the highest-level position in the information systems security department. In some institutions, they report to the chief information systems officers; in others, Infosec Managers report to the chief executive officers or presidents of the institutions.

Infosec Managers can pursue further advancement by way of salary increases and changes in title, such as to chief security officer or vice president of information security. Some Infosec Managers also pursue career growth by finding employment with companies that have new or developing infosec departments. In addition, some Infosec Managers become consultants or start their own firms in information systems security.

Education and Training

Requirements vary from employer to employer. Most employers prefer candidates with at least a bachelor's degree. Many employers prefer advanced degrees. Some employers are willing to hire candidates without any college degree if they have the experience in information systems security.

Experience and Skills

Applicants generally need between five and ten years of information systems security experience, depending on the responsibilities of the jobs that they are applying for. Along with infosec experience, employers look for experience in security management, project management, and application development. Furthermore, employers want candidates who have a general background in the employers' industry—banking, insurance, publishing, or others. In addition, applicants should have excellent writing, communication, and interpersonal skills as well as organizational, project management, and supervisory abilities.

Unions/Associations

Two professional groups specifically organized for infosec professionals are ICSA, Inc. (formerly called International Computer Security Association) and Information Systems Security Association. In addition to membership with these organizations, Infosec Managers might belong to computer groups, such as Association for Computing Machinery and security organizations such as American Society for Industrial Security. Joining such organizations gives Infosec Managers the opportunity for networking with peers and obtaining professional support and services such as certified training, continuing education, technical information, and job listings.

Tips for Entry

1. Join professional organizations and attend professional conventions to take advantage of networking with peers who may know of job openings.

2. The growing trend among employers is to hire certified security professionals. Enhance your employability by obtaining professional certification such as *Certified Information Systems Security Professional* (CISSP) from a recognized organization.

3. To get an idea of the extent of different responsibilities an Information Security Manager has at different companies, browse job openings on the Internet. In a job bank, such as "Career Mosaic," enter the phrase *information systems security manager* or *Infosec Manager.*

COMPUTER FORENSICS SPECIALIST

CAREER PROFILE

Duties: Conduct investigations of computer crime and computer-related crimes; examine computers to discover and recover electronic data that may be potential evidence of crimes

Alternate Title: Computer Investigative Specialist

Salary Range: $41,000 to $91,000

Employment Prospects: Limited

Advancement Prospects: Limited
Prerequisites:
Special Requirements—Must first become a law enforcement officer
Education—Requirements vary with the different law enforcement agencies
Experience—Requirements vary with the different law enforcement agencies
Special Skills—Computer skills; critical thinking, writing, and communication skills; interpersonal skills

CAREER LADDER

Unit Commander

Computer Forensics Specialist

Computer Forensics Specialist Trainee

Position Description

Computer Forensics Specialists are law enforcement officers who use technical expertise to investigate computer crimes and computer-related crimes. They discover and recover data from computers to determine potential evidence for arresting and convicting criminals. In law enforcement agencies, Computer Forensics Specialists are part of special details called computer crime units or high-technology crime units.

They conduct a wide range of computer crime investigations, including theft of computer systems, trade secrets, and information assets (data) as well as destruction or damage of computer files. They also conduct or assist in investigations in which computers were used to commit a crime such as embezzlement, credit fraud, selling narcotics, kidnapping, or murder. For example, a bank employee might keep a file of all the customer account numbers from which she steals money on her personal computer at home.

Before examining the data in a computer, Computer Forensics Specialists first gather information about the crime for which the data is potential evidence. With those facts, they plan what they should look for on the computer's hard disk and backup media. Throughout their examination, they follow standard procedures so that potential evidence is not destroyed or damaged thus establishing a chain of custody so that the evidence can be admitted at a court trial. Computer Forensics Specialists also make sure that all the data in a computer system is safe and intact throughout their examination.

Using special software and utilities, they perform a thorough search for relevant data, looking for and examining existing files as well as hidden files. They find and access relevant encrypted files and files that are protected by passwords. They probe every portion of unused space in the computer disk, searching for sites that may have evidence that had been created and then deleted, or erased. After completing their examination, they prepare a well-detailed report of their findings, including a list of files that may be potential evidence and how the files were discovered or recovered.

Computer Forensics Specialists perform other investigative duties, including interviewing witnesses and victims, interrogating suspects, performing surveillance or undercover work, participating in evidence searches and seizures, and arresting criminals.

Like all law enforcement officers, Computer Forensics Specialists work a 40-hour week with many overtime hours. They are on call 24 hours a day, seven days a week.

Salaries

Salaries vary for Computer Forensics Specialists working in law enforcement agencies. For example, Computer Forensics Specialists working for the Federal Bureau of Investigation (FBI) might earn between $40,700 and $91,000 per year. In local law enforcement departments, computer forensics is a voluntary special detail; thus, officers receive a salary based on their rank and level. Some departments may pay officers additional compensation for performing computer forensics duty. In its 1996 "Occupational Compensation Survey," the Bureau of Labor Statistics (of the U.S. Department of Labor) reported that many police officers who performed one or more special police duties, such as computer forensics duty, earned a salary between $40,924 to $56,160 per year (or between $787 to $1,080 per week).

Employment Prospects

Computer Forensics Specialists are part of computer crime or high-technology crime units in city, county, state, federal law enforcement agencies, and U.S. military forces. Some Computer Forensics Specialists are private consultants or work for computer forensics firms.

Most job opportunities become available when officers retire, resign, transfer to other positions, or become promoted to higher positions. Employment prospects in this field are limited, but have potential to grow due to the increase in computer crimes nationwide. However, the creation or expansion of a computer investigation unit is dependent on an agency's needs and budget.

Advancement Prospects

Computer investigation is a voluntary assignment. In all law enforcement agencies, officers can pursue supervisory and administrative positions. In local agencies, officers may have to resign from computer investigation duty in order to perform supervisory or administrative duties. Supervisory and administrative positions within computer investigation detail are limited to unit commanders.

Many retired law enforcement and military Computer Forensics Specialists start a second career by becoming computer forensics consultants, working for a private computer forensics firm, or starting their own firm.

Special Requirements

Computer Forensics Specialists must first become law enforcement officers with police departments, sheriff's departments, state police departments, or federal agencies such as the FBI, DEA, or U.S. Secret Service. (Read about special requirements for different law enforcement agencies in the "Police Work" section.)

Education and Training

Education requirements depend upon the entry requirements to the different law agencies. Because this is a new field, applicants do not need a computer science degree, but must have computer savvy—either self-taught or formally trained.

Depending on the law enforcement agencies, entry-level Computer Forensic Specialists receive formal training, on-the-job training, or a combination of both.

Experience and Skills

Every agency has it own requirements for eligibility to special assignments such as computer investigations details. Generally, agencies choose candidates who are skilled in computers and have the potential for being taught the necessary skills for conducting computer forensics investigations. In addition, candidates should have strong critical thinking, writing, and communication skills as well as good interpersonal skills.

Unions/Associations

Computer Forensics Specialists from both law enforcement and the private sector might belong to the High Technology Crime Investigation Association. Law enforcement officers might also belong to the International Association of Computer Investigative Specialists. Joining such organizations allows Computer Forensics Specialists to network with peers and obtain professional support and services, such as training, continuing education programs, and technical information.

Tips for Entry

1. When you apply or interview for a law enforcement position, let the agency known of your interest in computer forensics investigations.

2. Obtain employment with federal law enforcement agencies or join the U.S. military to get computer training as well as valuable investigative experience for this field.

3. Take college courses in criminal justice, law, police science, computer science, and other related fields. A college degree in any of these subjects is a valuable asset in this field.

4. You can learn more about the forensics computing field on the Internet. To look at web sites about law enforcement crime units, enter the phrase *high-technology crime* or *computer crime units* in a search engine. To look at web sites of computer forensics consultants, enter the phrase *forensics computer* or *forensics computing*.

QUALITY ASSURANCE SPECIALIST

CAREER PROFILE

Duties: Evaluate the performance and integrity of new software before it is sold to the public; check that programs work according to specifications; find flaws in the programs

Alternate Titles: Software Tester, Software Test Engineer

Salary Range: $16,000 to $50,000

Employment Prospects: Good

Advancement Prospects: Good
Prerequisites:
Education—Varies with the different employers
Experience—Have a computer background
Special Skills—Computer skills; communication skills, interpersonal skills, teamwork skills; problem-solving skills and organizational skills

CAREER LADDER

```
┌─────────────────────────────────────┐
│  Senior Quality Assurance Specialist │
└─────────────────────────────────────┘

┌─────────────────────────────────────┐
│     Quality Assurance Specialist     │
└─────────────────────────────────────┘

┌─────────────────────────────────────┐
│  Quality Assurance Specialist Trainee │
└─────────────────────────────────────┘
```

Position Description

Quality Assurance Specialists evaluate the performance and integrity of software before it is sold to the public. They check that software programs work according to developers' instructions, making sure that the software is compatible with the various computer systems on which they will be used. Furthermore, they look for bugs, or flaws, in the applications while testing them.

Upon completion of the final version of new software or updated versions of existing software, developers turn the software over to Quality Assurance Specialists. They also provide a set of specifications upon which Quality Assurance Specialists create a test plan. The specifications include information such as:

- who will use a software and the kind of environment (office, elementary school, medical lab) where the software will be used
- the purpose and objectives for the software
- the different platforms upon which the software can be used
- how the software is expected to work
- any specific features thay need to be tested
- specific types of tests that are needed
- when the testing needs to be completed

In addition Quality Assurance Specialists review any accompanying documents such as charts, diagrams, programmers' notes and correspondence, and reviews by customers who tested beta, or developmental, versions of the software.

Once they understand the specifications, Quality Assurance Specialists begin planning the test processes. They develop test scenarios; they estimate the number of tests they must perform and how many times they will perform each test; and they create time schedules.

They keep well-detailed notes for each test they perform, writing down positive results as well as problems. They describe any bugs, and note the number of times they appear. Each time the program crashes, they reconstruct the moves or computer commands that brought on a crash and write down the sequence for programmers to examine and fix. Throughout the testing, they submit written and oral progress reports to their managers. As part of their final report, Quality Assurance Specialists might include suggestions for improving applications, such as how to make them easier to use.

On occasion, Quality Assurance Specialists are given software to evaluate without any specifications. They must then define test procedures for the software. Usually that involves talking with programmers as well as customers who have tested the software to gather enough information to create a specifications outline from which to work.

Quality Assurance Specialists generally work 40 hours a week, but may work more hours to meet deadlines.

Salaries

Wages vary from employer to employer and depend on an employee's job duties and experience. According to a 1996 survey by the American Society for Quality Control, the average annual salary of its membership was $50,480. The Computer Museum (http://www.tcm.org) reports that annual salaries for quality assurance technicians are between $16,000 and $32,000.

Generally, quality assurance professionals who work in large cities and metropolitan areas receive higher wages. Also, professionals who have college degrees earn higher wages.

Employment Prospects

Quality Assurance Specialists work for software and hardware companies as well as for software quality assurance consulting firms. They also work for large companies and institutions. Job opportunities are readily available and are expected to grow due to the spread of standards in software and the increase of consumer dependence on high-quality software.

Advancement Prospects

Quality Assurance Specialists have several options to pursue. Within the quality assurance field, they can become quality assurance analysts as well as pursue supervisory and managerial positions. They might also consider changing into other positions such as programmers.

Education and Training

Education requirements for entry-level positions vary with different employers. Many employers prefer applicants who have college degrees with some classes in computer science or a related field. Some are willing to hire applicants who have a high school or general equivalency diploma.

Training varies with the employers as well. Some employers provide entry-level Quality Assurance Specialists with formal training programs while others give new employees informal on-the-job training.

Experience and Skills

Many companies hire applicants without any previous experience for entry-level positions as long as they have a computer background (trained or self-taught) and show that they have the potential to be trained to have quality assurance skills. Regardless of applicants' previous work experience, employers look for applicants with good communication skills as well as good interpersonal and teamwork skills. They also need strong problem-solving and organizational abilities.

Unions/Associations

Quality Assurance Specialists might belong to the American Society for Quality Control, which offers networking opportunities, training and education programs, job listings, research resources, and other professional services.

Tips for Entry

1. Contact the software quality assurance department at companies for which you are interested in working and ask about job openings that are available or may soon be available.

2. Gain experience by becoming volunteer testers for software companies. Contact software companies directly, and ask them if they need beta testers for the types of software of which you are familiar.

3. You can learn more about the software quality assurance field on the Internet. In a search engine, enter the phrase *software quality assurance*. You will get a list of web sites that include consulting firms, professional organizations, and general information.

CORRECTIONS

BAILIFF

CAREER PROFILE

Duties: Call courts to order; maintain order in courtrooms; protect judges, juries, and all those in attendance at trials

Salary Range: $15,000 to $50,000

Employment Prospects: Fair

Advancement Prospects: Limited
Prerequisites:
Special Requirements—For state courts, first become a deputy sheriff; for federal courts, first become a deputy U.S. marshal
Education—Varies with the different law enforcement agencies
Experience—Knowledge of office practices, court procedures, and legal terminology and forms
Special Skills—Reading and writing skills; communication and interpersonal skills

CAREER LADDER

```
┌─────────────────────────────┐
│      Unit Commander         │
└─────────────────────────────┘

┌─────────────────────────────┐
│          Bailiff            │
└─────────────────────────────┘

┌─────────────────────────────┐
│      Deputy Sheriff         │
└─────────────────────────────┘
```

Position Description

Bailiffs are law enforcement officers who provide security in courtrooms during court trials. In the state court systems, deputy sheriffs perform bailiff duty, which is part of a special detail in the sheriff's departments. In the federal court system, Bailiffs are deputy U.S. marshals.

As officers of the court, Bailiffs usually work in groups of two or more, performing a variety of tasks. They inspect courtrooms for security and cleanliness before court sessions begin. They also check that courtrooms have sufficient light, heat, and ventilation. It is the duty of the Bailiffs to call the court to order and announce the entry of the judge. During court sessions, Bailiffs call defendants and witnesses to the stand as well as swear them in before they testify before the court. In addition, Bailiffs maintain order in the court, warning persons who are disturbing court procedures, and, if necessary, physically removing unruly persons from courtrooms.

Bailiffs are responsible for the security of juries throughout court trials. They must also prevent jurors from talking about a trial with the public lest a mistrial is called—that is, the trial is stopped and the suspects are set free. So, Bailiffs escort juries between courtrooms and jury rooms as well as stand guard outside the jury rooms. In addition, Bailiffs attend to the jurors' needs, such as relaying their requests or questions to the judges. Bailiffs also arrange for food to be delivered to the juries or escort them to restaurants.

Bailiffs may run personal errands for jurors if they are sequestered (held overnight or longer). Furthermore, they make any necessary arrangements for jurors, such as overnight lodging or transportation.

Bailiffs work under the supervision of judges or court administrators, performing any errands or tasks that are required by the court. Upon the request of judges, Bailiffs might summon attorneys to the judge's chambers. They might maintain court documents and exhibits during trials. They might deliver court files, court minutes, and law books to judges or other court personnel. They might fetch necessary supplies or forms. When courts are not in session, Bailiffs might do routine clerical tasks such as photocopying court calendars and completing forms. Bailiffs who have legal training might serve as legal assistants to the judge.

Bailiffs perform other duties, which depend on the specific needs of the courts they serve. For example, in criminal courts, Bailiffs might guard and escort defendants (the persons who are accused of committing crimes) into courtrooms.

Bailiffs work regular court hours, Monday to Friday.

Salaries

As deputy sheriffs or deputy U.S. marshals, Bailiffs receive a salary based on their rank and pay scale. In 1996, most deputy sheriffs earned an annual salary between $15,900 and

$48,400. Annual salaries for new deputy U.S. marshals, in 1998, ranged from $24,000 to $35,000.

Employment Prospects

Bailiffs work for state and federal court systems, but they must first become deputy sheriffs or deputy U.S. marshals. Job opportunities in the state courts depend on court needs; and most opportunities become available as officers retire or transfer to other assignments.

Advancement Prospects

Bailiff duty is part of a deputy U.S. marshal's regular duties. For deputy sheriffs, the Bailiff detail is a voluntary assignment. Deputy sheriffs can stay with the detail for as long as they are qualified for the job or until they are transferred to other departments. Supervisory positions are limited to unit commanders.

Special Requirements

To become a Bailiff, an applicant must first become a deputy sheriff or deputy U.S. marshal. For either position, certain requirements must be met which vary with the different sheriff's departments and the U.S. Marshal Service. (Read about special requirements for deputy sheriffs on page 8 and for deputy U.S. marshals on page 14.)

Education and Training

Education requirements vary with the different agencies. Most sheriff's departments require Bailiffs to have a high school or general equivalency diploma. Some departments require an associate's degree or a minimum of 60 credits from an accredited college, preferably with course work in police science or other related fields. To become deputy U.S. mar-shals, applicants must have bachelor's degrees in law, criminal justice or other related field.

Experience and Skills

Deputy sheriffs may volunteer for Bailiff duty after serving a specific number of years on their force. They should have knowledge of office practices, court procedures, and legal terminology and forms. It's important that applicants have adequate reading and writing skills along with good communication and interpersonal skills.

Unions/Associations

Bailiffs, who are deputy sheriffs, belong to regional or state sheriff unions and associations. They might also join the National Sheriffs' Association or its affiliate, the American Deputy Sheriffs' Association. The International Association of Court Officers and Services, Inc. is another organization that Bailiffs might join. These organizations allow Bailiffs the opportunity to network with peers, obtain continuing education and training, and other professional services and support.

Tips for Entry

1. As a deputy sheriff, let the unit commander know of your interest, especially before you are eligible or before an opening is available.
2. Courses in paralegal, law, and criminal justice can provide you with valuable knowledge and skills for this position.
3. To learn more about state and federal court systems on the Internet, enter the phrase *judicial systems* or *state court systems* in a search engine to get a list of web sites.

CORRECTIONAL OFFICER (SHERIFF'S DEPARTMENT)

CAREER PROFILE

Duties: Maintain order, enforce rules and regulations, supervise prisoners and their activities in county jails and other county correctional facilities

Alternate Titles: Jailer, Detention Officer

Salary Range: $11,000 to $50,000

Employment Prospects: Excellent

Advancement Prospects: Good
   Prerequisites:
   Special Requirements—Must be a U.S. citizen; have no criminal record; fulfill age and other requirements; pass a selection process
   Education—High school diploma
   Experience—Requirements vary with the different sheriff's departments
   Special Skills—Critical thinking skills; interpersonal skills; supervisory and observational skills; communication and writing skills; self-management skills

CAREER LADDER

```
┌─────────────────────────┐
│        Sergeant         │
└─────────────────────────┘

┌─────────────────────────┐
│   Correctional Officer  │
└─────────────────────────┘

┌─────────────────────────┐
│ Correctional Officer Trainee │
└─────────────────────────┘
```

Position Description

Sheriff's Correctional Officers supervise inmates in county jails and other correctional facilities. In addition, they maintain a safe, secure, and orderly environment within correctional facilities. Unlike prisons, jails hold persons who have been arrested and are awaiting court hearings or trials along with persons who have been convicted of crimes and sentenced to serve time in jails. State and federal prisoners are sometimes housed in county correctional facilities when there is insufficient space for them in state or federal prisons.

As sworn law enforcement officers, Correctional Officers supervise prisoners and their activities, such as eating, exercising, showering, working, seeing visitors, and making phone calls. When needed, Correctional Officers obtain or provide medical help for inmates. In addition, they settle arguments or break up fights between inmates. They enforce discipline when prisoners become disorderly or break regulations. And when it is warranted, Correctional Officers use physical means to control inmates who become violent. Correctional officers keep a daily record of every inmate's activities, such as what they did, who visited them and any violations they committed.

Correctional Officers make routine checks throughout the institution for unsanitary conditions and fire hazards as well as signs of tampering around windows, doors, locks, or gates. They also perform routine inspections of cells and of prisoners for weapons, drugs, and other contraband. Furthermore, Correctional Officers monitor mail and screen visitors for any prohibited items.

In direct supervision jails, Correctional Officers work in the same space where prisoners live. There are no bars or gates to separate the Correctional Officers from the prisoners. In addition, Correctional Officers do not carry firearms. To maintain order and enforce regulations among prisoners, Correctional Officers use interpersonal and communication skills. Surveillance equipment is also used to help Correctional Officers monitor prisoner activity.

Sheriff's Correctional Officers may have other duties, such as:

- book prisoners into the facilities, which includes preparing arrest reports, fingerprinting prisoners, and taking their photographs
- interrogate prisoners about the charges against them

- take prisoner's belongings into custody, maintain them, and return them when prisoners are released
- distribute commissary items such as candy, snacks, and toilet articles as well as record payments on vouchers
- escort inmates to locations inside the jail as well as outside, such as to courtrooms and medical facilities
- help investigate any disturbances or crimes that are committed within the facilities
- search for escaped prisoners
- admit visitors as well as release them
- perform office tasks such as maintaining jail records

Correctional Officers work rotating shifts that include night, weekends, and holidays. On occasion, they may be required to work overtime.

Salaries

The Bureau of Labor Statistics (a division of the U.S. Department of Labor) estimates that Correctional Officers earn an annual wage between $11,960 and $50,439. The American Jail Association reports that Correctional Officer trainees who live in rural areas earn between $13,000 and $14,000 per year while trainees in urban areas may earn $30,000 or more per year. Correctional Officers also receive overtime pay.

Employment Prospects

Correctional Officers for county jails and other correctional facilities are employed by sheriff's departments. In many sheriff's departments, rookie deputy sheriffs are assigned to jail duty for a certain length of time before performing patrol duty. Some sheriff's departments have two distinct career lines—Correctional Officers and deputy sheriffs.

Job opportunities for qualified applicants are expected to stay favorable through the year 2006 for several reasons—the increasing rate of arrests and convictions; the expansion of construction of county correctional facilities; and the low salaries for Correctional Officers. The demand for most jobs is expected to be for large regional jails.

Advancement Prospects

With experience and further education and training, Correctional Officers can advance through the ranks of sergeant, lieutenant, and captain. Some Correctional Officers pursue other careers in corrections such as specialists, instructors, and parole officers.

Special Requirements

Most sheriff's departments require applicants to be U.S. citizens who have no criminal records. In addition, they must meet age, residency, vision and other requirements, which vary from department to department.

Applicants must pass every step of a selection process that includes any or all of the following: job application, written exam, oral interview, medical examination, physical aptitude or agility test, background investigation, psychological review, polygraph examination, and drug testing.

Education and Training

Sheriff's departments require a high school or general equivalency diploma. Some departments require an associate's degree or a minimum of 60 credits from an accredited college, preferably with course work in police science, psychology, criminal justice, or other related field.

Many departments have a formal training program that trainees must complete before starting on the job or within their probationary period. Trainees receive instruction on institutional policies, regulations, and operations; custody and security procedures; self-defense and use of firearms; and other pertinent subject matter. Upon graduation, trainees are assigned to field training officers.

Experience and Skills

Requirements vary with the different sheriff's departments. Many departments hire applicants without any previous work experience in corrections. In departments that have no career Correctional Officer positions, applicants must first qualify as deputy sheriffs. (To learn more about deputy sheriff requirements, read page 8.)

For sheriff's Correctional Officers, departments look for physically fit applicants who project authority and have strong critical thinking skills. Applicants should have good interpersonal skills as well as good supervisory and observational skills. They should also have good communication and writing abilities, and need strong self-management skills—the ability to get to work on time, follow directions, take initiative, work safely, stay calm while working under pressure and so on.

Unions/Associations

Sheriff's Correctional Officers might belong to the American Jail Association, an organization that provides professional support, networking, and training programs for jail personnel. In addition, Correctional Officers might join regional and state deputy sheriff's associations or correctional officer organizations.

Tips for Entry

1. Contact sheriff's departments or police departments to learn about job requirements and opportunities.
2. Obtain a bachelor's degree in criminal justice, public administration, social services, or other related field, if

you are interested in pursuing a career in jail management and administration.

3. To learn about different county jail systems on the Internet, enter the phrase *county jail* or *county corrections facility* in a search engine to get a list of web sites.

PROBATION OFFICER

CAREER PROFILE

Duties: Conduct pre-sentence investigations of convicted offenders to help courts determine the appropriate type of sentence; supervise convicted offenders while they complete the terms of their probations

Salary Range: Approximately $26,000 to $62,000

Employment Prospects: Fair

Advancement Prospects: Limited
  Prerequisites:
  Special Requirements—Must be a U.S. citizen; fulfill certain requirements; pass a selection process
  Education—Bachelor's degree; certified training
  Experience—One to two years of related work experience
  Special Skills—Communication and interpersonal skills; writing and investigative skills; organizational and supervisory skills

CAREER LADDER

Senior Probation Officer

Probation Officer

Probation Officer Trainee

Position Description

Probation Officers work with convicted offenders who receive suspended sentences—that is, they are placed on probation rather than serve time in jail or prison. Often characterized as part police officer and part social worker, Probation Officers oversee juvenile or adult probationers, or offenders. They make sure that probationers are completing the specified court plans under which they were conditionally released back into their communities. In addition, Probation Officers ensure the safety and protection of the communities. Because of the danger involved in their jobs, some Probation Officers are authorized to carry firearms.

Probation Officers perform several duties. One major duty is conducting pre-sentence investigations on offenders to help the courts determine suitable sentences for them, which may include probation, jail or prison sentence, or both. Probation Officers gather background information about the offenders, including their criminal history, work history, and so on. They review various records such as police reports, police records, medical files, and personnel records. They interview victims, police officers, and other individuals who have relevant information about the crime or offense. In addition, they interview offenders, family members, employers, counselors, and other individuals and professionals who may have pertinent facts about the offenders. Probation Officers evaluate all the facts and recommend rehabilitation or treatment plans for the offenders.

Another major duty is supervising convicted offenders who are on probation. All probationers have their own set of conditions for probation. For example, a convicted offender might get these conditions to complete during her 12 months on probation: do 500 hours of community service; meet regularly with a psychologist to deal with emotional problems; and stay away from certain individuals.

Probation Officers make sure each client (probationer who is on their caseload) understands the terms of his or her probation. They help every client obtain proper services and enroll in appropriate programs that may help him or her. In addition, Probation Officers make sure each client pays the fines, restitution, or reparations that courts have ordered him or her to pay. They keep in contact with every client, meeting regularly with each one. Furthermore, Probation Officers keep accurate case records on each client's progress and file written or oral reports with their supervisors. If progress for any client becomes negative, Probation Officers may submit a recommendation to court to suspend a client's probation.

In some agencies, Probation Officers are also assigned to work with parolees, or prisoners who are released before their sentence is completed. Probation Officers may have additional responsibilities, such as:

- represent the probation department in court to present probation reports or answer questions about probation recommendations
- operate work furloughs or other community correction programs
- perform intake services (the interviewing of offenders to determine if they should be placed under supervision rather than be brought to trial)
- enforce court orders such as arresting clients, performing searches for specific evidence, and seizing evidence
- train probation assistants and volunteers

Probation Officers frequently travel within their cities and sometimes to other cities for meetings with clients and other people. They work 40 hours a week, which may include nights and Saturdays to accommodate meetings with individuals who are unavailable during the day or weekdays. Probation Officers are on call 24 hours a day.

Salaries

Salaries vary according to agency, depending on factors such as a Probation Officer's experience and departmental budget. For example, the salary ranges for Probation Officers in three states are:

- $26,000 to $58,000 for county positions in California
- $30,800 to $42,000 for state positions in Nevada
- $26,000 to $62,000 for federal positions in Florida

Employment Prospects

Probation Officers are hired by probation departments at the county, state, and federal government levels. Most job opportunities are created to replace Probation Officers who retire, resign, or are promoted to higher positions. This field may expand because of the increasing rate of overcrowding in jails and prisons and the use of sanctions such as electronic monitoring and work furloughs; however, the creation of additional positions or maintenance of current level of staffing is dependent upon agencies' budgets.

Advancement Prospects

Supervisory and management opportunities in probation departments are limited to a few positions—supervisors, chief probation officers, and directors of probation departments. Many Probation Officers pursue career growth by way of salary increases and complexity of new assignments.

Special Requirements

As government employees, Probation Officers must be U.S. citizens. Applicants must also meet other requirements that vary from department to department. In addition, they must pass every step of a selection process that includes any or all of the following: job application, written exam, oral interview, medical examination, background investigation, psychological review, and drug testing.

Education and Training

In most agencies, the minimum education requirement is a bachelor's degree, preferably in criminal justice, social work, sociology, or other related field. Some agencies require an additional year of graduate level studies.

Probation Officer trainees must complete certified formal training as well as field training within their first year of employment.

Experience and Skills

Requirements for entry-level positions vary from agency to agency. Many agencies hire recent college graduates without any previous related work experience. Some agencies hire non-college graduates if they have two years of full-time work experience in related areas, such as intake work, rehabilitation counseling, or community work that involves supervising ex-offenders.

Employers look for emotionally stable candidates who can handle heavy caseloads, meet deadlines, and work alone. They are able to work with many different people as well as handle individuals who may be disturbed, upset, angry, hostile, or manipulative. In addition, candidates should have strong communication and interpersonal skills along with good writing and investigative skills. They also need organizational and supervisory abilities.

Unions/Associations

Probation Officers might belong to regional and state correctional associations as well as probation and parole officer associations. Two national organizations that Probation Officers might belong to are the American Probation and Parole Association and the American Correctional Association. Joining such organizations allows Probation Officers an opportunity to network with peers and obtain continuing education, training, and other professional services and support.

Tips for Entry

1. Contact probation departments directly, to learn about job openings, or job requirements.
2. While in college, do internships with probation departments, juvenile halls, or community-based programs that work with ex-offenders.
3. Many county probation departments use volunteers to assist probation officers with some of their routine office tasks. Find out if there are any programs in your area and join one to obtain valuable experience.
4. Many county probation departments have web sites on the Internet. To get a list of web sites, enter the phrase *probation department* in a search engine.

CORRECTIONAL OFFICER
(STATE OR FEDERAL)

CAREER PROFILE

Duties: Enforce regulations of state or federal prisons and other correctional facilities; supervise the conduct and activities of prisoners; maintain the general well-being of prisoners

Alternate Title: Corrections Officer

Salary Range: $17,000 to $32,000

Employment Prospects: Excellent

Advancement Prospects: Good
Prerequisites:

Special Requirements—Must be a U.S. citizen; have no criminal record; fulfill age and other requirements; pass a selection process

Education—High school diploma for state facilities; bachelor's degree for federal facilities; formal training and field training

Experience—Varies with the different institutions

Special Skills—Leadership skills; supervisory and interpersonal skills; writing and communication skills; observational and self-management skills

CAREER LADDER

```
┌─────────────────────────────┐
│   Supervisor or Sergeant    │
└─────────────────────────────┘

┌─────────────────────────────┐
│    Correctional Officer     │
└─────────────────────────────┘

┌─────────────────────────────┐
│ Correctional Officer Trainee │
└─────────────────────────────┘
```

Position Description

State and federal Correctional Officers work in state or federal prisons, penitentiaries, and other correctional facilities. They are responsible for maintaining a safe, secure, and orderly environment for adults or juvenile prisoners. Along with enforcing institutional policies and regulations, Correctional Officers supervise the conduct and activities of the prisoners.

Assigned to a variety of duty posts, Correctional Officers oversee prisoners 24 hours a day. They supervise inmates while they eat, bathe, exercise, work, attend educational programs, talk with visitors and pursue other activities. They conduct accurate counts of inmates. They keep constant watch for violations as well as for signs of unruly and unusual behavior that may turn into fights or disturbances. If inmates need medical attention, Correctional Officers provide basic first aid, CPR, or get medical help. In some facilities, Correctional Officers provide individual or group counseling.

Correctional Officers also make routine inspections of cells and of prisoners for weapons, drugs and other contra-band. Furthermore, Correctional Officers monitor mail and screen visitors for any prohibited items. Correctional Officers escort high-security inmates to locations within the facilities. Correctional Officers may also transport prisoners to outside locations such as courts, medical centers, and other correctional facilities.

When fights or disturbances occur, Correctional Officers break them up immediately, using physical force, firearms, chemical agents, and other necessary equipment, if necessary. In addition, Correctional Officers make daily written and oral reports of prisoners' activities—what activities they did, who visited them, any violations they committed, and so on.

Security duties are also part of Correctional Officers' jobs. They perform routine security and safety checks throughout the institution. They also stand guard at gates and in courtyards as well as hold security positions in security towers above the premises.

Depending on the facilities, Correctional Officers may have specialized duties. In maximum security facilities where very dangerous offenders are housed, Correctional Officers monitor inmates' activities with surveillance equipment from a centralized control center. In direct supervision prisons, Correctional Officers do not carry firearms. They work in the same space where prisoners live without any bars or gates to separate them from the prisoners. In these facilities, Correctional Officers use interpersonal communication skills to maintain order and enforce regulations among prisoners.

Correctional Officers work eight-hour days, five days a week. They work rotating shifts, which include nights, weekends, and holidays. They are sometimes required to work overtime.

Salaries

Wages vary from state to state as well as among the different correctional facilities. In general, entry-level Correctional Officers receive an annual salary between $17,000 and $20,000. They also receive compensation for overtime.

In federal prison systems, entry-level Correctional Officers earn an annual salary between $24,000 and $32,000. Salaries are typically higher in areas where the cost of living is higher. Federal Correctional Officers receive extra compensation for working overtime, night duty, and Sundays.

Employment Prospects

State and federal prisons, penitentiaries, community correctional work centers, and other correctional facilities hire Correctional Officers. Most job opportunities are for replacements for Correctional Officers who are retiring, resigning, or transferring to other positions. This field is considered one of the fastest-growing occupations through the year 2006. Additional positions are expected to be created due to the increasing rate of criminal convictions and longer sentencing as well as the expansion and construction of prisons and other correctional facilities.

Advancement Prospects

With additional experience, education, and training, Correctional Officers can advance to supervisory and administrative positions, including warden—the highest position in corrections. They can also pursue other careers within corrections, such as probation and parole officers, specialists, and instructors.

Federal Correctional Officers are eligible for retirement after 25 years of service or upon reaching age 50 if they have 20 years of service.

Special Requirements

In general, applicants must be U.S. citizens who are between 18 and 21 years old and must have no felony convictions. The maximum age for federal applicants is 36 years old. Applicants must meet other requirements that vary with the state and federal institutions.

Furthermore, applicants must pass every step of a selection process that includes any or all of the following: job application, written exam, oral interview, medical examination, physical aptitude or agility test, background investigation, psychological review, polygraph examination, and drug testing.

Education and Training

State institutions require applicants to have a high school or general equivalency diploma. Federal institutions require bachelor's degrees unless applicants fulfill the work experience requirement.

Entry-level Correctional Officers must complete formal instruction and field training, which cover areas such as institutional regulations and operations, constitutional law, cultural awareness, self-defense, and use of firearms. Federal Correctional Officer trainees complete specialized instruction at the Federal Bureau of Prisons residential training center in Glynco, Georgia.

Experience and Skills

Experience requirements vary with the different state institutions. Some institutions require previous work experience in corrections or other related area, including military service. For federal entry-level Correctional Officer positions, applicants without bachelor's degrees must have three years of general work experience that has involved supervision, teaching, social casework, rehabilitation counseling, management, or professional sales.

All employers look for applicants who show leadership abilities with good supervisory and interpersonal skills as well as good writing and communication skills. In addition, applicants should have strong observational and self-management abilities.

Unions/Associations

Correctional Officers might belong to regional or state professional Correctional Officer associations, including labor unions. Two national organizations that Correctional Officers might join are the International Association of Correctional Officers and the American Correctional Association. Joining such organizations affords Correctional Officers the opportunity to network with peers and obtain certification, continuing education, job listings, and other professional services and support.

Tips for Entry

1. Contact the state or federal correctional facility at which you are interested in working, and obtain information about job requirements and openings.
2. To enhance your opportunities in this field, take college courses in psychology, criminal justice, police science, criminology, and other related areas.

3. Participate in volunteer programs that work with juvenile and adult offenders and prisoners to gain valuable experience as well as learn if corrections is the field you want to pursue.

4. Many state correctional facilities have web sites on the Internet. To get a list of web sites, enter the phrase *state department of corrections.* To learn about the federal prison systems, visit the Federal Bureau of Prisons web site. Its address is *http://www.bop.gov.*

PAROLE OFFICER

CAREER PROFILE

Duties: Help parolees adjust to living and working in their communities; supervise and counsel parolees until they have completed their sentences

Alternate Title: Parole Agent

Salary Range: $20,000 to $70,000

Employment Prospects: Fair

Advancement Prospects: Limited
  Prerequisites:
  Special Requirements—Must be a U.S. citizen; fulfill certain requirements; pass a selection process
  Education—Bachelor's degree; certified training
  Experience—Some casework experience
  Special Skills—Communication, writing, and interpersonal skills; investigative skills; organizational and supervisory skills

CAREER LADDER

```
┌─────────────────────────────┐
│    Senior Parole Officer     │
└─────────────────────────────┘

┌─────────────────────────────┐
│       Parole Officer         │
└─────────────────────────────┘

┌─────────────────────────────┐
│    Parole Officer Trainee    │
└─────────────────────────────┘
```

Position Description

Parole Officers work with prisoners who have been granted a conditional release from prison before the end of their prison sentences. They help juvenile and adult prisoners adjust to living and working within society and staying away from further criminal activities. In addition, Parole Officers watch over parolees for the public safety, supervising them until they have completed the time left on their prison sentences.

As part of their responsibilities, Parole Officers help their clients (parolees who are on their caseloads) find jobs and residences. They refer clients to educational and training programs, counseling services, drug rehabilitation programs, and other services or programs that may help their clients make honest livings and lead productive lives. In addition, they enforce any fines or other payments that their clients are ordered to pay for their crimes.

Furthermore, Parole Officers monitor the progress of their clients by maintaining regular contact with them. For some clients, Parole Officers might contact them once every two weeks; with others, contact may be needed every few days. Parole Officers meet with their clients in parole offices and sometimes in clients' homes. Parole Officers may also talk with employers, family members, counselors, and others to learn how their clients are doing.

Parole Officers maintain accurate records on their clients, and submit regular oral and written reports to their supervisors and parole board on their clients' progress. If a client violates any terms of his or her parole, Parole Officers may recommend to the parole board that the client's parole be suspended. If the parole board agrees, the client is sent back to prison.

On occasion, Parole Officers may enforce court orders such as arresting their clients, conducting searches, and seizing evidence. Because of the danger involved in their jobs, some Parole Officers are authorized to carry firearms.

Many Parole Officers also perform pre-parole investigations to help parole boards decide whether prisoners should be granted parole and, if so, determine the terms of their parole. Parole Officers review prisoner records and any other pertinent reports. They interview correction officers and other correction staff. Through interviews with prisoners, family members, and others in the community, Parole Officers gather facts about prisoners' lives before their incarceration along with information about their families and job prospects.

Depending on the agency, Parole Officers might also work with probationers, or convicted offenders who receive suspended prison or jail sentences and instead serve probation under specified conditions.

Parole Officers often travel in their job to meet with clients and other individuals pertinent to their clients. They work 40 hours a week, usually with a flexible schedule in order to accommodate meetings with clients and others who are unavailable during the day and weekdays. Parole Officers are on call 24 hours a day.

Salaries

Salaries vary with the different agencies, depending on factors such as education, experience, job responsibilities, location, and an agency's budget. Most Parole Officers start at an annual salary between $20,000 and $30,000 per year, and may eventually earn between $40,000 and $50,000 per year. Those working for federal agencies may be able to earn as much as $70,000 per year.

Employment Prospects

Parole Officers are hired by parole divisions at the county, state, and federal government levels. The growing rate of overcrowding in jails and prisons should keep job opportunities readily available. Most openings become available when Parole Officers retire, resign, or become promoted to higher positions. The creation of additional positions or maintenance of current level of staffing is dependent upon agencies' budgets.

Advancement Prospects

Supervisory and management opportunities are limited to a few positions—supervisors, unit managers, and directors. Many Parole Officers pursue career growth by way of salary increases and complexity of new assignments.

Special Requirements

Applicants must be U.S. citizens and meet other requirements that vary from department to department. In addition, they must pass every step of a selection process that includes any or all of the following: job application, written exam, oral interview, medical examination, background investigation, psychological review, and drug testing.

Education and Training

Most agencies require applicants to have bachelor's degrees, preferably in criminal justice, social work, sociology, or other related field. Some employers require an additional year of graduate level studies. Some employers are willing to hire applicants without college degrees if they have sufficient work experience.

Parole Officer trainees must complete certified training within their first year of employment.

Experience and Skills

Many agencies require entry-level applicants to have one to three years of casework experience in a social service, correctional institution, or other agency.

Due to the emotional demands of the job, employers look for applicants who are able to work independently and meet with many different people of whom some may be disturbed, upset, angry, hostile, or manipulative. Applicants should be able to handle the additional stress that comes from handling heavy caseloads and meeting deadlines. Along with strong communication, writing and interpersonal skills, applicants should have good investigative skills. Also important are excellent organizational and supervisory abilities.

Unions/Associations

Parole Officers might belong to regional and state correctional associations and probation and parole officer associations. Two national organizations that they might belong to are the American Probation and Parole Association and the American Correctional Association. Joining such organizations gives Parole Officers the opportunity to network with peers and obtain continuing education, training, and other professional services and support.

Tips for Entry

1. To learn about job openings or job requirements, contact parole divisions directly.
2. While in college, do internships with probation departments, juvenile halls, or community programs that work with ex-offenders.
3. Volunteer with police departments or sheriff's departments to gain useful experience for this field.
4. To learn about some parole divisions on the Internet, enter the phrase *parole division* or *parole services* in a search engine to get a list of web sites.

EMERGENCY SERVICES

PUBLIC SAFETY DISPATCHER

CAREER PROFILE

Duties: Handle telephone requests for police, fire, rescue, and emergency medical help; dispatch appropriate units and equipment to emergency and non-emergency sites

Alternate Titles: Emergency Communications Officer, 911 Operator, Police Dispatcher

Salary Range: $12,000 to $40,000

Employment Prospects: Limited

Advancement Prospects: Limited
Prerequisites:

Special Requirements—Must be a U.S. citizen; meet department qualifications; pass a selection process

Education—High school diploma

Experience—Varies from agency to agency; some experience preferred

Special Skills—Organizational skills; communication, reading, and writing skills; teamwork and interpersonal skills; telephone skills and word processing or data entry skills

CAREER LADDER

```
┌─────────────────────────────────┐
│            Supervisor           │
└─────────────────────────────────┘

┌─────────────────────────────────┐
│      Public Safety Dispatcher   │
└─────────────────────────────────┘

┌─────────────────────────────────┐
│  Public Safety Dispatcher Recruit │
└─────────────────────────────────┘
```

Position Description

Public Safety Dispatchers process telephone calls from citizens requesting police, fire, rescue, or emergency medical help. Working in emergency communication centers, many Public Safety Dispatchers are law enforcement officers, firefighters, or emergency medical personnel who perform dispatch duties on a part-time or full-time basis.

Public Safety Dispatchers receive emergency and non-emergency requests for help. For example, they receive calls about thefts, burglaries, shootings, vandalism, heart attacks, injuries, fires, chemical spills, car accidents, missing persons, suicide attempts, bomb threats, illegal parking, traffic hazards, prowling wild animals, and obnoxious drunks. Some Public Safety Dispatchers also handle requests from public safety agencies such as police departments and fire departments.

Upon receiving requests, Public Safety Dispatchers ask standard questions to determine what type of units and equipment should be dispatched. They write information on cards or enter information directly into computer-aided dispatch (CAD) systems. For example, for a call requesting police help for a theft, a Public Safety Dispatcher would gather facts about the crime, location, suspects, victims, and injuries.

Public Safety Dispatchers transmit orders by radio or computer to the appropriate police, fire, rescue, or ambulance units. They monitor dispatched units, answering requests for additional backup or for other services such as rescue units.

In medical emergencies, Public Safety Dispatchers stay on the line with callers and relay updated information about the patients' conditions to hospital or emergency medical staff. Public Safety Dispatchers who are certified emergency medical service personnel may give certain medical assistance when necessary.

In large communication centers, Public Safety Dispatchers work in teams. Some dispatchers perform as call-takers (or 911 Operators). They answer calls, gather information, then transfer the information to other Public Safety Dispatchers who send out the appropriate response units.

Public Safety Dispatchers maintain well-detailed daily reports and logs. In addition, they perform other duties such as filing and other routine office tasks; monitoring city-wide radio channels; checking weather monitors; and operating mobile communications vans. In law enforcement agencies, dispatchers might process police records, process prisoners, and conduct computer searches for warrants and other data.

Sitting for long periods of time, Public Safety Dispatchers work with computers, telephones, two-way radios, and other electronic equipment. Their job is very stressful as they perform multitask duties and handle many highly emotional callers.

Emergency communication centers are open 24 hours a day. Thus, Public Safety Dispatchers work rotating shifts that include weekends and holidays.

Salaries

Salaries vary greatly, depending on factors such as experience, work hours (part-time or full-time), job responsibilities, location, and an agency's budget. *Dispatch Monthly* magazine reports that entry-level call-takers may earn a salary as low as $14,000 per year while Public Safety Dispatchers with line supervision responsibilities may earn up to $40,000 per year. The Bureau of Labor Statistics (a division of the U.S. Department of Labor) estimates that in 1997, the annual salary for most Public Safety Dispatchers was between $12,000 and $40,000.

Employment Prospects

Public Safety Dispatchers are hired by law enforcement agencies, fire departments, emergency medical services, and 911 centers. Job opportunities are expected to grow more slowly than the average for all occupations throughout the year 2006. One reason is due to the consolidation of police, fire, and emergency service communication centers into shared facilities.

Advancement Prospects

Supervisory and management positions are available, but limited. Many Public Safety Dispatchers pursue career growth by way of wage increases and complexity of new assignments. For some, this position is a stepping stone for pursuing a career as a police officer, deputy sheriff, firefighter, emergency medical technician, or other protective service career.

Special Requirements

Qualifications vary with every agency. In general, applicants must be U.S. citizens who are at least 18 years old and do not have felony convictions.

Applicants must pass every step of a selection process that includes any or all of the following: job application, written exam, typing test, oral interview, medical examination, audiogram, background investigation, drug test, psychological review, and polygraph examination.

Education and Training

Education requirements vary with the different agencies. Most agencies require that applicants have a high school or general equivalency diploma. Some agencies require some college work in police science or other related field.

Recruits must complete training programs, which vary with the different agencies. Some agencies supplement field training with formal study at law enforcement academies or community colleges where trainees study topics such as basic radio broadcasting, public safety telecommunications systems, and interpersonal communications.

Experience and Skills

Requirements vary from agency to agency. Some agencies prefer applicants with previous experience in dispatching or working with the public. With some agencies, applicants must be sworn law enforcement officers, firefighters, or emergency medical service personnel.

Agencies look for mature applicants who can handle constantly stressful situations and work with little supervision. Applicants should have excellent memories and be able to judge situations and make decisions quickly. They also need organizational skills, communication, reading, writing and telephone skills along with strong teamwork and interpersonal skills. Furthermore, applicants should have the ability to type a minimum number of words per minute, which varies with the different agencies.

Unions/Associations

The Association of Public-Safety Communication Officials (APCO) International, Inc. and the International Municipal Signal Association are two national organizations for Public Safety Dispatchers. The National Emergency Number Association is an organization specifically for 911 Operators. Joining such organizations allows Public Safety Dispatchers the opportunity to network with peers and obtain certification, continuing education, job listings, and other professional services and support.

Tips for Entry

1. Contact police departments or other public safety agencies directly to learn about job openings.
2. Enroll in Public Safety Dispatcher training courses that are offered in community colleges in your area.
3. Obtain work experience in which you deal directly with the public. Sales clerks, receptionists, hotel clerks, and customer service representatives are some workers who use work skills similar to those that dispatchers need.
4. Many emergency communications centers have web sites on the Internet. To get a list of web sites, enter the phrase *emergency communications center* or *police communications center* in a search engine.

FIREFIGHTER

CAREER PROFILE

Duties: Control and put out fires; save lives and property; inspect buildings for fire hazards; provide fire safety and fire prevention information; respond to other emergency calls

Salary Range: $12,000 to $50,000

Employment Prospects: Limited

Advancement Prospects: Good

Prerequisites:

Special Requirements—Meet department qualifications; pass a selection process

Education—High school diploma

Experience—No previous experience necessary

Special Skills—Communication, reading, and writing skills; teamwork and interpersonal skills; self-management skills

CAREER LADDER

```
┌─────────────────────────────────────┐
│   Fire Lieutenant; or a specialty    │
│       such as Firefighter/EMT,       │
│      Firefighter/Driver Operator     │
└─────────────────────────────────────┘

┌─────────────────────────────────────┐
│             Firefighter              │
└─────────────────────────────────────┘

┌─────────────────────────────────────┐
│         Firefighter Recruit          │
└─────────────────────────────────────┘
```

Position Description

Firefighters are responsible for protecting lives and property from fire in their communities. They use their knowledge of fire, building materials, and other factors to best control and suppress fires. Firefighters may be employees or volunteers. In many areas, particularly rural areas, fire departments are staffed by all-volunteer Firefighters.

Because firefighting is dangerous and complex work, Firefighters work in a very organized and coordinated manner, each performing preassigned tasks. They connect hose lines to hydrants; operate pumps; and hold hoses to direct water or chemicals on the fires. They enter burning buildings to rescue people or to reach the source of a fire. They raise and place ladders to climb to windows. They use axes or saws to hack their way into or through buildings. They also use cutting torches, saws, and other rescue equipment to retrieve people trapped within. Furthermore, Firefighters provide first aid and emergency medical treatment to victims.

After fires are put out, Firefighters help salvage property, such as ventilating smoke-filled rooms, removing broken glass, or covering objects to prevent water damage. They inspect utilities and appliances to make sure they can be safely turned on. They may help search for clues that show how a fire started; and if arson is suspected, they may help search for evidence.

In most communities, Firefighters respond to other emergency requests that consist of emergency medical calls; search and rescue missions; cleanups of hazardous materials such as oil spills; and requests for help in natural disasters such as floods, mudslides, earthquakes, and hurricanes.

Between calls, Firefighters clean and service fire trucks and firefighting equipment as well as maintain fire stations and grounds. They practice fire drills and do physical training. They also do office work, prepare reports, and study new firefighting technology.

Some Firefighters perform inspection services in their communities, checking homes, schools, hospitals, and other buildings for fire hazards. Some Firefighters teach fire safety and fire prevention classes and make presentations to schools and civic organizations.

While on duty, Firefighters work and live at their fire stations, which have kitchens, dining rooms, sleeping quarters, and training rooms. Most Firefighters work one of two types of work shifts:

- the 24-hour duty tour—after working 24 hours, they get either 48 hours or 72 hours off
- the split-shift tour—after working 9-hour or 10-hour day tours, Firefighters get about 72 hours off; after working 15-hour or 14-hour night tours, they get 48 hours off

Firefighters sometimes work overtime during fires and emergency situations. They are constantly at risk of being injured as well as being exposed to smoke, gases, chemicals, and hazardous materials that may affect their health.

Salaries

Salaries vary greatly, depending on factors such as experience and the size of a department's jurisdiction. Wages are generally higher in large cities and less in small cities and rural areas. In some smaller cities and rural areas, Firefighters are volunteers and receive no compensation. The International Association of Fire Fighters reports that the average annual salary for Firefighters in 1996 was $38,000 for a 56-hour workweek. According to the Bureau of Labor Statistics (a division of the U.S. Department of Labor), most Firefighters earned an annual salary between $12,000 and $50,000 in 1997.

Employment Prospects

Most Firefighters work for municipal or county fire departments. Some Firefighters work for other employers such as airports, refineries, factories, military bases, and forest protection agencies.

The competition for paid positions is high, and the turnover rate for these positions is low. Job openings are expected to increase more slowly than the average for all occupations through the year 2006. Most job openings will become available as personnel retire or transfer to other positions.

Advancement Prospects

Firefighters can develop satisfying and diverse fire protection careers. With further training, they can apply for specialized positions such as emergency medical technicians, fire equipment drivers/operators, fire dispatchers, and fire equipment mechanics. They can also pursue careers such as fire inspectors, fire investigators, or fire protection engineers.

Advancement through the ranks—engineer, lieutenant, captain, battalion chief, assistant chief, deputy chief, and chief—is based on competitive exams, job performance, interviews, and seniority. In many fire departments, candidates for battalion chief or beyond, must have a bachelor's degree, preferably in fire science, public administration, or a related field.

Special Requirements

Every fire department has specific age, residency, medical, and other qualifications that applicants must fulfill. In addition, applicants must pass a selection process that includes any or all of the following steps: job application, written exam, oral interview, medical exam, background investigation, psychological review, and drug test. Applicants must also pass a physical exam that tests physical strength, stamina, coordination, and agility.

Education and Training

Most fire departments require a high school or general equivalency diploma. Some fire departments require a minimum of college work; and some prefer applicants with associate's or bachelor's degrees in fire science or other related fields.

Recruits usually complete several weeks of formal training at a fire academy, vocational school, or community college. Their studies include firefighting techniques, fire prevention, emergency medical procedures, local building codes, and hazardous materials. They also learn to use firefighting and rescue equipment such as ladders, axes, saws, fire hoses, and fire extinguishers.

Many fire departments require recruits to become certified Firefighters within one year of their appointment. Some fire departments require all Firefighters to be certified emergency medical technicians.

Experience and Skills

In general, fire departments choose physically fit candidates who have strong leadership qualities and a sense of community service. Candidates must show that they have good communication, reading, and writing skills. They should also show that they have teamwork and interpersonal skills, as well as good self-management, such as the ability to get to work on time, follow directions, take initiative, work safely, and stay calm while working under pressure.

Unions/Associations

Most professional Firefighters belong to the International Association of Fire Fighters, a firefighting union that represents Firefighters throughout the United States and Canada. Many Firefighters also belong to the National Fire Protection Association as well as to local and state professional Firefighter associations. Joining such organizations allows Firefighters the opportunity to network with peers and obtain certification, continuing education, job listings, and other professional services and support.

Tips for Entry

1. Contact the fire departments for whom you would like to work to learn about their job requirements and opportunities.
2. To prepare for a firefighting career, take chemistry, physics, mathematics, English, physical education, computer, and industrial arts classes in high school.
3. Gain valuable firefighting experience by becoming a volunteer Firefighter.

4. Some fire departments offer cadet or apprenticeship programs for young people. Find out if these programs are available in your community.

5. You can read about different fire departments on the Internet. In a search engine, enter the phrase *fire department* to get a list of web sites to browse.

EMERGENCY MEDICAL TECHNICIAN

CAREER PROFILE

Duties: Provide emergency treatment for ill or injured persons and transport them to hospital emergency rooms

Salary Range: $12,000 to $40,000

Employment Prospects: Excellent

Advancement Prospects: Limited
Prerequisites:
Special Requirements—State certification; fulfill employer's qualifications; pass a selection process
Education—High school diploma
Experience—Varies with the different employers
Special Skills—Communication, teamwork, and interpersonal skills; reading and writing skills; physical strength and coordination abilities; driving skills.

CAREER LADDER

```
┌─────────────────────────────────┐
│      Emergency Medical          │
│   Technician—Paramedic          │
└─────────────────────────────────┘

┌─────────────────────────────────┐
│      Emergency Medical          │
│   Technician—Intermediate       │
└─────────────────────────────────┘

┌─────────────────────────────────┐
│ Emergency Medical Technician—Basic │
└─────────────────────────────────┘
```

Position Description

Emergency Medical Technicians (EMTs) provide ill and injured persons with emergency medical care and transport them to hospital emergency rooms. Receiving orders from public safety dispatchers, EMTs drive to emergency scenes in ambulances equipped with special communication equipment, medical equipment, and medical supplies. They attend to emergency medical situations such as heart attacks, gun wounds, car accident injuries, drug overdoses, unconsciousness, drowning, broken hips, and unexpected child births.

EMTs respond to emergencies according to their certified skill level. All EMTs are certified to perform these medical procedures: provide first aid, restore breathing (by giving oxygen or doing pulmonary or cardiopulmonary resuscitation), control bleeding, treat for shock, bandage wounds, and immobilize fractures. They can treat and help heart attack victims, using automated external defibrillators; treat poison and burn victims; manage emotionally disturbed patients; or assist in childbirth.

Emergency Medical Technicians with more advanced training can use more intensive care procedures. For example, they can administer intravenous fluids; use manual defibrillators to give lifesaving shocks to a stopped heart; and use advanced techniques and equipment to help patients with respiratory emergencies. The most advanced EMTs—or EMT-Paramedics—provide advanced emergency care such as administering drugs and interpreting electrocardiograms (EKGs).

EMTs usually work in teams of two. Upon reaching emergency scenes, they examine the patients to determine the nature and degree of their illness or injury. In addition, EMTs learn whether patients have any pre-existing medical conditions such as diabetes, epilepsy, or heart disease. Following standard operating procedures, EMTs provide appropriate medical treatment that they are certified to perform. They monitor patients' vital signs and give additional care, if necessary, as they transport them to hospital emergency rooms. With complicated problems, EMTs provide care according to instructions given by medical personnel over two-way radios.

After each response call, EMTs prepare and maintain written logs and reports. They clean and sterilize ambulances and equipment as well as restock supplies. They also make sure that ambulances are in top maintenance form.

EMTs work both indoors and outdoors in all types of weather. They risk back injuries from lifting patients and may be exposed to diseases such as Hepatitis-B and AIDS. From time to time, they may handle violent or distressed patients and bystanders.

EMTs typically work between 45 to 60 hours a week—working nights, weekends, and holidays. In some fire and police departments, EMTs are on call.

Salaries

Earnings vary, depending on employer, location, experience, and certification level. For example, an EMT-Paramedic working for a fire department in a large city usually earns higher wages than an EMT-Basic working for a private ambulance service in a small city. According to *Journal of Emergency Medical Services,* the average annual salary for EMT-Paramedics was $30,407 per year; for EMT-Basics, $25,051 per year. The Bureau of Labor Statistics (a division of the U.S. Department of Labor) estimates that most Emergency Medical Technicians earned a salary between $12,000 and $40,000 per year in 1997.

Employment Prospects

EMTs work for hospitals, ambulance services, emergency medical service centers, rescue squads, fire departments, and police departments. In many communities, especially rural areas, Emergency Medical Technicians are volunteers.

The turnover rate is generally high, and jobs are expected to be continuously available. Competition is higher for EMT positions with fire, police, and rescue squad departments due to job security, higher pay, and generous benefits packages.

Job openings for EMT-Paramedics are expected to increase as more states allow them to perform primary medical care on the scene.

Advancement Prospects

Technical advancement—to a basic, intermediate, or paramedic position—requires completion of certified training programs and passing state license examinations.

Supervisory and management opportunities are available in emergency medical services, but most EMTs would no longer be able to do field work. For many EMTs, their training and experience are stepping-stones to careers as firefighters, public safety dispatchers, nurses, and doctors.

Special Requirements

To apply for EMT positions, applicants must possess state EMT licenses. In most states, EMTs must register with the National Registry of Emergency Medical Technicians (NREMT) and re-register every few years to maintain their certifications.

Applicants must meet their prospective employer's qualifications, such as age or residency requirements. In addition they must pass every step of a selection process that includes any or all of the following: job application, written exam, interview, medical exam, physical aptitude test, drug testing, background investigation, psychological review, and polygraph examination.

Education and Training

To become EMTs, applicants need a high school or general equivalency diploma. They must complete formal EMT training programs offered at colleges and universities, in hospitals, or by police, fire, and health departments. (To qualify for EMT training programs, applicants must be at least 18 years old, have valid driver's licenses, and no felony records.)

EMT training has three progressive levels: EMT-Basic, the entry-level position, EMT-Intermediate, and EMT-Paramedic. Upon completing each level of training, students are eligible to take the state or NREMT certification examination.

Experience and Skills

Requirements vary with the different employers. To be EMTs with police and fire departments, applicants must be qualified police officers or firefighters. To apply for EMT-basic positions in hospitals and ambulance services, work experience is not necessary, but preferred.

Employers generally choose mature applicants who are willing to perform community service. Applicants must have communication, teamwork, and interpersonal skills along with adequate reading and writing skills. They also must be physically fit, agile, strong, and have the stamina and coordination to lift, carry, and balance heavy loads. In addition, applicants must have excellent driving abilities.

Unions/Associations

Many EMTs belong to the National Association of Emergency Medical Technicians. Many also join local and state professional EMT associations. Joining such organizations allows Emergency Medical Technicians the opportunity to network with peers and obtain certification, continuing education, job listings, and other professional services and support.

Tips for Entry

1. To learn about EMT training and job openings with emergency medical services, contact offices in the counties in which you want to work.
2. To enhance your qualifications, join professional associations and register with the National Registry of Emergency Medical Technicians.
3. Take health, science, and driver's education classes in high school to prepare for an EMT career.
4. Many emergency medical services offices and divisions have web sites on the Internet. Enter the phrase *emergency medical services* or *EMS* links in any search engine to get a list of web sites.

RESCUE TECHNICIAN

CAREER PROFILE

Duties: Perform search and rescue missions for missing and lost persons; perform *technical rescues* such as rescuing people stuck on high ledges, in crushed vehicles, under collapsed buildings, or in rushing water

Alternate Title: Rescue Specialist

Salary Range: Voluntary; no salary or additional pay

Employment Prospects: Good

Advancement Prospects: Limited
   Prerequisites:
   Special Requirements—Varies from agency to agency
   Education—High school diploma; completion of certified training programs
   Experience—No experience necessary
   Special Skills—Varies with the type of rescue work to be performed

CAREER LADDER

```
┌─────────────────────────────┐
│     Rescue Team Leader       │
└─────────────────────────────┘

┌─────────────────────────────┐
│     Rescue Technician        │
└─────────────────────────────┘

┌─────────────────────────────┐
│      Rescue Trainee          │
└─────────────────────────────┘
```

Position Description

Rescue Technicians are emergency responders who perform search and rescue missions for lost or missing persons in urban and wilderness settings. Furthermore, they search for victims in fires, collapsed buildings, airplane crashes, hurricanes, earthquakes, and other man-made or natural disasters.

Many rescues are performed in dangerous situations that call for Rescue Technicians who are trained in particular technical disciplines. For example:

- those trained in high-angle rescue might recover people who are stranded on high cliff ledges
- those trained in confined-space rescue might recover people who are lodged in manholes
- those trained in water rescue might save people who are caught in rushing flood waters
- those trained in vehicle-extrication rescue might remove people trapped in crushed cars

Rescue Technicians work for rescue squads or search-and-rescue units that are administered by police departments, sheriff's offices, fire departments, public safety departments, or emergency service offices. Typically, rescue squads are volunteer units composed of law enforcement officers, firefighters, emergency medical personnel, and private citizens.

Rescue work is performed quickly, but deliberately, in organized teams. Standard procedures are followed in every aspect of rescue work, from planning to finding and removing victims.

Each rescue situation begins with careful planning and assigning appropriate rescue teams. Rescue Technicians learn about a victim's identity and current mental and physical state to decide which rescue and first aid/lifesaving equipment is needed. They assess both real and potential hazards present within the area to be searched. In a *technical rescue,* such as a confined space rescue, Rescue Technicians must decide the best way to enter a site, perform the rescue, and exit without causing any injury to the victims or themselves.

Rescue Technicians search hills, forests, ditches, culverts, ponds, rivers, swamps, and other areas that are not easily accessible. Searches may be performed by foot, horse, mountain bikes, all-terrain vehicles, boats, skis, helicopters, or other specialized means of transportation. Some Rescue Technicians are trained as canine handlers to track missing or lost persons.

Upon locating or reaching victims, Rescue Technicians check vital signs and examine victims for trauma and injuries.

They provide first aid and emergency medical help for which they are trained—apply bandages and splints, immobilize fractures, for example—and secure victims to stretchers or backboards for carrying or hoisting out of the site.

As part of their duties, Rescue Technicians attend regular meetings, drills, and training sessions. They maintain rescue and lifesaving equipment, making sure all equipment is clean, in working order, and always ready to be used. Rescue Technicians also prepare and maintain incident reports, activity logs, staff files, and training records.

Rescue squads often work with other local, regional, and state rescue squads. They are on call 24 hours a day, 365 days a year.

Salaries

Rescue work is a voluntary assignment. Law enforcement officers, firefighters, emergency medical personnel, and park rangers rarely receive additional compensation for Rescue Technician duties. Salary is determined according to one's core duty.

Employment Prospects

Police departments, sheriff's departments, fire departments, public safety departments, emergency service offices, and federal and state park services have rescue squads. New rescue squads form every year. Existing rescue squads continually welcome new volunteers, including private citizens.

Advancement Prospects

Rescue Technician duty is a voluntary assignment. Volunteers stay with this work as long as they are interested and qualified. Supervisory positions are limited to team and squad leaders.

Becoming certified instructors or rescue equipment sales representatives or manufacturing consultants are other career paths for Rescue Technicians.

Special Requirements

Private citizen volunteers must meet certain qualifications which vary from squad to squad. Some rescue squads require volunteers to pass police background checks and/or driving record checks.

Most agencies require Rescue Technicians to be certified in each type of technical rescue work that they will perform, such as vehicle extrication, confined space rescue, high-angle rescue, diving rescue, tracking, canine handling, and cadaver recovery.

Education and Training

Generally, applicants need a high school or general equivalency diploma in order to obtain the necessary rescue work certifications.

Rescue Technicians must complete certified training in basic land search and rescue techniques, first aid, and life-saving skills. Some squads require Rescue Technicians to become certified as first emergency responders or emergency medical technicians.

Experience and Skills

Applicants do not need any previous experience, but they should have the basic skills for the type of rescue work they will perform. For example, volunteers for wilderness rescue units should have outdoor survival skills, and volunteers for water rescue units should have strong swimming skills.

Rescue squads typically look for mature, confident volunteers who have positive attitudes and strong commitments to serve the public. They show that they have the ability to react quickly to situations and stay calm under stressful conditions. In addition, applicants must be in excellent health with excellent physical strength and stamina.

Unions/Associations

The National Association for Search and Rescue, the International Rescue and Emergency Care Association, and the Mountain Rescue Association are national organizations that Rescue Technicians might join. In addition, they might join regional and state professional organizations. Joining such organizations allows Rescue Technicians the opportunity to network with peers and obtain certification, continuing education, technical information, and other professional services and support.

Tips for Entry

1. As a police officer, firefighter, park ranger, or emergency service staff member, let your supervisor or rescue squad commander know of your interest in joining the rescue squad.
2. Teenagers might be able to join rescue squads as part of a participating Explorer group. Or, they might join as Members in Training, which allows participation in training sessions and, sometimes, in search and rescue missions.
3. Learn first aid, CPR, wilderness survival skills, knot-tying skills, and other skills that are useful for professional rescue work. Also maintain a regular exercise program to stay physically fit.
4. Many rescue units have web sites on the Internet. Enter the phrase *rescue squad* or *search and rescue unit* in a search engine to get a list of web sites.

LIFEGUARD

CAREER PROFILE

Duties: Prevent drownings, injuries, and other accidents at swimming pools, water parks, oceans, lakes, and rivers

Alternate Titles: Water Safety Officer, Ocean Water Lifeguard

Salary Range: $5.15 to $14.00 per hour

Employment Prospects: Fair

Advancement Prospects: Limited
Prerequisites:

Special Requirements—Vary with the different employers; pass a selection process

Education—High school diploma; lifeguard training programs

Experience—Varies with the different employers

Special Skills—Leadership skills; interpersonal and teamwork skills; communication and writing skills

CAREER LADDER

```
┌─────────────────────────────┐
│   Head (Pool) Lifeguard or  │
│    (Beach) Team Leader       │
└─────────────────────────────┘

┌─────────────────────────────┐
│          Lifeguard           │
└─────────────────────────────┘

┌─────────────────────────────┐
│       Lifeguard Trainee      │
└─────────────────────────────┘
```

Position Description

Lifeguards supervise all water activity and prevent drownings, injuries, and other accidents within their assigned areas. Pool Lifeguards protect swimmers at public and private swimming pools and water parks, while Beach Lifeguards protect swimmers in open beach areas at oceans, rivers, and lakes.

Usually working in pairs, Lifeguards observe swimmers, often with the help of binoculars, from towers and stations. Using megaphones and bullhorns, they warn swimmers about unsafe areas as well as unruly behavior. They also keep an eye out for poor swimmers and summon them back from deep waters.

Upon seeing swimmers in danger, Lifeguards respond immediately to rescue them. They provide first aid, CPR, or other appropriate emergency medical attention that they are qualified to provide. Lifeguards also complete necessary reports such as emergency incident reports, medical treatment reports, and daily activity logs.

In addition, Pool Lifeguards enforce facility safety rules such as "no running around the pool." They also inspect dressing rooms for cleanliness and safety hazards. Plus, they clean and refill the pool. This includes determining the chlorine content and pH value of the water. Pool Lifeguards may give swimming lessons, help at swim meets, and do cashier duties at snack bars.

Beach Lifeguards patrol public beach areas by foot or by vehicle, enforcing ordinances, rules, and regulations that govern beach activities and shore water usage. In addition, Beach Lifeguards are responsible for identifying ocean and beach hazards such as high surf and strong currents. Some Beach Lifeguards act as harbor police officers with limited law enforcement authority; however, they do not carry firearms.

Rescue work for Beach Lifeguards involves both ocean rescues and cliff rescues. They operate rescue boats and all-terrain vehicles as well as emergency medical equipment such as resuscitators. They also operate switchboards or two-way radios to coordinate activities with emergency rescue units.

Lifeguards may work part time or full time, year round or temporarily during the summer months. Many Beach Lifeguards in California, Florida, and Hawaii work full time on a year-round basis, with some agencies providing 24-hour service.

Salaries

Salaries vary and depend on factors such as a Lifeguard's experience, job duties, and work hours (full-time or part-time, permanent or seasonal) as well as an employer's size and location. Most Lifeguards earn an hourly wage, which ranges from as low as the federal minimum wage to as high as $14 an hour. Typically, Lifeguards with more experience and responsibilities can expect to earn higher wages.

Listed below are examples of salaries for full-time permanent Lifeguards at two agencies:

- $18,876 to $28,550 for the city of Delray, Florida
- $27,912 to $43,776 for the California State Parks

Employment Prospects

Lifeguards are hired by local, state, and national parks; hotels and resorts; campgrounds and water parks; health and fitness centers; and colleges and universities.

Job opportunities for Pool and Beach Lifeguard positions are available year round; most openings are available for summer positions. Mostly high school and college students fill these seasonal positions, and the turnover rate is high.

Competition for permanent positions and for Beach Lifeguard positions—permanent and seasonal—is high. Returning seasonal Lifeguards generally receive better work schedules and assignments. Some employers hire permanent Beach Lifeguards from seasonal Lifeguard ranks.

Advancement Prospects

Advancement opportunities for Pool Lifeguards are limited to head lifeguard, swim instructor, swim coach, assistant facility manager, and facility manager.

Beach Lifeguards have better promotion opportunities, advancing up the ranks from team leader to sergeant, lieutenant, and then chief. In addition, Beach Lifeguards can pursue specialized duty such as rescue boat patrol, underwater recovery unit, marine firefighting, cliff rescue, and river rescue.

Special Requirements

Requirements vary with the different employers as well as for seasonal and permanent work. For example, applicants must be at least 16 years old to apply for some seasonal Lifeguard jobs while 18 years old is usually the minimum age requirement for permanent positions or Beach Lifeguard positions.

Applicants may also be required to be certified in performing first aid and cardiopulmonary resuscitation (CPR). Applicants for Beach Lifeguards may be required to obtain certification as first responders or emergency medical technicians.

In addition, applicants must pass a selection process that includes any or all of the following: application, written exam, interview, physical exam, hearing test, vision test, drug test, background investigation, and a performance exam that tests swimming ability, strength, and stamina.

Education and Training

For permanent employment, most employers require applicants to possess a high school or general equivalency diploma. Some employers prefer applicants with college degrees.

Applicants for Pool Lifeguards must have completed certified lifeguard training programs from the Red Cross or another recognized organization. Beach Lifeguard applicants must complete a certified training program that meets the curriculum requirements of the United States Lifesaving Association.

Experience and Skills

Requirements vary with the different employers. In general, employers look for candidates who are responsible, professional, reliable, and have the ability to enforce safety rules. Candidates should have excellent interpersonal and teamwork skills. They also need good communication and writing skills. They show that they have the ability to react quickly and calmly to emergency situations as well as have the ability to handle large, and sometimes rowdy, crowds.

For entry-level Beach Lifeguards, previous experience in lifeguarding, law enforcement, and boating is desired by some ocean lifeguard operations.

Unions/Associations

The United States Lifesaving Association is a professional organization for Beach Lifeguards. Beach Lifeguards might also belong to regional and state beach lifeguard associations. Joining such organizations allows Lifeguards the opportunity to network with peers and obtain certification, continuing education, job listings, and other professional services and support.

Tips for Entry

1. Most employers hire for summer seasonal Lifeguards in the spring. Contact the employers for whom you want to work at the beginning of the year to find out when they are recruiting for summer Lifeguard jobs.

2. Open to 8-to 17-year-olds, the Junior Lifeguarding program teaches basic water safety and first aid techniques and provides valuable training for future Lifeguards. To find out about programs in your area, contact aquatic programs at YMCA, community parks, or community colleges.

3. You do not have to wait until you get a Lifeguard job to obtain first aid, CPR, and Red Cross Lifeguard certifications. You can enroll in these certification programs at any time. Contact local Red Cross offices, community colleges, or community parks to find out about Lifeguard training programs.

4. To read about some Lifeguard operations, associations, or lifeguarding on the Internet, enter the phrase *lifeguard operations* or *lifeguarding* to get a list of web sites to browse.

COMPLIANCE INSPECTIONS

FOOD INSPECTOR

CAREER PROFILE

Duties: Make sure that slaughterhouses and food processing plants comply with federal laws and regulations that establish standards for producing raw meat, chicken, and eggs and their byproducts

Salary Range: $21,000 to $50,000

Employment Prospects: Fair

Advancement Prospects: Limited
  Prerequisites:
  Special Requirements—Meet strict physical requirements; pass a selection process
  Education—Bachelor's degree
  Experience—Work experience in the food industry or a food processing environment
  Special Skills—Physical coordination and manual dexterity; teamwork, communication, and writing skills; observational skills

CAREER LADDER

```
┌─────────────────────────────┐
│    Senior Food Inspector    │
└─────────────────────────────┘

┌─────────────────────────────┐
│       Food Inspector        │
└─────────────────────────────┘

┌─────────────────────────────┐
│    Food Inspector Trainee   │
└─────────────────────────────┘
```

Position Description

Federally employed Food Inspectors perform inspections at meat and poultry slaughterhouses and processing plants. They work for the Food Safety and Inspection Service, a division of the United States Department of Agriculture. Their job is to make sure that companies comply with federal laws and regulations which establish standards for producing raw meat, chicken, and eggs and their byproducts.

They inspect all raw beef, pork, lamb, chicken, and turkey and eggs to make sure that products are wholesome and free of disease. In addition, they inspect about 250,000 different processed meat and poultry products. These include hams, sausage, soups, stews, pizzas, frozen dinners, and any product containing 2% or more of cooked poultry or at least 3% of raw meat. They also inspect liquid, frozen, and dried egg products.

Food Inspectors normally work in teams at the sites. At slaughterhouses, they perform antemortem (before animals are slaughtered) and postmortem (after animals are slaughtered) inspections. Antemortem inspections involve visual examinations of livestock or poultry in confined areas where they are kept. Food Inspectors also make sure that sanitary equipment and handling practices are used. The postmortem inspection involves examining carcasses and animal body parts for visible defects that can affect safety and quality.

Food Inspectors use sharp steel knives or hooks to perform their inspections, working rapidly and accurately.

At processing plants, Food Inspectors monitor all stages of the processing operations to ensure that approved procedures are followed. Food Inspectors not only inspect the processed meat and poultry but also all the other ingredients that make up the final products. Furthermore, they test for the presence of salmonella and other bacteria that may cause food poisoning. They also check that nutrition guidelines and safe food handling labels are accurate.

Food Inspectors work in hazardous working environments. They must be attentive to slippery floors, vats of extremely hot water, high voltage equipment, and large machines. In addition, they work in extreme climates (cold, damp, dry) throughout the plant. Furthermore, their duties often require moderate lifting, walking, and long hours of standing throughout their shift.

Salaries

Federally employed Food Inspectors receive a salary based on a pay schedule called *General Schedule*. The pay schedule starts at the GS-1 grade and goes up to the GS-15 grade, with each grade having ten steps. Food Inspectors start at the GS-5 grade ($21,000 to $27,000 per year) or the GS-7 grade ($26,000 to $33,000 per year).

In 1997, most Food Inspectors earned an annual salary between $23,000 and $50,000, according to the Bureau of Labor Statistics (a division of the U.S. Department of Labor). Inspectors with more education and experience typically earn higher wages, as do inspectors with harder job responsibilities (such as supervisory duties). Those who live in metropolitan areas and large cities where the cost of living is higher usually earn higher wages, too.

Employment Prospects

The Food Safety and Inspection Service employs Food Inspectors for field offices throughout the United States. Job growth is expected to be slower than the average for all jobs through the year 2006. Most job opportunities will become available as Food Inspectors retire, resign, or become promoted. The creation of additional job openings depends on the agency's needs and budget.

Advancement Prospects

Supervisory and management opportunities are available, but limited. Many Food Inspectors pursue career growth by way of wage increases and complexity of new assignments.

Special Requirements

Applicants must meet strict physical requirements, such as having good eyesight and having no chronic skin conditions. In addition, applicants must pass the agency's selection process which includes the following: job application, written exam, oral interview, medical examination, background investigation, and drug testing.

Education and Training

Applicants must have Bachelor's degrees with at least twelve semester hours in biology, physical science, mathematics, or agricultural science. Food Inspector trainees also complete both classroom and on-the-job training that include study of federal laws and inspection procedures.

Experience and Skills

Applicants must have one year of work experience in the food industry or in a food processing environment at which they followed specific standards of quality and approved production methods to make food products.

In addition, applicants must be physically and mentally able to efficiently perform job functions in hazardous work settings. They must be able to lift and carry objects up to 44 pounds as well as have good eye-hand coordination and dexterity of the arms, hands, and fingers.

Employers look for responsible candidates who have excellent teamwork, communication, writing and observational skills and the ability to perform detailed work.

Unions/Associations

Most federally employed Food Inspectors join the American Federation of Government Employees, the largest federal employee union. In addition to union representation, members can obtain legal representation, technical expertise, informational services, and other professional support and services.

Tips for Entry

1. For current recruitment information, contact a Food Safety and Inspection Service office. You might find a listing in the U.S. Government pages of your telephone book under *Department of Agriculture*. Another source for job announcements is the U.S. Office of Personnel Management (OPM), which also may be listed in your telephone book. Or visit the OPM web site (*http://www.usajobs.opm.gov*) on the Internet.

2. Many Food Safety and Inspection Service offices hire Food Inspectors for part-time work or for an on-call basis. These positions may eventually lead to full-time work.

3. You can learn more about the Food Safety and Inspection Service on the Internet. Its web address is *http://www.fsis.usda.gov/*.

AGRICULTURAL COMMODITY GRADER

CAREER PROFILE

Duties: To inspect, grade, and certify the quality of over 200 commodities based on federal regulations and standards

Salary Range: $21,000 to $50,000

Employment Prospects: Fair

Advancement Prospects: Limited
  Prerequisites:
  Special Requirements—Must be a U.S. citizen; have a driver's license; agree to relocation; pass a selection process
  Education—Bachelor's degree
  Experience—Three years work experience without a bachelor's degree
  Special Skills—Problem-solving skills; communication, report-writing, and interpersonal skills; organizational and self-management skills

CAREER LADDER

```
┌─────────────────────────────────────────┐
│  Senior Agricultural Commodity Grader    │
└─────────────────────────────────────────┘

┌─────────────────────────────────────────┐
│     Agricultural Commodity Grader        │
└─────────────────────────────────────────┘

┌─────────────────────────────────────────┐
│  Agricultural Commodity Grader Trainee   │
└─────────────────────────────────────────┘
```

Position Description

Agricultural Commodity Graders work for the Agricultural Marketing Service, a division of the United States Department of Agriculture (USDA). Their job is to inspect, grade, and certify the quality of over 200 commodities, including cotton and cotton products, dairy products, dried beans, eggs, fruits, live cattle, meat, peanuts, poultry and poultry products, rabbits, sheep, swine, tree nuts, tobacco, vegetables, and wool.

USDA standards are developed for each particular product. For example, Agricultural Commodity Graders would follow a set of standards for grading each type of milk product—whole milk, low-fat milk, buttermilk, cream, non-fat dry milk, and so on.

When performing an inspection, Agricultural Commodity Graders choose samples from the container, lot, or line of products that are to be certified. They examine the samples to determine their conformance to weight, quantity, packing, packaging, labeling, and other specifications. They also look for abnormal growths, spoilage, and other defects. They may collect samples of suspected material or pests and send them to laboratories for analysis.

Upon completing their evaluation of the samples, Agricultural Commodity Graders assign a grade to the commodity being certified. For example, a container of fresh apples may be given one of seven grades, of which the top three are U.S.

Extra Fancy, U.S. Fancy, and U.S. No. 1. Agricultural Commodity Graders issue certification papers or apply official grade markings directly to products or containers.

Agricultural Commodity Graders also perform inspections of processing plants and other facilities to determine their compliance with regulations. They check that sanitation is maintained throughout the plant as well as proper processing, packaging, storage, and transportation procedures are in compliance. Furthermore, they make sure only approved chemicals and pesticides are used.

The Agricultural Commodity Graders meet with owners or their representatives to discuss their findings. They may suggest to owners methods of improving quality or correcting any problems. In addition, Agricultural Commodity Graders complete all necessary reports and records.

Agricultural Commodity Graders work in many different settings, such as meat plants, fruit canneries, fish processing plants, milk processing plants, cheese factories, and chicken ranches. Whatever the setting, their duties often require moderate lifting, walking, and long hours of standing throughout their shift.

Salaries

Agricultural Commodity Graders receive a salary based on a pay schedule called *General Schedule*. The pay schedule starts at the GS-1 grade and goes up to the GS-15 grade, with each grade having ten steps. Agricultural Commodity Inspectors start at the GS-5 grade ($21,000 to $27,000 per year) or the GS-7 grade ($26,000 to $33,000 per year).

In 1997, most Agricultural Commodity Inspectors earned an annual salary between $23,000 and $50,000, according to the Bureau of Labor Statistics (a division of the U.S. Department of Labor). Inspectors with more education and experience typically earn higher wages, as do inspectors with greater job responsibilities (such as supervisory duties). Those who live in metropolitan areas and large cities where the cost of living is higher usually earn higher wages, too.

Employment Prospects

Agricultural Commodity Graders are stationed at Agricultural Marketing Service field offices throughout the United States. Job growth for Agricultural Commodity Graders is expected to be slower than the average for all jobs through the year 2006. Most job opportunities will become available as officers retire, resign, or become promoted. The creation of additional job openings depends on the agency's needs and budget.

Advancement Prospects

Supervisory and management opportunities are available, but limited. Many Agricultural Commodity Graders pursue career growth by way of wage increases and complexity of new assignments.

Special Requirements

Applicants must be United States citizens. For many positions, applicants need a valid driver's license. Applicants must also agree to reassignments to other geographical locations throughout their careers. Furthermore, applicants must pass the agency's selection process that includes the following: job application, oral interview, medical examination, and background investigation.

Education and Training

Applicants who have no work experience need a bachelor's degree to qualify at the GS-5 grade. A combination of college credits and work experience may also qualify applicants at GS-5. To qualify at the GS-7 grade (without work experience), applicants must have a bachelor's degree and meet specific academic achievements, or have one year of graduate work, or possess a master's degree.

Trainees must successfully complete a training program that combines classroom and field training.

Experience and Skills

Applicants who have no college degree need at least three years of responsible work experience to qualify at the GS-5 grade. Applicants should be knowledgeable about the commodities they would be grading as well as be able to determine product quality and condition. To qualify at the GS-7 grade, applicants must have one year of experience performing compliance or regulatory work; or, one year of experience applying knowledge about United States laws, regulations, and procedures for importing and exporting merchandise; or, a combination of education and work experience.

The agency looks for responsible candidates who have problem-solving skills along with communication, report-writing, and interpersonal skills. In addition, candidates should have organizational skills as well as self-management skills—the ability to get to work on time, follow directions, take initiative, work safely, and stay calm while working under pressure.

Unions/Associations

The American Federation of Government Employees is a union for many federal employees, including Agricultural Commodity Graders.

Tips for Entry

1. For further career information or job opportunities, contact a local Agricultural Marketing Service office. You might find a listing in the U.S. Government pages of your local telephone book under *Department of Agriculture.* Another source for job announcements is the U.S. Office of Personnel Management (OPM), which may also be listed in your telephone book. Or visit the OPM web site *(http://www.usajobs.opm.gov)* on the Internet.

2. As of 1998, the Agricultural Marketing Service offers two student work experience programs with part-time and full-time trainee positions. Upon graduation, trainees are offered full-time employment. The Poultry Student Career Experience program is open to students pursuing a high school or general equivalency diploma, a vocational or a technical certificate, or any college degree. The Livestock and Seed Career Program is open to students pursuing bachelor's or master's degrees. For more information, contact your school's job counseling or cooperative education department.

3. You can learn more about the Agricultural Marketing Service on the Internet. Its web address is *http://www.ams.usda.gov/.*

CONSUMER SAFETY INSPECTOR

CAREER PROFILE

Duties: To enforce federal and state laws that govern the production, handling, storing, and marketing of products that are sold to the public

Salary Range: $18,000 to $90,000

Employment Prospects: Fair

Advancement Prospects: Limited
Prerequisites:
Special Requirements—Meet an agency's special requirements and selection process
Education—Bachelor's degree
Experience—Varies from agency to agency
Special Skills—Communication and report-writing skills; teamwork and interpersonal skills; observational and problem-solving skills

CAREER LADDER

> **Senior Consumer Safety Inspector**

> **Consumer Safety Inspector**

> **Consumer Safety Inspector Trainee**

Position Description

Consumer Safety Inspectors make sure that companies comply with federal and state laws that govern the production, handling, storing, and marketing of products that are sold to the public. These products include foods, infant formulas, animal feeds, drugs, medical equipment, blood products, vaccines, cosmetics, fabrics, clothing, toys, household products, appliances, furniture, sports equipment, computer software, paints, pesticides, bicycles, vehicles, and many others.

Working individually or in teams, Consumer Safety Inspectors examine products as well as the facilities where they are manufactured or processed. They make routine inspections and conduct investigations of complaints made by customers, employees, vendors, or consumer activist groups.

When examining products, Consumer Safety Inspectors look for impurities and defects that may be harmful to health. They use various tools—such as portable scales, cameras, ultraviolet lights, thermometers, chemical testing kits, and radiation monitors—to identify substances and sources of contamination. They may send product samples, collected as part of their examinations, to laboratories for analysis. Furthermore, Consumer Safety Inspectors check for improper packaging and labeling that may be deceptive or inaccurate.

As part of their facility inspections, Consumer Safety Inspectors monitor manufacturing practices or production processes and review quality control systems. They watch for violations of standards. After completing their inspections, they discuss their findings with plant managers or officials, cite violations, and suggest corrective measures.

Consumer Safety Inspectors prepare comprehensive reports and correspondence regarding their inspections; and, when necessary, compile evidence that may be used in legal proceedings. In addition, Consumer Safety Inspectors may be called to testify as expert witnesses on their findings and inspection methods.

Consumer Safety Inspectors work irregular hours. Some compliance officers work part-time or on an on-call basis. For many positions, officers travel to other cities and states to perform their duties.

Salaries

Salaries vary from agency to agency. The estimated annual salaries for Consumer Safety Inspectors in 1997 ranged from $18,000 to $90,000, according to the Bureau of Labor Statistics (a division of the U.S. Department of Labor). Inspectors with more education and experience typically earn higher wages as do inspectors with harder job responsibilities (such as supervisory and administrative duties). Those who live in metropolitan areas and large cities where the cost of living is higher usually earn higher wages too.

Employment Prospects

Consumer Safety Inspectors work for various federal and state agencies that regulate products and processes that affect the public good. The Food and Drug Administration, the Consumer Product Safety Commission, and the Environmental Protection Agency are just a few federal agencies that employ Consumer Safety Inspectors.

Job growth for all compliance officers, including Consumer Safety Inspectors, is expected to be slower than the average for all jobs through the year 2006. Most job opportunities will become available as officers retire, resign, or become promoted. The creation of additional job openings depends on an agency's needs and budget.

Advancement Prospects

Supervisory and management opportunities are available, but limited. Promotion is generally based on agency needs and individual merit. Many Consumer Safety Inspectors pursue career growth by way of wage increases and complexity of new assignments.

Special Requirements

Every agency has specific job qualifications that applicants must meet. For example: the Food and Drug Administration requires applicants to be U.S. citizens and possess a valid driver's license; and for some positions, applicants must agree to be relocated to other geographical locations throughout their careers.

In addition, applicants must pass an agency's selection process which includes the following: job application, oral interview, medical examination, and background investigation.

Education and Training

Education requirements vary with the different agencies. In general, entry-level applicants must have a bachelor's degree, preferably in subjects that are related to the areas in which applicants would work. For example, Consumer Safety Inspectors who perform fish processing inspections might have a bachelor's degree in biological sciences, chemistry, food technology, nutrition, veterinary medical science, or other related scientific field.

Consumer Safety Inspectors must successfully complete training in applicable laws and inspection procedures. Training programs vary with the different agencies, but generally combine classroom and on-the-job training.

Experience and Skills

Experience requirements vary with the different agencies. In general, applicants should have knowledge of the properties and characteristics of the products they would be inspecting along with basic skills in the techniques of collecting samples and performing field tests and examinations.

Agencies look for candidates with communication and report-writing skills as well as teamwork and interpersonal skills. In addition, candidates should have strong observational problem-solving abilities.

Tips for Entry

1. To learn about job vacancies in local and state governments, contact your state employment office. For federal government vacancies, contact a local U.S. Office of Personnel Management (OPM); or visit its web site *(http://www.usajobs.opm.gov/)* on the Internet.

2. Many federal agencies allow undergraduate and graduate students to apply for positions nine months before their graduation date. They may be offered jobs that they will begin after graduation.

3. The Food and Drug Administration (FDA) and the Consumer Product Safety Commission (CPSC) are two regulatory agencies that hire consumer safety inspectors. To learn more about these agencies, visit their web sites on the Internet. The web address for the FDA is *http://www.fda.gov;* for CPSC, *http://www.cpsc.gov.*

ENVIRONMENTAL HEALTH OFFICER

CAREER PROFILE

Duties: To enforce federal, state, and local laws and regulations that protect the public from environmental health hazards

Alternate Titles: Sanitarian, Environmental Health Inspector

Salary Range: $18,000 to $90,000

Employment Prospects: Fair

Advancement Prospects: Limited
Prerequisites:
Special Requirements—Meet an agency's special qualifications and selection process
Education—Bachelor's degree
Experience—Varies from agency to agency
Special Skills—Communication, writing, and interpersonal skills; critical thinking and self-management skills

CAREER LADDER

Senior Environmental Health Officer

Environmental Health Officer

Environmental Health Officer Trainee

Position Description

Environmental Health Officers work for local, state, and federal public health departments. Their job is to enforce laws and regulations that protect the public from environmental health hazards such as unsanitary food handling, pest infestations, air pollution, and tainted water supplies. They inspect restaurants, food processing plants, schools, public buildings, apartment buildings, sewage disposal systems, waste disposal sites, recreational areas, swimming pools, refineries, factories, or other public and private establishments. These are just a few of the types of inspections they conduct:

- They examine the way food is handled, processed, and served in restaurants, hospitals, schools, and other institutions.
- They check the cleanliness and safety of food and drink as they are produced in food and beverage processing plants. In addition, they examine how sewage, refuse, and garbage are treated and disposed.
- They determine the nature and cause of air or water pollution in refineries, factories, and other facilities; and if necessary, initiate action to stop further pollution.
- They inspect private and public dwellings and buildings for insect and rodent infestation.

- They survey swimming pools and other public bathing places for unsanitary conditions.

In large public health departments, Environmental Health Officers usually specialize in a particular area such as waste control, institutional sanitation, or water pollution. In rural areas and small towns, Environmental Health Officers are responsible for all environmental health inspections.

Environmental Health Officers perform routine inspections as well as investigate consumer or employee complaints. Their inspections involve performing visual examinations as well as conducting field tests and collecting samples that they send to laboratories for analysis.

Upon completing an inspection, they review their findings with owners or employers and issue citations for any violations. Environmental Health Officers may initiate court complaints if violations are not corrected. Some inspectors have the authority to issue citations for owners or employers to appear in court. Furthermore, Environmental Health Officers help in preparing evidence and testifying in court trials.

In addition, Environmental Health Officers perform these duties:

- evaluate license applications and construction plans to make sure owners would be in compliance with codes covering solid waste collection and disposal, hazardous waste collection and disposal, sewage treatment and disposal, or other relevant environmental health codes
- provide education and training programs about public health and environmental standards
- investigate sudden epidemic outbreaks of hepatitis, tuberculosis, or other diseases within their communities
- recommend new or revised environmental health ordinances

Environmental Health Officers spend most of their time on field inspections and investigations that often require long hours of walking, standing, stooping, and climbing. Their work also involves accurately documenting inspections and preparing official reports and correspondence. They work a 40-hour week, and may sometimes work irregular hours.

Salaries

In 1997, the estimated annual salaries for Environmental Health Officers ranged from $18,000 to $90,000, according to the Bureau of Labor Statistics (a division of the U.S. Department of Labor). Officers with more education and experience typically earn higher wages, as do those with greater job responsibilities (such as supervisory and administrative duties). Those who live in metropolitan areas and large cities where the cost of living is higher usually earn higher wages too.

Employment Prospects

Most Environmental Health Officers work for local and state public health agencies. Some work for federal agencies that have environmental regulatory responsibilities, such as the Department of Energy and the Environmental Protection Agency.

Job growth for Environmental Health Officers is expected to be slower than the average for all jobs through the year 2006. Most job opportunities will become available as inspectors retire, resign, or become promoted. The creation of additional job openings depends on the agency's needs and budget.

Advancement Prospects

Supervisory and management opportunities are available, but limited to lead officer, supervisor, assistant chief, and director positions. Many Environmental Health Officers pursue career growth by way of wage increases and complexity of new assignments.

Research work, teaching, consultation work, or employment in the private sector are other career paths that Environmental Health Officers might pursue.

Special Requirements

Special job requirements vary from agency to agency. Most agencies, for example, require applicants to hold a current driver's license. In addition, applicants are required to possess state or national certification as Environmental Health Officers. Entry-level candidates may be expected to obtain certification with the first few months or first year of employment.

Furthermore, applicants must pass an agency's selection process that may include any of the following: application, written exam, oral interview, medical examination, background investigation, and drug test.

Education and Training

In general, applicants must have a bachelor's degree in environmental health or in the physical or biological sciences. Some agencies accept a combination of college study and work experience. Trainees must successfully complete their agency's training program on applicable laws and inspection methods and techniques.

Experience and Skills

Experience requirements vary from agency to agency. Normally, entry-level applicants must have a practical knowledge of basic environmental health concepts, principles, methods, and techniques.

Agencies look for neat, responsible candidates who can perform detailed work. Candidates should have excellent communication, writing, and interpersonal skills as well as critical thinking and self-management abilities.

Unions/Associations

The National Environmental Health Association and the American Public Health Association are two national professional groups for Environmental Health Officers. Joining such organizations gives Environmental Health Officers the opportunity to network with peers and obtain professional support and services, such as certified training, continuing education programs, technical information, and job resources.

Tips for Entry

1. For career information and job vacancies at the local level, contact the local Public Health Department or Office of Environmental Health.

2. Network with professionals to learn more about the field and job opportunities. Attend professional conferences as well as join professional associations that allow student memberships.

3. High school courses that may help you prepare for a career in environmental health are math, life science, physical sciences, and English composition.

4. Many local public health departments have web sites on the Internet. To get a list of web sites to browse, enter the phrase *local public health department* in a search engine.

COMPLIANCE SAFETY AND HEALTH OFFICER

CAREER PROFILE

Duties: Enforce federal and state occupational safety and health laws and regulations; inspect work sites for unsafe or unhealthy working conditions

Alternate Titles: Safety Compliance Officer, OSHA Inspector, Safety and Occupational Health Specialist

Salary Range: $23,000 to $50,000

Employment Prospects: Fair

Advancement Prospects: Limited
Prerequisites:
Special Requirements—Fulfill an agency's special qualifications and pass its selection process
Education—Bachelor's degree
Experience—Varies from agency to agency
Special Skills—Interpersonal skills; communication, writing, and reading skills; observational problem-solving skills

CAREER LADDER

```
┌─────────────────────────────────┐
│  Senior Compliance Safety and   │
│         Health Officer          │
└─────────────────────────────────┘

┌─────────────────────────────────┐
│ Compliance Safety and Health    │
│           Officer               │
└─────────────────────────────────┘

┌─────────────────────────────────┐
│     Compliance Safety and       │
│    Health Officer Trainee       │
└─────────────────────────────────┘
```

Position Description

Compliance Safety and Health Officers are government inspectors who enforce federal and state laws that provide for safe and healthful working conditions in all workplaces, such as factories, warehouse centers, medical facilities, construction sites, office buildings, stores, transportation companies. Their job is to look for hazards that may cause death or serious injury and illness to workers. This includes inspecting the work environment as well as the machinery and equipment at the work sites.

Compliance Safety and Health Officers follow routine procedures for performing inspections. They learn about the companies that they will inspect, and gather the necessary equipment and materials for testing health and safety hazards at the work sites. At the start of inspections, they meet with the employers, safety directors, or other authorized representatives where the Compliance Safety and Health Officers explain the reason for their inspections. Examples are: a random inspection; an employee complaint; a recent serious accident; the company has a high rate of worker's compensation claims; or the company is in a high-hazard industry such as construction.

Usually accompanied by the employers or their representatives, inspectors walk through entire work sites or specific areas. They observe workers to determine compliance with safety precautions and the use of safety equipment. They also interview workers to learn about work practices, or, if it is the purpose of the inspection, about recent accidents. Compliance Safety and Health Officers might take photographs of the work environment. In addition, they review documents such as injury and illness records, safety training programs, and emergency action plans.

Compliance Safety and Health Officers have the authority to issue citations for any violations of safety and health standards. Upon completing their inspections, they discuss these violations with employers and may suggest ways to correct them. They give deadlines for correcting the violations as well as explain the penalties that may be imposed if violations are not corrected. They also explain to employers what their rights are.

If Compliance Safety and Health Officers find conditions that may cause imminent danger, they can ask employers to voluntarily correct the hazards immediately or remove workers from the areas. When employers are not willing to comply to the requests, they can initiate court complaints against them. Compliance Safety and Health Officers complete detailed inspection reports, which may be placed as evidence in legal proceedings. In addition, they may be asked to testify at court trials.

Their jobs are stressful; they sometimes handle employers' hostile objections to their inspections. In addition, officers are at risk of the same injuries and illnesses that workers are exposed to in hazardous work sites.

Compliance Safety and Health Officers often work irregular hours.

Salaries

In 1997, the Bureau of Labor Statistics (a division of the U.S. Department of Labor) estimates that most compliance Safety and Health Officers earned an annual salary between $23,000 and $50,000. Inspectors with more education and experience typically earn higher wages, as do inspectors with greater job responsibilities (such as supervisory and administrative duties). Those who live in metropolitan areas and large cities where the cost of living is higher usually earn higher wages, too.

Employment Prospects

Compliance Safety and Health Officers work for state occupational safety and health departments as well as for the Occupational Safety and Health Administration (OSHA), a division under the U.S. Department of Labor.

Job growth for Compliance Safety and Health Officers is expected to be slower than the average for all jobs through the year 2006. Most job opportunities will become available as officers retire, resign, or become promoted. The creation of additional job openings depends on an agency's needs and budget.

Advancement Prospects

Supervisory and managerial prospects are rather limited. Many officers pursue career growth by way of wage increases and complexity of new assignments.

Two other career paths for Compliance Safety and Health Officers are working for private employers or becoming consultants.

Special Requirements

As prospective employees of a government agency, applicants must pass every step of a selection process that includes any of the following: job application, written exam, panel in-

terview, medical examination, background investigation, and drug testing.

Education and Training

Education requirements vary with the different agencies. Employers prefer applicants who have a bachelor's degree with a major in safety, occupational health, industrial hygiene, or other related field.

Compliance Safety and Health Officers must successfully complete a training program that includes the study of occupational safety laws and regulations; industrial processes and hazards; and investigation and inspection techniques. Training programs usually involve both classroom and field training.

Experience and Skills

Experience requirements vary from agency to agency. Entry-level applicants should have general experience in scientific or technical work using basic principles and concepts of the occupational safety and health field.

Agencies look for responsible candidates who have excellent interpersonal skills along with good communication, writing, and reading skills. Also, candidates show that they can work accurately and enjoy doing detailed work. In addition, they have good observational skills and problem-solving skills.

Tips for Entry

1. To learn about job vacancies in local and state governments, contact your state employment office. For federal government vacancies, contact a local Office of Personnel Management (OPM). Or visit its web site (*http://www.usajobs.opm.gov*) on the Internet.

2. High school courses that are valuable for a career in occupational safety and health is chemistry, biology, math, psychology, writing, and communication. Enrolling in any of these college courses is also valuable: safety, occupational health, industrial hygiene, occupational medicine, toxicology, public health, mathematics, physics, chemistry, biological sciences, engineering, and industrial psychology.

3. Obtaining certification as a Certified Safety Professional (CSP), Certified Industrial Hygienist (CIH), or Certified Health Physicist may enhance your chances for obtaining positions in this competitive field.

4. You can learn about the Occupational Safety and Health Administration on the Internet. Its web address is *http://www.osha.gov/*.

AVIATION SAFETY INSPECTOR

CAREER PROFILE

Duties: Enforce federal laws and regulations that govern the quality, performance, and safety of aircraft equipment and personnel

Salary Range: $31,000 to $59,000

Employment Prospects: Fair

Advancement Prospects: Limited
Prerequisites:
Special Requirements—Must be a U.S. citizen; have a driver's license; fulfill job qualifications; pass the selection process
Education—High school diploma
Experience—Depends on the type of inspection to be performed
Special Skills—Communication and report-writing skills; interpersonal skills

CAREER LADDER

```
┌──────────────────────────────────┐
│          Supervisor              │
└──────────────────────────────────┘

┌──────────────────────────────────┐
│     Aviation Safety Inspector    │
└──────────────────────────────────┘

┌──────────────────────────────────┐
│ Aviation Safety Inspector Trainee│
└──────────────────────────────────┘
```

Position Description

Aviation Safety Inspectors work for the Federal Aviation Administration (FAA), a division of the U.S. Department of Transportation. Their job is to enforce the FAA regulations that govern the quality, performance, and safety of aircraft equipment and personnel.

Aviation Safety Inspectors specialize in inspecting either commercial aircraft (such as air carriers) or general aviation aircraft (single and multi-engine aircraft used for pleasure, air taxi, industry, and agriculture). In addition, Aviation Safety Inspectors specialize in different inspection areas, or options.

Some Aviation Safety Inspectors perform maintenance inspections. They evaluate aircraft mechanics and repair facilities as well as training programs for mechanics. In addition, these Aviation Safety Inspectors evaluate aircraft and related equipment for airworthiness. Other Aviation Safety Inspectors perform avionics (electronics systems) inspections. This includes the evaluation of avionics technicians and repair facilities as well as training programs for avionics technicians. These Aviation Safety Inspectors also inspect aircraft and related equipment for airworthiness in regard to avionics programs.

Operations inspections is another option in which some Aviation Safety Inspectors specialize. These inspectors perform the evaluation of commercial and other aviation operations. In addition, they certify pilots, flight instructors, and

other airmen. These Aviation Safety Inspectors also evaluate flight training programs along with their equipment and facilities.

Another option that some Aviation Safety Inspectors specialize in is manufacturing inspections. They evaluate any manufacturing facility that makes or modifies aircraft, aircraft equipment, and avionics equipment. They also inspect any originally built or modified aircraft, aircraft parts, and avionics equipment. Furthermore, they issue FAA certificates for all civil aircraft, such as imports, amateur-built planes, and modified planes.

Aviation Safety Inspectors have irregular work schedules, which may include weekends and holidays. They may work different hours from one day to the next, depending on the tasks that they are performing. Some inspections require traveling to other geographical locations for extended periods of time.

Salaries

Aviation Safety Inspectors receive a salary based on a pay schedule called *General Schedule*. The pay schedule starts at the GS-1 grade and goes up to the GS-15 grade, with each grade having ten steps. An Aviation Safety Inspector's base salary falls within the range of GS-9, GS-11, or GS-12. An additional compensation is added to the base salaries for those Aviation Safety Inspectors who work in large cities and metropolitan areas where the cost of living is higher. The base salaries in 1999 ranged from $31,000 to $59,000.

Employment Prospects

Aviation Safety Inspectors work for the FAA (Federal Aviation Administration). Those inspectors performing air carrier, aviation avionics, maintenance, and operations inspections work out of Flight Standards division and district offices throughout the United States and Puerto Rico. Those performing manufacturing inspections work out of 30 Manufacturing Inspection division and district offices.

Competition for Aviation Safety Inspector jobs is high; and most job opportunities become available when inspectors retire, resign, or are promoted to higher positions. The creation of additional positions depends on the agency's needs.

Advancement Prospects

Supervisory and management opportunities are available, but limited. Advancement is competitive, based on agency needs and individual merit. Many Customs Inspectors pursue career growth by way of wage increases and complexity of new assignments.

Special Requirements

Applicants must be U.S. citizens with a valid driver's license. They must not have more than two FAA violations within the last five years prior to application. They must also be fluent in the English language, meet physical requirements, and have no chemical dependencies or drug abuse problems. Those applying for operation inspections must possess an FAA first-class medical certificate.

Furthermore, they must pass every step of the FAA's selection process that includes the following: job application, oral interview, and background investigation. Those applying for operation inspections must also pass a medical examination and drug test.

Education and Training

Applicants must have at least a high school or general equivalency diploma. In addition, applicants for positions as air-carrier-maintenance or general-aviation-maintenance inspectors need FAA mechanic certificates with particular ratings, such as airframe ratings. Applicants for air carrier operations or general aviation operations inspections must have either an airline transport or commercial pilot certificate.

Aviation Safety Inspectors must successfully complete FAA training, which includes the study of FAA laws and in-spection procedures. Furthermore, their first year of employment is probationary.

Experience and Skills

Requirements vary with the different positions. Applicants must have extensive work experience in the area of inspections that they would be performing. For maintenance inspections, applicants must have performed aviation maintenance in the last three years as well as have at least three years of supervisory experience. For avionics inspections, applicants must have performed avionics work in the last three years as well as have at least three years of supervisory experience.

For operations inspections, applicants must have a minimum number of flight hours as well as minimum number of flight hours for the last three and five years respectively. Also, applicants for general-aviation operations inspections must have some aviation work experience within the last ten years.

For manufacturing inspections, applicants must have experience in quality control and quality assurance systems as well as knowledge of the methods and techniques in the manufacture of aircraft, aircraft engines, and other aircraft parts. Alternatively, applicants must have experience issuing certificates or approvals for the airworthiness of aircraft and aircraft parts; or in managing programs that lead to such issuance.

Furthermore, candidates should have excellent communication, report-writing, and interpersonal skills to handle the many different people they will work with and meet.

Unions/Associations

Aviation Safety Inspectors might join the American Federation of Government Employees, a union for federal employees.

Tips for Entry

1. To obtain career information or learn about job vacancies, contact: FAA, Mike Monroney Aeronautical Center, Aviation Careers Division, P.O. Box 26650, Oklahoma City, OK 73126. Another source for job announcements is the U.S. Office of Personnel Management (OPM), which may be listed in the U.S. Government pages in your telephone book. Or visit the OPM web site (*http://www.usajobs.opm.gov*) on the Internet.
2. You can learn more about the FAA on the Internet. Its web site address is *http://www.faa.gov/.*

POSTAL INSPECTOR

CAREER PROFILE

Duties: Enforce federal postal laws; conduct management and financial audits in the U.S. Postal Service; conduct investigations of postal crime

Salary Range: $23,000 to $50,000

Employment Prospects: Fair

Advancement Prospects: Limited
  Prerequisites:

  Special Requirements—Must be a U.S. citizen between 21 and 37 years old; meet health requirements; have a driver's license; have no criminal record; pass a selection process

  Education—Bachelor's degree; 14-week training program

  Experience—Meet one of the six experience requirements

  Special Skills—Teamwork and interpersonal skills; communication, researching, and writing skills

CAREER LADDER

```
┌─────────────────────────────┐
│        Team Leader          │
└─────────────────────────────┘

┌─────────────────────────────┐
│      Postal Inspector       │
└─────────────────────────────┘

┌─────────────────────────────┐
│   Postal Inspector Trainee  │
└─────────────────────────────┘
```

Position Description

Postal Inspectors work for the United States Postal Inspection Service, the law enforcement arm of the United States Postal Service. They are responsible for enforcing more than 200 federal laws that relate to the U.S. Mail, the U.S. Postal Service, and postal employees.

Postal Inspectors perform two major duties. One duty is conducting management and financial audits of major programs and projects of the U.S. Postal Service. These audits help Postal Inspectors identify potential areas of crime risk along with ways to run the U.S. Postal Service more efficiently and economically. The other—and more prevalent—duty is conducting investigations of postal crime such as:

- theft of U.S. mail, postal money orders, and equipment
- assault or murder of postal employees
- burglary of a postal facility
- mailings of bombs, obscene material, child pornography, or drugs
- counterfeiting of postmarks, postage stamps or postal money orders
- extortion
- mail fraud (the use of the mails to scam the public)

As with any criminal investigation, Postal Inspectors gather accurate information to link suspects to their crimes. They gather physical evidence, interrogate suspects, interview victims and witnesses and, if needed, do surveillance and undercover work. When Postal Inspectors have sufficient evidence for a case, they present it to U.S. Attorneys or other Department of Justice officials who decide what action should be taken. Postal Inspectors may help prepare evidence and provide testimony if a case is prosecuted in court.

Postal Inspectors carry firearms, and have the authority to serve warrants and subpoenas. They have, however, limited powers to arrest criminals. Postal Inspectors may only arrest persons who are committing a felony within their presence or if they have reasonable grounds to believe that persons are committing or have committed postal crimes.

On occasion, Postal Inspectors work with local, state, and other federal law enforcement officers on joint investigations in which the U.S. mail, the U.S. Postal Service, or postal employees are involved. For example, some Postal Inspectors might work on a special task force to investigate a group of people who are sending fraudulent insurance claims through the mail.

Postal Inspectors work long and irregular hours. Their duties often involve frequent travel to other cities and states.

Postal Inspectors may be reassigned to any Postal Inspection Service office at any time in their careers.

Salaries

In 1997, the Bureau of Labor Statistics (a division of the U.S. Department of Labor) estimates that most Postal Inspectors earned an annual salary between $23,000 and $50,000. Inspectors with more education and experience typically earn higher wages, as do inspectors with harder job responsibilities (such as supervisory and administrative duties). Those who live in metropolitan areas and large cities where the cost of living is higher usually earn higher wages, too.

Employment Prospects

Postal Inspectors work in U.S. Postal Inspection Service field offices throughout the United States. Job growth for Postal Inspectors is expected to be slower than the average for all jobs through the year 2006. Most job opportunities will be created to replace Postal Inspectors who are retiring, resigning for other occupations, or being promoted. Competition for the positions is high.

Advancement Prospects

Supervisory and management opportunities are available, but limited. Many Postal Inspectors pursue career growth by way of wage increases and complexity of new assignments.

Special Requirements

Applicants must be U.S. citizens who are at least 21 years old and no older than 37 years old upon receiving an appointment. In addition they must meet standard health requirements, have a valid driver's license, and have no criminal record.

Applicants must pass every step of the agency's long, complex selection process, which includes the following: job application, written exam, skills assessment, panel interview, medical examination, physical aptitude test, background investigation, polygraph examination, and drug testing. If applicable, applicants must also pass a language proficiency test.

Education and Training

Applicants must have a bachelor's degree (no specific major is required) as well as fulfill one of the experience requirements.

Postal Inspector recruits must complete a 14-week training program at the Inspection Service Academy in Potomac, Maryland. Trainees study subjects such as federal postal laws, court procedures, postal operations, audit functions, search and seizure procedures, arrest techniques, defensive tactics, and use of firearms.

Experience and Skills

Applicants must meet at least one of these requirements:

- have two years of postal service experience as either a supervisor, a U.S. Postal Inspection Service employee, or a postal employee who has performed injury compensation, postal technology, or other specialized work
- have two years of law enforcement experience with arrest authority and criminal investigation duty
- have two years of internal auditing experience, or be currently certified as a certified public accountant, certified management accountant, certified internal auditor, or certified information systems auditor
- have two years experience as a commissioned military officer
- be a currently licensed lawyer who has a juris doctorate and is a member of a state bar
- be a fluent speaker in a foreign language

In addition, applicants should have excellent teamwork and interpersonal skills as well as strong communication, researching, and writing skills.

Unions/Associations

Postal Inspectors might join the Federal Law Enforcement Officers Association, which offers networking opportunities, education programs, and other professional services and support.

Tips for Entry

1. For current recruitment information, contact a U.S. Postal Inspection Service office or a local U.S. Office of Personnel Management (OPM). You might find a listing for either agency in the U.S. Government pages of your local telephone book.
2. Gain work experience with the U.S. Postal Service as well as with the U.S. Postal Inspection Service, as many Postal Inspectors are recruited from within the U.S. Postal Services.
3. You can learn more about the United States Postal Inspection Service on the Internet. Its web address is *http://www.usps.gov/websites/depart/inspect*. To visit the United States Postal Service web site, go to *http://www.usps.gov/*.

IMMIGRATION INSPECTOR

CAREER PROFILE

Duties: Enforce United States immigration laws; check the eligibility of all people entering the United States from other countries

Salary Range: $21,000 to $50,000

Employment Prospects: Fair

Advancement Prospects: Limited
Prerequisites:

Special Requirements—Must be a U.S. citizen; have no criminal record; pass a selection process

Education—Bachelor's degree; 16-week training program

Experience—Three years of work experience, without a bachelor's degree

Special Skills—Problem-solving skills; communication, writing; and interpersonal skills

CAREER LADDER

```
┌─────────────────────────────────┐
│         Team Leader             │
└─────────────────────────────────┘

┌─────────────────────────────────┐
│      Immigration Inspector      │
└─────────────────────────────────┘

┌─────────────────────────────────┐
│   Immigration Inspector Recruit │
└─────────────────────────────────┘
```

Position Description

Immigration Inspectors are law enforcement officers for the Immigration and Naturalization Service, a division of the United States Department of Justice. They enforce all federal laws relating to the rights of persons to enter the United States and its territories—Puerto Rico, Guam, and the Virgin Islands. Immigration Inspectors screen all travelers arriving into the United States from other countries. This includes immigrants and foreign visitors as well as American citizens who are returning home.

As uniformed law enforcement officers, Immigration Inspectors have the authority to carry firearms. They work at the ports of entry into the United States—airports in major American cities, stations along the Mexican and Canadian borders, and seaports along the Pacific and Atlantic coasts. Some work in pre-inspection locations in foreign countries.

Upon entering the United States from another country, people must go through immigration checkpoints. There, they present their passports, visas, and other pertinent documents to Immigration Inspectors. These compliance officers review the documents and question people to determine:

- people's identity (by checking picture identification as well as ship or airplane passenger lists)

- people's citizenship status
- non-citizens' legal status (such as tourist, U.S. permanent resident, or foreign student status) to enter the country
- the authenticity of passports, visas, and all other relevant documents

If Immigration Inspectors suspect people's eligibility to enter the United States, they question these people further. Immigration Inspectors may place dangerous people or those who are considered to be a flight risk in holding cells until their cases are resolved. Upon completion of their examinations, persons are either admitted to the United States or detained and turned over to proper law enforcement authorities. Immigration Inspectors also have the authority to deport ineligible people and place them on planes back to their native countries.

In addition, Immigration Inspectors perform other duties related to the inspection process that includes preparing reports and maintaining records.

Immigration Inspectors work a 40-hour week, but are often required to work overtime. They sometimes travel, being away from their duty stations for extended periods of time. Immigration Inspectors are on call 24 hours, seven days a week.

Salaries

The Immigration Inspectors receive a salary based on a pay schedule called *General Schedule*. The pay schedule starts at the GS-1 grade and goes up to the GS-15 grade, with each grade having ten steps. Immigration Inspectors start at the GS-5 grade ($21,000 to $27,000 per year) or the GS-7 grade ($26,000 to $33,000 per year).

In 1997, most Immigration Inspectors earned an annual salary between $23,000 and $50,000, according to the Bureau of Labor Statistics (a division of the U.S. Department of Labor). Inspectors with more education and experience typically earn higher wages as do inspectors with harder job responsibilities (such as supervisory duties). Those who live in metropolitan areas and large cities where the cost of living is higher usually earn higher wages, too. In addition, they receive overtime pay and uniform allowances. If they serve at overseas posts, they receive housing allowances.

Employment Prospects

INS has over 250 ports (air, sea, and land) of entry into the United States at which Immigration Inspectors are stationed. Competition for jobs is high; and most job opportunities become available when Immigration Inspectors retire, resign, or are promoted to higher positions. The creation of additional positions depends on the agency's needs.

Advancement Prospects

Supervisory and management opportunities are available, but limited. Many Immigration Inspectors pursue career growth by way of wage increases and complexity of new assignments.

Special Requirements

Applicants must be U.S. citizens without criminal records. For duty at some stations, applicants must be proficient in Spanish, or acquire proficiency. In addition, applicants must pass every step of the agency's selection process which includes the following: job application, written exam, interview, medical examination, background investigation, and drug testing.

Education and Training

Applicants must have a bachelor's degree if they do not have the required work experience. Having a combination of college study and work experience may also be acceptable.

Immigration Inspector recruits must complete 16 weeks of training at the Federal Law Enforcement Training Center in Glynco, Georgia. Recruits study courses such as Spanish, immigration law, police training, physical training, and use of firearms. Upon completion, recruits are assigned to a duty station and work under the supervision of field training officers.

Experience and Skills

If applicants do not have a bachelor's degree, they need a minimum of three years of responsible work experience or a combination of education and work experience. In addition, applicants must have strong problem-solving skills as well as the ability to make sound, fair, and accurate decisions based on complex laws and regulations. They must also show that they have good communication and writing abilities along with good interpersonal skills.

Unions/Associations

Many Immigration Inspectors join the Federal Law Enforcement Officers Association, a professional organization for all federal law enforcement officers. It offers networking opportunities, education programs, and other professional services and support.

Tips for Entry

1. For current recruitment information, contact an INS office or the local U.S. Office of Personnel Management (OPM). You might find a listing for either agency in your local telephone book under U.S. Government.
2. You can apply for Immigration Inspector positions at different locations at the same time. But you must submit a separate application for each location.
3. Recent college graduates with a 3.5 GPA may apply for available Immigration Inspector positions under the Outstanding Scholar Program.
4. To learn more about INS, visit its web site on the Internet. Its web address is *http://www.ins.usdoj.gov/.*

CUSTOMS INSPECTOR

CAREER PROFILE

Duties: Enforce federal laws that govern imports entering the United States as well as exports leaving the country

Salary Range: $21,000 to $50,000

Employment Prospects: Fair

Advancement Prospects: Limited
Prerequisites:

Special Requirements—Must be a U.S. citizen; have a valid driver's license; have no criminal record; pass a selection process

Education—Bachelor's degree; 11-week training program

Experience—Three years of work experience without a college degree

Special Skills—Interpersonal, communication, and writing skills; problem-solving and self-management skills

CAREER LADDER

```
┌─────────────────────────────┐
│        Team Leader          │
└─────────────────────────────┘

┌─────────────────────────────┐
│      Customs Inspector      │
└─────────────────────────────┘

┌─────────────────────────────┐
│  Customs Inspector Recruit  │
└─────────────────────────────┘
```

Position Description

Customs Inspectors are uniformed law enforcement officers for the U.S. Customs Service, a division of the Department of Treasury. They enforce federal laws that govern imports entering the United States as well as exports leaving the country.

Customs Inspectors work at ports of entry in airports in major cities, at border stations along the boundaries with Canada and Mexico, and in seaports along the Pacific and Atlantic oceans. Customs Inspectors may board vessels, trains, or aircraft and inspect vehicles entering or leaving the United States. They examine cargo and baggage in addition to inspecting clothing worn or carried by people.

All imports and exports are declared on U.S. Customs forms with their descriptions, values, and countries of origin. Customs Inspectors review these declaration forms and other pertinent documents such as invoices, crew lists, passenger lists, and permits. They also examine the declared items and may weigh, measure, or gauge them in order to determine their values. In addition, Customs Inspectors make sure no items are undeclared, and may take any undeclared items into custody.

If necessary, Customs Inspectors may take a sample of an item in question and have it appraised. Customs Inspectors calculate the amount of taxes, or duties, that persons must pay and collect payment from them. In instances of violations, such as declaring a lower value on items, Customs Inspectors may impose fines.

Customs Inspectors also check for illegal drugs, merchandise, arms, stolen property, and other contraband that may be smuggled into the United States. Upon finding any contraband, Customs Inspectors have the authority to seize the contraband. In addition, they have the authority to detain and apprehend persons who have broken laws.

Furthermore, Customs Inspectors maintain daily records of their transactions, and write formal reports of any violations or other incidents that they may handle.

Customs Inspectors often work closely with other federal agencies, such as the Immigration and Naturalization Services, FBI, and the Border Patrol to ensure the overall security of U.S. borders.

Customs inspection work is physically demanding; and depending on their stations, Customs Inspectors may work outside in all types of weather. These officers are required to work many long hours in overtime.

Salaries

Customs Inspectors receive a salary based on a pay schedule called *General Schedule.* The pay schedule starts at the GS-1 grade and goes up to the GS-15 grade, with each grade having ten steps. Customs Inspectors start at the GS-5 grade

($21,000 to $27,000 per year) or the GS-7 grade ($26,000 to $33,000 per year).

In 1997, most Immigration Inspectors earned an annual salary between $23,000 and $50,000, according to the Bureau of Labor Statistics (a division of the U.S. Department of Labor). Inspectors with more education and experience typically earn higher wages, as do inspectors with greater job responsibilities (such as supervisory duties). Those who live in metropolitan areas and large cities where the cost of living is higher usually earn higher wages too. Customs Inspectors can earn up to $30,000 more in overtime.

Employment Prospects

The U.S. Customs Service has over 300 ports (air, sea, and land) of entry at which Customs Inspectors are stationed. Competition for jobs is high; and most job opportunities become available when officers retire, resign, or are promoted to higher positions. The creation of additional positions depends on the agency's needs.

Advancement Prospects

Supervisory and management opportunities are available, but limited. Many Customs Inspectors pursue career growth by way of wage increases and complexity of new assignments.

Special Requirements

Applicants must be U.S. citizens with a valid driver's license and have no criminal record. In addition, they must pass every step of the agency's selection process, which includes the following: job application, written examination, oral interview, medical examination, physical agility test, background investigation, and drug testing. This process usually takes eight months. Successful applicants are placed on eligibility lists for the geographical areas where they want to work, and are offered positions when vacancies become open.

Education and Training

Applicants without any work experience can qualify at the GS-5 grade with a bachelor's degree. A combination of college credits and work experience may also qualify applicants at GS-5. To qualify at the GS-7 grade (without work experience), applicants must have a bachelor's degree and meet specific academic achievements; or, have one year of graduate work; or, possess a master's degree.

Customs Inspectors trainees must complete an 11-week training program at the Federal Law Enforcement Training Center in Glynco, Georgia. Their study includes behavioral sciences, bombs and explosives, narcotics, use of firearms, and physical training. They also learn customs laws as well as search, seizure, arrest, entry, and merchandise control procedures.

Experience and Skills

Applicants without college degrees can qualify at the GS-5 grade with three or more years of responsible work experience involving meeting and dealing with people. To qualify at the GS-7 grade, applicants must have one year of experience performing compliance or regulatory work; one year of work applying knowledge about federal laws, regulations, and procedures for importing and exporting merchandise; or, a combination of education and work experience.

The U.S. Customs Service looks for neat, responsible persons who have good interpersonal, communication, and writing skills. In addition, applicants must have good problem-solving skills and the ability to get to work on time, follow directions, take initiative, work safely, and stay calm while working under pressure.

Unions/Associations

Customs Inspectors might belong to the Federal Law Enforcement Officers Association, which offers networking opportunities, education programs, and other professional services and support.

Tips for Entry

1. Contact a U.S. Customs Service office to learn more about career opportunities. You might find a listing in your local telephone book under U.S. Treasury. Or, call the agency's toll-free number, (800) 944-7725.
2. Having law enforcement or military experience is valuable for a career in this field. So is the ability to speak and understand a foreign language fluently.
3. Recent college graduates with a 3.5 GPA may enhance their chances for employment by applying under the Outstanding Scholar Program.
4. You can learn more about the U.S. Customs Service on the Internet. Its web site address is *http://www.customs.ustreas.gov*.

PARK RANGER

CAREER PROFILE

Duties: Enforce laws that protect local, state, and federal parks; provide for public safety within park boundaries

Alternate Titles: Park Police, Park Guide, Park Interpreter

Salary Range: $18,000 to $90,000

Employment Prospects: Fair

Advancement Prospects: Limited
Prerequisites:
Special Requirements—Vary with the different agencies
Education—Bachelor's degree or some college study
Experience—Knowledge of natural resources and park work
Special Skills—Problem-solving, teamwork, and interpersonal skills; communication, reading, and writing skills

CAREER LADDER

```
┌─────────────────────────────┐
│     Senior Park Ranger      │
└─────────────────────────────┘

┌─────────────────────────────┐
│        Park Ranger          │
└─────────────────────────────┘

┌─────────────────────────────┐
│   Seasonal Park Ranger or   │
│     Park Ranger Trainee     │
└─────────────────────────────┘
```

Position Description

Park Rangers are responsible for protecting local, state, and federal parks and providing for public safety within park boundaries. They work in urban, rural, and wilderness settings that include parks, historical sites, nature reserves, and recreation areas. They wear many hats on their job: They are inspectors, tour guides, conservationists, historians, firefighters, teachers, rescue technicians, and some are also law enforcement officers. (They are not, however, forest rangers or wildlife conservation officers, which are different occupations.)

Park Rangers have various duties of which enforcing park regulations is one example. They also patrol park grounds—including the back country—for criminal activity, cleanliness, fire prevention, and safety hazards; collect park entrance and campground fees; register vehicles and visitors; and issue special permits for back country and off-road vehicle use. On occasion, especially in larger parks, Park Rangers monitor and control traffic and visitor use to the facilities. Park Rangers also deal with complaints and accidents; they may evict violators or report them to appropriate law enforcement officers.

Some Park Rangers are sworn law enforcement officers with the authority to carry firearms. They give verbal or written warnings as well as issue citations and make arrests. They also conduct investigations of unsolved crime within their jurisdiction.

Park Rangers help visitors learn about the natural, cultural, and historical aspects of their parks. They answer questions about such topics as natural resources, recreational activities, and topography. In addition, they prepare exhibits and create written materials. They also conduct group hikes, history presentations, crafts classes, and other recreational programs.

Park Rangers are always ready to respond to emergency situations, ranging from fighting fires to searching for lost campers to rescuing hikers from high cliffs to transporting injured campers to emergency rooms. Some Park Rangers are certified as emergency medical technicians and rescue technicians.

Another duty is the care and management of natural resources. They do regular maintenance jobs such as garbage pickup, landscaping, or trail repair. They may supervise or participate in special programs such as habitat restoration, monitoring wildlife behavior, or monitoring air quality.

Park Rangers perform strenuous work in all types of weather and terrain. They work rotating shifts, including weekends and holidays. During tourist seasons, they frequently work overtime. Many Park Rangers are on call 24 hours a day.

Salaries

In 1997, estimated annual salaries for Park Rangers were between $18,000 and $90,000, according to the Bureau of Labor Statistics (a division of the U.S. Department of Labor).

Park Rangers with more education and experience typically earn higher wages, as do those with greater job responsibilities (such as supervisory and administrative duties). Those who live in metropolitan areas and large cities where the cost of living is higher usually earn higher wages too. Most Park Rangers receive overtime pay and uniform allowances.

Employment Prospects

Park Rangers work for national, state, and local parks. Competition for jobs—both permanent and seasonal—is high, especially at larger popular parks. Most job opportunities become available when officers retire, resign, or are promoted to higher positions. Positions are often filled by experienced seasonal employees.

Advancement Prospects

Supervisory and management opportunities are available, and based on an agency's needs and individual merit. Possessing a master's degree is helpful for advancement to high supervisory positions such as federal district ranger or state park manager.

Park Rangers with law enforcement units can apply for specialized units, such as bike patrol and canine patrol. With their diverse work experience, Park Rangers might enter other fields such as law enforcement, zookeeping, or environmental protection.

Special Requirements

Every agency has special requirements that applicants must meet. For example: to apply for a position with law enforcement duties in the National Park Service, applicants must be U.S. citizens between 21 and 37 years old without criminal records.

Applicants must pass every step of an agency's selection process, which includes any or all of the following: job application, written exam, panel interview, medical examination, physical aptitude or agility test, background investigation, psychological review, polygraph examination, and drug testing.

In addition, applicants may need current CPR, Emergency Medical Technician or other certifications, upon being appointed or within a certain time after being hired.

Education and Training

Requirements for career positions vary with the different agencies as well as for the type of positions. Most agencies require that applicants have either a college degree or two years of college study, preferably in park and recreation manage-

ment, natural science, history, natural resource management, criminal justice, police science, or other related field.

Recruits must complete training programs, which vary with the different agencies as well as with the particular duties that are to be performed. For example, Park Rangers with police duties must complete a police officer training program.

Experience and Skills

Applicants generally need three years of related work experience, if they do not fulfill the education requirements. Park agencies look for responsible candidates who have basic knowledge of natural resources and park work. In addition, candidates should be problem-solvers with the ability to work independently as well as have the flexibility and patience to handle constant changes and contact with various people. Candidates should have teamwork and interpersonal skills as well as communication, reading, and writing abilities.

Unions/Associations

Three national organizations that Park Rangers might belong to are: Park Law Enforcement Association; U.S. Park Ranger Lodge (part of the Fraternal Order of Police); and National Society for Park Resources (part of the National Recreation and Park Association). Furthermore, Park Rangers might join state professional associations. Joining such organizations gives Park Rangers the opportunity to network with peers and obtain professional support and services, such as continuing education and job resources.

Tips for Entry

1. The National Park Service (NPS) recruits several months ahead of time for seasonal jobs. To learn about upcoming recruitment periods, write to: Seasonal Employment Program, Human Resources Office, National Park Service, P.O. Box 37127, Mail Stop 2225, Washington DC 20013-7129. Or visit the NPS web site at: *http://www.nps.gov/.*

2. Obtain work experience by doing volunteer work or getting part-time or seasonal positions in a park system.

3. Recent college graduates with a 3.5 GPA may enhance their chances for federal employment by applying under the Outstanding Scholar Program.

4. Many national and state parks have web sites on the Internet. To learn about national parks, start at the NPS web site, *http://www.nps.gov/.* For state parks, enter the name of the state plus *State Parks* in a search engine to get a list of web sites (Example: *Idaho State Parks*).

BANK EXAMINER

CAREER PROFILE

Duties: Investigate banking institutions to make sure they are safe, sound operations and are in compliance with federal or state banking laws

Salary Range: $23,000 to $50,000

Employment Prospects: Fair

Advancement Prospects: Limited
  Prerequisites:
  Special Requirements—Qualifications vary with the different agencies; pass a selection process
  Education—Bachelor's degree
  Experience—Varies with the different agencies
  Special Skills—Problem-solving, teamwork, and interpersonal skills; communication, writing, research, and computer utilities

CAREER LADDER

```
┌─────────────────────────────────┐
│      Senior Bank Examiner        │
└─────────────────────────────────┘

┌─────────────────────────────────┐
│         Bank Examiner            │
└─────────────────────────────────┘

┌─────────────────────────────────┐
│       Assistant Examiner         │
└─────────────────────────────────┘
```

Position Description

Bank Examiners make sure that banks are following federal and state banking laws and that banks are safe, sound operations. Working for either a state or federal agency, Bank Examiners conduct investigations on banks, savings banks, credit unions, home financing institutions, or other banking institutions.

Usually working in teams of two or more, Bank Examiners make regularly scheduled inspections on banks within their assigned districts in addition to conducting investigations of consumer complaints. Their examinations involve auditing financial records as well as reviewing bank procedures, board policies, and other relevant data. They may also interview bank officers and employees.

Upon compiling all pertinent data, Bank Examiners analyze the information to determine:

- the bank's financial condition
- how well management runs the bank
- whether there are adequate internal controls
- if there are any unsafe and unsound practices
- if the bank has violated any federal or state laws and regulations

Bank Examiners meet with bank officials after completing their assessments. The inspectors discuss their findings and make appropriate suggestions for correcting any weaknesses. In addition, Bank Examiners write a well-detailed report of their examinations and recommendations.

Bank Examiners work a 40-hour week, five days a week. Overnight travel is a frequent part of their job.

Salaries

Salaries vary with the different state and federal bank regulatory agencies. In 1997, most Bank Examiners earned an annual salary between $23,000 and $50,000, according to the Bureau of Labor Statistics (a division of the U.S. Department of Labor). Salaries are typically higher in geographical locations where the cost of living is higher. Travel costs, including food, lodging, and transportation, are usually reimbursed if Bank Examiners present proper invoices and receipts.

Employment Prospects

Bank Examiners are employed by state banking departments as well as by these federal regulatory agencies: Office of the Controller of the Currency (OCC), Federal Reserve System, and Federal Deposit Insurance Corporation (FDIC).

Job growth for all compliance officers, including Bank Examiners, is expected to be slower than the average for all jobs through the year 2006. Most job opportunities will become available as Bank Examiners retire, resign, or become promoted.

Advancement Prospects

Bank Examiners usually start in the position of Assistant Examiners or Bank Examiner trainees. After a few years, Assistant Examiners can advance to Bank Examiners (which may involve additional written and oral exams). Further advancement into supervisory and management positions is possible, but limited. Promotions are competitive, based on an agency's needs and on individual merit.

Special Requirements

Special requirements vary with the different agencies. To work for federal agencies, applicants must be U.S. citizens. For most agencies, applicants must possess a valid driver's license. In many agencies, applicants must be eligible for obtaining a fidelity bond. Some agencies may require applicants to live in (or agree to be relocated to) the geographic location where they would be assigned.

Applicants may be ineligible to apply at an agency if they are customers or own stock in banks that the agency regulates. In addition, they may be ineligible if they are related to any employee or paid consultant of any bank that the agency regulates.

Furthermore, applicants must pass every step of an agency's selection process, which may include any of the following: application, written examination, oral interview, and background investigation.

Education and Training

In general, entry-level applicants must have a bachelor's degree in finance, accounting, business administration, economics or other related field. In addition, applicants must have completed a minimum number of semester hours in accounting. (Many agencies allow a combination of education and experience to be substituted for the education requirement.)

Trainees must successfully complete training programs that include classroom, self-study, and on-the-job training. In addition, Bank Examiners must undergo regular training throughout their careers to keep up with constantly changing laws and financial products and services.

Experience and Skills

Requirements vary with the different agencies. For example, federal agencies require applicants without a bachelor's degree to have three years of work experience in a financial institution reviewing, analyzing, recommending, or approving loan applications or investment decisions. In addition, applicants must have knowledge of accounting or auditing principles.

All agencies look for candidates who have strong problem-solving skills as well as teamwork and interpersonal skills. Candidates also show that they have strong communication and writing skills to present technical information clearly and effectively. In addition, they have research skills and computer skills, especially with word processing and spread sheet programs.

Tips for Entry

1. To learn about career opportunities, contact state banking departments and appropriate federal agencies directly. For federal positions, you can also learn about Bank Examiner vacancies through a local U.S. Office of Personnel Management, or visit its web site (*http://www.usajobs.opm.gov/*) on the Internet.

2. Some state banking departments have Bank Examiner trainee programs for which persons who have little or no required work experience may apply. Contact a state banking department to find out if they have trainee programs.

3. On the Internet, you can learn about various state and federal bank regulatory agencies. To read about state agencies, enter the phrase *state banking department* or *department of commerce* to get a list of web sites to browse. Web addresses for federal agencies are: Office of the Comptroller of the Currency, *http://www.occ.treas.gov;* Federal Reserve System, *http://www.bog.frb.fed.us;* and Federal Deposit Insurance Corporation, *http://www.fdic.gov/.*

REVENUE OFFICER

CAREER PROFILE

Duties: Collect delinquent taxes for the federal or state governments

Alternate Titles: Revenue Compliance Officer, Revenue Agent (states)

Salary Range: $23,000 to $50,000

Employment Prospects: Fair

Advancement Prospects: Limited
Prerequisites:
Special Requirements—Qualifications vary with the different agencies; pass a selection process
Education—Bachelor's degree
Experience—Varies from agency to agency
Special Skills—Problem-solving and organizational skills; interpersonal skills; communication, report-writing, telephone, and interviewing abilities

CAREER LADDER

```
┌─────────────────────────────────┐
│   Supervisory Revenue Officer   │
└─────────────────────────────────┘

┌─────────────────────────────────┐
│        Revenue Officer          │
└─────────────────────────────────┘

┌─────────────────────────────────┐
│     Revenue Officer Trainee     │
└─────────────────────────────────┘
```

Position Description

Revenue Officers are responsible for collecting delinquent taxes that are owed to the United States government or to a state government by individuals, organizations, businesses, and corporations. This includes collection of income tax, excise tax, sales tax, franchise tax, inheritance tax, estate tax, and so on.

Employed by the federal or a state government revenue department, Revenue Officers are assigned specific types of tax collections, such as inheritance or excise taxes, within geographical districts. From time to time, they may need to conduct collections outside of their assigned district.

Their caseloads are heavy; for example, federal Revenue Officers may be responsible for 40 to 100 cases of delinquent tax returns. With each case, Revenue Officers examine the tax return, checking the accuracy of the math as well as the taxpayer's compliance with tax laws. Upon reviewing a case, they send a collection notice to the taxpayer. They might also call or visit the taxpayer in person. If the Revenue Officers do not have current addresses, they then use professional skiptracing methods to locate taxpayers.

Revenue Officers conduct interviews with taxpayers and their representatives to gather more information for determining the amount of tax liability. They also hold meetings with taxpayers to discuss how they plan to resolve their unpaid tax debts. Revenue Officers may negotiate payment schedules (a minimum amount every month over a period of time) with taxpayers; but final approval for any payment schedule is made by their superiors.

When taxpayers do not pay, Revenue Officers conduct investigations into their financial background, learning what assets—wages, bank accounts, houses, cars, and other personal and real property—taxpayers own. Some Revenue Officers work complex or sensitive cases that involve surveillance as well as seizures of taxpayers' assets, which are done with warrants and other appropriate legal notices.

As part of their duty, Revenue Officers keep detailed, up-to-date records on all their cases. If any of their cases are brought to trial, they may help prepare documentary evidence for court officials. In addition, they may testify as witnesses in court.

Revenue Officers work independently under the supervision of a senior officer. They normally work five days a week, 40 hours per week. Some travel is required on their job.

Salaries

In 1997, most Revenue Officers earned an annual salary between $23,000 and $50,000, according to the Bureau of Labor Statistics (a division of the U.S. Department of Labor). Revenue Officers with more education and experience typically earn higher wages, as do officers with greater job responsibilities (such as supervisory duties). Those who live in metropolitan areas and large cities where the cost of living is higher usually earn higher wages too.

Employment Prospects

Revenue Officers work for state revenue departments as well as for the federal revenue department—the Internal Revenue Service (IRS), a division of the U.S. Department of the Treasury.

Job growth for all compliance officers, including Revenue Officers, is expected to be slower than the average for all jobs through the year 2006. Most job opportunities become available when officers retire, resign, or are promoted to higher positions. The creation of additional positions depends on an agency's needs and budget.

Advancement Prospects

Supervisory and management opportunities are available, but limited. Many Revenue Officers pursue career growth by way of wage increases and complexity of new assignments.

Revenue Officers might pursue other paths within this field, such as tax auditor or criminal investigator.

Special Requirements

Requirements vary from agency to agency. For example, to apply for a federal job, applicants must be U.S. citizens.

In addition, applicants must pass an agency's selection process, which includes the following: job application, written examination, oral interview, and background investigation. Applicants may also need to pass a tax compliance check.

Education and Training

For entry-level positions, applicants must have a bachelor's degree, preferably with a major in business administration, accounting, public administration, law, police science, or other related field. (Experience or a combination of education and experience may substitute for the education requirement.)

Revenue Officer trainees must complete their agency's training program in tax laws and collection techniques. In many agencies, the program is one year long and includes both classroom and field training.

Experience and Skills

Experience requirements vary from agency to agency. Some agencies may require one or more years of relevant experience along with possessing a bachelor's degree. They look for candidates with experience in personal finance, law enforcement, claims adjustment, collection work, or other directly related field.

Applicants should have excellent problem-solving and organizational skills plus the ability to handle angry or upset clients. Also, applicants should have effective communication and good report-writing abilities as well as telephone and interviewing skills. Being tactful, adaptable, and resourceful are also important.

Tips for Entry

1. To learn about job vacancies for the IRS, contact the IRS office at which you would like to work. You can also contact a local branch of the U.S. Office of Personnel Management to learn about job vacancies, or visit its web site (*http://www.usajobs.opm.gov*) on the Internet.

2. To get an idea if this is a field you would like to work in, obtain a job with the IRS or your state's revenue office. Many seasonal full-time and part-time positions as customer service representatives and tax examining clerks are available during tax periods.

3. Almost all state revenue departments have web sites. To learn about a department, enter the name of the state and the phrase *department of revenue*. (Example: *Tennessee Department of Revenue*). You can also check out the IRS web site on the Internet. Its web address is *http://www.irs.treas.gov/*.

BUILDING AND CONSRUCTION INSPECTIONS

PLAN REVIEWER

CAREER PROFILE

Duties: Review construction plans and specifications to make sure they are in compliance with building codes, regulations, and standards

Alternate Title: Plan Examiner

Salary Range: $20,000 to $60,000

Employment Prospects: Fair

Advancement Prospects: Limited
  Prerequisites:
  Special Requirements—Pass a selection process; have a profession license or certification
  Education—High school diploma
  Experience—Have several years of experience in construction supervision or in building inspections
  Special Skills—Writing, communication, and customer service skills; problem-solving skills and the ability to interpret written materials, drawings, and other forms

CAREER LADDER

```
┌─────────────────────────────┐
│    Senior Plan Reviewer     │
└─────────────────────────────┘

┌─────────────────────────────┐
│       Plan Reviewer         │
└─────────────────────────────┘

┌─────────────────────────────┐
│    Plan Reviewer Trainee    │
└─────────────────────────────┘
```

Position Description

Plan Reviewers examine construction plans for residential, commercial, and industrial projects—houses, schools, churches, restaurants, banks, shopping centers, apartment buildings, high-rise office buildings, parking garages, factories, prisons, and other structures. Projects may be new constructions or renovations on existing structures. Plan Reviewers make sure that construction plans and specifications are in compliance with building codes, regulations, and standards. Building permits are issued to owners or contractors once Plan Reviewers approve their construction plans.

For every project, Plan Reviewers review all construction documents such as architectural and site plan drawings, structural design calculations, and soil reports. They also go over plans and specifications for some or all of the following installations, checking against appropriate codes:

- structural construction (foundation, walls, ceilings, doors, roofs, chimneys, and other parts of buildings)
- electrical installations (electrical wiring and fixtures for lighting systems, heating systems, and security systems)
- plumbing installations (water-supply systems, sewer systems)

- mechanical installations (heating, ventilation, air conditioning, and cooling systems)

They also make sure that construction plans are in compliance with fire protection regulations and zoning laws as well as appropriate state statutes that enforce such matters as energy conservation and access to the disabled.

Approval is not given if Plan Reviewers find any noncompliance with codes or problems such as the wrong types of building materials being used. Plan Reviewers record the deficiencies and later meet with owners and design professionals to explain code violations or other problems. When documents are corrected, they are resubmitted to Plan Reviewers for another examination.

Plan Reviewers also have other duties, which vary from agency to agency. Some duties may include:

- keeping status reports of all construction plans under review up to date
- explaining building codes, laws, and standards to the public, contractors, architects, and other building officials
- maintaining a library of building codes and related documents

- coordinating plan reviews among various building inspectors
- Conducting structural, electrical, or other type of building inspection
- Helping with the training of new or inexperienced Plan Reviewers

In addition, Plan Reviewers must keep up with code and regulatory changes as well as with new construction technology.

Plan Reviewers work a regular 40-hour week, performing most of their duties in their offices.

Salaries

Salaries vary from agency to agency. In 1996, Plan Reviewers earned between $21,600 and $55,800 per year. (The median annual salary was $33,700 per year.) Earnings are generally higher in metropolitan areas where the cost of living is higher.

Employment Prospects

Plan Reviewers work for building departments with city, county, and state governments. Some Plan Reviewers work for private architectural and engineering firms as well as for code-consulting businesses and model code agencies that provide plan review services.

Job opportunities are expected to grow as fast as the average for all occupations through the year 2006. Most job openings, however, will become available as Plan Reviewers retire or transfer to other jobs or positions.

Advancement Prospects

Advancement opportunities for government-employed Plan Reviewers are available, but limited. Many Plan Reviewers pursue career growth by way of wage increases and complexity of new assignments.

Another career path is working in the private sector as consultants or as staff members of architectural and engineering firms.

Special Requirements

Applicants must pass an agency's selection process that may include any of the following: application, written exam, oral interview, medical examination, background investigation, and drug test.

Plan Reviewers must have state or local licenses or be certified by a recognized organization in the categories (e.g., electrical, plumbing) and type of plans (e.g., single dwellings, multiple dwellings, commercial) that they would be reviewing. Many agencies allow trainees to obtain proper certification within a certain time period.

Education and Training

Requirements vary from agency to agency. Applicants must have a high school or general equivalency diploma. Most agencies require additional college study in architecture, engineering, the construction trades, building inspection, or a related field. Many agencies prefer associate's or bachelor's degrees.

Under the supervision of senior officials, Plan Reviewers receive on-the-job training.

Experience and Skills

Requirements vary from agency to agency. But applicants should have several years of experience in construction supervision or in building inspections. Applicants should be able to read construction plans and drawings and understand engineering and architectural definitions and symbols.

Agencies look for tactful, independent applicants who have good technical-writing, communication, and customer service skills—the ability to present information effectively and answer questions from the general public, architects, contractors, and other building officials. In addition, applicants need problem-solving skills and the ability to interpret information from verbal instructions, written materials, diagrams, and other forms.

Unions/Associations

Plan Reviewers might join any of these major professional associations: the International Conference of Building Officials, the Building Officials and Code Administrators International, Inc., and the Southern Building Code Congress International, Inc. In addition, Plan Reviewers might join regional and state professional groups. Joining professional organizations gives Plan Reviewers the opportunity for networking with peers and obtaining professional support and services such as certified training, continuing education, and job resources.

Tips for Entry

1. Check out job listings with professional associations. Many associations post vacancies—for private firms and public agencies—that are available in different parts of the country.
2. Learn basic computer skills as more and more Plan Reviewers are using computers in their work.
3. Many building departments have web sites on the Internet. Some describe the plan's review process. To get a list of web sites to browse, enter the phrase *building inspections department* in a search engine.

BUILDING INSPECTOR

CAREER PROFILE

Duties: Conduct inspections of new constructions as well as renovations and repairs to make sure that all structural installations comply with building codes, regulations, and standards

Salary Range: $21,000 to $90,000

Employment Prospects: Fair

Advancement Prospects: Limited
   Prerequisites:
   Special Requirements—Pass a selection process; have a professional license or certification; have a current driver's license
   Education—High school diploma
   Experience—Be a construction worker at the journeyman level with supervisory or management experience
   Special Skills—Decision-making skills; teamwork and interpersonal skills; reading, writing, and communication abilities; management skills

CAREER LADDER

```
┌─────────────────────────────────┐
│    Senior Building Inspector    │
└─────────────────────────────────┘

┌─────────────────────────────────┐
│       Building Inspector        │
└─────────────────────────────────┘

┌─────────────────────────────────┐
│    Building Inspector Trainee   │
└─────────────────────────────────┘
```

Position Description

Building Inspectors are code enforcement officials for local, state, or federal government agencies. They conduct on-site inspections of residential, commercial, and industrial construction projects—including homes, schools, stores, hospitals, apartment buildings, office buildings, high-rise complexes, parking garages, factories, refineries, and prisons. They make sure all structural parts (foundation, floors, walls, doors, windows, roofs, chimneys, and so forth) meet building codes, regulations, and standards.

Usually working alone, Building Inspectors examine construction projects several times until their completion. (Projects may involve new constructions as well as repairs or renovations on existing buildings.) They review the quality and safety of the work as well as the materials being used. They check that all work follows the pre-approved construction plans and specifications. At each visit, they examine a specific phase of construction that they must approve before builders can go on to the next phase. For example, a Building Inspector would examine and approve the framework for a building's foundation before concrete is poured.

Their inspection is mostly visual; but they also use tape measures, surveying instruments, metering devices and test equipment. In addition, they keep a running log of their inspections throughout the project. Upon completion of all construction, Building Inspectors perform a comprehensive inspection, and issue an occupancy certificate if everything is in compliance.

When Building Inspectors find problems with a construction phase, they notify owners or contractors and explain the problems—such as code violations, unacceptable materials, or noncompliance with approved preconstruction plans. Building Inspectors have the authority to issue "stop work" orders, if problems are not corrected.

As part of their duties, Building Inspectors keep up with new building codes and construction legislation as well as with changing construction technology. In addition, they perform other tasks, which vary from agency to agency. For example, they might:

- review and approve preconstruction building plans and specifications
- issue building permits
- advise building contractors and property owners about appropriate building codes and regulations
- investigate complaints of unsafe buildings or construction work being done without proper permits
- perform electrical, plumbing, mechanical, or other nonstructural inspections.
- make recommendations for new building codes

Building Inspectors work 40 hours a week. Most of their time is spent in the field conducting inspections.

Salaries

In 1997, the estimated annual salaries for Building Inspectors ranged from $21,000 to $90,000, according to the Bureau of Labor Statistics (a division of the U.S. Department of Labor). Inspectors with more experience typically earn higher wages, as do those with greater job responsibilities (such as supervisory and administrative duties). Those who live in metropolitan areas and large cities where the cost of living is higher usually earn higher wages too.

Employment Prospects

Most Building Inspectors work for building departments at the city and county government level. Some work for state governments or federal agencies such as the U.S. Army Corps of Engineers, the U.S. Department of Agriculture, or the U.S. Department of Housing and Urban Development. Some also work for engineering and architectural firms that offer building inspection services.

Job opportunities are expected to grow as fast as the average for all occupations through the year 2006. The concern for public safety and the quality of construction should fuel a growing demand for inspectors. Most job openings, however, will become available as inspectors retire or transfer to other jobs or positions.

There is potential growth in the private sector for Building Inspectors due to the tendency of governments to contract out inspection work.

Advancement Prospects

Advancement opportunities are available; but engineering or architectural degrees are usually required for supervisory and administrative positions. Many Building Inspectors pursue career growth by way of wage increases and complexity of new assignments. Some choose to specialize in specific types of structural inspections, such as the inspection of reinforced concrete.

Another career path is to become a consultant or work for engineering, architectural, and management services firms in the private sector.

Special Requirements

Applicants must pass an agency's selection process, which may include any of the following: application, written exam, oral interview, medical examination, background investigation, and drug test.

In most agencies, Building Inspectors must have appropriate state or local licenses or certification from recognized professional organizations. (Trainees may be given a time period upon which to obtain proper licensing or certification.) In addition, most agencies require applicants to possess a valid driver's license.

Education and Training

Education requirements vary from agency to agency. Applicants need at least a high school or general equivalency diploma. More and more agencies prefer applicants with a bachelor's or associate's degree—or at least two years of formal study—in construction technology, engineering, architecture, or code work.

Building Inspectors receive on-the-job training to learn local codes, ordinances, and regulations; contract specifications; inspection techniques; and recordkeeping and reporting duties.

Experience and Skills

Experience requirements depend on the job duties that applicants would perform. In general, applicants should have a thorough knowledge of construction practices and skills along with an understanding of building codes and regulations. Most agencies hire applicants who are journeyman construction workers with supervisory or management experience.

Agencies typically look for physically fit candidates who are able to interpret building plans and codes, make critical decisions, be tactful and impartial, and work independently. Applicants should have teamwork and interpersonal skills in addition to reading, writing, and communication abilities. Furthermore, applicants should have good management skills as the job involves handling several projects and tasks at the same time.

Unions/Associations

Three major professional associations for Building Inspectors are: the International Conference of Building Officials, the Building Officials and Code Administrators International, Inc., and the Southern Building Code Congress International, Inc. Joining professional organizations gives Building Inspectors the opportunity for networking with peers and obtaining professional support and services, such as certified training, continuing education, technical information, and job resources.

Tips for Entry

1. Many local governments have job hotlines—phone numbers for recorded messages of current job announcements. In the city or county government listings of your phone book, look for "Job Hotline" under *Personnel or Human Resources Department*.
2. To prepare for a career in building inspections, take construction courses along with blueprint, algebra, geometry, and English classes in high school.

3. To enhance your chances of employment, enroll in a certificate or associate degree program in building inspection technology.

4. Many building departments have web sites on the Internet. To get a list of web sites to browse, enter the phrase *building inspections department* in a search engine.

MECHANICAL INSPECTOR

CAREER PROFILE

Duties: Conduct on-site inspections of mechanical installations (heating, ventilation, air conditioning, and cooling systems) to make sure they comply with mechanical codes, regulations, and standards

Salary Range: $21,000 to $90,000

Employment Prospects: Fair

Advancement Prospects: Limited
Prerequisites:
Special Requirements—Pass a selection process; have a professional license or certification; have a current driver's license
Education—High school diploma
Experience—Have several years of experience installing mechanical equipment along with supervisory experience
Special Skills—Math, reading, and writing abilities; communication and interpersonal skills; problem-solving and management skills

CAREER LADDER

```
┌─────────────────────────────────┐
│   Senior Mechanical Inspector   │
└─────────────────────────────────┘

┌─────────────────────────────────┐
│      Mechanical Inspector       │
└─────────────────────────────────┘

┌─────────────────────────────────┐
│   Mechanical Inspector Trainee  │
└─────────────────────────────────┘
```

Position Description

Mechanical Inspectors are code enforcement officials for local, state, and federal government agencies. They conduct on-site inspections of mechanical installations in residential, commercial, and industrial construction projects. Their job is to make sure that the installation of new or modified heating, ventilation, air conditioning, and cooling systems complies with mechanical codes and regulations. They inspect air distribution systems; boilers and water heaters; gas piping systems; furnaces, fireplaces, chimneys, and vents; air-conditioning components; refrigeration systems; incinerators, commercial kitchen appliances and exhaust equipment; and so on.

Inspection is mostly visual; but Mechanical Inspectors also use measuring tools, calipers, scales, gauges, testing instruments, and other tools to check the quality and safety of workmanship or equipment. They also check that air quality and energy conservation standards are met. In addition, they make sure that installations comply with pre-approved construction plans and specifications.

Mechanical Inspectors give final approval for all mechanical installations and mark appropriate records that are displayed at construction sites. When work is in noncompliance of codes or pre-approved plans, Mechanical Inspectors contact owners, contractors, or supervisors and explain what problems must be corrected before approval can be given. If problems are not corrected within a specified period of time, Mechanical Inspectors may issue a "stop work" order.

As part of their job, Mechanical Inspectors maintain well-detailed records and prepare reports and correspondence about their inspections. In addition, Mechanical Inspectors keep up with new mechanical codes and regulations as well as with changing technology.

Mechanical Inspectors perform other duties, which vary from agency to agency. For example, they might:

- review and approve pre-construction electrical plans and specifications
- issue mechanical permits
- advise the public, contractors, and other building officials regarding mechanical codes and regulations
- make recommendations for new building codes

Usually working alone, Mechanical Inspectors work 40 hours per week, mostly in the field.

Salaries

In 1997, the estimated annual salaries for Mechanical Inspectors ranged from $21,000 to $90,000, according to the Bureau of Labor Statistics (a division of the U.S. Department of Labor). Inspectors with more experience typically earn higher wages as do those with greater job responsibilities (such as supervisory and administrative duties). Those who live in metropolitan areas and large cities where the cost of living is higher usually earn higher wages too.

Employment Prospects

Most Mechanical Inspectors work for building departments at the city and county government level. Some work for state governments or federal agencies such as the U.S. Department of Housing and Urban Development. Some Mechanical Inspectors work for private sector engineering firms that offer mechanical inspection services.

Job opportunities are expected to grow as fast as the average for all occupations through the year 2006. Most job openings will become available as Mechanical Inspectors retire or transfer to other jobs or positions.

Advancement Prospects

Advancement opportunities are available; but engineering or architectural degrees are usually required for supervisory and administrative positions. Many Mechanical Inspectors pursue career growth by way of wage increases and complexity of new assignments. Some Mechanical Inspectors become private consultants.

Special Requirements

Applicants must pass an agency's selection process, which may include any of the following: application, written exam, oral interview, medical examination, background investigation, and drug test.

In addition, Mechanical Inspectors must have appropriate state or local licenses or professional certification from recognized organizations. (Trainees may be given a time period to obtain proper licensing or certification.) Also, most agencies require applicants to possess a valid driver's license.

Education and Training

Applicants need at least a high school or general equivalency diploma. In some states, to obtain a Mechanical Inspectors license, a bachelor's degree in architecture or civil or structural engineering is required.

Mechanical Inspectors receive on-the-job training to learn local codes, ordinances, and regulations; contract specifications; inspection techniques; and recordkeeping and reporting duties.

Experience and Skills

Requirements vary from agency to agency. Applicants should have several years of experience installing mechanical equipment along with supervisory experience. Some agencies also accept applicants' experience of performing mechanical inspections as part of their duties as general building inspectors. In addition, applicants should be able to analyze, interpret, and accurately check heating, ventilation and air-conditioning equipment, plans, and specifications.

Also, applicants should have good math, reading, writing, and communication skills. Furthermore, they need interpersonal skills, and problem-solving and management abilities.

Unions/Associations

Mechanical Inspectors might belong to the International Association of Plumbing and Mechanical Officials, the International Conference of Building Officials, the Building Officials and Code Administrators International, Inc., or the Southern Building Code Congress International, Inc. Joining professional organizations gives Mechanical Inspectors the opportunity to network with peers and obtain professional support and services, such as certified training, continuing education, technical information, and job resources.

Tips for Entry

1. Network with mechanical inspectors and other building officials to learn about current job openings or jobs that may become available soon.

2. Keep up with changes in building codes, construction practices, and technical developments by self-study, enrolling in college or correspondence courses, or attending seminars sponsored by professional organizations.

3. Many building departments have web sites on the Internet with specific information about mechanical inspections. To get a list of web sites, enter the phrase *building inspections department* in a search engine.

ELECTRICAL INSPECTOR

CAREER PROFILE

Duties: Conduct inspections of electrical installations in construction projects to make sure work is in compliance with electrical codes, regulations, and standards

Salary Range: $21,000 to $90,000

Employment Prospects: Fair

Advancement Prospects: Limited
Prerequisites:
Special Requirements—Pass a selection process; have a professional license or certification; have a current driver's license
Education—High school diploma
Experience—Be a journeyman electrician with supervisory experience
Special Skills—Problem-solving and management skills; writing and communication abilities; interpersonal skills

CAREER LADDER

```
┌─────────────────────────────────────┐
│     Senior Electrical Inspector      │
└─────────────────────────────────────┘

┌─────────────────────────────────────┐
│        Electrical Inspector          │
└─────────────────────────────────────┘

┌─────────────────────────────────────┐
│     Electrical Inspector Trainee     │
└─────────────────────────────────────┘
```

Position Description

Electrical Inspectors are code enforcement officials for local, state, and federal government agencies. They review installations for electrical wiring and fixtures in residential, commercial, or industrial construction projects. These projects may be new installations or alterations to existing electrical systems such as power, lighting, heating, air-conditioning, sound, and security systems. Electrical Inspectors make sure all work is in compliance with electrical codes, regulations, and standards.

Electrical inspections are done on a visual basis along with the use of inspection tools, such as metering devices and test equipment, to check the quality and safety of materials and workmanship. For example, Electrical Inspectors verify that electrical circuits can operate without overloads. As part of their inspections, Electrical Inspectors review pre-approved electrical plans and specifications to make sure that they have been followed. They also make sure work is done by licensed electricians.

Electrical Inspectors give final approvals for all electrical installations and mark appropriate records that are displayed at construction sites. When work is in noncompliance of codes or pre-approved plans, Electrical Inspectors contact owners, contractors, or supervisors and explain what prob-

lems must be corrected before approval can be given. Electrical Inspectors may issue a "stop work" order if problems are not corrected within a specified period of time.

As part of their job, Electrical Inspectors maintain well-detailed records and prepare reports and correspondence regarding their inspections. In addition, Electrical Inspectors keep up with new electrical codes and standards as well as changing technology.

Depending on the agency, Electrical Inspectors perform other duties. For example, they might:

- review and approve pre-construction electrical plans and specifications
- issue electrical permits
- advise the public, contractors, and other building officials about electrical codes, regulations, and standards
- help train new or inexperienced inspectors
- make recommendations for new electrical codes

Usually working alone, Electrical Inspectors work a 40-hour week. Their hours are spent at the construction work site as well as in a field office, reviewing blueprints, answering correspondence or telephone calls, writing reports, and scheduling inspections.

Salaries

In 1997, the estimated annual salaries for Electrical Inspectors ranged from $21,000 to $90,000, according to the Bureau of Labor Statistics (a division of the U.S. Department of Labor). Inspectors with more experience typically earn higher wages, as do those with broader job responsibilities (such as supervisory and administrative duties). Those who live in metropolitan areas and large cities where the cost of living is higher usually earn higher wages too.

Employment Prospects

Most Electrical Inspectors work for building departments at the city and county government level. Some work for state governments or federal agencies such as the U.S. Army Corps of Engineers and the U.S. Department of Housing and Urban Development. Some inspectors also work for engineering firms that offer electrical inspection services.

Job opportunities for building inspectors, including Electrical Inspectors, is expected to grow as fast as the average for all occupations through the year 2006. The concern for public safety and the quality of construction should fuel a growing demand. Most job openings for Electrical Inspectors will become available as inspectors retire or transfer to other jobs.

Advancement Prospects

Job opportunities are available, but limited. Many Electrical Inspectors pursue career growth by way of wage increases and complexity of new assignments. Some Electrical Inspectors become private consultants.

Special Requirements

Every agency has its own set of requirements that applicants must fulfill. Most agencies require applicants to have state or local electrical inspector licenses or certification from a professional code association prior to being appointed or within a certain time period upon being hired. In addition, Electrical Inspectors may be required to maintain certification as journeyman line workers. Applicants must also have a valid driver's license.

Furthermore, applicants must pass an agency's selection process that may include any of the following: application, written exam, oral interview, medical examination, background investigation, and drug test.

Education and Training

Education requirements vary with the different agencies. Most agencies require applicants to have a high school or general equivalency diploma. More and more agencies prefer applicants who have enrolled in electrical training at colleges, technical schools, or vocational schools. Some agencies prefer applicants to have bachelor's degrees in electrical engineering.

Electrical Inspectors receive on-the-job training to learn local codes, ordinances, and regulations; contract specifications; inspection techniques; and recordkeeping and reporting duties.

Experience and Skills

Requirements vary with different agencies. In general, applicants must be journeyman electricians with supervisory experience. They should have knowledge of electrical codes and ordinances in addition to the principles of electrical inspection.

Applicants must have problem-solving and management skills, as well as excellent writing and effective communication abilities. In addition, applicants need interpersonal skills.

Unions/Associations

Electrical Inspectors might belong to the International Association of Electrical Inspectors, the International Conference of Building Officials, the Building Officials and Code Administrators International, Inc., or the Southern Building Code Congress International, Inc. Joining professional organizations gives Electrical Inspectors an opportunity to network with peers and obtain professional support and services, such as certified training, continuing education, technical information, and job resources.

Tips for Entry

1. Contact city and county building departments directly to learn about job openings, or contact city and county government personnel (human resources) offices.

2. Some agencies allow applicants to substitute voluntary professional certification for one or more years of required work experience.

3. Many building departments have web sites on the Internet with specific information about electrical inspections. Enter the phrase *building inspections department* in a search engine to get a list of web sites.

PLUMBING INSPECTOR

CAREER PROFILE

Duties: Conduct on-site inspections of plumbing installations in construction projects to make sure they are in compliance with plumbing codes, sanitation standards, and construction specifications

Salary Range: $21,000 to $90,000

Employment Prospects: Fair

Advancement Prospects: Limited
  Prerequisites:
  Special Requirements—Pass a selection process; have a professional license or certification; have a current driver's license
  Education—High school diploma
  Experience—Several years of work experience in plumbing and sewer systems with supervisory experience
  Special Skills—Communication and writing abilities; interpersonal skills; problem-solving and management skills

CAREER LADDER

```
┌──────────────────────────────────────┐
│      Senior Plumbing Inspector       │
└──────────────────────────────────────┘

┌──────────────────────────────────────┐
│         Plumbing Inspector           │
└──────────────────────────────────────┘

┌──────────────────────────────────────┐
│     Plumbing Inspector Trainee       │
└──────────────────────────────────────┘
```

Position Description

Plumbing Inspectors are code enforcement officials for local, state, and federal government agencies. They make sure all plumbing installations in residential, commercial, and industrial construction projects are in compliance with plumbing codes, sanitation standards, and construction specifications. They inspect new plumbing systems as well as repairs or replacements to existing plumbing systems. These include water supply systems, water distribution systems, drainage systems, sewer systems, private disposal systems, water heater installations, fire sprinkler systems, and so on.

Their site visits involve visual inspections as well as the use of inspection tools and testing equipment to check on the quality and safety of the workmanship and materials. They check for proper installation of plumbing systems and that approved materials (such as back-flow prevention devices) are being used.

In addition, Plumbing Inspectors review pre-approved plumbing plans and specifications to verify that they have been followed. They also check that the plumbers doing the work possess valid certification or licensing.

When work is in noncompliance, Plumbing Inspectors notify owners, contractors, or supervisors and explain what problems must be corrected before approval can be given. If problems are not corrected within a specified period of time, Plumbing Inspectors may issue a "stop work" order.

Maintaining detailed records of their inspections is an essential part of their duties. In addition, they keep up with new plumbing codes and standards as well as changing technology.

Plumbing Inspectors perform other duties, which vary from agency to agency. For example, they might:

- review and approve pre-construction plumbing plans and specifications
- issue plumbing permits
- advise the general public, contractors, plumbers, and other building officials about plumbing codes as well as installation and permit requirements
- investigate complaints of plumbing code violations

Usually working alone, Plumbing Inspectors work 40 hours per week, mostly in the field. They may be full-time or part-time staff members or work for building departments on a contractual basis.

Salaries

In 1997, the estimated annual salaries for Plumbing Inspectors ranged from $21,000 to $90,000, according to the Bureau of Labor Statistics (a division of the U.S. Department of Labor). Inspectors with more experience typically earn higher wages, as do those with greater job responsibilities (such as supervisory and administrative duties). Those who live in metropolitan areas and large cities where the cost of living is higher usually earn higher wages too.

Employment Prospects

Most Plumbing Inspectors work for building departments at the city and county government level. Some work for state governments or federal agencies such as the U.S. Department of Housing and Urban Development. Some Plumbing Inspectors also work for engineering firms that offer plumbing inspection services.

Job opportunities for Plumbing Inspectors is expected to grow as fast as the average for all occupations through the year 2006. Most job openings for Plumbing Inspectors will become available as inspectors retire or transfer to other jobs.

Advancement Prospects

Job opportunities are available, but limited. Many Plumbing Inspectors pursue career growth by way of wage increases and complexity of new assignments. Some inspectors become private consultants.

Special Requirements

Specific qualifications vary from agency to agency. A state or local Plumbing Inspector license or professional certification from a recognized organization must be obtained before becoming appointed or within a time period upon being employed. A valid driver's license is also required.

Furthermore, applicants must pass an agency's selection process, which may include any of the following: application, written exam, oral interview, medical examination, background investigation, and drug test.

Education and Training

Agencies require applicants to have at least a high school or general equivalency diploma. More and more agencies prefer additional college course work or the completion of technical or trade school curriculum in plumbing, mechanical engineering, or other related fields.

Plumbing Inspectors receive on-the-job training to learn local codes, ordinances, and regulations; contract specifications; inspection techniques; and recordkeeping and reporting duties.

Experience and Skills

Requirements vary from agency to agency. Applicants should have several years of work experience in plumbing and sewer systems as well as supervisory experience. In addition, they should have knowledge of codes and laws governing plumbing installations.

Agencies look for physically fit candidates who are able to communicate clearly and effectively, both orally and in writing. Interpersonal skills are essential. Also, likely candidates have good problem-solving and management abilities to handle the various projects and tasks of their job.

Unions/Associations

Plumbing Inspectors might belong to the International Association of Plumbing and Mechanical Officials, the International Conference of Building Officials, the Building Officials and Code Administrators International, Inc., or the Southern Building Code Congress International, Inc. Joining professional organizations gives Plumbing Inspectors the opportunity to network with peers and obtain professional support and services, such as certified training, continuing education, technical information, and job resources.

Tips for Entry

1. To learn more about code enforcement careers or job vacancies, contact a Plumbing Inspector or Building Inspector at a local building department.
2. Obtain voluntary professional certification from recognized professional associations, such as the International Conference of Building Officials, to enhance your chances of being hired.
3. Many building departments have web sites on the Internet with specific information about plumbing inspections. To get a list of web sites to browse, enter the phrase *building inspections department* in a search engine.

CONSTRUCTION INSPECTOR

CAREER PROFILE

Duties: Conduct on-site inspections of the construction or repairs of streets, highways, sewer systems, and other public works to make sure the projects are in compliance with construction codes, regulations, and standards

Alternate Titles: Public Works Inspector, Transportation Construction Inspector

Salary Range: $18,000 to $90,000

Employment Prospects: Fair

Advancement Prospects: Limited
Prerequisites:

Special Requirements—Pass a selection process; have appropriate professional license or certification; have a current driver's license

Education—High school diploma

Experience—Have several years of work experience in public works, engineering inspections, or construction along with supervisory or management experience

Special Skills—Reading and math skills; communication and writing skills; problem-solving skills and management skills; people and teamwork skills

CAREER LADDER

Senior Construction Inspector

Construction Inspector

Construction Inspector Trainee

Position Description

Construction Inspectors are code enforcement officials for local, state, and federal government agencies. They make sure that the construction of streets, highways, sewer systems, and other public works is in compliance with construction codes and regulations. They also make sure that construction work follows pre-approved plans and specifications.

Local Construction Inspectors (also known as Public Works Inspectors) conduct on-site inspections of the construction or repair of streets, sidewalks, driveways, water systems, sewer systems, streetlights, and traffic signals as well as the excavations and trenches dug by private utility companies. State and federal Construction Inspectors inspect the construction and repair of roads, highways, freeways, bridges, tunnels, dams, and other structures.

Construction Inspectors check the quality and safety of the workmanship and the materials being used. For example, they may check delivery tickets to verify the quality of materials; calculate quantities of material used, such as concrete, to compare with bid estimates; observe materials being laid, fin-

ished, and compacted; check alignment of pipe and quality of joints; and test pavement thickness.

Construction Inspectors may reject any unsatisfactory materials. They also consult with site supervisors about any deviations from pre-approved plans and specifications. When code violations and other problems occur, Construction Inspectors notify contractors and explain what must be corrected. They make follow-up inspections to see that problems are corrected. If problems are not corrected within a specified period of time, inspectors may issue "stop work" orders.

Construction Inspectors keep well-detailed records and complete all necessary correspondence and reports. In addition, they keep up with changing construction codes and regulations as well as construction materials and technology.

Construction Inspectors perform other duties as required by their particular agencies. For example, they may conduct maintenance inspections, going on patrol to look for poor conditions in streets, sidewalks, driveways, traffic control devices and other items, and issue notices to appropriate agencies or homeowners to make necessary repairs.

Construction Inspectors typically work a 40-hour week. State and federal Construction Inspectors may be required to travel, including overnight trips, to various sites throughout their state or region.

Salaries

In 1997, the estimated annual salaries for Construction Inspectors ranged from $21,000 to $90,000, according to the Bureau of Labor Statistics (a division of the U.S. Department of Labor). Inspectors with more experience typically earn higher wages, as do those with greater job responsibilities (such as supervisory and administrative duties). Those who live in metropolitan areas and large cities where the cost of living is higher usually earn higher wages too.

Employment Prospects

Construction Inspectors work for city and county public works departments as well as for state transportation departments. Some work for federal agencies such as the U.S. Department of Transportation or the U.S. Army Corps of Engineers. Some also work with engineering and architectural firms that offer construction inspection services.

Job opportunities are expected to grow as fast as the average for all occupations through the year 2006. Most job openings will become available as Construction Inspectors retire or transfer to other jobs or positions. The creation of additional positions depends on a department's needs and budget.

Advancement Prospects

Construction Inspectors who have a combination of extensive work experience and college degrees have better chances for promotion. However, advancement opportunities are limited. Many Construction Inspectors pursue career growth by way of wage increases and complexity of new assignments. Some become private consultants.

Special Requirements

Applicants must fulfill qualifications, such as citizenship and residency, that an agency requires. Also, they must have appropriate state or local licenses or certifications from professional code organizations. (Trainees are usually given a time period within which to obtain certification.) In addition, most agencies require applicants to possess a valid driver's license.

Furthermore, applicants must pass an agency's selection process that may include any of the following: application, written exam, oral interview, medical examination, background investigation, and drug test.

Education and Training

Requirements vary with the different agencies. Applicants should have at least a high school or general equivalency diploma. Many agencies prefer applicants who have graduated from an apprenticeship program; have at least two years of study in engineering or architecture; or have an associate's degree with courses in construction technology, blueprint reading, mathematics, building inspection, or related subjects.

Construction Inspectors receive on-the-job training to learn local codes, ordinances, and regulations; contract specifications; inspection techniques; and recordkeeping and reporting duties.

Experience and Skills

Requirements vary from agency to agency. In general, applicants should have several years of work experience in public works, engineering inspections, or construction work along with experience performing supervisory or management duties.

Applicants must have adequate reading and math skills. They also must have excellent communication and writing abilities to clearly express and describe technical information. In addition, they should have problem-solving and management skills to handle various projects and tasks, as well as good interpersonal and teamwork skills.

Unions/Associations

Public Works Inspectors might belong to the International Conference of Building Officials, the Building Officials and Code Administrators International, Inc., or the Southern Building Code Congress International, Inc. Some might join the American Public Works Association. Joining professional organizations affords Construction Inspectors an opportunity for networking with peers and obtaining professional support and services, such as certified training, continuing education, technical information, and job resources.

Tips for Entry

1. For job information at the local government level, contact public works departments; and at the state level, contact transportation departments.
2. Sometimes state transportation departments hire Construction Inspectors as seasonal employees, usually from March to November.
3. Many agencies allow related education, such as an associate's degree in engineering technology, to be substituted for experience, on a year-by-year basis.
4. On the Internet, check out various public works or transportation departments. Enter either *public works department* or *state transportation department* in a search engine to get a list of web sites. To learn more about the U.S. Department of Transportation, go to *http://www.dot.gov/*.

WORKPLACE SAFETY AND SECURITY

INDUSTRIAL HYGIENIST

CAREER PROFILE

Duties: Examine work sites for occupational hazards and diseases; identify any risks and eliminate or control them

Alternate Titles: Industrial Hygiene Engineer; Environment, Safety, and Health Officer

Salary Range: $35,000 to $130,000 or higher

Employment Prospects: Fair

Advancement Prospects: Limited
   Prerequisites:
   Education—Bachelor's degree
   Experience—Varies with the different employers
   Special Skills—Problem-solving; teamwork and interpersonal skills; communication and writing abilities; computer skills

CAREER LADDER

```
┌─────────────────────────────────┐
│   Senior Industrial Hygienist    │
└─────────────────────────────────┘

┌─────────────────────────────────┐
│      Industrial Hygienist        │
└─────────────────────────────────┘

┌─────────────────────────────────┐
│   Industrial Hygienist Trainee   │
└─────────────────────────────────┘
```

Position Description

Industrial Hygienists examine and monitor work sites for potential hazards that may affect the health, comfort, or efficiency of employees. To identify potential hazards, Industrial Hygienists work closely with engineers, management officers, and employees. Potential hazards, for example, may include:

- exposure to lead, asbestos, pesticides, or other hazardous agents
- poor indoor air quality
- high noise levels
- radiation discharges
- work tasks that could lead to repetitive stress injuries, carpal tunnel syndrome, or other cumulative trauma disorders

In addition, Industrial Hygienists help employers comply with local, state, and federal safety, health, and environmental laws and regulations.

Industrial Hygienists use skills from chemistry, physiology, toxicology, physics, and engineering disciplines. Their work involves conducting scientific research to provide data on potentially harmful conditions. They might collect samples of suspected toxic materials such as dust, gases, and vapors to analyze in the laboratory. They might take relevant measurements—noise levels or measurements of carbon monoxide in the air, for example. They might also observe and interview workers.

Upon analyzing their findings, Industrial Hygienists then look for methods to eliminate or control potential hazards. For example, they might recommend that workers wear special protective clothing or equipment, such as goggles or respirators. When corrective measures are in effect, Industrial Hygienists monitor the programs to make sure that hazards have been eliminated or are under control.

As part of their work, Industrial Hygienists prepare comprehensive reports that include their observations, inspections, analyses of laboratory results and other findings. They are responsible for record keeping and maintaining medical monitoring programs in the workplace. They may also teach safety and health procedures to employees so as to reduce their risk of injuries and illnesses.

Some Industrial Hygienists also attend to safety and environmental duties. They might, for example, develop and administer safety and/or environmental programs and policies; perform safety inspections; conduct safety awareness training classes; coordinate the disposal of company waste; and monitor compliance with environmental laws and regulations.

Industrial Hygienists work 40 hours a week.

Salaries

According to the American Industrial Hygiene Association, entry-level Industrial Hygienists can earn between $35,000 and $40,000 per year. Middle-to high-level Industrial Hygienists can earn between $40,000 and $130,000 or more.

Employment Prospects

Industrial Hygienists are employed by manufacturing companies, chemical companies, government agencies, public utilities, hospitals, colleges and universities, and other businesses or organizations. They also work for safety consulting firms that provide industrial hygiene services.

Job opportunities for Industrial Hygienists are expected to be readily available with competition high for experienced positions. Currently, the fastest growing categories of this field are self-employed and consulting Industrial Hygienists. In addition, professionals predict that in the next few years:

- more Industrial Hygienists will be performing safety and environmental management responsibilities in addition to their technical duties
- more companies will hire consulting firms to perform industrial hygiene services

Advancement Prospects

Advancement opportunities are available for supervisory and management positions, but competition is high. Industrial Hygienists typically need extensive experience, advanced education, and professional certification (such as Certified Industrial Hygienist) for those positions.

Industrial Hygienists can pursue other options as consultants, compliance inspectors, researchers, and instructors or trainers. In addition, they may transfer their experience and skills to safety management, human resources, sales, and other areas.

Education and Training

Requirements vary with different employers. Most employers prefer applicants with a bachelor's degree in industrial hygiene, engineering, chemistry, biology, physical science, health, or other related field.

Industrial Hygienists must complete their employers' training programs, which may include both formal instruction and on-the-job training.

Experience and Skills

Requirements vary from employer to employer; many employers hire recent college graduates. In general, applicants should have knowledge of industrial hygiene concepts, principles, and practices as well as be familiar with the industry (such as manufacturing or public utilities) in which they would work. More and more employers prefer candidates who are knowledgeable of state and federal occupational safety and health regulations and who have experience in developing safety programs.

In addition, employers look for candidates who have excellent problem-solving skills as well as teamwork and interpersonal skills. Good candidates also have the communication and writing abilities to effectively explain technical terms and concepts in nontechnical language. Furthermore, candidates should be computer literate.

Unions/Associations

Among the many professional organizations that Industrial Hygienists might belong to are the National Safety Council and the American Industrial Hygiene Association. Joining professional organizations gives Industrial Hygienists the opportunity to network with peers and obtain professional support and services, such as certified training, continuing education, technical information, and job resources.

Tips for Entry

1. To learn about available part-time and full-time jobs or student internships, contact the human resource (or personnel) offices of companies where you would like to work.
2. To stay competitive in the job market, many professionals are earning environmental or safety degrees or both. Also, they are obtaining safety professional certification as they become eligible.
3. To learn about Industrial Hygienists on the Internet, visit the American Industrial Hygiene Association web site at *http://www.aiha.org/*. Or, enter the phrase *industrial hygiene* in a search engine to get a list of web sites to browse regarding associations, equipment, consulting firms, and other aspects of this field.

SAFETY MANAGER

CAREER PROFILE

Duties: Manage an organization's safety program and make sure it is in compliance with employer's policies as well as with relevant local, state, and federal laws

Alternate Titles: Safety Officer; Environmental Health and Safety Manager

Salary Range: $25,000 to $70,000

Employment Prospects: Good

Advancement Prospects: Limited
Prerequisites:
Education—Bachelor's degree
Experience—Varies from employer to employer
Special Skills—Supervisory, organizational, and problem-solving skills; teamwork and interpersonal skills; communication and writing abilities; computer skills

CAREER LADDER

```
┌─────────────────────────────────┐
│         Safety Director         │
└─────────────────────────────────┘

┌─────────────────────────────────┐
│         Safety Manager          │
└─────────────────────────────────┘

┌─────────────────────────────────┐
│  Safety Management Trainee or   │
│        Safety Assistant         │
└─────────────────────────────────┘
```

Position Description

Safety Managers oversee the occupational safety and health programs in industrial plants, corporations, universities, hospitals, government agencies, and other workplaces. They are responsible for instituting safety policies and procedures that maintain safe and healthy work environments.

While consulting department managers as well as employees, Safety Managers develop various safety plans. These include contingency plans for fires, gas spills, and other disasters as well as safety training programs for employees. Safety Managers are also responsible for alerting employees to the danger of working with hazardous substances such as toxic fumes or chemicals.

Another major duty is conducting safety inspections to detect existing or potential accident and health hazards. Safety Managers make sure work sites are in compliance with federal and state OSHA (Occupational Safety and Health Administration) regulations, local fire and public health regulations, and insurance industry requirements.

Upon finding actual or potential safety problems, Safety Managers take necessary action to resolve them. For example, they might direct staff Industrial Hygienists to examine the air quality at a work site to determine the potential danger to employees. In addition, Safety Managers supervise or conduct investigations of all safety accidents.

As representatives of their employers, Safety Managers are contact persons for OSHA and other regulatory agencies. Safety Managers also prepare studies of industrial accidents, causes, and hazards to health for public relation uses.

Some Safety Managers are responsible for environmental issues as well. For example, they may be in charge of disposing hazardous waste or conducting inspections to make sure the workplace is in compliance with federal, state, and local environmental laws and regulations.

Furthermore, Safety Managers attend to managerial tasks such as supervising safety staff, preparing budgets, and making purchases. They also complete and maintain paperwork, such as OSHA records, accident reports, permits, employee records and invoices.

Safety Managers usually work more than their regular 40-hour week to complete their responsibilities.

Salaries

Salaries vary, depending on size and type of employer, geographical location, job duties, and personal qualifications. For example, experienced Safety Managers who work for large companies can earn $70,000 or more per year.

According to the Board of Certified Safety Professionals, entry-level safety professionals with a bachelor's degree can earn between $25,000 to $35,000 per year. Those in the middle of their careers can earn between $50,000 to $70,000 per year.

Employment Prospects

Safety Managers work in many different industries such as manufacturing, construction, utilities, transportation, insurance, government, education, nonprofit agencies, and health care. The job outlook for safety professionals is expected to remain stable into the future.

Advancement Prospects

Safety Managers can advance to administrative positions, such as safety directors. Many Safety Managers change jobs or locations to move up to Safety Manager positions with higher pay or more challenging responsibilities.

Another career move for Safety Managers is to become private consultants or start their own businesses providing safety management services.

Education and Training

Requirements vary from employer to employer. More and more employers prefer applicants with a bachelor's degree in safety management, industrial hygiene, engineering, physical science, or other related field. Some employers accept applicants with business degrees if they have the required experience. In addition, more and more employers are requiring professional certification such as the Certified Safety Professional (CSP) designation.

Employers may require their Safety Managers to attend training seminars and continuing education classes in order to stay current with changing technologies as well as with safety and health laws and regulations.

Experience and Skills

Requirements vary with the different employers. Applicants may need as few as two years of occupational safety and health experience or as many as eight or more years. Typically, applicants must have knowledge of the daily business operations of the industry—healthcare, transportation, construction—in which they would be working. Also, they must be knowledgeable of occupational safety and health laws and regulations.

Employers look for candidates who have strong supervisory, organizational, and problem-solving abilities. In addition, candidates must have excellent teamwork and interpersonal skills along with superior communication and writing abilities.

Having computer skills, including the use of word-processing, spreadsheets, and graphic presentation programs, is also essential.

Unions/Associations

Safety Managers might join professional organizations such as the American Society of Safety Engineers, the National Safety Council, the System Safety Society, or the American Industrial Hygiene Association. Joining professional organizations provides Safety Managers an opportunity for networking with peers and obtaining professional support and services, such as certified training, continuing, education, technical information, and job resources.

Tips for Entry

1. Join professional organizations and network with other safety professionals to learn of jobs that are currently open or may be available soon.

2. Many safety professionals have backgrounds or advanced study in business administration, education, engineering, physical sciences, social sciences, or other fields to enhance their employability and chance for promotions.

3. As a college student, develop a portfolio to document your course work, internships, work experience, and related extracurricular activities. You can then submit copies of your portfolio with your applications for employment or graduate schools.

4. To learn more about occupational safety issues on the Internet, visit the National Safety Council web site at *http://www.nsc.org/*.

LOSS CONTROL REPRESENTATIVE

CAREER PROFILE

Duties: Help insurance clients develop effective safety plans; identify hazards in clients' workplace that may lead to the loss of lives, property, money, and other assets; make recommendations for reducing risks

Alternate Title: Loss Control Specialist

Salary Range: $20,000 to $70,000 and over

Employment Prospects: Good

Advancement Prospects: Limited
Prerequisites:
Education—Bachelor's degree
Experience—One to three years of safety experience; knowledge of industries (transportation, construction, healthcare, etc.) in which an individual would be working
Special Skills—Problem-solving, negotiation, and organizational skills; communication, writing, and presentation abilities; computer skills

CAREER LADDER

```
┌─────────────────────────────────────────┐
│   Senior Loss Control Representative     │
└─────────────────────────────────────────┘

┌─────────────────────────────────────────┐
│      Loss Control Representative         │
└─────────────────────────────────────────┘

┌─────────────────────────────────────────┐
│         Loss Control Trainee             │
└─────────────────────────────────────────┘
```

Position Description

Loss Control Representatives work for insurance companies. Like safety officers, Loss Control Representatives help businesses and organizations develop effective safety plans. Their job is to evaluate the workplaces of insurance clients and identify hazards that may lead to the loss of lives, property, money, and other assets. In addition, Loss Control Representatives gather information for insurance underwriters who will use the data to determine the price of insurance policies for new insurance clients.

While managing caseloads, Loss Control Representatives make regular inspections of their clients' work sites. They must keep up with changes in all local, state, and federal regulations and laws that affect their clients' businesses. Loss Control Representatives also conduct investigations of any sizable losses suffered by their clients.

To determine the quality and effectiveness of their clients' safety programs, Loss Control Representatives perform various tasks. For example, during inspection visits, they might:

- review safety policies and procedures
- survey the facilities and equipment (for example, checking for fire hazards, obstructions blocking emergency exits, noncompliant storage of toxic chemicals, defective equipment, or broken electrical ground wires)
- observe the workers to evaluate their safety habits (such as using tools properly or wearing proper safety protection)
- audit past losses
- review safety inspection programs or accident investigation procedures
- examine records of state or federal Occupational Safety and Health Administration (OSHA) audits

When Loss Control Representatives find real or potential hazards, they make recommendations for reducing risks. These include mandatory recommendations that clients must correct in order to be in compliance with insurance companies' requirements or OSHA laws and regulations. Loss Control Representatives prepare reports of their findings and recommendations. They submit the reports to their clients as well as hold meetings to discuss them.

Loss Control Representatives may travel throughout their state or region to visit clients. Overnight travel is often required. Furthermore, Loss Control Representatives may be reassigned to other locations throughout their career with an employer.

Salaries

Salaries vary with different employers. Salaries also depend on employees' education, experience, and job duties.

Wages are typically higher in large metropolitan areas where the cost of living is higher.

The American Society of Safety Engineers reports that in 1997, the average salary of their membership, which includes Loss Prevention Representatives, was $54,000 per year. Entry-level Loss Prevention Representatives earn a salary in the low $20,000 range while managers and directors earn over $70,000.

Employment Prospects

Most Loss Control Representatives are employed by insurance companies; many are employed by manufacturers and government agencies as well. Many also work for consulting firms that offer loss control services as part of their occupational safety and health services.

The job outlook for Loss Control Representatives is considered to be good into the future. Experienced Loss Control Representatives can expect to find available job opportunities.

Advancement Prospects

Loss Control Representatives can pursue managerial and administrative positions as Loss Control Managers and Loss Control Directors. Typically, the larger a company is, the greater opportunity there is for advancement.

Furthermore, Loss Control Representatives may use their loss control experiences to move into other areas of insurance such as sales, human resources, underwriting, and risk management.

Education and Training

Requirements differ from employer to employer. Employers generally look for applicants with a bachelor's degree in occupational safety and health, fire science, industrial hygiene, engineering, physical science, business, or other related fields.

Loss Control trainees must complete training programs, which vary with different employers. Some employers provide formal training to develop technical and business skills in addition to on-the-job training under the supervision of senior Loss Control Representatives.

Experience and Skills

Requirements vary from employer to employer. Most employers prefer candidates who have at least one to three years of safety experience that includes planning and implementing safety and loss prevention programs. Larger companies sometimes hire recent college graduates without any previous work experience in loss control.

In addition, applicants should have knowledge of the industries (transportation, food industry, security firms, construction, agriculture, healthcare) in which they would be making loss control assessments. And, applicants should be familiar with the practical realities of running daily business operations.

Employers look for self-disciplined candidates who require little supervision and who demonstrate that they have problem-solving, negotiation, and organizational skills along with communication, writing, and presentation (or public-speaking) abilities. Also important is having computer skills that include using wordprocessing, spreadsheets, and graphic presentation software.

Unions/Associations

Loss Control Representatives might belong to professional safety organizations such as the System Safety Society and the American Society of Safety Engineers. In addition, they might join professional groups such as the Risk and Insurance Management Society, Inc., Public Risk Management Association, and National Fire Protection Association. Joining professional organizations gives Loss Control Representatives the opportunity to network with peers and obtain professional support and services, such as certified training, continuing education, technical information, and job resources.

Tips for Entry

1. Many insurance companies attend job fairs at colleges and universities to recruit applicants as well as to provide career information. Contact nearby colleges and universities to learn about upcoming job fairs.

2. To enhance your employability and advancement opportunities, obtain professional certification when you become eligible—such as Certified Safety Professional (CSP), Associate in Risk Management (ARM), or Associate in Loss Control Management (ALCM).

3. Many insurance companies have web sites on the Internet with specific information about loss control services. To get a list of web sites to browse, enter the phrase *loss control services* in a search engine.

SECURITY CONSULTANT

CAREER PROFILE

Duties: Provide expert advice in designing effective security programs to protect clients' assets—lives, property, data, and so forth—against fire, theft, vandalism, threats, workplace violence, and other criminal acts

Alternate Titles: Security Management Consultant; Security Engineer; Technical Security Consultant

Salary Range: less than $50,000 to $200,000

Employment Prospects: Excellent

Advancement Prospects: Limited
  Prerequisites:
  Education—No standard requirements
  Experience—Security and/or law enforcement experience
  Special Skills—Security management skills; organizational and interpersonal skills; communication and writing skills; ability to run a business

CAREER LADDER

```
┌─────────────────────────────────┐
│      Security Consultant        │
└─────────────────────────────────┘

┌─────────────────────────────────┐
│  Staff positions with security  │
│     firms, security             │
│     departments, or             │
│     law enforcement agencies    │
└─────────────────────────────────┘
```

Position Description

Security Consultants are self-employed specialists in physical security, personnel security, computer security, retail security, and other types of security. They offer their particular expertise to clients—businesses, corporations, and institutions—for a fee. They help clients develop effective security measures to protect lives, property, data, and other assets against arson, theft, vandalism, threats, workplace violence, and other criminal acts.

Security Consultants specialize in one or more industries such as: financial, telecommunications, retail, warehousing, hospitality, entertainment, healthcare, pharmaceutical, education, utilities, transportation, construction, or manufacturing. Clients hire them to perform specific services; for example, Security Consultants might be hired to:

- perform security surveys and audits to evaluate existing security systems
- perform risk and threat assessments to find potential areas of loss within the business and recommend security countermeasures
- develop overall security policies and procedures
- develop response plans against workplace violence and against various criminal actions such as armed robbery, extortion, kidnapping, arson, and bombings

- oversee the installation of security systems (Note: Security Consultants are not connected in any way with firms that sell security equipment or services.)
- design security awareness training programs that teach employees how to incorporate security policies and procedures on their jobs
- provide executive protection (bodyguard services to executives)
- provide expert witness testimony in lawsuits that involve security personnel, technology, or other matters

One service Security Consultants do not provide is investigation work, as that is a different activity from security consulting, according to the International Association of Professional Security Consultants.

Security Consultants gather all information that is relevant to their projects. They might observe daily operations; discuss security procedures and policies with appropriate staff members; review relevant records, documents, and other materials; test security systems; and so on. Upon studying and analyzing all information, Security Consultants design plans that fit their clients' goals and objectives as well as budgets.

The work of Security Consultants involves meeting deadlines and providing clients with both oral and written progress reports. In addition, they prepare final reports that detail their findings and recommendations. Supporting documents are also included with these reports. Security Consultants usually make oral presentations of these comprehensive reports as well.

Security Consultants usually handle several projects at the same time. While working at their own offices as well as at their clients' offices, Security Consultants create their own work schedules.

Along with their consultation work, Security Consultants oversee daily business operations. For example, they may supervise support staffs, do accounts, invoice clients, pay bills, and do routine office work.

Salaries

Security Consultants charge an hourly fee that varies from $50 to $300 or more per hour. They may also charge a flat fee per project.

Annual earnings depend on their location and the size and type of projects as well as the consultant's experience and ambition. Experienced consultants may earn $50,000 to $100,000 or more per year; and it is not uncommon for top-notch Security Consultants to earn more than $200,000 per year.

Employment Prospects

Security Consultants are sole proprietors of their own businesses. They are contracted by businesses, corporations, institutions, government agencies, and private individuals for their consulting services.

Security is one of the fastest-growing fields worldwide due to the increased concern about workplace violence, theft, terrorism, and white-collar crime. Job opportunities within all levels of the security industry, including Security Consultants, are expected to increase favorably through 2006.

Advancement Prospects

Security Consultants might seek further career growth by way of increased business income, complexity of new projects, or expansion of their businesses.

Education and Training

There are no standard education requirements for Security Consultants. However, clients prefer hiring Security Consultants who have a college degree as well as professional certifications, such as Certified Protection Professional.

Experience and Skills

Security Consultants typically have had many years of experience in security, having held manager and director positions for several years. Many Security Consultants also have law enforcement backgrounds, having worked for local, state, or federal agencies.

Successful Security Consultants have excellent security management skills as well as organizational and interpersonal skills. They also have superior communication and writing skills, such as the ability to present technical terms and concepts in nontechnical vocabulary. In addition, Security Consultants must have the necessary skills to run a successful business.

Unions/Associations

Organizations that Security Consultants might belong to are: the International Association of Professional Security Consultants and the American Society for Industrial Security. Joining professional organizations gives Security Consultants the opportunity to network with peers and obtain professional support and services, such as certified training, continuing education, technical information, and job resources.

Tips for Entry

1. Security Consultants often obtain new clients through recommendations from other consultants and specialists in security.

2. Having published professional articles and books demonstrates to many clients a Security Consultant's expertise in current security technology and issues.

3. To learn more about the security consulting field, visit the International Association of Professional Security Consultants web site on the Internet. Its web address is *http://www.iapsc.org/.* In addition, many Security Consultants have web sites on the Internet. To get a list to browse, enter the phrase *security consultant* or *security management consulting* in a search engine.

AVIATION SAFETY
AND SECURITY

AIR TRAFFIC CONTROLLER

CAREER PROFILE

Duties: Make sure air traffic is flowing safely, orderly, and smoothly; give pilots permission and instruction for aircraft taxiing, takeoffs, and landings; monitor aircraft in flight

Alternate Titles: Air Traffic Specialist; Air Traffic Service Provider; Flight-Service-Station Controllers are also known as Flight Service Specialists

Salary Range: $26,000 to $90,000

Employment Prospects: Limited

Advancement Prospects: Limited
Prerequisites:
Special Requirements—Must be a U.S. citizen; be less than 31 years old for airport tower or en route center positions; pass a selection process
Education—Bachelor's degree: FAA Academy
Experience—Three years experience without college degree; pilot, navigator, or military air traffic controller experience preferred
Special Skills—Concentration and memory skills; teamwork and interpersonal skills; communication and problem-solving skills

CAREER LADDER

```
┌─────────────────────────────────────┐
│   Air Traffic Control Supervisor     │
└─────────────────────────────────────┘

┌─────────────────────────────────────┐
│      Air Traffic Controller          │
└─────────────────────────────────────┘

┌─────────────────────────────────────┐
│    Air Traffic Control Trainee       │
└─────────────────────────────────────┘
```

Position Description

Air Traffic Controllers manage several aircraft at the same time, constantly communicating with pilots and with each other to make sure air traffic is flowing safely and smoothly. They also give pilots permission and instruction for takeoffs and landings. Air Traffic Controllers monitor aircraft in flight with radar and provide pilots with weather, navigational sites, air traffic, and other important information.

Air Traffic Controllers work in three types of facilities. At *terminal facilities,* they work in air towers or in radar-approach centers, which are usually housed within air towers. They separate aircraft as they arrive or depart from an airport and as they taxi on the ground. Air Traffic Controllers manage air traffic below 17,000 feet and within a radius of 3 to 30 miles of an airport. Tower controllers may also manage air traffic at smaller airports that fall within their airspace.

Air Traffic Controllers at *en route* (or air route) *control centers* manage aircraft that fly through their airspace, which might cover a radius of 200 miles, for example. The airspace is divided into sections and assigned to units of two or three

Air Traffic Controllers who monitor aircraft as they pass through their assigned airspace. They give pilots air traffic clearance and instructions as well as advise about flight conditions in their particular jurisdiction.

At *automated flight service stations,* Air Traffic Controllers provide pilots with preflight, in-flight, and emergency help. These Air Traffic Controllers are experts on the terrain, airports, and navigational sites in their jurisdiction.

Many different Air Traffic Controllers guide and monitor aircraft from takeoff to landing. For example: Imagine that a jet is ready to depart. A tower controller assigns the jet a runway, and—watching it from the tower—guides it from the gate to the runway. Another controller relays information about weather, speed and direction of wind, and visibility to the pilots as well as gives permission for the jet to depart when all is clear. A radar-approach controller guides the pilot out of the airport's airspace and notifies the appropriate en route control center as the jet enters its airspace.

Each time the jet enters a different airspace, a new en route controller monitors the jet and gives pertinent information to the pilots. For example, if the jet is scheduled to arrive at the same time, location, and altitude as another aircraft in the next airspace, the controller instructs the pilots on how to change course. Flight service station traffic controllers also keep contact with the pilots, and keep them up to date with conditions, such as wind turbulence, that may affect flight.

As the jet approaches its destination, a pilot radios the terminal, and a radar-approach controller assigns the pilot a runway and gives landing clearance. That controller (or another controller) guides the jet the last few miles to the runway. When the jet nears the runway, the pilot communicates with tower controllers who delay any departures that might interfere with the jet's landing. Once landed, the jet is guided to its assigned gate by a tower controller using only his or her sight. (Radar is used when visibility is poor.)

Air Traffic Controllers work 40-hour weeks, often working four-hour stretches without a break. At larger airports, controllers often put in many hours of overtime and sometimes work six-day shifts.

Salaries

Air Traffic Controllers receive a salary based on a pay schedule called *General Schedule*. The pay schedule starts at the GS-1 grade and goes up to the GS-15 grade, with each grade having ten steps. Air Traffic Controllers start at the GS-7 grade ($26,000 to $33,000 per year).

In 1997, most Air Traffic Controllers earned an annual salary between $40,000 and $90,000, according to the Bureau of Labor Statistics (a division of the U.S. Department of Labor). Those who live in metropolitan areas and large cities where the cost of living is higher usually earn higher wages too.

Employment Prospects

The majority of civilian Air Traffic Controllers in the United States work for the Federal Aviation Administration (FAA), part of the U.S. Department of Transportation. Some civilian controllers work for the U.S. Department of Defense or for non-FAA airports.

There are a limited number of positions and the creation of more openings depends on FAA needs and the availability of funds. Job turnover is low, and Air Traffic Controllers are seldom laid off.

Advancement Prospects

Supervisory and management positions are available, but limited. Many Air Traffic Controllers pursue career growth by way of wage increases and increased responsibilities. Air Traffic Controllers might also pursue research, instructor, or administrative positions with the FAA.

Special Requirements

Applicants must be U.S. citizens; those applying for airport tower or en route center positions must be less than 31 years old.

Applicants must also pass every step of the FAA's selection process, which includes the following: job application, written test, oral interview, aptitude tests, physical exam, drug test, psychological exam, and background investigation.

Each year, Air Traffic Controllers must pass a physical exam as well as a job performance examination, which is given twice a year. Furthermore, they must retire when they become 56 years old.

Education and Training

Entry-level applicants need bachelor's degrees, preferably in air traffic control, airport science, or airport management. The FAA also accepts applicants with a combination of education and work experience.

Recruits must complete seven months of training at the FAA Academy in Oklahoma City, where they study FAA regulations, the airway system, controller equipment, and other basics. Upon completion of the program, they are assigned to a facility and complete on-the-job training under a senior officer as well as participate in further classroom instruction and independent study. (It takes several years before recruits become full-fledged Air Traffic Controllers.)

Experience and Skills

Without a bachelor's degree, entry-level applicants must have three years of experience showing that they are capable of becoming Air Traffic Controllers, or have previous experience as pilots, navigators, or military Air Traffic Controllers.

The FAA looks for applicants who are alert and precise with excellent concentration and memory skills. They must also have excellent teamwork and interpersonal skills as well as superior communication abilities. In addition, they should have problem-solving skills and the ability to make wise decisions quickly and effectively.

Unions/Associations

Air Traffic Controllers might belong to the National Air Traffic Controllers Association, a labor union. Flight-service-station air controllers might belong to the National Association of Air Traffic Specialists, also a labor union.

Tips for Entry

1. To learn about job openings, contact a U.S. Office of Personnel Management (OPM) office, which may be listed under the U.S. government pages in your telephone book. Or visit the OPM web site *(http://www.usajobs.opm.gov)* on the Internet.
2. Visit the different air traffic control facilities and see which environment might suit you best.

3. Learn computer skills. Most, if not all, facilities will have automation technology in place by the year 2005.

4. Many air traffic control towers have web sites on the Internet. To get a list of web sites to browse, enter the phrase *air traffic control tower* in a search engine.

AIRCRAFT DISPATCHER

CAREER PROFILE

Duties: Manage daily airline flight operations, including the preparation of flight plans and the monitoring of flights in progress; be jointly responsible with airline captains for flight safety and operations.

Alternate Title: Airline Dispatcher

Salary Range: $18,000 to $80,000 or more

Employment Prospects: Excellent

Advancement Prospects: Fair
  Prerequisites:
  Special Requirements—FAA Aircraft Dispatcher certificate
  Education—High school diploma
  Experience—Varies with the different airlines
  Special Skills—Decision-making and communication skills; teamwork and interpersonal skills; organizational and self-management skills

CAREER LADDER

```
┌─────────────────────────────────────┐
│     Aircraft Dispatcher Supervisor   │
└─────────────────────────────────────┘

┌─────────────────────────────────────┐
│         Aircraft Dispatcher          │
└─────────────────────────────────────┘

┌─────────────────────────────────────┐
│     Aircraft Trainee or Assistant    │
│         Aircraft Dispatcher          │
└─────────────────────────────────────┘
```

Position Description

Aircraft Dispatchers are licensed by the Federal Aviation Administration (FAA) to manage daily flight operations. They are hired by the various airlines, which may have regional, nationwide, or international flights. They have joint responsibility with airline captains for flight safety and operations, and are often described as the "captains (or pilots) on the ground."

Unlike captains, Aircraft Dispatchers are responsible for many flights at the same time, working from airline dispatch centers, or system operation control centers. These dispatch centers are usually located at airlines' main headquarters.

Aircraft Dispatchers prepare flight plans, complying with airline regulations as well as FAA and international laws. They also pay attention to safety and economic aspects. When selecting flight routes, they weigh factors such as weather, altitudes, and air traffic flow. As part of their planning process, Aircraft Dispatchers also compute the amount of fuel needed to complete the flight while considering various factors such as the type of aircraft, distance of flight, weather, and any maintenance limitations that an aircraft might have.

Aircraft Dispatchers also prepare the dispatch release form, a legal document that gives authorization for a flight to depart. This document must be co-signed by captains and Aircraft Dispatchers. If Aircraft Dispatchers think conditions may threaten the safety of a flight, they will delay or cancel it.

In addition, Aircraft Dispatchers are responsible for monitoring the progress of each flight under their control and for monitoring weather, aircraft position reports, and aeronautical navigation charts. They provide captains with updates of conditions that may affect the successful completion of their flights. For example, they warn captains of sudden changes in weather, air traffic, or airport field conditions. When necessary, Aircraft Dispatchers recommend changes in the flight plans—such as changing altitudes or landing at different airports—for safety and economic reasons. Furthermore, Aircraft Dispatchers assist in any flight emergencies.

As liaisons between flight crews and ground service operations, Aircraft Dispatchers prepare and distribute flight information to other employees, including those working at reservation desks and gate stations. Their data is usually the source for all information that is provided to the traveling public.

In order to perform their tasks, Aircraft Dispatchers must be knowledgeable in many different areas. For example, they must be familiar with all airports and airline routes; the different types of aircraft operated by their airlines, including takeoff, cruising, and landing characteristics; meteorology;

air traffic control procedures; and instrument flight procedures.

Aircraft Dispatchers keep up with changing technologies, company policies, and FAA regulations by participating in regular training sessions as well as continuing education programs and self-study. In addition, the FAA requires Aircraft Dispatchers to ride in the cockpit with flight crews at least five hours each year to observe flight routes, working conditions.

Dispatch centers operate on a 24-hour basis; thus, Aircraft Dispatchers work rotating shifts that include weekends and holidays. They may also work overtime.

Salaries

Salaries vary with different airlines. Major airlines usually pay more than smaller regional airlines. In general, entry-level Aircraft Dispatchers can expect to start with a salary between $18,000 and $27,000 per year. Experienced Aircraft Dispatchers at major airlines can earn a salary of $70,000 to $80,000 or more per year. Aircraft Dispatchers can earn additional pay by working overtime.

Employment Prospects

Aircraft Dispatchers work for regional, national, and international airlines as well as for large freight carriers such as United Parcel Service and Federal Express.

The job market is currently strong and expected to remain strong in the future. Much of this is due to the fact that since 1997, all Aircraft Dispatchers must have FAA certification. In addition, the turnover in jobs is high, especially with the smaller regional airlines.

Advancement Prospects

Supervisory and management positions, which vary from airline to airline, are available. Many Aircraft Dispatchers pursue career growth by way of wage increases and additional responsibilities that often involve changing jobs or locations.

Special Requirements

Applicants must posses the FAA aircraft dispatcher certificate. Applicants for this certificate must be at least 23 years old and fulfill one of these other requirements before applying for the certification:

- two years of experience in scheduled air carrier or military aviation operations, or in other aircraft operations such as a flight pilot, flight radio operator, flight navigator, or meteorologist
- two years of experience as an air route traffic controller or certified air traffic control tower operator
- one year of experience as an assistant Aircraft Dispatcher

- completion of an Aircraft Dispatcher training program from an FAA-approved school

Education and Training

Applicants must have a high school or general equivalency diploma; however, more and more airlines are requiring college degrees.

Trainees must complete airline training programs that include company orientation and formal flight dispatcher training. Trainees then receive on-the-job training under the supervision of senior Aircraft Dispatchers. Field training may last several weeks or months or even over a year, depending on the airline.

Experience and Skills

Requirements vary with different airlines. Many airlines hire applicants who have no prior dispatch work experience but have completed FAA-approved training programs and hold FAA certification.

Airlines look for candidates who can think clearly and quickly with the ability to make sound decisions that affect many people's lives. Candidates should have excellent communication skills. In addition, they should have teamwork and interpersonal skills as well as the ability to get to work on time, follow directions, take initiative, work safely and work calmly under pressure.

Unions/Associations

The Airline Dispatchers Federation is a professional organization that many Aircraft Dispatchers join. It offers opportunities for networking with peers, educational programs, job resources, and other professional services and support.

Tips for Entry

1. After submitting job applications, contact personnel offices on a regular basis by phone or mail to let them know you are still available. Many Flight Dispatchers have been hired because they contacted an airline at a time when an opening just became available.
2. Individuals who are at least 21 years old and are eligible for the FAA Aircraft Dispatcher certificate can take the test. If they pass, they will be issued a Letter of Aeronautical Competency and receive the Aircraft Dispatcher certificate upon reaching their 23rd birthday.
3. To learn more about Aircraft Dispatchers, visit the Airline Dispatchers Federation web site on the Internet. Its web address is *http://www.dispatcher.org/*.

AIRPORT FIREFIGHTER

CAREER PROFILE

Duties: Respond to all aircraft emergencies; rescue passengers and crews; put out all fires at airports; provide emergency medical care services

Salary Range: $12,000 to $50,000

Employment Prospects: Limited

Advancement Prospects: Good
Prerequisites:
Special Requirements—Meet department qualifications
Education—High school diploma; FAA-approved training program
Experience—Previous firefighting experience
Special Skills—Teamwork and interpersonal skills; communication, reading, and writing abilities

CAREER LADDER

```
┌─────────────────────────────────┐
│          Lieutenant             │
└─────────────────────────────────┘

┌─────────────────────────────────┐
│       Airport Firefighter       │
└─────────────────────────────────┘

┌─────────────────────────────────┐
│   Airport Firefighter Trainee   │
└─────────────────────────────────┘
```

Position Description

Airport Firefighters are specially trained to provide aircraft rescue and firefighting services. They respond to all aircraft emergencies, rescuing crew and passengers, and putting out aircraft fires. They also provide fire protection for all airport facilities including terminal buildings, parking lots, aircraft hangars and ramps, maintenance shops, fuel farms, runways, and taxiways. And they provide emergency medical services and public assistance to airport employees, tenants, passengers, and visitors. They may respond to calls within an immediate radius of the airports. Some Airport Firefighters are also certified peace officers who perform police duties at the airport.

Fire stations are located at airports, near runways, and are equipped with special heavy-duty and complex aircraft rescue and firefighting vehicles and equipment. Firefighters are required to reach aircraft emergencies within a few minutes. As they cross runways to reach an emergency, they are alert to incoming and outgoing flights. In addition, they are in communication with the airport control tower, the local fire dispatcher, and, at some airports, with the National Guard.

Airport Firefighters perform a different strategy than that of structural or building firefighting. Their first priority is to rescue the passengers and crew, who will be suffering from traumatic injuries and burns, and may need to be extricated from the aircraft. Airport Firefighters must work quickly, as aviation fuels burn at temperatures between 3,000 and 4,000 degrees Fahrenheit, and the aircraft cabin can reach unbearable temperatures within minutes.

They fight only that part of the fire that interferes with the rescue to allow more time for the rescue. For example, they might spray the outside of the fuselage with overflowing streams of foam or water to draw off heat from the inside of the aircraft. Once a rescue is completed, Airport Firefighters then redirect their energies to suppressing the fire.

Firefighters perform other duties that may include:

* conducting routine fire inspections of fuel farms, hangars, and other airport property
* teaching fire safety training classes to airport and airline employees
* participating in routine drills and training sessions
* performing routine inspections and maintenance of all rescue and firefighting vehicles and equipment
* maintaining fire stations and grounds
* performing desk watch duty

Aircraft rescue and firefighting work is hard and dangerous. Airport Firefighters are exposed to high noise levels, extreme heat, toxic chemicals (such as nitrogen dioxide and carbon monoxide), and hazardous materials. They often lift and carry persons or objects weighing over 100 pounds.

Airport Firefighters live and work at their fire stations during their duty tours, which vary from department to department.

Salaries

Salaries vary greatly, depending on factors such as experience and the size of the department's jurisdiction. Airport Firefighters typically receive overtime pay and uniform allowances. The International Association of Fire Fighters reports that the average annual salary for Firefighters in 1996 was $38,000 for a 56-hour workweek. According to the Bureau of Labor Statistics (a division of the U.S. Department of Labor), most Firefighters earned annual salaries between $12,000 and $50,000 in 1997.

Employment Prospects

Most Airport Firefighters work for local or state fire departments. Some work for private firms that offer aircraft rescue and firefighting services.

Job openings for firefighters, including Airport Firefighters, are expected to increase more slowly than the average for all occupations through the year 2006. Most job openings will become available as personnel retire or transfer to other positions. The turnover rate for Airport Firefighter positions is low, and the competition for available positions is high.

Advancement Prospects

Advancement through the ranks—engineer, lieutenant, captain, battalion chief, assistant chief, deputy chief, and chief—is based on competitive exams, job performance, interviews, and seniority. With further training, Airport Firefighters can apply for specialized positions such as fire equipment drivers/operators or firefighter/paramedics. They might pursue other firefighting careers such as fire inspectors, fire investigators, or fire protection engineers.

Special Requirements

Every fire department has specific age, residency, medical, and other qualifications that applicants must fulfill. Applicants may be required to hold firefighting and emergency medical technician certifications as well as a valid driver's license.

Education and Training

Fire departments require a high school or general equivalency diploma. Some departments require additional college work or college degrees, preferably in fire science or other related field.

Recruits must complete Federal Aviation Administration (FAA) approved training programs. Among the subjects that trainees study are airport operations; aircraft construction and equipment; personnel safety; airport emergency plans; use of aircraft rescue and firefighting equipment and appliances; and emergency aircraft evacuation.

Furthermore, all Airport Firefighters are required to complete a live-fire drill at least once a year. This drill includes a pit fire with an aircraft mock-up to simulate the type of aircraft fire they may encounter.

Experience and Skills

Requirements vary from department to department. For example, some departments hire only applicants who have aircraft rescue and firefighting experience. In general, applicants should have previous firefighting and rescue technician experience.

Fire departments typically choose dependable candidates who can stay calm and have the strength and agility to work under harsh and stressful conditions for long periods of time. The best candidates have excellent teamwork and interpersonal skills. In addition, they have superior communication skills as well as good reading and writing abilities.

Unions/Associations

Airport Firefighters can join the International Association of Fire Fighters, a union, as well as local and state professional Firefighter associations. In addition, they might join the Aircraft Rescue and Fire Fighting Working Group, an organization specifically for Airport Firefighters. Many also join the National Fire Protection Association. Joining such organizations allows Firefighters the opportunity to network with peers and obtain certification, continuing education, job listings, and other professional services and support.

Tips for Entry

1. Improve your chances of getting a job at the fire departments where you would like to work by being able to fill all required—as well as desired—job qualifications. For example, if having paramedic certification or particular technical rescue (confined space rescue, high level rescue) certification is a high priority, then obtain the necessary certification.

2. As a firefighter, let the commander of the aircraft rescue and firefighting unit know of your interest even if positions are not currently available.

3. To learn more about Airport Firefighters on the Internet, enter the phrase *aircraft rescue and firefighting* to get a list of relevant web sites to browse. Or, visit the Aircraft Rescue and Fire Fighting Working Group at *http://www.arffwg.org/*.

AIRPORT POLICE OFFICER

CAREER PROFILE

Duties: Enforce local and state laws, preserve the peace, protect life and property, and provide public service at airports; provide security to airports; enforce FAA regulations

Alternate Titles: Airport Safety Officer; Airport Public Safety Officer

Salary Range: $19,200 to $64,500

Employment Prospects: Good

Advancement Prospects: Excellent
Prerequisites:

Special Requirements—Must be a U.S. citizen; have a driver's license; have no criminal record; meet department qualifications; pass a selection process
Education—High school diploma; police academy training, airport security training
Experience—Previous law enforcement experience preferred
Special Skills—Observational and problem-solving skills; teamwork and interpersonal skills; communication, reading, and writing abilities

CAREER LADDER

```
┌──────────────────────────────────┐
│  Special Assignments, Detective,  │
│         or Sergeant               │
└──────────────────────────────────┘

┌──────────────────────────────────┐
│      Airport Police Officer       │
└──────────────────────────────────┘

┌──────────────────────────────────┐
│   Airport Police Officer Trainee  │
└──────────────────────────────────┘
```

Position Description

Airport Police Officers enforce state and local laws at airports as well as preserve the peace, protect life and property, and provide public service. In addition, they are responsible for airport security, enforcing airport security policies and procedures that are in accordance with Federal Aviation Administration (FAA) regulations.

As uniformed officers, Airport Police Officers carry firearms and have the authority to issue warnings and citations and make arrests. Their work involves patrolling assigned areas (terminal buildings, parking lots, runways, and grounds), and keeping an eye out for theft, trespassing, vandalism, and all other criminal activity. They make their rounds by foot, in patrol vehicles, or on bicycles.

Airport Police Officers also receive dispatches to help airport employees, tenants, travelers, and the general public. Airport Police Officers investigate trouble such as shoplifting, theft, assault, rape, or other criminal activity, and look into problems such as lost items or missing persons. They also respond to emergency situations such as vehicle accidents,

heart attacks, or childbirth, and provide first aid, CPR (cardiovascular pulmonary resuscitation), or other emergency medical care that they are certified to perform.

Other tasks Airport Police Officers perform are:

- screen passengers for guns, bombs, and other contraband
- coordinate police efforts for special events (such as the arrival of visiting dignitaries) that require heightened security
- enforce traffic laws in the airport
- provide traffic control in and out of airports and on nearby highways during emergencies or special events
- provide general information about airport facilities to travelers and the general public

At some airports, Airport Police Officers are part of departments that oversee all law enforcement, aircraft rescue and firefighting, and emergency medical care activities. These officers are cross-trained to provide all these services on their work shifts.

Furthermore, Airport Police Officers cooperate with other local and state law enforcement agencies as well as federal agencies (such as the FBI, the Drug Enforcement Administration, the U.S. Secret Service, the U.S. Customs, and the Immigration and Naturalization Service) on various activities such as narcotics surveillance or antiterrorism programs.

As part of their duties, Airport Police Officers keep a daily field notebook on their activities as well as complete accidents and incidents reports. All logs and reports must be accurate and detailed, as they become permanent public records that can be placed as evidence in trials.

Airport Police Officers work rotating shifts that include nights, weekends, and holidays. Officers who also perform aircraft rescue and firefighting duty work a shift that schedules those duties.

Salaries

Salaries vary from department to department. In 1996, the annual salary for police officers, including Airport Police Officers, ranged from as low as $19,200 to as high as $64,500. Police officers with supervisory duties typically earn more than those with nonsupervisory duties. Also, Police Officers who work in metropolitan areas—such as New York, Miami, Chicago, Dallas, Los Angeles, and Seattle—generally earn higher wages. In some departments, Police Officers receive additional pay for special unit assignments. In addition to their base salary, Police Officers also receive compensation for working overtime—hours worked beyond their regular work shift—as well as for working weekends, holidays, and late-night shifts. Most Police Officers receive uniform allowances.

Employment Prospects

Airport Police Officers work for city, county, or state police departments. Job opportunities for police officers, in general, are expected to grow as fast as all other jobs until 2006. Most openings will be created to replace officers who retire, resign, or are promoted to higher positions. The creation of additional positions will depend on departments' needs and budgets.

Advancement Prospects

Officers interested in supervisory or administrative duties can seek promotions as sergeants, lieutenants or captains. They must have additional experience and education as well as pass competitive exams and reviews.

In larger airport police departments, officers can volunteer for special duty, such as canine patrol or hostage negotiations, when they become eligible.

Special Requirements

Most departments require applicants to be U.S. citizens with a valid driver's license and with no criminal record. They must meet certain vision, weight, and height requirements. Other qualifications, such as age, vary from department to department.

Applicants must pass every step of a selection process, which includes any or all of the following: job application, written exam, panel interview, medical examination, physical aptitude or agility test, background investigation, psychological review, polygraph examination, and drug testing.

Education and Training

Applicants must have a high school or general equivalency diploma. Many departments also require applicants to have a minimum of college credits with courses in police science or other related study. Some police departments require applicants to have either an associate's or bachelor's degree.

Recruits must complete police academy training along with separate airport security training, which covers use of firearms; procedures for detentions, search, arrest, and other aviation security activities; and law enforcement responsibilities in airport security. Those recruits who will perform aircraft rescue and firefighting duties must also complete fire academy training. Along with formal training, recruits complete field training under the supervision of senior officers.

Experience and Skills

Requirements vary from department to department. Most departments prefer one or more years of experience in law enforcement. For positions with aircraft rescue and firefighting duty, departments prefer applicants with structural firefighting or aircraft rescue and firefighting experience.

Police departments look for honest and dependable candidates who need little supervision and can handle stressful situations. They have good observational and problem-solving skills as well as teamwork and interpersonal skills. In addition, they have adequate communication, reading, and writing abilities.

Unions/Associations

Airport Police Officers might join local and state police associations as well as national organizations such as the American Federation of Police and Fraternal Order of Police. Officers who perform aircraft rescue and firefighting duties might join the Aircraft Rescue and Fire Fighting Working Group. Joining such organizations allows Airport Police Officers the opportunity to network with peers and obtain professional support and services, such as continuing education and technical information.

Tips for Entry

1. To learn about job openings or career information, contact airport police units or stations. In the city, county, or state government pages of your telephone book, look under *Airports* or *Airport Commissions*.

2. As a police officer, let the commander of the airport patrol unit or division know of your interest even if positions are not currently available.

3. Some airport police departments have web sites on the Internet. To get a list of web sites to browse, enter the phrase *airport police* in a search engine.

APPENDIXES

APPENDIX I
COLLEGES AND UNIVERSITIES

Listed below are selected college degree programs that are offered at two-year colleges or four-year colleges and universities. Degree programs for law enforcement, police science, criminal justice, chemistry, math, natural sciences, airport technology, computer science, sociology, emergency medical technology, and other protective-services related majors are not listed here because they are typically offered at colleges and universities throughout the country. Also, keep in mind that there are other colleges and universities that offer the selected degree programs in this section.

To learn about other schools or majors, talk with school or career counselors as well as with professionals. In addition, you can look up schools in college directories produced by Peterson's, Barron's, or other publishers, which can be found in school or public libraries.

(Note: Web site addresses change from time to time. If you come across an address that no longer works, you may be able to find a new one by entering the name of the school in a search engine.)

A. TWO-YEAR COLLEGES

AIR TRAFFIC CONTROL

California

Cuyamaca College
900 Rancho San Diego Parkway
El Cajon, CA 92019-4304
http://www.cuyamaca.gcccd.cc.ca.us

Mt. San Antonio College
Aeronautics & Transportation
1100 North Grand Avenue
Walnut, CA 91789
http://www.mtsac.edu

Southwestern College
900 Otay Lakes Boulevard
Chula Vista, CA 91910
http://www.swc.cc.ca.us

Florida

Miami-Dade Community College
Aviation Department
500 College Terrace
Homestead, FL 33030
http://www.mdcc.edu

Maryland

Catonsville Community College
CCBC Catonsville
800 South Rolling Rd.
Baltimore, MD 21228
http://www.cat.cc.md.us/info.html

Minnesota

Inver Hills Community College
2500 East 80th Street
Inver Grove Heights, MN 55076-3224
http://www.ih.cc.mn.us

Minneapolis Community and Technical College
10100 Flying Cloud Drive
Eden Prairie, MN 55347
http://www.tec.mn.us

Pennsylvania

Community College of Beaver County
Aviation Science Center
125 Cessna Drive
Beaver Falls, PA 15010-1060
http://www.ccbc.cc.pa.us

Washington

Green River Community College
12401 Southeast 320th Street
Auburn, WA 98092
http://www.greenriver.ctc.edu

OCCUPATIONAL SAFETY AND HEALTH

Arizona

Gateway Community College
108 North 40th Street
Phoenix, AZ 85034
http://www.gwc.maricopa.edu

California

Mt. San Antonio College
1100 North Grand Avenue
Walnut, CA 91789
http://www.mtsac.edu

San Diego City College
1313 Twelfth Avenue
San Diego, CA 92101

Colorado

Trinidad State Junior College
600 Prospect
Trinidad, CO 81082
http://www.tsjc.cccoes.edu

Hawaii

University of Hawaii-Honolulu Community College
874 Dillingham Boulevard
Honolulu, HI 96817
http://www.hcc.hawaii.edu

Iowa

Clinton Community College
1000 Lincoln Blvd.
Clinton, IA 52732
http://www.eiccd.cc.ia.us

Muscatine Community College
152 Colorado Street
Muscatine, IA 52761
http://www.eiccd.cc.ia.us

Maryland

Catonsville Community College
CCBC Catonsville
800 South Rolling Rd.
Baltimore, MD 21228
http://www.cat.cc.md.us/info.html

Nevada

Great Basin College
1500 College Parkway
Elko, NV 89801
http://www.scs.unr.edu/gbc/

Truckee Meadows Community College
Mail Station #15
Reno, NV 89512
http://www.scs.unv.edu

New Jersey

Camden County College
P.O. Box 200
College Drive
Blackwood, NJ 08012
http://www.camdenc.edu

New York

Broome Community College
P.O. Box 1017
Binghamton, NY 13902
http://www.sunybroome.edu

North Carolina

**Durham Technical Community
    College**
1637 Lawson Street
Durham, NC 27703
http://www.dtcc.nc.us

Oklahoma

Tulsa Community College
6111 East Skelly Drive
Tulsa, OK 74135
http://www.tulsa.cc.ok.us

Pennsylvania

**Northampton County Area
    Community College**
3835 Green Pond Road
Bethlehem, PA 18020
http://www.nrhm.cc.pa.us

Tennessee

State Technical Institute at Memphis
5983 Macon Cove
Memphis, TN 38134
http://www.stim.tec.tn.us

Texas

Kilgore College
1100 Broadway
Kilgore, TX 75662
http://www.kilgore.cc.tx.us

San Jacinto College, Central Campus
4624 Fairmont Parkway
Pasadena, TX 77501
http://www.sjcd.cc.tx.us

SAFETY AND SECURITY TECHNOLOGIES

Indiana

Ivy Tech State College–Northwest
1440 East 35th Avenue
Gary, IN 46409
http://www.ivy.tec.in.us

Louisiana

Delgado Community College
501 City Park Avenue
New Orleans, LA 70119
http://www.dcc.edu

Michigan

Macomb Community College
14500 E. 12 Mile Road
Warren, MI 48093
http://www.macomb.cc.mi.us

Oakland Community College
George A. Bee Administration Center
2480 Opdyke Road
Bloomfield Hills, MI 48304
http://www.occ.cc.mi.us

Minnesota

Pine Technical College
1000 Fourth Street
Pine City, MN 55063
http://www.ptc.tec.mn.us

Nevada

Truckee Meadows Community College
Mail Station #15
Reno, NV 89512
http://www.scs.unv.edu

New Jersey

Hudson County Community College
168 Sip Avenue
Jersey City, NJ 07306
http://www.hudson.cc.nj.us

Ohio

**Cuyahoga Community College,
    Western Campus**
11000 Pleasant Valley Road
Parma, OH 44130
http://www.tri-c.cc.oh.us/west

B. FOUR-YEAR COLLEGES

AIR TRAFFIC CONTROL

Alaska

University of Alaska Anchorage
2811 Merrill Field Drive
Anchorage, AK 99501
http://www.uaa.alaska.edu

Delaware

Delaware State University
1200 North DuPont Highway
Dover, DE 19901-2277
http://www.dsc.edu

Wilmington College
320 DuPont Highway
New Castle, DE 19720-6491
http://www.wilmcoll.edu

Florida

Embry-Riddle Aeronautical University
600 South Clyde Morris Boulevard
Daytona Beach, FL 32114-3900
http://www.db.erau.edu

Indiana

Purdue University
1080 Schleman Hall
West Lafayette, IN 47907-1080
http://www.purdue.edu

Maryland

University of Maryland, Eastern Shore
Backbone Road
Princess Anne, MD 21853
http://www.umes.umd.edu

Minnesota

Saint Cloud State University
720 4th Avenue South
Saint Cloud, MN 56301-4498
http://www.stcloudstate.edu

New Hampshire

Daniel Webster College
Aviation Division
20 University Drive
Nashua, NH 03063-1699
http://www.dwc.edu

New Jersey

Thomas Edison State College
101 West State Street
Trenton, NJ 08608
http://www.tesc.edu

New York

Dowling College
Idle Hour Boulevard
Oakdale, NY 11769-1999
http://www.dowling.edu

North Dakota

University of North Dakota
University Station
Grand Forks, ND 58202
http://www.und.edu

Tennessee

Middle Tennessee State University
1301 E. Main Street
Murfreesboro, TN 37132
http://www.ntsu.edu

Virginia

Averett College
420 Main Street
Danville, VA 24541
http://www.averett.edu

Hampton University
Office of Admissions
Hampton, VA 23668
http://www.hampton.edu

CONSERVATION LAW ENFORCEMENT

Maine

Unity College
Office of Admissions
P.O. Box 532
Unity, ME 04988-0532
http://www.unity.edu

CORRECTIONS

Alabama

Auburn University
100 Mary Martin Hall
Auburn, AL 36849
http://www.auburn.edu

Troy State University, Troy
241 Adams Administration
Troy, AL 36082
http://www.troyst.edu

Arkansas

University of Arkansas at Pine Bluff
UAPB, Box 17
1200 University Drive
Pine Bluff, AR 71601-2799
http://www.uapb.edu

Arizona

Prescott College, Adult Degree Program
220 Grove Avenue
Prescott, AZ 86301
http://www.prescott.edu

California

California State University, Fresno
5241 North Maple Avenue
Fresno, CA 93740
http://www.csufresno.edu

California State University, Hayward
25800 Carlos Bee Blvd.
Hayward, CA 94542
http://www.csuhayward.edu

California State University, Long Beach
1250 Bellflower Blvd.
Long Beach, CA 90840
http://www.csulb.edu

Colorado

University of Southern Colorado
2200 Bonforte Blvd.
Pueblo, CO 81001
http://www.uscolo.edu

Connecticut

University of New Haven
300 Orange Avenue
West Haven, CT 06516
http://www.newhaven.edu

Florida

Florida State University
A2500 University Center
Tallahassee, FL 32306-1009
http://www.fsu.edu

Illinois

Chicago State University
95th Street at King Drive
Chicago, IL 60628
http://www.csu.edu

Indiana

University of Indianapolis
1400 East Hanna Avenue
Indianapolis, IN 46227-3697
http://www.uindy.edu

Kansas

Washburn University of Topeka
1700 SW College
Topeka, KS 66621
http://www.wuacc.edu

Kentucky

Eastern Kentucky University
521 Lancaster Avenue
Richmond, KY 40475-3101
http://www.eku.edu

Murray State University
1st Floor Sparks Hall
Murray, KY 42071-0009
http://www.mursuky.edu

University of Kentucky
11 Funkhouser Building
Lexington, KY 40506-0032
http://www.uky.edu

Massachusetts

Northeastern University
360 Huntington Avenue
Boston, MA 02115-5096
http://www.neu.edu

Michigan

Northern Michigan University
1401 Presque Isle Avenue
Marquette, MI 49855
http://www.nmu.edu

Minnesota

Mankato State University
P.O. Box 8400
MSU55
Mankato, MN 56002-8400
http://www.mankato.msus.edu

Saint Cloud State University
720 4th Avenue South
Saint Cloud, MN 56301-4498
http://www.stcloudstate.edu

Winona State University
P.O. Box 5838
Winona, MN 55987-5838
http://www.winona.msus.edu

Missouri

Central Missouri State University
Office of Admissions
Administration 104
Warrensburg, MO 64093
http://www.cmsu.edu

College of the Ozarks
Office of Admissions
Point Lookout, MO 65726
http://www.cofo.edu

New Jersey

Jersey City State College
2039 Kennedy Boulevard
Jersey City, NJ 07305-1957
http://www.jcstate.edu

New York

**John Jay College of Criminal Justice,
the City University of New York**
899 10th Avenue
New York, NY 10019-1093
http://www.jjay.cuny.edu

Utica College of Syracuse University
1600 Burrstone Road
Utica, NY 13502-4892
http://www.ucsu.edu

Ohio

Kent State University
161 Michael Schwartz Center
Kent, OH 44242-0001
http://www.kent.edu

Oklahoma

Langston University
Office of Admissions
P.O. Box 838
Langston, OK 73050
http://www.lunet.edu

Oregon

Western Oregon University
Admissions Office
Monmouth, OR 97361
http://www.wou.edu

Pennsylvania

Mercyhurst College
Office of Admissions
Erie, PA 16546
http://eden.mercy.edu

York College of Pennsylvania
Office of Admissions
York, PA 17405-7199
http://www.ycp.edu

Rhode Island

Salve Regina University
100 Ochre Point Avenue
Newport, RI 02840-4192
http://www.salve.edu

Tennessee

**University of Tennessee at
Chattanooga**
615 McCallie Avenue
Chattanooga, TN 37403-2598
http://www.utc.edu

Texas

Lamar University
P.O. Box 10009
Beaumont, TX 77710
http://www.lamar.edu

Sam Houston State University
Admissions Office
P.O. Box 2418
Huntsville, TX 77341-2418
http://www.shsu.edu

Utah

Weber State University
1001 University Circle
Ogden, UT 84408-1001
http://www.weber.edu

Virginia

Averette College
420 Main Street
Danville, VA 24541
http://www.averett.edu

Virginia Commonwealth University
821 West Franklin Street
Box 842526
Richmond, VA 23284-9005
http://www.vcu.edu

Washington

Eastern Washington University
EWUMS-148
Cheney, WA 99004-2431
http://www.ewu.edu

FIRE PROTECTION ENGINEERING

California

**California State University, Los
Angeles**
5151 State University Drive
Los Angeles, CA 90032-8530
http://www.calstatela.edu

Connecticut

University of New Haven
300 Orange Avenue
West Haven, CT 06516
http://www.newhaven.edu

Kentucky

Eastern Kentucky University
521 Lancaster Avenue
Richmond, KY 40475-3102
http://www.eku.edu

Maryland

University of Maryland
Office of Admissions
College Park, MD 20742
http://www.umcp.umd.edu

Massachusetts

Worcester Polytechnic Institute
Center for Firesafety Studies
100 Institute Road
Worcester, MA 01609
http://www.wpi.edu

Ohio

University of Cincinnati
Mail Location 91
100 Edwards Center
Cincinnati, OH 45221-0091
http://www.uc.edu

Oklahoma

Oklahoma State University
104 Whitehurst
Stillwater, OK 74078
http://www.okstate.edu

FORENSIC SCIENCE

Alabama

Jacksonville State University
700 Pelham Road
Jacksonville, AL 36265-9982
Http://www.jsu.edu

Connecticut

University of New Haven
300 Orange Avenue
West Haven, CT 06516
http://www.newhaven.edu

Florida

University of Central Florida
P.O. Box 160111
Orlando, FL 32816
http://www.ucf.edu

Hawaii

Chaminade University of Honolulu
3140 Waialae Avenue
Honolulu, HI 96816-1578
http://www.chaminade.edu

Illinois

Southern Illinois University at Carbondale
New Student Admissions
Mail Code 4710
Carbondale, IL 62901-6806
http://www.siu.edu/cwis

Indiana

Indiana University Bloomington
300 North Jordan Avenue
Bloomington, IN 47405
http://www.indiana.edu/~iuadmit

Kentucky

Eastern Kentucky University
521 Lancaster Avenue
Richmond, KY 40475-3101
http://www.eku.edu

Missouri

College of the Ozarks
Office of Admissions
Point Lookout, MO 65726
http://www.cofo.edu

New York

John Jay College of Criminal Justice, the City University of New York
899 10th Avenue
New York, NY 10019-1093
http://www.jjay.cuny.edu

St. John's University
8000 Utopia Parkway
Jamaica, NY 11439
http://www.stjohns.edu

State University of New York College at Buffalo
1300 Elmwood Avenue
Buffalo, NY 14222-1095
http://www.buffalostate.edu or

Ohio

Ohio University
Office of Admissions
120 Chubb Hall
Athens, OH 45701-2979
http://www.ohiou.edu

Oklahoma

University of Central Oklahoma
100 N. University Drive
Edmond, OK 73034
http://www.ucok.edu

Pennsylvania

Point Park College
201 Wood Street
Pittsburgh, PA 15222-1984
http://www.ppc.edu

West Chester University of Pennsylvania
100 West Rosedale Avenue
West Chester, PA 19383
http://www.wcupa.edu

Washington, D.C.

George Washington University
2121 Eye Street, NW
Washington, DC 20052
http://www.gwu.edu/index.html

INFORMATION SYSTEMS SECURITY

Indiana

Purdue University
1080 Schleman Hall
West Lafayette, IN 47907-1080
http://www.purdue.edu

INDUSTRIAL HYGIENE

California

California State University, Northridge
18111 Nordhoff Street
Northridge, CA 91330
http://www.csun.edu

Indiana

Purdue University
1080 Schleman Hall
West Lafayette, IN 47907-1080
http://www.purdue.edu

Kentucky

Western Kentucky University
1 Big Red Way
Bowling Green, KY 42101-3576
http://www.wku.edu

Ohio

Ohio University
Office of Admissions
120 Chubb Hall
Athens, OH 45701-2979
http://www.ohiou.edu

OCCUPATIONAL SAFETY AND HEALTH

Alabama

University of North Alabama
University Station
Florence, AL 35632-0001
http://www.una.edu

Jacksonville State University
700 Pelham Rd.
Jacksonville, AL 36265-9982
http://www.jsu.edu

California

California State University, Fresno
5241 North Maple Avenue
Fresno, CA 93740
http://www.csufresno.edu

California State University, Northridge
18111 Nordhoff Street
Northridge, CA 91330
http://www.csun.edu

National University
11255 North Torrey Pines Road
La Jolla, CA 92037-1011
http://www.nu.edu

Connecticut

University of New Haven
300 Orange Avenue
West Haven, CT 06516
http://www.newhaven.edu

Indiana

Purduc University
1080 Schleman Hall
West Lafayette, IN 47907-1080
http://www.purdue.edu

Ball State University
Department of Admissions
Muncie, IN 47306-1099
http://www.bsu.edu

Indiana University Bloomington
300 North Jordan Avenue
Bloomington, IN 47405
http://www.indiana.edu/~iuadmit

Kentucky

Murray State University
112 Sparks Hall
Murray, KY 42071-0009
http://www.mursuky.edu

Michigan

Ferris State University
PRK 110
Big Rapids, MI 49307-2742
http://www.ferris.edu

Grand Valley State University
1 Campus Drive
Allendale, MI 49401-9403
http://www.gvsu.edu

Madonna University
36600 Schoolcraft Road
Livonia, MI 48150-1173
http://www.munet.edu

Oakland University
357 Hannah Hall
Rochester, MI 48309-4401
http://mars.acs.oakland.edu

Missouri

Central Missouri State University
Office of Admissions
Administration 104
Warrensburg, MO 64093
http://www.cmsu.edu

Montana

Montana Tech of the University of Montana
1300 West Park Street
Butte, MT 59701-8997
http://www.mtech.edu

New Hampshire

Keene State College
229 Main Street
Keene, NH 03435-1701
http://www.keene.edu

New York

Clarkson University
Holcroft House
P.O. Box 5605
Potsdam, NY 13699
http://www.clarkson.edu

Mercy College
555 Broadway
Dobbs Ferry, NY 10522-1189
http://www.mercynet.edu

North Carolina

North Carolina Agricultural and Technical State University
1601 East Market Street
Greensboro, NC 27411
http://www.ncat.edu

Saint Augustine's College
1315 Oakwood Avenue
Raleigh, NC 27610-2298

North Dakota

University of North Dakota
Box 8382
Grand Forks, ND 58202
http://www.und.nodak.edu

Ohio

Ohio University
Office of Admissions
120 Chubb Hall
Athens, OH 45701-2979
http://www.ohiou.edu

Oklahoma

Southeastern Oklahoma State University
Office of Enrollment Management
P.O. Box 4225
Durant, OK 74701
http://www.sosu.edu

Oregon

Oregon State University
Department of Admissions
Corvallis, OR 97331-4501
http://www.orst.edu

Pennsylvania

**Allegheny University of the Health
   Sciences**
201 North 15th Street
Mail Stop 506
Philadelphia, PA 19102-1192
http://www.allegheny.edu

Millersville University of Pennsylvania
Office of Admissions
P.O. Box 1002
Millersville, PA 17551-0302
http://www.millersv.edu

**Pennsylvania State University,
   University Park Campus**
Undergraduate Admissions
201 Shields Building
University Park, PA 16802
http://www.psu.edu

South Carolina

Clemson University
P.O. Box 345124
Clemson, SC 29634
http://www.clemson.edu

Tennessee

East Tennessee State University
P.O. Box 70731
ETSU
Johnson City, TN 37614-0734
http://www.etsu-tn.edu

Washington

Central Washington University
400 East 8th Avenue
Ellensburg, WA 98926
http://www.cwu.edu

West Virginia

Fairmont State College
Director of Admissions
1201 Locust Avenue
Fairmont, WV 26554
http://www.fscwv.edu

SAFETY AND SECURITY TECHNOLOGIES

California

University of Southern California
University Park
Los Angeles, CA 90089-0911
http://www.usc.edu

Illinois

Illinois State University
Office of Admissions
Campus Box 2200
Normal, IL 61790-2200
http://www.ilstu.edu

Indiana

Indiana State University
210 North Seventh Street
Terre Haute, IN 47809-1401
http://www.indstate.edu

Kentucky

Eastern Kentucky University
521 Lancaster Avenue
Richmond, KY 40475-3101
http://www.eku.edu

Missouri

Central Missouri State University
Office of Admissions
Administration 104
Warrensburg, MO 64093
http://www.cmsu.edu

Southeast Missouri State University
One University Plaza
Cape Girardeau, MO 63701-4799
http://www.semo.edu

New Jersey

Jersey City State College
2039 Kennedy Boulevard
Jersey City, NJ 07305-1957
http://www.jcstate.edu

New York

**John Jay College of Criminal Justice,
   the City University of New York**
899 10th Avenue
New York, NY 10019-1093
http://www.jjay.cuny.edu

Mercy College
555 Broadway
Dobbs Ferry, NY 10522-1189
http://www.mercynet.edu

Saint John's University
8000 Utopia Parkway
Jamaica, NY 11439
http://www.stjohns.edu

Oklahoma

Oklahoma State University
104 Whitehurst
Stillwater, OK 74078
http://www.okstate.edu

University of Central Oklahoma
100 N. University Drive
Edmond, OK 73034
http://www.ucok.edu

Pennsylvania

Indiana University of Pennsylvania
216 Pratt Hall
Indiana, PA 15705
http://www.iup.edu

Texas

**Texas A&M University, College
   Station**
Admissions and Records
P.O. Box 30014
College Station, TX 77842-3014
http://www.tamu.edu

Vermont

Southern Vermont College
Monument Avenue
Bennington, VT 05201
http://www.svc.edu

Virginia

Virginia Commonwealth University
821 West Franklin Street
Box 842526
Richmond, VA 23284-9005
http://www.vcu.edu

West Virginia

Marshall University
400 Hal Greer Boulevard
Huntington, WV 25755-2020
http://www.marshall.edu

Wisconsin

University of Wisconsin-Whitewater
Office of Admissions
Whitewater, WI 53190-1790
http://www.uww.edu

APPENDIX II
TECHNICAL AND VOCATIONAL SCHOOLS

The following technical and vocational schools offer training programs for some of the professions in this book. To learn about other training programs for these professions or for other occupations that are not listed here, talk with professionals or professional organizations. Job counselors in schools and employment programs may be able to help you as well.

Addresses and phone numbers are listed below so you can contact the schools directly for information. Some schools also have their web site addresses listed. Keep in mind that web site addresses change from time to time. If you come across an address that no longer works, you may be able to find a new address by entering the name of the school in a search engine.

AIRPORT FIREFIGHTER

Texas

DFW International Airport Fire Rescue Training Academy
P.O. Drawer 610687
DFW Airport, TX 75261-0687
(972) 574-5534; fax: (972) 574-4385
http://www.dfwairport.com/dps

BODYGUARD

Colorado

Executive Security International Private Training School
2128 Railroad Avenue
Department Web
Rifle, CO 81650
(800) 874-0888
http://www.esi-lifeforce.com

North Carolina

Corporate Security International, Inc.
2918 Manufactures Drive
Greensboro, NC 27406-4606
(800) 731-8733 or (336) 574-1773
fax: (336) 574-1779
http://www.csi-nc.com

FLIGHT DISPATCHER

Arizona

Flight Control Academy
1002 E. Valencia Road, Suite B
Tucson, AZ 85706
(520) 573-3467; fax: (520) 573-3502
http://www.flash.net/~jjcaz

California

Sierra Academy Of Aeronautics
P.O. Box 2429
Oakland International Airport
Oakland, CA 94614
(800) 243-6300; fax: (510) 568-6116
http://www.sierraacademy.com

Florida

Embry-Riddle Aeronautical University
600 S. Clyde Morris Boulevard
Daytona Beach, FL 32114- 3900
(904) 226-7051 or (904) 226-6976;
fax: (904) 226-7641
http://www.db.erau.edu

Sheffield School Of Aeronautics
499 N.W. 70th Avenue, Suite 110
Ft. Lauderdale, FL 33317
(954) 581-6022; fax: (954) 584-8980
http://www.sheffield.com

Georgia

Airline Career Training, Inc.
567 Parkway Drive
Atlanta, GA 30354
(404) 763-9835; fax: (606) 384-7823
http://www.flightdispatch.com

Illinois

Lewis University
Route 53, Box 285
Romeoville, IL 60446
(815) 836-5225; fax: (815) 834-6106
http://www.lewisu.edu

Kentucky

Airline Ground Schools Inc.
10901 Kimberly Drive
Union, KY 41091
(606) 384-7821; fax: (606) 384-7823
http://memers.aol.com/agsdanny/AGS/index.htm

Minnesota

Aviation Training, Inc.
3050 Metro Drive, Suite 200
Minneapolis, MN 55425
(800) 292-9149 or (612) 851-0066;
fax: (612) 851-0094
http://www.academyeducation.com

New York

Academics Of Flight
43-49 45th Street
Sunnyside, NY 11104
(800) 291-9785 or (718) 937-5716
http://memers.aol.com/flywithaof/MainPage.html

Texas

Airline Flight Dispatcher Training Center
400 Fuller Wiser Road, Suite 222
Euless, TX 76039
(817) 571-5046; fax: (817) 571-0772
http://www.airlinedispatcher.com

International Aviation & Travel Academy
4846 South Collins Drive
Arlington, TX 76018
(800) 678- 0700; fax: (817) 784-7022
http://www.iatac.com

LOCKSMITH

California

Golden Gate School of Locksmithing
3722 San Pablo Avenue
Oakland, CA 94608
(510) 654-2677

San Francisco Lock School
4002 Irving Street
San Francisco, CA 94122-1219
(415) 566-5545 or (415) 347-2222

School of Lock Technology
1049 Island Avenue
San Diego, CA 92101
(619) 234-1036; fax: (619) 234-5937

School of Lock Technology
302 W. Katelia
Orange, CA 92667
(714) 633-1366; fax: (714) 633-0199

Valley Technical Institute
5408 N. Blackstone
Fresno, CA 93710
(209) 436-8501; fax: (209) 439-3814

Universal School of Master Locksmithing
3201 Fulton Avenue
Sacramento, CA 95821
(916) 482-4216; fax: (916) 485-9385

Colorado

Colo2rado Locksmith College, Inc.
4991 W. 80th Avenue, Unit 103A
Westminster, CO 80030
(303) 427-7773

Florida

Lock and Safe Institute of Technology, Inc.
1650 N. Federal Highway
Pompano Beach, FL 33062
(800) 457-LOCK or (305) 785-0444

Illinois

Acme School
Locksmithing Division
11350 S. Harlem
Worth, IL 60482
(708) 361-3750; fax: (708) 448-9306

Indiana

Locksmith School, Inc.
3901 S. Meridian Street
Indianapolis, IN 46217
(317) 632-3979; fax: (317) 784-2945

Kentucky

Lockmasters, Inc.
5085 Danville Road
Nicholasville, KY 40356
(800) 654-0637 or (606) 885-6041;
fax: (606) 887-0810

Louisiana

Southern Locksmith Training Institute
1387 Airline Drive
Bossier City, LA 71112
(318) 227-9458; fax: (318) 746-1734

Missouri

Foley-Beisaw Institute
6301 Equitable Road
Kansas City, MO 64120
(800) 821-3452 or (816) 483-4200;
fax: (816) 483-5010

Nevada

American Locksmith Institute of Nevada
875 S. Boulder Highway
Henderson, NV 89015
(702) 565-8811; fax: (702) 565-7017

New Jersey

Locksmithing Institute of America, Inc.
116 Fairfield Road
Fairfield, NJ 07004
(800) 526-0890 or (201) 575-5225;
fax: (201) 808-1948

Security Systems Management Schools
116 Fairfield Road
Fairfield, NJ 07004
(800) 526-0890 or (201) 575-5225

Tennessee

Messick Vo-Technical Center
703 South Greer
Memphis, TN 38111
(901) 325-4840; fax: (901) 325-4842

Texas

School of Lock Technology
509 Rio Grande Street
Austin, TX 78701
(888) 511-8874 or (512) 473-8874;
fax: (512) 472-4838

PARK RANGER

The following schools are approved by the National Park Service to offer the Seasonal Law Enforcement Training Program (SLETP), which trains individuals to become seasonal Park Rangers. Upon completion of the program and background investigations, graduates are granted a Level II Law Enforcement Commission to perform limited law enforcement duties.

For further information from the National Park Service, contact:
Law Enforcement Employee Development Center
National Park Service Federal Law Enforcement Training Center
Building 64, Room 219
Glynco, GA 31524
(912) 267-2795 or (912) 267-2246
http://www.ustreas.gov/fletc/index.htm

Alaska

University of Alaska Southeast, Sitka Campus
Law Enforcement Certificate Program
1332 Seward Avenue
Sitka, AK 99835
(907) 747-6611; fax: (907) 747-5606

Arizona

Northern Arizona University
Park Ranger Training Program
School of Forestry
P.O. Box 15018
Flagstaff, AZ 86011-5018
(520) 523-0228; fax: (520) 523-1080
http://www.for.nau.edu/prm/rangers

California

Santa Rosa Junior College
Santa Rosa Training Center
609 Tomales Road
Petaluma, CA 94952-9612
(707) 776-0721; fax: (707) 776-0814

Colorado

Colorado Northwestern Community College
Criminal Justice Program
500 Kennedy Drive (Hill Hall)
Rangely, CO 81648
(800) 562-1105; fax: (970) 675-3291

Minnesota

Vermilion Community College
NPS Seasonal Ranger Training
1900 East Camp Street
Ely, MN 55731-1996
(800) 657-3608; fax: (218) 365-7207

Massachusetts

University of Massachusetts at Amherst
Seasonal Law Enforcement Training Program
608 Goodell Building
Amherst, MA 01003-3260
(413) 545-2484; fax: (413) 545-3351

North Carolina

Southwestern Community College
Macon County Center
152 Industrial Park Road
Franklin, NC 28734
(828) 369-7331; fax: (828) 369-2428

Ohio

Cuyahoga Community College
Ranger Academy, Continuing & Professional Education Office
11000 Pleasant Valley Road
Parma, OH 44130
(216) 937-5081; fax: (440) 884-4373

Hocking College
National Ranger Training Institute
3301 Hocking Parkway
Nelsonville, OH 45764-9582
(740) 753-3200; fax: (740) 753-9411

Pennsylvania

Slippery Rock University
Seasonal Ranger Training
Department of Parks and Recreation/ Environmental Education
Slippery Rock, PA 16057-1326
(724) 738-2596; fax: (724) 738-2959

South Dakota

Western Dakota Tech Institute
Law Enforcement Technology
800 Mickelson Drive
Rapid City, SD 57701
(800) 544-8765

Washington

Skagit Valley College
Administration of Justice Program
2405 E. College Way
Mount Vernon, WA 98273-5899
(360) 416-7829; fax: (360) 416-7890

POLYGRAPH EXAMINER

Arizona

Arizona School of Polygraph Sciences
3106 W Thomas Road, Suite 1114
Phoenix, AZ 85017
(602) 272-8123; fax: (602) 272-9735

California

Backster School of Lie Detection
861 Sixth Avenue, Suite 403
San Diego, CA 92101-6379
(619) 233-6669; fax: (619) 233-3441

Georgia

Argenbright International Institute of Polygraph
4854 Old National Highway, Suite 210
Atlanta, GA 30337-6222
(800) 305-9559 or (404) 763-3552;
fax: (404) 305-0822

Florida

Academy of Forensic Psychophysiology
801 W Bay Drive, Suite 509
Largo, FL 33770-3220
(888) 793-1131 or (813) 588-9668;
fax: (813) 581-7758
http://www.polygraph.net

International Academy of Polygraph
1885 W Commercial Boulevard, Suite 125
Fort Lauderdale, FL 33309-3066
(954) 771-6900; fax: (954) 776-7687

Maryland

Maryland Institute of Criminal Justice
8424 Veterans Highway, Suite 3
Baltimore, MD 21108-0458
(800) 493-8181 or (410) 987-6665;
fax: (410) 987-4808

Michigan

American Institute of Polygraph
25000 Ford Road, Suite 1A
Dearborn Heights, MI 48127-3106
(313) 274-3810; fax: (313) 565-7901

Oregon

Western Oregon University School of Polygraphy
Division of Extended and Summer Studies
Western Oregon University
Monmouth, OR 97361
(503) 838-8483; fax: (503) 838-8473
http://www.wou.edu/Provost/ Extendedpolygraph.html

Pennsylvania

**Academy of Scientific Investigative
  Training**
1704 Locust Street, 2nd Floor
Philadelphia, PA 19103
(215) 732-3349; fax: (215) 545-1773
http://www.polygraph-training.com

Texas

**Texas Department of Public Safety
  Law Enforcement**
Polygraph School
P.O. Box 4087
Austin, TX 78773-0001
(512) 424-5912; fax: (512) 424-5766

Virginia

Virginia School of Polygraphy
7909 Brookfield Road
Norfolk, VA 23518-3279
(757) 583-1578; fax: (757) 588-0305

PRIVATE INVESTIGATOR

California

Detective Training Institute
P.O. Box 909
San Juan Capistrano, CA 92693
(888) 425-9338; fax: (714) 498-4751
http://www.detectivetraining.com

Oregon

Academy of Legal Investigators
3303 Ward Court N.E.
Salem, OR 97305
(800) 842-7421
http://wimall.com/alijohn/

Pennsylvania

Lion Investigation Academy
Admissions Office
553 Main Street
Stroudsburg, PA 18360
(717) 223-5627
http://www.advsearch.com/lionacademy.htm

RESCUE TECHNICIAN

California

CMC Rescue School
CMC Rescue, Inc.
P.O. Drawer 6870
Santa Barbara, CA 93160-6870
(800) 235-5741; fax: (800) 235-8951
http://www.cmcrescue.com

**North Tree Fire Education and
  Training**
P.O. Box 863
Marina, CA 93933
(877) 347-3338
http://www.ntftraining.com

Rescue 3 International
9075 Elk Grove Boulevard, #200
P.O. Box 519
Elk Grove, CA 95759-0519
(800) 45-RESCUE or (916) 685-3066;
fax: (916) 685-6969
http://www.rescue3.com

Colorado

Dive Rescue International
201 North Link Lane
Fort Collins, CO 80524-2712
(970) 482-0887; fax: (970) 482-0893
http://www.diverescueintl.com

Mountain Rescue Association
710 Tenth Street, Suite 105
Golden, CO 80401
(503) 658-4165
http://www.mra.org

North Carolina

**National Association For Search and
  Rescue**
Rescue Training
Education Department
P.O. Box 339
Glen Alpine, NC 28628-0339
(704) 584-1768; fax: (704) 584-6858
http://www.nasar.org/prod/edu.htm

Pennsylvania

Technical Rescue Specialists
P.O. Box 1574
Southampton, PA 18966
(800) 830-3088; fax: (215) 364-8311
*http://www.rit.edu/~jeb2858/start/
programs.htm*

APPENDIX III
PROFESSIONAL UNIONS
AND ASSOCIATIONS

The following headquarter offices are for the professional organizations that are mentioned in this book. You can contact these groups or visit their web sites on the Internet to learn about careers, job opportunities, training programs, seminars, conferences, professional certification, and so on. Most of these organizations have branch offices throughout the country; contact an organization's headquarters to find out if a branch is in your area.

There are also local, regional, and state professional associations and unions that can be contacted for information. To learn about any organizations that may be in your area, talk with local professionals.

(Note: Web site addresses change from time to time. If you come across an address that no longer works, you may be able to find a new address by entering the name of the organization in a search engine.)

POLICE WORK

American Federation of Police
3801 Biscayne Boulevard
Miami, FL 33137

Fraternal Order of Police
Grand Lodge
1410 Donelson Pike, Suite A17
Nashville, TN 37217
(615) 399-0900; fax: (615) 399-0400
http://www.grandlodgefop.org

International Association of Women Police
5413 West Sunnyside Avenue
Chicago, IL 60630
(617) 298-5808
http://www.iawp.org

International Union of Police Associations
1421 Prince Street, Suite 330
Alexandria, VA 22314-2805
(800) 247-4872 or (703) 549-7473
http://www.sddi.com/iupa

International Homicide Investigators Association
P.O. Box 520
Barnstable, MA 02630
(800) 742-1007 or (508) 362-3470
http://www.ihia.org

International Narcotics Interdiction Association
P.O. Box 1118
Pinehurst, NC 28374
(954) 491-5056
http://www.inia.org

International Association of Crime Analysts
P.O. Box 937
Arvada, CO 80001
(214) 670-3763
http://www.iaca.net

National Sheriffs' Association
1450 Duke Street
Alexandria, VA 22314-3490
(703) 836-7827
http://www.sheriffs.org

American Deputy Sheriffs' Association
15915 Katy Freeway #350
Houston, TX 77094
(800) 937-7940; fax: (281) 398-5521
http://www.neosoft.com/~adsa

North American Wildlife Enforcement Officers Association
c/o Gary Martin, Compliance Promotion
    Specialist
Enforcement Section 6th Floor South
Ontario Ministry of Natural Resources
300 Water Street
Peterborough, ON K9J 8M5
(705) 755-1512
http://www.naweoa.com

Federal Law Enforcement Officers Association
Membership Services
P.O. Box 508
East Northpoint, NY 11731-0472
(516) 368-6117; fax: (516) 368-6429
http://www.fleoa.org

National Drug Enforcement Officers Association
2020 Pennsylvania Avenue NW, Suite 299
Washington, DC 20006
(202) 298-9653
http://www.ndeoa.org

National Border Patrol Council
Secretary/Treasurer
P.O. Box 2101
Laredo, TX 78044
http://www.nbpc.net

SPECIAL POLICE UNITS

International Police Mountain Bike Association
1612 K Street, NW, Suite 401
Washington, DC 20006
(202) 822-1333; fax: (202) 822-1334
*http://www.bikeleague.org/ipmba2/
    ipmbaprg.htm*

Law Enforcement Bicycle Association
823 Snipe Ireland Road
Richmond, VT 05477-9604
(802) 434-7077
http://www.leba.org

North American Police Work Dog Association
4222 Manchester Avenue
Perry, OH 44081
(888) 4CANINE; fax: (440) 259-3170
http://www.napwda.com

United States Police Canine Association
http://www.minn.net/uspca
Contact persons are:

- Skip Brewster
  National Secretary USPCA
  11780 Beaconsfield
  Detroit, MI 48224
- James Nichols
  National President USPCA
  P.O. Box 973
  Punta Gorda, FL 33951
- Kevin Conroy
  National Treasurer USPCA
  #4 Coed Lane
  Farmingville, NY 11738

Airborne Law Enforcement Association
P.O. Box 3683
Tulsa, OK 74101-3683
(918) 599-0705; fax: (918) 583-2353
http://www.alea.org

Law Enforcement Thermographers' Association
P.O. Box 6485
Edmond, OK 73083-6485
(405) 330-6988
http://www.leta.org

International Association of Bomb Technicians and Investigators
P.O. Box 8629
Naples, FL 34101

American Special Operations Sniper Association
e-mail: asosa@cros.net
http://www.geocities.com/Pentagon/8732
or *http://www.cros.net/asosa*

National Tactical Officers Association
P.O. Box 529
Doylestown, PA 18901
(800) 279-9127
http://www.ntoa.org

International Society of Crime Prevention Practitioners
266 Sandy Point Road
Elmenton, PA 16373
(724) 867-1000; fax: (724) 867-1200

http://ourworld.compuserve.com/homepages/ISCPP

American Society for Industrial Security
1625 Prince Street
Alexandria, VA 22314-2818
(703) 519-6200; fax: (703) 519-6299
http://www.asisonline.org

FORENSIC SCIENCE

International Association for Identification
2535 Pilot Knob Road, Suite 117
Mendota Heights, MN 55120-1120
telephone: (651) 681-8566;
fax: (651) 681-8443
http://www.theiai.org

The Association of Crime Scene Reconstruction
P.O. Box 20149
Oklahoma City, OK 73156-0149
http://www.acsr.com

American Academy of Forensic Sciences
Mailing address:
P.O. Box 669
Colorado Springs, CO 80901-0669
Street address:
410 North 21st Street, Suite 203
Colorado Springs, CO 80904-2798
(719) 636-1100; fax: (719) 636-1993
http://www.aafs.org

Association of Firearm and Toolmark Examiners
c/o Lannie G. Emanuel, AFTE Secretary
SW Institute of Forensic Sciences
5230 Medical Center Dr.
P.O. Box 35728
Dallas, TX 75235-0728
(214) 920-5979; fax: (214) 920-5957
http://www.povn.com/~4n6/afte.htm

American Society of Questioned Document Examiners
P.O. Box 382684
Germantown, TN 38183-2684
(901) 759-0729
http://www.asqde.org

National Association of Document Examiners
20 Nassau Street
Princeton, NJ 08542
(609) 924-8193; fax: (609) 924-1511
http://expertpages.com/org/nade.htm

National Association of Medical Examiners
1420 S. Grand Boulevard
St. Louis, MO 63104
(314) 577-8298; fax: (314) 268-5124
http://www.thename.org/index.html

American Society of Clinical Pathologists
2100 W. Harrison
Chicago, IL 60612
(312) 738-1336
http://www.ascp.org

American Medical Association
(800) AMA-3211
http://www.ama-assn.org
Headquarters
515 North State Street
Chicago, IL 60610
(312) 464-5000
Washington office
1101 Vermont Avenue NW
Washington, D.C. 20005
(202) 789-7400

American Polygraph Association
P.O. Box 8037
Chattanooga, TN 37414-0037
or:
951 Eastgate Loop Suite 800,
Chattanooga, TN 37411-5608
(800) APA-8037; fax: (432) 894-5435
http://www.polygraph.org

American Association of Police Polygraphists
P.O. Box 2155
Upland, CA 91785-2155
(888) 743-5479
http://www.polygraph.org/states/aapp

PRIVATE INVESTIGATORS

National Association of Investigative Specialists
P.O. Box 33244
Austin, TX 78764
(512) 719-3595; fax: (512) 719-3594
http://www.pimall.com/nais/home.html

International Association of Arson Investigators
300 S. Broadway, Suite 100
St. Louis, MO 63102-2808
(314) 621-1966; fax: (314) 621-5125
http://www.fire-investigators.org

International Association of Special Investigation Units
5024-R Campbell Boulevard
Baltimore, MD 21236-5974
(410) 933-3480; fax: (410) 931-8111
http://www.iasiu.com/source/home.asp

National Society of Professional Insurance Investigators
National Chapter
P.O. Box 88
Delaware, OH 43015-0888
(888) NSPII-98; fax: (614) 369-7155
http://www.nspii.com

National Association of Legal Investigators
6109 Meadowwood
Grand Blanc, MI 48439
(800) 266-6254; fax: (810) 694-7109
http://www.nali.com

Association of Certified Fraud Examiners
The Gregor Building
716 West Avenue
Austin, TX 78701
(800) 245-3321 or (512) 478-9070;
fax: (512) 478-9297
http://www.cfenet.com

International Association of Financial Crimes Investigators
1620 Grant Avenue
Novato, CA 94945
(415) 897-8800; fax: (415) 898-0798
http://www.iafci.org/start.html

American Institute of Certified Public Accountants
1211 Avenue of the Americas
New York, NY 10036-8775
(212) 596-6200; fax: (212) 596-6213
http://www.aicpa.org

International Association of Personal Protection Specialists
World Headquarters
1190 Homestead Road
Santa Clara, CA 95050
http://www.iapps.org

SECURITY

Associated Locksmiths of America, Inc.
3003 Live Oak Street
Dallas, TX 75205
(214) 827-1701; fax: (214) 827-1810
http://www.aloa.org

Institutional Locksmiths Association
National Board Office
P.O. Box 1275
Waldorf, MD 20604-1275
(888) 552-LOCK/ (888) 552-5625
http://www.mindspring.com/~inhouse/startila.htm

National Burglar and Fire Alarm Association
7101 Wisconsin Avenue #901
Bethesda, MD 20814
(301) 907-3202
http://www.alarm.org

Society of Fire Protection Engineers
7315 Wisconsin Avenue, Suite 1225W
Bethesda, MD 20814
(301) 718-2910; fax: (301) 718-2242
http://www.sfpe.org

National Fire Protection Association
1 Batterymarch Park
Quincy, MA 02269-9101
(617) 770-3000; fax: (617) 770-0700
http://www.nfpa.org

National Society of Professional Engineers
1420 King Street
Alexandria, VA 22314-2794
(888) 285-6773 or (703) 684-2800;
fax: (703) 836-4875
http://www.nspe.org

International Foundation for Protection Officers
3106 Tamiami Trail N, #269
Naples, FL 34103
(941) 430-0534; fax: (941) 430-0533
http://www.ifpo.com

American Society for Industrial Security
1625 Prince Street
Alexandria, VA 22314-2818
(703) 519-6200; fax: (703) 519-6299
http://www.asisonline.org

COMPUTER SECURITY

ICSA, Inc.
12379-C Sunrise Valley Drive
Reston, VA 20191-3422
(703) 453-0500; fax: (703) 620-6540
http://www.icsa.net

Information Systems Security Association
7044 S. 13th Street
Oak Creek, WI 53154
(414) 768-8000; fax: (414) 768-8001
http://www.issa-intl.org

SIGMOD (Special Interest Group on Management of Data)
Association for Computing Machinery
Headquarters Office
Onc Astor Plaza
1515 Broadway
New York, NY 10036
(212) 869-7440; fax: (212) 944-1318
http://www.acm.org/sigmod

Association for Computing Machinery
Headquarters Office
One Astor Plaza
1515 Broadway
New York, NY 10036
(212) 869-7440; fax: (212) 944-1318
http://www.acm.org

American Society for Industrial Security
1625 Prince Strcct
Alexandria, VA 22314-2818
(703) 519-6200; fax: (703) 519-6299
http://www.asisonline.com

High Technology Crime Investigation Association
3567 Benton Street, Suite 370
Santa Clara, CA 95051
http://htcia.org

The International Association of Computer Investigative Specialists
P.O. Box 21688
Keizer, OR 97307-1688
Phone/Fax: (503) 557-1506
http://cops.org

American Society for Quality
611 East Wisconsin Avenue
P.O. Box 3005
Milwaukee, WI 53201-3005
(800) 248-1946; fax: (414) 272-1734
http://www.asq.org

CORRECTIONS

National Sheriffs' Association
1450 Duke Street
Alexandria, VA 22314-3490
(703) 836-7827
http://www.sheriffs.org

American Deputy Sheriffs' Association
15915 Katy Freeway #350
Houston, TX 77094
(800) 937-7940; fax: (281) 398-5521
http://www.neosoft.com/~adsa

International Association of Court Officers and Services, Inc.
1450 Duke Street, Suite 206
Alexandria, VA 22314-3490
(703) 836-7827
http://www.sheriffs.org/iacos.html

American Jail Association
2053 Day Road, Suite 100
Hagerstown, MD 21740- 9795
(301) 790-3930; fax: (301) 790-2941
http://www.corrections.com/aja

American Probation and Parole Association
P.O. Box 11910
2760 Research Park Drive
Lexington, KY 40578-1910
(606) 244-8203; fax: (606) 244-8001
http://www.csg.org/appa

American Correctional Association
4380 Forbest Boulevard
Lanham, MD 20706-4322
(800) 222-5646
http://www.corrections.com/aca

International Association of Correctional Officers
P.O. Box 81826
Lincoln, NE 68501-1826
(800) 255-2382; fax: (402) 464-5931
http://www.acsp.uic.edu/iaco

EMERGENCY SERVICES

Association of Public Safety Communications Officials International, Inc.
2040 S. Ridgewood Avenue
South Daytona, FL 32119-8437
(904) 322-2500 or (888) APCO 9-1-1;
fax: (904) 322-2501
http://www.apcointl.org

International Municipal Signal Association
P.O. Box 539
165 East Union Street
Newark, NY 14513-0539
(800) 723-4672; fax (315) 331-8205
http://www.imsasafety.org

National Emergency Number Association
47849 Papermill Road
Coshocton, OH 43812
(740) 622-8911; fax: (740) 622-2090
http://www.nena9-1-1.org

International Association of Fire Fighters
1750 New York Avenue NW
Washington, DC 20006
(202) 737-8484; fax: (202) 737-8418
http://www.iaff.org

National Fire Protection Association
1 Batterymarch Park
Quincy, MA 02269-9101
(617) 770-3000 (617) 770-0700
http://www.nfpa.org

National Association of Emergency Medical Technicians
408 Monroe
Clinton, MS 39056-4210
(800) 34-NAEMT; fax: (601) 924-7325
http://www.naemt.org

National Association for Search and Rescue
4500 Southgate Place, Suite 100
Chantilly, VA 20151-1714
(703) 222-6277; fax: (703) 222-6283
http://www.nasar.org

International Rescue and Emergency Care Association
8630 M Guildford, Suite 319
Columbia, MD 21046
(800) 221-3435
http://www.emsrescue.org

Mountain Rescue Association
710 Tenth Street, Suite 105
Golden, CO 80401
http://www.mra.org

United States Lifesaving Association
P.O. Box 366
Huntington Beach, CA 92648
http://www.usla.org

COMPLIANCE INSPECTIONS

American Federation of Government Employees
80 F Street NW
Washington, DC 20001
(202) 737-8700
http://www.afge.org

The National Environmental Health Association
720 S. Colorado Boulevard
South Tower, Suite 970 South
Denver, CO 80246-1925
(303) 756-9090; fax: (303) 691-9490
http://www.neha.org

American Public Health Association
1015 15th Street NW
Washington, DC 20005-2605
(202) 789-5600; fax: (202) 789-5661
http://www.apha.org

Federal Law Enforcement Officers Association
Membership Services
P.O. Box 508
East Northpoint, NY 11731-0472
(516) 368-6117; fax: (516) 368-6429
http://www.fleoa.org

U.S. Park Ranger Lodge
Membership
P.O. Box 151
Fancy Gap, VA 24238
http://home.earthlink.net/~bikeranger

Park Law Enforcement Association
1715 Baltimore, Suite C
Kansas City, MO 64108
(877) PARKLAW or (877) 727-5529
http://www.parkranger.com

National Recreation and Park Association
22377 Belmont Ridge Road
Ashburn, VA 20148-4501
(800) 626-6772 or (703) 858-0784
http://www.npra.org

CONSTRUCTION AND BUILDING INSPECTIONS

International Conference of Building Officials
5360 Workman Mill Road
Whittier, CA 90601-2298
(800) 284-4406 or (523) 699-0541;
fax: (562) 692-3853
http://www.icbo.org

Building Officials and Code Administrators International, Inc.
4051 W. Flossmoor Road
Country Club Hills, IL 60478-5795
(708) 799-2300; fax: (708) 799-4981
http://www.bocai.org

Southern Building Code Congress International, Inc.
900 Montclair Road
Birmingham, AL 35213-1206
(205) 591-1853; fax: (205) 591-0775
http://www.sbcci.org

International Association of Plumbing and Mechanical Officials
20001 E Walnut Drive South
Walnut, CA 91789-2825
(909) 595-8449; fax: (909) 594-3690
http://www.iapmo.org

International Association of Electrical Inspectors
P.O. Box 830848
901 Waterfall Way, Suite 602
Richardson, TX 75080-0848
(927) 235-1455; fax: (972) 235-3855
http://www.vaxxine.com/iaei

American Public Works Association
2345 Grand Boulevard, Suite 500
Kansas City, MO 64108-2641
(816) 472-6100; fax: (816) 472-1610
http://www.pubworks.org

WORKPLACE SAFETY AND SECURITY

National Safety Council
1121 Spring Lake Drive
Itasca, IL 60143-3201
(630) 285-1121; Fax: (630) 285-1315
http://www.nsc.org

American Industrial Hygiene Association
2700 Prosperity Avenue, Suite 250
Fairfax, VA 22031
(703) 849-8888; fax: (703) 207-3561
http://www.aiha.org

The American Society of Safety Engineers
Customer Service
1800 E Oakton Street
Des Plaines, IL 60018
(847) 699-2929; fax: (847) 768-3434
http://www.asse.org

System Safety Society
P.O. Box 70
Unionville, VA 22567-0070
(800) 747-5744
http://www.system-safety.org

Risk and Insurance Management Society, Inc.
655 Third Avenue
New York, NY 10017
telephone: (212) 286-9292
http://www.rims.org

Public Risk Management Association
1815 N. Fort Myer Drive Suite 1020
Arlington, VA 22209
(703) 528-7701; fax (703) 528-7966
http://www.primacentral.org

National Fire Protection Association
1 Batterymarch Park
Quincy, MA 02269-9101
(617) 770-3000; fax: (617) 770-0700
http://www.nfpa.org

International Association of Professional Security Consultants
1444 I Street, Suite 700
Washington, DC 20005-2210
telephone: (202) 712-9043
fax: (202) 216-9646
http://www.iapsc.org

American Society for Industrial Security
1625 Prince Street
Alexandria, VA 22314-2818
(703) 519-6200; fax (703) 519-6299
http://www.asisonline.org

AVIATION SAFETY AND SECURITY

National Air Traffic Controllers Association
1150 17th Street NW, Suite 701
Washington, DC 20036
(202) 223-2900
http://newc.com/natca

National Association of Air Traffic Specialists
11303 Amherst Avenue, Suite 4
Wheaton, MD 20902
(301) 933-6228; fax: (301) 933-3902
http://www.naats.org

Airline Dispatchers Federation
700 13th Street, Suite 950
Washington, DC 20005
(800) OPN-CNTL
http://www.dispatcher.org

Aircraft Rescue & Fire Fighting Working Group
1701 W. Northwest Highway
Grapevine, TX 76051
(817) 329-5092; fax (817) 329-5094
http://www.arffwg.org

International Association of Fire Fighters
1750 New York Avenue NW
Washington, DC 20006
(202) 737-8484; fax: (202) 737-8418
http://www.iaff.org

National Fire Protection Association
1 Batterymarch Park
Quincy, MA 02269-9101
(617) 770-3000; fax: (617) 770-0700
http://www.nfpa.org

American Federation of Police
3801 Biscayne Boulevard
Miami, FL 33137

Fraternal Order of Police
Grand Lodge
1410 Donelson Pike, Suite A17
Nashville, TN 37217
(615) 399-0900; fax: (615) 399-0400
http://www.grandlodgefop.org

APPENDIX IV
PROFESSIONAL CERTIFICATIONS

The following are some organizations where you can get further information regarding professional certifications. In addition, talk with professional individuals and organizations to learn about other professional certifications you might obtain to enhance your employability and advancement opportunities.

You can usually find information about professional certifications at these organizations' web sites. Keep in mind that organizations change web site addresses from time to time. If you come across an address that no longer works, you may be able to find a new one by entering the name of the organization in a search engine.

COMPUTER SECURITY

For information about CISSP—Certified Information Systems Security Practitioner—certification, contact:

(ICS)2, Inc.
415 Boston Turnpike, Suite 105
Shrewsbury, MA 01545-3469
(508) 845-9200; fax: (508) 845-2420
http://www.isc2.org
For information about CCP (Certified Computing Professional) and ACP (Associate Computing Professional) certifications, contact:

Institute for Certification of Computer Professionals
2200 East Devon Avenue, Suite 247
Des Plaines, IL 60018
(847) 299-4227; fax: (847) 299-4280
http://www.iccp.org

CONSTRUCTION INSPECTION

The following organizations offer certification programs for various building/construction plan examinations and inspections:

Building Officials and Code Administrators International, Inc.
4051 W. Flossmoor Road
Country Club Hills, IL 60478-5795
(708) 799-2300; fax: (708) 799-4981
http://www.bocai.org

International Conference of Building Officials
5360 Workman Mill Road
Whittier, CA 90601-2298
(800) 284-4406 or (523) 699-0541;
fax: (562) 692-3853
http://www.icbo.org

Southern Building Code Congress International, Inc.
900 Montclair Road
Birmingham, AL 35213-1206
(205) 591-1853; fax: (205) 591-0775
http://www.sbcci.org

EMERGENCY SERVICES

For information about certification in aircraft rescue and firefighting, contact:

Aircraft Rescue and Firefighting Certification Program
American Association of Airport Executives
4212 King Street
Alexandria, VA 22302
contact: Craig Williams, (703) 824-0500 × 151
http://www.airportnet.org/depts/regaff/arff/arffcert.htm

For information about certification in search and rescue skills as well as specialized rescue skills such as Search and Rescue Medical Responder, contact:

National Association for Search and Rescue
4500 Southgate Place, Suite 100
Chantilly, VA 20151-1714
(703) 222-6277; fax: (703) 222-6283
http://www.nasar.org

For information about professional certification in various fire service job categories, contact:

National Board on Fire Service Professional Qualifications
P.O. Box 492
Quincy, MA 02269

For information about professional registration as certified Emergency Medical Technicians, contact:

National Registry of Emergency Medical Technicians
Rocco V. Morando Building
6610 Busch Boulevard
P.O. Box 29233
Columbus, OH 43229
(614) 888-4484; fax: (614) 888-8920
http://www.bairdit.com/nremt/index.htm

For information about open-water lifeguard certification, contact:

USLA Lifeguard Agency Certification
P.O. Box 9009
San Diego, CA 92169-0009
http://www.usla.org/Train+Cert/agenciescert.shtml

FINANCE AND INSURANCE

For information about CFE—Certified Fraud Examiner—certification, contact:

The Association of Certified Fraud Examiners
The Gregor Building
716 West Avenue
Austin, TX 78701
(800) 245-3321 or (512) 478-9070;
fax: (512) 478-9297
http://www.cfenet.com/index.html

For information about CPA—Certified Public Accountant—certification, contact:

American Institute of Certified Public Accountants
1211 Avenue of the Americas
New York, NY 10036-8775
(212) 596-6200; fax: (212) 596-6213
http://www.aicpa.org

FORENSIC SCIENCE

For information about general examination and trace evidence examination certification, contact:

American Board of Criminalistics
ABC Registrar
P.O. Box 1123
Wausau, WI 54402-1123
(715) 845-3684; fax: (715) 845-4156
http://www.criminalistics.com

For information about forensic document examination certification, contact:

**American Board of Forensic
    Document Examiners, Inc.**
7887 San Felipe, Suite 122
Houston TX 77063
(713) 784-9537
http://www.asqde.org/abfde.htm

For information about advanced or specialized polygraph examination certification, contact:

American Polygraph Association
P.O. Box 8037
Chattanooga, TN 37414-0037
or:
951 Eastgate Loop, Suite 800
Chattanooga, TN 37411-5608
(800) APA-8037; fax: (423) 894-5435
http://www.polygraph.org

For information about certification in crime scene investigation, latent print examination, footwear and tire track examination, bloodstain pattern examination, and other areas, contact:

**International Association for
    Identification**
2535 Pilot Knob Road, Suite 117
Mendota Heights, MN 55120-1120
(651) 681-8566; fax: (651) 681-8443
http://www.iaibbs.org or
http://206.241.48.46

OCCUPATIONAL HEALTH AND SAFETY

For information about CIH—Certified Industrial Hygienist—certification, contact:

American Board of Industrial Hygiene
6015 West St. Joseph, Suite 102
Lansing, MI 48917-3980
(517) 321-2638; fax: (517) 321-4624
http://www.ABIH.org

For information about CSP—Certified Safety Professional—certification, contact:

Board of Certified Safety Professionals
208 Burwash Avenue
Savoy, IL 61874
(217) 359-9263; fax: (217) 359-0055
http://www.bcsp.com

PRIVATE INVESTIGATION

For information about certifications in investigative specializations such as missing persons investigation, surveillance investigation, background investigation, and arson investigation, contact:

**National Association of Investigative
    Specialists, Inc.**
P.O. Box 33244, Austin, TX 78764
(512) 420-9292; fax: (512) 420-9393
http://www.pimall.com/nais/home.html

For information about CLI—Certified Legal Investigator—certification, contact:

**National Association of Legal
    Investigators**
6109 Meadowwood
Grand Blanc, MI 48439
(800) 266-6254; fax: (810) 694-7109
http://www.nali.com

SECURITY

For information about RL (Registered Locksmith), CRL (Certified Registered Locksmith), CPL (Certified Professional Locksmith), and CML (Certified Master Locksmith) certifications, contact:

Associated Locksmiths of America, Inc.
3003 Live Oak Street
Dallas, TX 75205
(214) 827-1701; fax: (214) 827-1810
http://www.aloa.org

For information about CPP—Certified Protection Professional—certification, contact:

**American Society for Industrial
    Security**
1625 Prince Street
Alexandria, VA 22314-2818
(703) 519-6200; fax: (703) 519-6299
http://www.asisonline.org

For information about CPO (Certified Protection Officer) and CSS (Certified Security Supervisor) certifications, contact:

**International Foundation for
    Protection Officers**
3106 Tamiami Trail N, #269
Naples, FL 34103
(941) 430-0534; fax: (941) 430-0533
http://www.ifpo.com

For information about certified alarm technicians, contact:

The National Training School
National Burglar and Fire Alarm
Association
7101 Wisconsin Avenue #901
Bethesda, MD 20814
(800) 702-1NTS
http://www.alarm.org

APPENDIX V
STATE PRIVATE INVESTIGATIVE LICENSING AGENCIES

The following is a list of state agencies that grant private investigator licenses. Addresses and phone numbers are given so you can contact the agency in your state for information. Also check with the city or country clerk and sheriff's or police department where you wish to practice for local licensing requirements.

(Note: Addresses, phone numbers, and web site addresses change from time to time. If an address or phone number is no longer available, contact your state police office for current information.)

Alabama

Alabama has no state private investigator licensing requirement (as of October 1999). Contact the local government clerk and police or sheriff's department where you wish to practice for local licensing requirements.

Alaska

Alaska has no state private investigator licensing requirement (as of October 1999). Contact the local government clerk and police or sheriff's department where you wish to practice for local licensing requirements.

Arizona

Security Guard and Private Investigator Licensing Unit

Arizona Department of Public Safety
2102 West Encanto Boulevard
Phoenix, AZ 85009
(602) 223-2361
http://www.dps.state.az.us/mq/dpsmqpi.htm

mailing address: P.O. Box 6328
Phoenix, AZ 85005

Arkansas

Private Investigator and Private Security Guard Licensing

Arkansas State Police
#1 State Police Plaza Dr.
Little Rock, Arkansas 72209
(501) 618-8610

California

Bureau of Security and Investigative Services

Department of Consumer Affairs
400 R Street, Suite 3040
Sacramento, CA 95814
(800) 952-5210, for application and general information
(916) 322-4000, for licensing and requirement questions
fax: (916) 323-1182
http:/www.dca.ca.gov/bsis

Colorado

Colorado has no state private investigator licensing requirement (as of October 1999). Contact the local government clerk and police or sheriff's department where you wish to practice for local licensing requirements.

Connecticut

Special Licensing and Firearms Unit

Connecticut State Police
1111 Country Club Road
Middletown, CT 06457-9294
(860) 685-8000; fax: (860) 685-8354
http://www.state.ct.us/dps/special.htm

Delaware

Licensing—Private Security and Detective

Delaware State Police
P.O. Box 430
Dover, DE 19903
(302) 739-5991

District of Columbia

Metropolitan Police Headquarters
300 Indiana Avenue NW
Washington, DC 20001
(202) 727-4081; fax: (202) 727-0580

Florida

Division of Licensing
Florida Department of State
P.O. Box 6687
Tallahassee, FL 32314-6687
(850) 487-0482; fax: (850) 488-2789
http://licgweb.dos.state.fl.us/investigations/index.html

Georgia

Board of Private Detective Security Agencies
166 Pryor Street SW
Atlanta, GA 30303-3465
(404) 656-2282; fax: (404) 657-4220
http://www.sos.state.ga.us/ebd-detective

Hawaii

Board of Private Detectives and Guards
Department of Commerce and Consumer Affairs
1010 Richards Street
Honolulu, HI 96813
(808) 586-3000

Idaho

Idaho has no state private investigator licensing requirement (as of October 1999). Contact the local government clerk and police or sheriff's department where you wish to practice for local licensing requirements.

Illinois

Illinois Department of Professional Regulation
320 West Washington Street, 3rd Floor
Springfield, IL 62786
(217) 785-0800; (217) 782-8556,
for application
fax: (217) 782-7645
http://www.state.il.us/dpr

Indiana

Private Detective Licensing Board
Professional Licensing Agency
302 West Washington Street, Room E-034
Indianapolis, IN 46204
(317) 232-2980; fax: (317) 233-5559
*http://www.state.in.us/pla/detect/
index.html*

Iowa

Private Investigative Agency Licensing
Iowa Department of Public Safety
Wallace State Office Building, 3rd Floor
Des Moines, IA 50319-0045
(515) 281-7610; fax: (515) 281-4569
*http://www.state.ia.us/iwd/ris/lmi/files/
licocc/private%20investig ator.htm*

Kansas

Private Detective Licensing
Kansas Bureau of Investigation
Office of the Attorney General
1620 SW Tyler
Topeka, KS 66612
(785) 296-8200
http://www.kapi.org

Kentucky

Kentucky Justice Cabinet
406 Wapping Street, 2nd Floor
Frankfort, KY 40601
(502) 564-7554

Louisiana

State Board of Private Investigator Examiners
2051 Silverside Dr., Suite 190
Baton Rouge, LA 70808
(800) 299-9696 or (225) 763-3556;
fax: (225) 763-3536
http://www.intersurf.com/~lsbpie

Maine

Administrative Licensing Unit
Maine Department of Public Safety
397 Water Street
Gardiner, ME 04345
(207) 624-8775
mailing address: 164 State House
Augusta, ME 04333-0164

Maryland

Licensing Division
Maryland Department of State Police
1201 Reisterstown Road
Pikesville, MD 21208-3899
(410) 799-0191

Massachusetts

Special Licensing Unit
Department of State Police
20 Somerset Street
Boston, MA 02108
(617) 727-6128

Michigan

Private Security & Investigator Section
Michigan Department of State Police
714 S. Harrison Road
East Lansing, MI 48823

Minnesota

Department of Public Safety
Private Detective & Protective Agent
Services Board
444 Cedar Street
St. Paul, MN 55101
(612) 215-1753

Mississippi

Mississippi has no state private investigator licensing requirement (as of October 1999). Contact the local government clerk and police or sheriff's department where you wish to practice for local licensing requirements.

Missouri

Missouri has no state private investigator licensing requirement (as of October 1999). Contact the local government clerk and police or sheriff's department where you wish to practice for local licensing requirements.

Montana

Board of Private Security Patrol Officers and Investigators
Division of Professional and Occupational
Licensing
Arcade Building, Lower Level
111 North Jackson
PO Box 200513
Helena, MT 59620-0513
(406) 444-3728; fax: (406) 444-1667
*http://www.com.state.mt.us/
License/POL/pol_boards/psp_board/
board_ page.htm*

Nebraska

Nebraska Secretary of State
State Capitol, Suite 2300
Lincoln, NE 68509-0800
(402) 471-2384
*http://www.nol.org/home/SOS/
privatedetectives/pd.htm*
mailing address: P.O. Box 94608
Lincoln, NE 68509-4608

Nevada

Private Investigator Board
Office of the Attorney General
100 N. Carson Street
Carson City, NV 89701-4717
(800) 992-0900 or (702) 687-5000
*http://www.leg.state.nv.us.NAC/
NAC-648.html*

New Hampshire

Secretary
New Hampshire State Police License
and Permits Division
10 Hazen Drive
Concord, NH 03301
(603) 271-3575
*http://www.state.nh/us/soiccnh/
private.htm*

New Jersey

Private Detective Unit
State Regulatory Bureau
Division of State Police
P.O. Box 7068
W. Trenton, NJ 08625
(609) 882-2000

New Mexico

Private Investigators Board
2055 Pacheco Street, Suite 400
Santa Fe, NM 87504
(505) 476-7100
*http://www.state.nm.us/rld/b&c/
private_investigators_board.htm*

New York

Division of Licensing Services
NYS Department of State
84 Holland Avenue
Albany, NY 12208
(518) 474-4429
*http://www.dos.state.ny.us/lcns/
pimain.html*

North Carolina

Private Protective Services Board
P.O. Box 29500
3320 Old Garner Rd.
Raleigh, NC 27626-0500
(919) 662-4387; fax: 919-662-4459
*http://www.jus.state.nc.us/Justice/
pps/pps.htm*

North Dakota

Private Investigative & Security Board
North Dakota Governor's Office
600 East Boulevard Avenue
Bismarck, ND 58505-0001
(701) 222-3063 or (701) 328-2200

Ohio

**Division of Real Estate and
     Professional Licensing**
Ohio Department of Commerce
77 South High Street, 20th floor
Columbus, OH 43266-0547
(614) 466-4130 or (614) 466-4100
*http://www.com.state.oh.us/real/
default.htm*

Oklahoma

**Council on Law Enforcement
     Education and Training**
P.O. Box 11476
Oklahoma City, OK 73136-0476
(405) 425-2775 or (405) 425-2770;
fax: (405) 425-7314

Oregon

Oregon Board of Investigators
State Office Building
800 Oregon Street
Portland, OR 97232
(503) 731-4359

Pennsylvania

Pennsylvania has no state private investigator licensing agency (as of October 1999). Contact the local government clerk and police or sheriff's department where you wish to practice for licensing requirements.

Rhode Island

Rhode Island has no state private investigator licensing agency (as of October 1999). Contact the local government clerk and police or sheriff's department where you wish to practice for licensing requirements.

South Carolina

State Law Enforcement Division
Regulatory Services
P.O. Box 21398
Columbia, SC 29221-1398
(803) 737-9000; fax: (803) 896-7041
*http://www.lpitr.state.sc.us/cgi-bin/
ntquest.exe*

South Dakota

South Dakota has no state private investigator licensing requirement (as of October 1999). Contact the local government clerk and police or sheriff's department where you wish to practice for local licensing requirements.

Tennessee

Private Investigators Division
Department of Commerce & Insurance
500 James Robertson Parkway
Nashville, TN 37243-1158
(615) 741-4827
*http://www.state.tn.us/commerce/
rbliStreethtml*

Texas

**Board of Private Investigators &
     Private Security Agencies**
4930 S. Congress, Suite C-305
Austin, TX 78745
(512) 463-5545 or (888) 544-4774;
fax: (512) 452-2307
http://www.tbpi.org
mailing address: P.O. Box 13509
Austin, TX 78711

Utah

**The Division of Law Enforcement and
     Technical Services**
Bureau of Criminal Identification
4501 South 2700 West
Salt Lake City, UT 84119
(801) 965-4404; fax: (801) 965-4756

Vermont

**Board of Private Investigative and
     Security Services**
Office of Professional Regulation
Redstone Building
26 Terrace Street
Montpelier, VT (802) 828-2191

Virginia

Private Security Section
Department of Crinminal Justice Services
P.O. Box 10110
Richmond, VA 13240-9998
(804) 786-4700

Washington

**Private Investigator Licensing
     Program**
Department of Licensing
2424 Bristol Court, SW
Olympia, WA 98504
(360) 664-9070; fax: (360) 753-3747
http://www.wa.gov/dol/bpd/pifront.htm
mailing address: P.O. Box 9649
Olympia, WA 98507-9649

West Virginia

Private Investigator Licensing Division
West Virginia Secretary of State
Building 1, Suite 157-K
1900 Kanawha Blvd. East
Charleston, WV 25305-0770
(304) 558-6000; fax: (304) 558-0900
http://www.state.wv.us/sos/

Wisconsin

Bureau of Direct Licensing & Real Estate—Private Detective
Department of Regulation & Licensing
1400 East Washington Avenue
P.O. Box 8935
Madison, WI 53708-8935
(608) 266-5511, extension 43
http://badger.state.wi.us:80/
agencies/drl/Regulation/html/dod124.html

Bureau of Direct Licensing & Real Estate—Private Detective
Department of Regulation & Licensing
1400 East Washington Avenue
P.O. Box 8935
Madison, WI 53708-8935
(608) 266-5511, extension 43
*http:///badger.state.wi.us:80/agencies/
drl/Regulation/html/dodl24. html*

Wyoming

Wyoming has no state private investigator licensing requirement (as of October 1999). Contact the local government clerk and police or sheriff's department where you wish to practice for local licensing requirements.

APPENDIX VI
PROFESSIONAL PERIODICALS

The following are some professional journals, magazines, newsletters, and other periodicals. Some of these periodicals may be found at college and university libraries or at larger public library branches. Usually, a sample copy may be bought directly from the publisher; call or write a publisher for price information.

Some publishers have limited on-line versions of their publications for free on the Internet. A few of the periodicals listed below only exist on-line. Keep in mind that publishers occasionally change their web addresses. If you come across an address that no longer works, you may be able to find a new one by entering the name of the periodical in a search engine.

To find out about other periodicals, contact professional individuals or organizations. In fact, many professional organizations have their own newsletters, magazines, or journals that are available to the public.

To find out about other periodicals, contact professional individuals or organizations. In fact, many professional organizations have their own newsletters, magazines, or journals that are available to the public.

AVIATION SAFETY

Air Traffic Control Quarterly
Air Traffic Control Association, Inc.
2300 Clarendon Boulevard, Suite 711
Arlington, VA 22201

The NATCA Voice
112 Juliann Drive #5
Wood Dale, IL 60191
The NATCA Voice Online
*http://www.natcavoice.org/news/
index.htm*

Flight Safety Digest
Flight Safety Foundation
601 Madison Street, Suite 300
Alexandria, VA 22314
(703) 739-6700 ext. 103;
fax: (703) 739- 6708
*http://www.flightsafety.org./flight_safety_
digest.html*

COMPLIANCE INSPECTION

Compliance Online
*http://www.ieti.com/taylor/
compliance.html*

Environmental Health Monthly
P.O. Box 6806
Falls Church, VA 22040
(703) 237-2249
*http://www.enviroweb.org/
publications/CCHW/ehm*

Safe and Healthy Workplace
U.S. HealthWorks—Preventive Services
605 Eastowne Drive
Chapel Hill, NC 27514
(800) 334-5478
*http://www.health-hygiene.com/
homepage.htm*

CONSTRUCTION INSPECTION

**Building Standards™, The
International Magazine for
Building Officials**
5360 Workman Mill Road
Whittier, CA 90601-2298
(562) 699-0541; fax: (562) 699-8031
Fax Information Service: (562) 699-4253
http://www.icbo.org

Codes Forum
The International Code Council
900 Montclair Road
Birmingham, AL 35213-1206
(205) 599-9777
http://www.intlcode.org

COMPUTER SECURITY

Cipher
Electronic Newsletter of the Technical Committee on Security and Privacy, A Technical Committee of the Computer Society of the IEEE
*http://www.itd.nrl.navy.mil/ITD/5540/
ieee/cipher*

ComputerWorld (on-line)
http://www.computerworld.com

**The EDP Audit, Control & Security
Newsletter**
CRC Press LLC
Customer Service
2000 NW Corporate Boulevard
Boca Raton, FL 33431
(800) 272-7737 or (561) 994-0555
fax: (800) 374-3401 or (561) 998-9114
http://www.auerbach-publications.com

Information Systems Security
CRC Press LLC
Customer Service
2000 NW Corporate Boulevard
Boca Raton, FL 33431
(800) 272-7737 or (561) 994-0555
fax: (800) 374-3401 or (561) 998-9114
http://www.auerbach-publications.com

ZDNNews (on-line)
http://www5.zdnet.com/zdnn

CORRECTIONS

American Jails
American Jail Association
2053 Day Road, Suite 100
Hagerstown, MD 21740-9795
(301) 790-3930
*http://www.corrections.com/aja/mags/
magazine.html*

Corrections Technology Management
1000 Skokie Boulevard
Wilmette, IL 60091
(800) 843-9764 or (847) 256-8555
fax: (847) 256-8574
http://hendonpub.ia.thirdcoast.net/ctm

Corrections Today
The American Correctional Association
4380 Forbes Boulevard
Lanham, MD 20706-4322
(800) 222-5646
*http://www.correcions.com/aca/cortoday/
index.html*

The Keepers' Voice
P.O. Box 81826
Lincoln, NE 68501-1826
(800) 255-2382; fax: (402) 464-5931
http://www.acsp.uic.edu/iaco

EMERGENCY SERVICES

American Lifeguard Magazine
31 Garfield Avenue
Avon-by-the-Sea, NJ 07717
http://www.usla.org/LGtoLG/mag.shtml

**9-1-1 Magazine: Public Safety
    Communications and Response**
P.O. Box 11788
Santa Ana, CA 92711
(800) 231-8911
http://www.9-1-1magazine.com

Carolina Fire & Rescue Journal
P.O. Box 25828
Charlotte, NC 28229-5828
http://207.71.2.201/cfrj

Dispatch Monthly
P.O. Box 8387
Berkeley, CA 94707-8387
(510) 528-7830; fax: (510) 558-3109
http://www.911dispatch.com

**EMS Insider, The Newsletter for EMS
    Managers**
Jems Communications
P.O. Box 2789
Carlsbad, CA 92018
(800) 266-JEMS or (760) 431-9797;
fax: (760) 431-8176
*http://wwwdotcom.com/jems/
insider/inside1.html*

Emergency Medical Services™
The Journal of Emergency Care Rescue and
Transportation
Summer Communications Inc.
7626 Densmore Avenue
Van Nuys, CA 91406-2042
(800) 224-4367 or (818) 786-4367;
fax: (818) 786-9246
http://www.emsmagazine.com

Fire-Rescue Magazine
Jems Communications
P.O. Box 2789
Carlsbad, CA 92018
(800) 266-JEMS or (760) 431-9797;
fax: (760) 431-8176
*http://wwwdotcom.com/jems/ffnews/
ffnews.html*

**JEMS (Journal of Emergency Medical
    Services)**
Jems Communications
P.O. Box 2789
Carlsbad, CA 92018
(800) 266-JEMS or (760) 431-9797;
fax: (760) 431-8176
*http://wwwdotcom.com/jems/jems/
jems1.html*

NFPA Journal
National Fire Protection Association
1 Batterymarch Park
Quincy, MA 02269-9101
(617) 770-3000; fax: (617) 770-0700
http://www.nfpa.org/journal.html

National Fire & Rescue
3000 Highwoods Boulevard, Suite 300
Raleigh, NC 27604-1029
(919) 872-5040; fax: (919) 876-6531
http://www.nfrmag.com/welcome.html

Wildfire Magazine
International Association of Wildland Fire
P.O. Box 328
Fairfield, WA 99012
fax: (509) 283-2264
*http://www.wildfiremagazine.com/
publications.shtml*

FORENSIC SCIENCE

**The American Journal of Forensic
    Medicine and Pathology**
Lippincott-Raven Publishers
227 East Washington Square
Philadelphia, PA 19106

**American Polygraph Association
    Newsletter**
American Polygraph Association
P.O. Box 8037
Chattanooga, TN 37414-0037
http://www.polygraph.org

Forensic Science International
Elsevier Science
P.O. Box 945
New York, NY 10159-0945
(888) 437-4636 or (212) 633-3730;
fax: (212) 633-3680
*http://www.elsevier.com/inca/
publications/store/5/0/5/5/1/2*

**Scientific Testimony: An Online
    Journal**
http://www.scientific.org

Wound Ballistics Review
International Wound Ballistics Association
P.O. Box 701
El Segundo, CA 90245-0701
(310) 640-6065
http://www.firearmstactical.com/wbr.htm

LAW ENFORCEMENT

American Police Beat Magazine
P.O. Box 382702
Cambridge, MA 02238-2702
(800) 234-0056 or (617) 491-8878;
fax: (617) 354-6515
http://www.apbweb.com

**The Backup: Law Enforcement
    Publication**
418 Coeur d'Alene Avenue
Cocur d'Alene, ID 83814
(208) 765-8062; fax: (208) 765-1059
http://www.thebackup.com

**CLEAF: Computers in Law
    Enforcement Advocacy Forum
    (on-line)**
*http://frontpage.dallas.net/~shinder/
CLEAF/forum.htm*

FBI Law Enforcement Bulletin
http://www.fbi.gov/leb/leb.htm
To subscribe, contact:
Superintendent of Documents
P.O. Box 371954
Pittsburgh, PA 15250-7954
(202) 512-1800; fax: (202) 512-2250

(NOTE: When contacting by mail, be sure to
write "FBI Law Enforcement Bulletin" in your
correspondence—and on your check, if sending
payment for a subscription.)

International Game Warden Magazine
P.O. Box 595
Edwardsville, IL 62025
(618) 656-1090
http://www.hci.net/~decoydoc/info/
IGW.html

Law Enforcement News
John Jay College
899 10th Avenue
New York, NY 10102-1093
http://www.lib.jjay.cuny.edu/len

The Marshals Monitor
http://www.usdoj.gov/marshals/pub.html

The Online Journal for Crime Scene Investigators
http://members.aol.com/identtec/
training.htm

On Patrol
116 West 8th Street, Suite 63
Georgetown, TX 78626
http://www.onpatrol.com

OCCUPATIONAL HEALTH AND SAFETY

AIHA Journal
American Industrial Hygiene Association
2700 Prosperity Avenue, Suite 250
Fairfax, VA 22031
(703) 849-8888; fax: (703) 207-3561
http://www.aiha.org/period.html

BNP's Industrial Safety & Hygiene News
201 King of Prussia Road
Radnor, PA 19089
(610) 964-4000; fax: (610) 964-4947
http://safetyonline.net/ishn/home.htm. or:
http://www.ishn.com

Industrial Hygiene News
Rimbach Publishing Company
8650 Babcock Boulevard
Pittsburgh, PA 15237
(888) 746-2224 or (800) 245-3182
http://www.rimbach.com/ihnpage/
products/PROD.HTM

Industrial Safety & Hygiene News
Suite 201
237 Lancaster Avenue
Devon, PA 19333
(610) 254-0766; fax: (610) 254-9877
http://safetyonline.net/ishn/home.htm

Professional Safety
Journal of the American Society of Safety Engineers
Customer Service
1800 E. Oakton Street
Des Plaines, IA 60018
(847) 699-2929; fax: (847) 768-3434
fax on demand: (800) 380-7101
http://www.asse.org/bprofe.htm

Safety and Health
National Safety Council
1121 Spring Lake Drive
Itasca, IL 60143-3201
(800) 621-7619 or (630) 285-1121;
fax: (630) 285-1315
http://www.nsc.org/pubs/sh.htm

PRIVATE INVESTIGATION

Accounting and Claims: The Newsletter of Investigative Accounting
National Association of Forensic Accountants
500 East Broward Boulevard, Suite 1650
Fort Lauderdale, FL 3394-3033
(800) 523-3680; fax: (305) 467-1381
http://www.nafanet.com

Claims Intelligence Report
64-5249 Kaukea Road
P.O. Box 1650
Kamuela, HI 96743-6180
(808) 885-5090
http://www.maui.net/~berit/CIR.html

P.I. Magazine
755 Bronx
Toledo, OH 43609
(419) 382-0967
http://pimall.com/pimag

SECURITY

Access Control & Security Systems Integration
P.O. Box 12993
Overland Park, KS 66282-2993
(800) 441-0294 or (913) 967-1707
http://www.securitysolution.com

Fire Engineering
(800) 752-9768
http://www.fire-eng.com

SDM (Security Distributing & Marketing) Magazine Online
http://www.sdmmag.com

Security Management Online
American Society for Industrial Security
http://www.securitymanagement.com

Security Online - Security Industry News
http://www.securityonline.com/news.htm

APPENDIX VII
FEDERAL AGENCIES

Federal agencies can be contacted directly for information about careers and job vacancies. Most agencies have web sites on the Internet that provide information. Some agencies even allow you to apply for jobs through the Internet.

Listed below are the federal agencies that were mentioned in this book with addresses to their headquarters in Washington, D.C. along with their web site addresses. These federal agencies also have regional or field offices throughout the country.

Addresses and phone numbers for the branch offices usually can be found at the agencies' web sites. In addition, look in the white pages of telephone books under *United States Government.*

(Note: Federal agencies may change their web addresses from time to time. If you come across an address that no longer works, you may be able to find a new one by entering the name of the federal agency in a search engine.)

Consumer Product Safety Commission
4330 East-West Highway
Bethesda, MD 20814
http://www.cpsc.gov

Environmental Protection Agency
401 M Street SW
Washington, DC 20460
http://www.epa.gov

**Federal Deposit Insurance
  Corporation**
550 17th Street NW
Washington, DC 20429
http://www.fdic.gov

Federal Reserve System
20th and Constitution Avenue NW
Washington, DC 20551
http://www.bog.frb.fed.us

Food and Drug Administration
U.S. Department of Health and Human Services
5600 Fishers Lane
Rockville, MD 20857
http://www.fda.gov

National Park Service
U.S. Department of Interior
1849 C Street NW
Washington, DC 20240
http://www.nps.gov

U.S. Department of Agriculture
14th & Independence Avenue SW
Washington, DC 20250
http://www.usda.gov

- **Agricultural Market Service**
  http://www.ams.usda.gov

Food Safety and Inspection Service
http://www.fsis.usda.gov

U.S. Army Corps of Engineers
U.S. Department of Defense
20 Massachusetts Avenue NW
Washington, DC 20314-1000
http://www.usace.army.mil

U.S. Department of Energy
1000 Independence Avenue SW
Washington, DC 20585
http://www.doe.gov

**U.S. Department of Housing and
  Urban Development**
451 7th Street SW
Washington, DC
http://www.hud.gov

U.S. Department of Justice
950 Pennsylvania Avenue NW
Washington, DC 20530-0001
http://www.usdoj.gov

- **Drug Enforcement Administration**
  Information Services Section (CPI)
  700 Army-Navy Drive
  Arlington, VA 22202
  http://www.usdoj.gov/dea

- **Federal Bureau of Investigation**
  935 Pennsylvania Avenue NW
  Washington, DC 20535
  http://www.fbi.gov

- **Federal Bureau of Prisons**
  320 First Street NW
  Washington, DC 20534
  http://www.bop.gov

- **Immigration and Naturalization
  Service**
  425 I Street NW
  Washington, DC 20536
  http://www.ins.usdoj.gov

- **United States Border Patrol**
  *http://www.ins.usdoj.gov/borderpatrol/
  default.htm*

- **United States Marshals Service**
  Employment and Compensation
  Division
  Field Staffing Branch
  600 Army-Navy Drive
  Arlington, VA 22202-4210
  http://www.usdoj.gov/marshals

U.S. Department of Labor
200 Constitution Avenue NW
Washington, DC 20210
http://www.dol.gov

- **Occupational Safety and Health
  Administration**
  http://www.osha.gov

U.S. Office of Personnel Management
1900 E Street NW
Washington, DC 20415-0001
http://www.opm.gov
—for information about federal careers
  and job vacancies, go to
  http://www.usajobs.opm.gov

U.S. Department of Transportation
400 7th Street
Washington, DC 20590
http://www.dot.gov

- **Federal Aviation Administration**
  800 Independence Avenue SW
  Washington, DC 20591
  http://www.faa.gov

U.S. Department of Treasury
1500 Pennsylvania Avenue NW
Washington, DC 20220
http://www.ustreas.gov

- **Comptroller of the Currency**
  250 E Street SW
  Washington, DC 20219-0001
  http://www.occ.treas.gov

- **Internal Revenue Service**
  1111 Constitution Avenue NW
  Washington, DC 20224
  http://www.irs.treas.gov

- **United States Customs Service**
  1300 Pennsylvania Avenue NW
  Washington, DC 20229
  http://www.customs.ustreas.gov

United States Secret Service
Personnel
1800 G Street NW, Suite 912
Washington, DC 20223
http://www.treas.gov/usss/index.htm

U.S. Postal Inspection Service
United States Postal Service
475 L'Enfant Plaza West
Washington, DC 20260
*http://www.usps.gov/websites/
department/inspect*

APPENDIX VIII
BIBLIOGRAPHY

The following are some books that may help you learn more about careers in law enforcement, security, forensic science, safety, compliance inspections, emergency services, or other protective service field. To learn about other books that may be helpful, ask professionals—individuals and organizations—as well as librarians for suggestions.

CAREER INFORMATION

Bureau of Labor Statistics, *Occupational Outlook Handbook 1997–98 (Bulletin 2500)*. Washington, D.C.: Bureau of Labor Statistics.

Camenson, Blyte, *People Working in Service Businesses*. Lincolnwood, Ill.: VGM Career Horizons, 1997.

Cohen, Paul and Shari, *Careers in Law Enforcement and Security*. New York: The Rosen Publishing Group, Inc., 1995.

Garter, Bob, *Careers in the National Parks*. New York: Rosen Publishing Group, Inc., 1993.

Jakubiak, Joyce (Editor), *Specialty Occupational Outlook: Trade and Technical*. Detroit: Gale Research, Inc., 1996.

Krannich, Ronald L. and Caryl Rae Krannich, *The Best Jobs for the 1990s and into the 21st Century*. Manassas Park, Va.: Impact Publications, 1995.

Lee, Mary Price, Richard S. Lee, and Carol Beam, *100 Best Careers in Crime Fighting*. New York: Macmillan, 1998.

Quintana, Debra *100 Jobs in the Environment*. New York: Macmillan, 1996.

Stinchcomb, James. *Opportunities in Law Enforcement and Criminal Justice*. Lincolnwood, Ill.: NTC/VGM Career Horizons, 1986.

Smith, Russ (Editor), *Federal Careers in Law Enforcement*. Manassas Park, Va.: Impact Publications, 1996.

U.S. Department of Labor, Employment and Training Administration, U.S. Employment Service, *Dictionary of Occupational Titles*. Washington, D.C.: Superintendent of Documents, US GPO, 1991.

COMPUTER SECURITY

Campen, Alan D., Douglas H. Dearth, and R. Thomas Goodden (Editors), *Cyberwar: Security, Strategy, and Conflict in the Information Age*. Fairfax, Va: AFCEA International Press, 1996.

Hafner, Katie and John Markoff, *Cyberpunk: Outlaws And Hackers On The Computer Frontier*. New York: Simon & Schuster, 1991.

Hoffman, Lance J. (Editor), *Rogue Programs: Viruses, Worms, and Trojan Horses*. New York: Von Nostrand Reinhold, 1991.

Hutt, Arthur E., Seymour Bosworth and Douglas B. Hoyt, eds., *Computer Security Handbook* New York, NY: John Wiley & Son, 1995.

Kabay, M. E., *The NCSA Guide to Enterprise Security: Protecting Information Assets*. New York: McGraw-Hill, 1996.

Markoff, John and Tsutomu Shimomura, *Takedown: The Pursuit and Capture of Kevin Mitnick, America's Most Wanted Computer Outlaw-By the Man Who Did It*. New York: Hyperion, 1996.

National Research Council, *Computers at Risk: Safe Computing in the Information Age*. Washington, D.C.: National Academy Press, 1991.

Quarantiello, Laura E., *Cyber Crime: How to Protect Yourself from Computer Criminals*. Lake Geneva, Wisc.: Limelight Books, 1997.

Rosenblatt, Kenneth S., *High-Technology Crime: Investigating Cases Involving Computers*. San Jose, Calif.: KSK Publications, 1995.

Siyan, Karanjiit & Chris Hare, *Internet Firewalls and Network Security*. Indianapolis: New Riders Press, 1995.

Stair, Lila B., *Careers in Computers*. Lincolnwood, Ill.: VGM Career Horizons, 1996.

Winkler, Ira, *Corporate Espionage: What It Is, Why It Is Happening In Your Company, What You Must Do About It*. Rocklin, Calif.: Prima Publishing, 1997.

CORRECTIONS

Abadinsky, Howard, *Probation and Parole: Theory and Practice*. Upper Saddle River, N.J.: Prentice Hall, 1997.

Allen, Harry E. and Clifford E. Simonsen, *Corrections in America: An Introduction*. Upper Saddle River, N.J.: Prentice Hall, 1997.

Champion, Dean J., *Probation, Parole, and Community Corrections*. Upper Saddle River, N.J.: Prentice Hall, 1998.

Goodman, Debbie J., *Enforcing Ethics: A Scenario-Based Workbook for Police and Corrections Recruits and Officers*. Upper Saddle River, N.J.: Prentice Hall, 1998.

Hammer, Hy (Editor), *Probation Officer, Parole Officer*. New York: Arco Publishing, 1996.

McCleary, Richard, *Dangerous Men: The Sociology of Parole*. New York: Harrow & Heston, 1992.

Petersilia, Joan (Editor), *Community Corrections: Probation, Parole and Intermediate Sanctions*. New York: Oxford University Press, 1997.

Steinberg, Eve P., *Correction Officer*. New York: NY: Arco Publishing, 1997.

Strinchcomb, Jeanne B. and Vernon Brittain Fox, *Introduction to Corrections*. Upper Saddle River, N.J.: Prentice Hall, 1998.

CONSTRUCTION INSPECTION

Bannister, Jay, *Building Construction Inspection: A Guide for Architects*. New York: John Wiley & Sons, Inc. 1991.

Kardon, Redwood, *Code Check: A Field Guide To Building a Safe House*. Newton, Conn.: Taunton Press, 1998.

O'Brien, James J., *Construction Inspection Handbook: Quality Assurance and Quality Control.* New York: Von Nostrand Reinhold, 1998.

EMERGENCY SERVICES

American Red Cross, *Emergency Response.* St. Louis, Mo.: Mosby Lifeline, 1997.

American Red Cross, *Lifeguarding: Instructor's Manual.* St. Louis, Mo.: Mosby Lifeline, 1995.

American Red Cross, *Basic Water Rescue.* St. Louis, Mo.: Mosby Lifeline, 1997.

American Rescue Dog Association, *Search and Rescue Dogs: Training Methods.* New York: Howell Books, 1991.

Association Press. *Lifeguard Training, Principles and Administration.* New York: Association Press, 1973.

Braunworth, Brent and Laurence W. Schlanger, *Street Scenarios for the EMT and Paramedic.* Englewood Cliffs, N.J.: Prentice Hall, 1994.

Brewster, B. Chris (Editor), *The United States Lifesaving Association Manual of Open Water Lifesaving.* Englewood Cliffs, N.J.: Prentice Hall, 1995.

Committee, International Fire Service Training Association, Lynne C. Murnane, ed., and Carl E. Goodson (Editor), *Aircraft Rescue and Fire Fighting.* Stillwater, Okla.: Fire Protection Publications, Oklahoma State University, 1992.

Delsohn, Steve, *The Fire Inside: Firefighters Talk About Their Lives.* New York: HarperCollins Publishers, 1996.

Ellis, Jeff, Jill E. White and Ellis Associates Staff, *National Pool and Waterpark Lifeguard CPR Training.* Boston: Jones & Barlett, 1998.

Fox, Deborah, *People at Work in Mountain Rescue.* Parsippany, N.J.: Silver Burdett, 1998.

Hempel, John C. and Steven Hudson, ed., *Manual of U.S. Cave Rescue Techniques.* Huntsville, AL: National Cave Rescue Commission, 1988.

Lloyd, Joan E. and Edwin B. Herman, *EMT: Race for Life.* New York: Ivy Books, 1998.

Miller, Charly D., *Jems EMS Pocket Book,* St. Louis, Mo.: Mosby-Year Book, Inc., 1996.

Mudd-Ruth, Maria, *Firefighting: Behind The Scenes.* Boston: Houghton Mifflin, 1998.

Paul, Caroline, *Fighting Fire.* New York: St. Martin's Press, 1998.

Peterson, Linda, *Emergencies.* Princeton, N.J.: Peterson's, 1993.

Ray, Slim, *Swiftwater Rescue: A Manual For The Rescue Professional.* Asheville, N.C.: CFS Press, 1997.

Tilton, Buck, *Rescue From The Backcountry: Basic Essentials.* Merrillville, Ind.: ICS Books, 1990.

FORENSIC SCIENCE

Abrams, Stanley, *The Complete Polygraph Handbook.* Lexington, Mass.: Lexington Books, 1989.

Curriden, Mark and Benjamin Wecht and Cyril Wecht, *Grave Secrets: A Leading Forensic Expert Reveals the Startling Truth about O.J. Simpson, David Koresh, Vincent Foster, and other Sensational Cases.* New York: E.P. Dutton, 1996.

Di Maio, Dominick J. and Vincent J. M. Di Maio, *Forensic Pathology.* Boca Raton, Fla.: CRC Press, 1993.

Dix, Jay, *Guide to Forensic Pathology.* Boca Raton, Fla.: CRC Press, 1998.

Fisher, David, *Hard Evidence: How Detectives Inside the FBI's Sci-Crime Lab Have Helped Solve America's Toughest Cases.* New York: Dell, 1996.

Ellen, David, *The Scientific Examination of Documents: Methods and Techniques.* Bristol, Penn.: Taylor & Francis, 1997.

Gardner, Robert, *Crime Lab 101: Experimenting With Crime Detection.* New York: Walker, 1992.

Hawthorne, Mark, *First Unit Responder: A Guide to Physical Evidence Collection for Patrol Officers.* Boca Raton, Fla.: CRC Press, 1998.

Heard, Brian, *Handbook of Firearms & Ballistics: Examining & Interpreting Forensic Evidence.* New York: John Wiley & Sons, 1996.

Hermann, Bernd and Susanne Hummel, ed., *Ancient DNA: Recovery and Analysis of Genetic Material from Paleontological, Archaeological, Museum, Medical, and Forensic Specimens.* New York: Springer Verlag, 1994.

Inman, Keith and Norah Rudin, *An Introduction to Forensic DNA Analysis.* Boca Raton, Fla.: CRC Press, 1997.

Kurland, Michael, *How to Solve a Murder: The Forensic Handbook.* New York: Macmillan Publishing, 1995.

Lee, Henry C., *Advances in Fingerprint Technology.* Boca Raton, Fla.: CRC Press, 1992.

Nickell, Joe, *Detecting Forgery: Forensic Investigation of Documents.* Lexington: University Press of Kentucky, 1996.

Saferstein, Richard, *Criminalistics: An Introduction to Forensic Science.* Upper Saddle River, N.J.: Prentice Hall, 1998.

Sheely, Robert, *Police Lab: Using Science To Solve Crimes.* New York: Silver Moon Press, 1993.

Zonderman, Jon, *Beyond the Crime Lab: The New Science of Investigation.* New York: John Wiley & Sons, 1990.

LAW ENFORCEMENT

Baker, Mark, *Cops: Their Lives in Their Own Words.* New York: Pocket Books, 1995.

Torres, Donald A., *Handbook of State Police, Highway Patrols, and Investigative Agencies.* New York: Greenwood Press, 1987.

Bryson, Sandy. *Police Dog Tactics.* New York: McGraw-Hill, 1996.

Butler, Daniel R., Leland Gregory, and Alan Ray, *America's Dumbest Criminals: Based on True Stories from Law Enforcement Officials Across the Country.* Nashville, Tenn.: Rutledge Hill Press, 1995.

Dempsey, Tom, *Contemporary Patrol Tactics: A Practical Guide For Patrol Officers.* Englewood Cliffs, N.J.: Prentice Hall Career & Technology, 1992.

Eden, R.S. *K9 Officer's Manual.* Bellingham, Wash.: Detselig Enterprises Ltd.: Temeron Books, 1993.

Fisher, David, *Hard Evidence: How Detectives Inside The FBI's Sci-Crime Lab Have Helped Solve America's Toughest Cases.* New York: Simon & Schuster, 1995.

Geberth, Vernon J., *Practical Homicide Investigation: Tactics, Procedures, and Forensic Techniques.* Boca Raton, Fla.: CRC Press, 1996.

Greenberg, Keith Elliot, *Bomb Squad Officer: Expert With Explosives.* Woodbridge, Conn.: Blackbirch Marketing, 1995.

Jeffreys, Diarmuid. *The Bureau: Inside the Modern FBI.* Boston: Houghton Mifflin Co., 1995.

Kessler, Ronald, *The FBI: Inside The World's Most Powerful Law Enforcement Agency.* New York: Pocket Books, 1993.

Lonsdale, Mark V., *Sniper II: A Guide to Special Response Teams.* Los Angeles: Specialized Tactical Training Unit, 1992.

Lyman, Michael D., *Criminal Investigation: The Art and the Science.* Upper Saddle River, N.J.: Prentice Hall Career & Technology, 1998.

Ragle, Larry, *Crime Scene.* New York: Avon Books, 1995.

Rowland, Desmond and James Bailey, *The Law Enforcement Handbook.* New York: Facts On File, Inc., 1985.

Snow, Robert L. *Swat Teams: Explosive Face-Offs With America's Deadliest Criminals.* New York: Plenum Press, 1996.

Stroud, Carsten, *Deadly Force: In The Streets with the U.S. Marshals.* New York: Bantam Books, 1996.

Weston, Paul B., Kenneth M. Wells, and Marlene Hertoghe, *Criminal Evidence for Police.* Englewood Cliffs, N.J.: Prentice Hall, 1995.

Winkleman, Katherine K., *Police Patrol.* New York: Walker and Co., 1996.

OCCUPATIONAL HEALTH AND SAFETY

American Industrial Hygienists Association, "Balancing Work, Health, Technology & Environment: Careers in Industrial Hygiene," (pamphlet). Fairfax, Va.: American Industrial Hygienists Association, 1997.

American Industrial Hygienists Association, "Industrial Hygienists: Dedicated to Protecting People in the Workplace and the Community" (brochure). Fairfax, Va.: American Industrial Hygienists Association.

Della-Giustina, Daniel E. *Safety and Environmental Management.* New York: Von Nostrand Reinhold, 1996.

Geller, Scott, *The Psychology of Safety: How to Improve Behaviors and Attitudes on the Job.* Radnor, Penn.: Chilton Book, 1996.

Goetsch, David L., *Occupational Safety and Health in the Age of High Technology: For Technologists, Engineers, and Managers.* Englewood Cliffs, N.J.: Prentice Hall, 1996.

Kaletsky, Rick, *OSHA Inspections: Preparations and Response.* New York: McGraw Hill, 1996.

Koren, Herman. *Illustrated Dictionary of Environmental Health and Occupational Safety.* Boca Raton, Fla.: CRC Press/Lewis Publishers and National Environmental Health Association, 1996.

Levin, Lester. *An Investigative Approach to Industrial Hygiene: Sleuth at Work.* New York: Von Nostrand Reinhold, 1996.

Peterson, Robert D. and Joel M. Cohen, *The Complete Guide to OSHA Compliance.* Boca Raton, Fla.: CRC Press, 1995.

Richardson, Margaret. *Managing Worker Safety and Health Excellence.* New York: John Wiley & Sons, Inc., 1997.

PRIVATE INVESTIGATION

Akin, Richard H., *The Private Investigator's Basic Manual.* Springfield, Ill.: Charles C. Thomas Publisher, 1979.

Anderson, Kingdon Peter, *Undercover Operations: A Manual for the Private Investigator.* Boulder, Colo.: Paladin Press, 1998.

Dempsey, John S., *An Introduction to Public and Private Investigations.* Minneapolis/St. Paul, Minn.: West Publishing Co., 1996.

Golec, Anthony M., *Techniques of Legal Investigation.* Springfield, Ill.: Charles C. Thomas Publisher, 1995.

Kirk, Paul Leland and John D. Dehaan, *Kirk's Fire Investigation, 4th ed.* Upper Saddle River, N.J.: Prentice Hall, 1997.

National Fire Protection Association, *NFPA 921, Guide for Fire and Explosion Investigations: 1998 ed.* Boston: National Fire Protection Association, 1998.

Redsicker, David R. and John J. O'Connor, *Practical Fire and Arson Investigation, 2nd ed.* Boca Raton, Fla.: CRC Press, 1996.

Riddle, Kelly E., *Insurance Investigations From A to Z, The Investigator's Guide to Uncovering Insurance Fraud.* Austin, Texas: Thomas Investigative Publications, Inc., 1998.

Thomas, Ralph D., *How to Investigate by Computer: 1998 ed.* Austin, Texas: Thomas Investigative Publications, Inc., 1998.

SECURITY

Bintliff, Russell L., *The Complete Manual of Corporate and Industrial Security.* Englewood Cliffs, N.J.: Prentice Hall, 1992.

Burstein, Harvey, *Introduction to Security.* Englewood Cliffs, N.J.: Prentice Hall, 1994.

Fischer, Robert J. and Gion Green, *Introduction to Security.* Woburn, Mass.: Butterworth-Heinemann, 1992.

Heitert, Robert D., *Security Officer's Training Manual.* Englewood Cliffs, N.J.: Prentice Hall, 1993.

Horan, Donald J., *The Retailer's Guide to Loss Prevention and Security.* Boca Raton, Fla.: CRC Press, 1996.

Icove, David, Karl Seger, and William Von Storch, *Computer Crime.* Sebastopol, Calif.: O'Reilly and Associates, 1995.

June, Dale L., *Introduction to Executive Protection.* Boca Raton, FL: CRC Press, 1998.

Lonsdale, Mark V., *Bodyguard: A Guide to VIP Protection.* Los Angeles: Specialized Tactical Training Unit, 1995.

Kehoe, Edward P., *The Security Officer's Handbook.* Boston: Butterworth-Heinemann, 1994.

Purpura, Philip P., *Criminal Justice: An Introduction.* Boston: Butterworth-Heinemann, 1997.

Purpura, Philip P., *Security and Loss Prevention: An Introduction.* Boston: Butterworth-Heinemann, 1990.

Rathjen, Joseph E., *Locksmithing: From Apprentice to Master.* New York: McGraw-Hill, 1995.

APPENDIX IX
INTERNET RESOURCES

The selected Internet web sites and web pages listed below can help you learn more about the occupations that are described in this book. Most of the web sites are of police departments, fire departments, organizations, companies, etc. Some web pages are articles about the various professions or about particular issues that are written by professionals. Other web pages provide links to other relevant web sites such as schools, associations, and agencies.

Upon completion of this book, the web sites below were all accessible. However, please keep in mind that web masters may remove web sites or web pages at any time or change web addresses. If you come across an address that no longer works, you may be able to find a new address by entering the name of the organization or web page title in a search engine.

Remember, the web sites mentioned here are just a sampling of what you can find on the Internet. They're just to get you started!

GENERAL INFORMATION

Career Information

These web sites can give you
  further general information
  about various careers:

**1998–99 Occupational Outlook
  Handbook**
Bureau of Labor Statistics
http://stats.bls.gov/ocohome.html

**California Employment Development
  Department, California
  Occupational Guides**
*http://www.calmis.cahwnet.gov/file/
  OCCGUIDE*

**The Princeton Review Guide to Your
  Career**
http://www.review.com/career/find

Job Banks

These web sites provide current
  listings for job opportunities:

**United States Office of Personnel
  Management**
http://www.usajobs.opm.gov

Federal Jobs Digest Home Page
http://www.jobsfed.com

America's Job Bank
http://www.ajb.dni.us/index.html

**America's Job Bank and State Job
  Banks**
http://safetynet.doleta.gov/jobbank.htm

Welcome to CareerMosaic
http://www.careermosaic.com

The Monster Board
http://www.monster.com

COMPLIANCE
INSPECTIONS

**American National Standards Institute
  (ANSI)**
http://web.ansi.org/default.htm

NIOSH Institute
http://www.cdc.gov/niosh

Aviation Safety Inspectors

Aviation Safety Information
http://www.faa.gov/asafety.htm

Aviation Safety Links
http://www.aviation.org/links.htm

**FAA Aviation Safety Inspector's
  Handbooks**
http://www.faa.gov/avr/afs/faa/home.html

FAA Technical Center
http://www.tc.faa.gov

*Building and Construction
Inspectors*

Code Check
http://www.CodeCheck.com

The International Code Council
http://www.codes.org

**"A Day in the Life of a Building
  Inspector," by Redwood Kardon**
http://www.codecheck.com/day.htm

**"Mission Possible: Inspectors Lead the
  Way," by Stuart H. Hersh**
*http://www.icbo.org/
  Building_Standards_Online/read.c
  Gi?file=./Features_and_Articles/
  archive/899913580.arc
  hive&action=Features_and_Articles*

Food Inspectors

The-Inspector.com
http://www.the-inspector.com

Health and Safety Inspectors

**The Environmental Health Officers
  Page**
http://www.ceejay.demon.co.uk

Environmental Health Resources
*http://www.CDC.GOV/nceh/
  programs/ehserve/EHSA/tome/TOC.htm*

NSF International
http://www.nsf.org

Public Safety sites
*http://www.geocities.com/
  Heartland/834/links.htm*

**The Public Health
  Inspector/Environmental Health
  Officer Home Page**
*http://www.ualberta.ca/~dalden/
  Index.html*

Park Rangers

Florida Ranger Home Page
http://www.geocities.com/Yosemite/6935

**National Park Service Human
Resource Employment Information**
http://www.nps.gov/personnel/index.html

Park Rangers on the Web
*http://www.geocities.com/~parkranger/
index.htm*

COMPUTER SECURITY

**Alta Associates (data and internet
security jobs)**
*http://www.altaassociates.com/
datajobs.html*

CMP Net, The Technology Network
http://www.techweb.com

**COAST (Computer Operations, Audit
and Security Technology)
Homepage**
*http://www.cs.purdue.edu/coast/
coast.html*

COAST Hotlist: Computer Security
*http://www.cs.purdue.edu/coast/
coast.hotlist*

**Computer Crime Investigation
bibliography, Global Technology
Research, Inc.**
*http://www.aracnet.com/~gtr/archive/
investigate.html*

**Computer & Internet Security
Resources**
http://virtuallibrarian.com/legal

**Computer Crime Investigation
Bibliography (Global Technology
Research, Inc.)**
*http://www.aracnet.com/~gtr/archive/
investigate.html*

The Computer Museum
http://www.tcm.org

Computer Society
http://computer.org

Cybercop Home Page
http://www.cybercop.org

**En Garde Systems—Secure Zone
(the computer security information
center)**
http://www.securezone.com

Gateway to Information Security
http://www.securityserver.com

**Information Systems Audit and
Control Association**
http://www.isaca.org/ainfo.htm

**Lawrence Livermore National
Laboratory Computer Security
Technology Center**
http://ciac.llnl.gov/cstc/CSTCHome.html

Readings on Computer Crime
*http://swissnet.ai.mitt.edu/6095/
readings-crime.html*

**Security Groups and
Organizations—Computer Security**
*http://www.alw.nih.gov/Security/
security-groups.html*

Welcome to Securityinfo.com
http://www.securityinfo.com/index.html

**"Secret Agents Need Not Apply," by
William P. Densmore**
*http://www.computerworld.com/home/
print9497.nsf/al
ISL9712car9171FA*

Computer Forensic Specialist

**Computer Crime Investigation
Bibliography (Global Technology
Research, Inc.)**
*http://www.aracnet.com/~gtr/archive/
investigate.html*

**"An Explanation of Computer
Forensics," by Judd Robbins**
*http://www.knock-knock.com/
forens01.htm*

**"Computer Crime: An Emerging
Challenge for Law Enforcement,"
by David L. Carte, Ph.D and Andra
J. Katz, Ph.D**
*http://www.inso-sec.com/access/
infoseczh.html-ssi*

**"Forensic Computer Examination," by
Daniel Hooper**
http://www.pimall.com/nais/n.forcom.html

**"Investigating Computer Crime is
Every Department's Concern," by
Bill Clede**
*http://ourworld.compuserve.com/
homepages/BillC/comprim.html*

Quality Assurance Specialist

**International Organization for
Standardization**
http://www.iso.ch

Quality Related Sites
*http://www.asq.org/abtquality/qualsite/
qualsite.html*

Software Testing Institute
http://www.ondaweb.com/sti

**"What Does a Software Quality
Assurance Professional do
anyway?"**
*http://www.computerworld.com/
features/970818bfd_qanda.html*

CORRECTIONS

The Corrections Connection
http://www.corrections.com

**Florida State University School of
Criminology Criminal Justice
Links**
http://www.criminology.fsu.edu/cj.html

National Institute of Corrections
http://www.nicic.org/inst

Overview of the U.S. Court Systems
http://www.wld.com/ldusover.htm

Prisons
http://www.prisons.com

**A Worldwide Resource for the
Corrections Industry**
http://www.prisons.com

U.S. Parole Commission
http://www.usdoj.gov/uspc/parole.htm

Parole Officer/Probation Officer

**Probation and Parole Officer/Agent
Forum**
*http://members.aol.com/paroleino/
index.htm*

**"Dealing with Hardened Ex-cons no
9-to-5 job," by Andy Furillo**
*http://www.sacbee.com/news/beetoday/
newsroom/local /111697/local104.html*

EMERGENCY SERVICES

Emergency Services WWW Site list
http://www.jellis.com/arp/links.htm

Fire & Emergency Information Network
http://www.fire-ems.net

Kentucky EMS Connection
http://hultgren.org

Kentucky EMS Connections: EMS Weblinks
http://hultgren.org/Library/links1.htm

Links to Public Safety Sites
http://www.geocities.com/Heartland/2834/links.html

Other Fire/Rescue/EMS Websites
http://warhammer.mcc.virginia.edu/cars/othrsite.html

Public Safety Information and Training Links
http://www.geocities.com/CollegePark/Lab/9211/public.htm

Red Cross
http://www.redcross.org

Welcome to Jems Communications
http://wwwdotcom.com/jems/mainmenu.html

"The Call," by Jennifer Simperman
http://www.warhammer.mcc.virginia.edu/cars/super.html

Airport Firefighter

ARFF ALERT Home Page
http://www.conknet.com/arffwg/arff1.html

International Aviation Fire & Rescue Information
http://www.fire.org.uk/aviation

Thirty Thousand Feet—Aviation Rescue and Firefighting Links
http://extra.newsguy.com/~ericmax/rescue.htm

Emergency Medical Technician

The Emergency and Medical Services Website
http://www.thirdstreet.com/ems/emsstate.html

"What is an Emergency Medical Technician, and How Do I Become One," Kentucky EMS Connection.
http://www.hultgren.org/Library/EMT_faq.htm

Firefighter

Directory of Fire Museums
http://www.firemuseumnetwork.org/dir.html

International Association of Fire Chiefs
http://www.ichiefs.org

Federal Emergency Management Agency (FEMA)
http://www.fema.gov

Fire Departments Online
http://www.fhouse.org/ffdept.htm

Fire Department Training Network
http://www.firescue.com

Firefighting-Dot-Com
http://www.firefighting.com

Firefighters Historical Society
http://www.fireengine.net/default.htm

Fire National Academy
http://www.usfa.fema.gov

Fire Protection and Information Sites
http://www.worldsafety.com/FireA.html

Stamford (CT) Fire and Rescue
http://www.stamfordfire.com

U.S. Fire Administration
http://www.usfa.fema.gov

Women in the Fire Service Network
http://www.geocities.com/Wellesley/4699

Lifeguard

Aquatic Safety and Water Rescue Issues
http:www.lifesaving.com/articles.htm

Ellis & Associates Lifeguarding, Acquatics
http://www.jellis.com

Ocean Safety and Lifeguard Services Division of the City and County of Honolulu's Emergency Services Department
http://www.aloha.com/~lifeguards/wsafety.html

Links to Lifeguarding Resources
http://www.ualberta.ca/~dhay/lifeguarding/links.htm

Lifeguarding links
http://www.ualberta.ca/~dray/lifeguarding/links.htm

Lifesaving and EMS Links
http://www.lifesaving.com/links.htm

Los Angeles County Lifeguard Operations
http://pen2ci.santa-monica.ca.us/laco-lifeguard

Red Cross—Health & Safety Services Acquatics
http://www.redcross.org/hss/aquatics.html

San Diego Lifeguard Services
http://www.sannet.gov/lifeguards

"The Ten Commandments of a Lifeguard."
http://www.cs.uwm.edu/~nicolas/lifeguard/tencommands.html

"What Does a Lifeguard Do?"
http://www.users.bigpond.com/Background/what.htm

Public Safety Dispatcher

Dispatcher's Glossary
http://www.911dispatch.com/glossary.html

Emergency Communications Center
http://www.911dispatch.com

Public Safety Dispatcher Job Office
http://www.911dispatch.com/job_file/job.html

Randy's 911 Dispatcher Page.
http://members.tripod.om/~dispatcher/index2.html

"Police Dispatching & Emergency Communications," by Matt Betz
http://www.1adventure.com/Law/career/dispatch.htm

"What Does It Take to be a Police Dispatcher?" Metro-Dade Police Department
http://www.mdpd.metro-dade.com/career2.html

Rescue Technician

SAR (Search and Rescue) Contacts
http://brmrg.med.virginia.edu/sar_contacts/index.html

Charlottesville-Albemarle Rescue Squad, Inc.
http://warhammer.mcc.Virginia.edu/cars/index.html or *http://www.warhammer.mcc.virginia.edu/cars*

Emergency Search and Rescue Links
http://www.esar.org/links.html

Emergency Services Sites
http://krypton.mankato.msus.edu/oakly/EMS.html

International Association of Dive Rescue Specialists
http://www.cet.com/~bell/iadrs.html

National Institute for Urban Search and Rescue
http://emergencyservices.com/niusr/press.html

SAR Teams
http://web20.mindlink.net/sarinfo/Sarteams.htm

SARINFO!
http://web20.mindlink.net/sarinfo

SARINFO's Tech Tips
http://web20.mindlink.net/sarinfo/Sartechs.htm

FORENSIC SCIENCE

American Society of Crime Lab Directors
http://www.ascld.org

Carpenter's Forensic Science Resources
http://www.tncrimlaw.com/forensic

Center for Forensic Studies
http://www.phys.edu/~menzel

Crimes and Clues: The Art and Science of Criminal Investigations
http://crimeandclues.com

Forensic Education and Consulting
http://pw2.netcom.com/~nrbiocom/Forensic_EducationConsulting/index.htm

Forensic Enterprises, Inc. (Hayden B. Baldwin)
http://www.feinc.net

Forensic Science Bookstore
http://www.corpus-delicti.com/general.html

Forensic Science Education Resource
http://www.geocities.com/CapeCanaveral/6635

Forensic Science related sites
http://gwis.circ.gwu.edu/~forensics/sites.html

Forensic Science web page
http://users.aol.om/mirror/page112.htm

The Forensic Sciences Foundation, Inc.
http://www.aafs.org

Institute of Science and Forensic Medicine
http://www.gov.sg/moh/isfm

Reddy's Forensic Home Page
http://haven.ios.om/~nyrc/homepage.html

UC Riverside Police
http://police2.ucr.edu

Zeno's Forensic Page
http://users.bart.nl/~geradts/forensic.html

Crime Scene Technician

California Criminalist Institute
http://www.ns.net/dleccil

"Crime Scene Interpretation," by M/Sgt. Hayden B. Baldwin
http://www.feinc.net/cs-int.htm

"Crime Scene Investigation"
http://police2.ucr.edu/csi.htm

"Crime Scene Processing Protocol," by M/Sgt. Hayden B. Baldwin
http://www.feinc.net/cs-proc.htm

"Crime Scene Response Guidelines: Personnel Duties and Responsibilities. "Crime Scene Processing Protocol," by M/Sgt. Hayden B. Baldwin
http://www.police2.ucr.edu/respon2.htm

"Examination and Documentation of the Crime Scene," by George Shiro
http://police2.ucr.edu/evidenc2.htm

Forensic Scientist/Criminalist

Forensic News from Iowa (Iowa Division International Association For Identification (I.A.I.)
http://hometown.aol.com/FNEWSIA/index.html

International Association of Bloodstain Pattern Analysts
http://www.shadow.net/~noslow/index.html

International Footprint Association
http://www.mscomm.com/~footprint

Latent Print Examination: Fingerprints, Palmprints, Footprints. . . .
http://onin.com/fp

Questioned Document Examination Page of Emily J. Will
http://www.webmasters.net/qde

Norwitch Document Laboratory
http://www.QuestionedDocuments.com/

The Society of Forensic Toxicologists
http://www.soft-tox.org/

U.S. Bureau of Alcohol, Tobacco, and Firearms
http://www.atf.treas.gov

"Firearms and Toolmarks Examinations" by Joe Saloom
http://www.adfs.com/firearms.htm

Forensic Pathologist

"Death Investigation"
http://www.adfs.com/di.htm

"So You Want to be a Medical Detective?" National Association of Medical Examiners
http://www.thename.org/career/career.htm

Polygraph Examiner

Academy of Forensic Psychophysiology
http://www.polygraph.net

"Standards and Principles of Practice," American Association of Police Polygraphists.
http://www.polygraph.org/states/aapp/aappsapp.htm

"What happens in a polygraph test?"
http://www.truthorlie.com/whatpoly.html

LAW ENFORCEMENT

American Police Hall of Fame and Museum
http://www.aphf.org

FBI Academy
http://www.fbi.gov/academy/academy.htm

Federal law enforcement career information
http://comp.uark.en/~explorer/fedjobs

Hampton Roads Law Enforcement Forum
http://www.exis.net/hrlef/resource.htm

Federal Law Enforcement Training Center
http://www.ustreas.gov/fletc

International Association of Chiefs of Police
http://www.theiacp.org

Law Enforcement Careers web site
http://www.gate.net/~fcfjobs

Law Enforcement Links
http://www.leolinks.com

Law Enforcement Sites On The Web Part 2 Of 8 (Ira Wilsker)
http://www.ih2000.net/ira/ira2.htm

Maryland Institute of Criminal Justice
http://www.micj.com

Mickey's Place in the Sun Law and Law Enforcement (links)
http://peole.delphi.com/mickjyoung/law.html

Mickey's Crime and Crime Prevention Resources
http://people.delphi.com/mickjyoung/crime.html

National Troopers Coalition
http://www.alpha.com/NTC.HTM

WD9T's Law Enforcement Page
http://members.primary.net/~carlos30/officer.html

WD9T's Favorite Law Enforcement Sites
http://members.primary.net/~carlos30/lawlinks.html

"Entering the World of Law Enforcement" by Lance R. Atchison
http://www.powernet.net/~kinsly/AtchisonEnterprises/background.htm

"How to Get a Job in Criminal Justice," Southeastern Louisiana University
http://www.selu.edu/Academics/Depts/Sociology/cjadv3.htm

"Law Enforcement Careers" The American Hall of Fame and Museum
http://www.aphf.org/p12_lawenfcareer.htm

Airport Officer

Aviation Security site
http://home.eunet.no/~steinesa/sesindex.htm

Civil Aviation Security
http://cas.faa.gov

Metropolitan Nashville Airport Authority
http://www.nashintl.com/police.html

Bike Patrol Officer

Bicycle Patrol, Highland Park Police Department
http://www.highlandpark.org/HPKCity/police/bike.htm

"Police on Bikes® Fact Sheet," IPMBA
http://www.bikeleague.org/ipmba2/factsht.htm

"Stealth Riding or Visibility: An Option and a Choice," by Noel T. Sevilla
http://www.1adventure.com/Law/police/specunit/stealth.htm

"Bicycling Cops Wheel Close to Community," by Deborah VanPelt
http://www.tampatrib.com/news/thur10fm.htm

"Bike 54, Where Are You?" by Kyle R. Wood
http://www.seattletimes.com/extra/browse/altbike_072596.html

Bomb Technician

Bureau of Alcohol, Tobacco, and Firearms
http://www.atf.treas.gov/core/explarson/explarson.htm

Explosive Ordnance Disposal Information Page
http://www.geocities.om/Pentagon/4347

FBI Explosives Unit—Bomb Data Center Lab
http://www.fbi.gov/lab/bombsum/eubdc.htm

Hazardous Devices School
http://www.logsa.army.mil/ommcs/hdd.html

Tallahassee Police Department Bomb Unit
http://www.state.fl.us/cityhtl/patrol/eod.html

Unofficial Anderson County Sheriff's Department
http://www.flywrite.net/ACSO

"Bomb Busters"
http://www.nextstep.com/stepback/cycle10/125/bomb.html

"Bomb Threats and Physical Security Planning" (National Security Institute)
http://nsi.org/Library/Terrorism/bombthreat.html

"The Chicago Police Department Bomb Squad," by Steve Macko
http://www.emergency.com/chbmbsqd.htm

Border Patrol Agent

"Border Patrol Hiring FAQ"
http://www.pe.net/~harris/bp_faq.html

LINKS—National Border Patrol Council, Local 1613, San Diego, California
http://www.borderpatrol1613.org/links.htm

The Border Patrol
http://www.usbp.com

Border Patrol Explorers
http://members.aol.com/post1997/post199.html

United States Border Patrol on-line application
http://www.usajobs.opm.gov/bpa1.htm

United States Border Patrol unofficial website
http://www.pe.net/~haris/bp_hire.html

Canine Handler

Bo's Nose Knows: The K-9 Unit of Valparaiso IN
http://www.netnitco.net/users/perrys/ww2

k9 Connection
http://www.k9nation.net/k9connection

Police Dog Home Page
http://www.policeK9.com

Conservation Officer

The Game Wardens Place
http://www.hci.net~decoydoc

Pennsylvania Association of Conservation Officers
http://www.pawco.org

Utah Division of Wildlife Resources Law Enforcement
http://www.nr.state.ut.us/dwr/!enfo.htm

Washington Game Warden Association
http://www.gamewardens.com

"So You Want to be a Fish and Wildlife Officer," by Tony De La Torre
http://www.gamewarden.com/WANNABE.HTM

"The Guardians," by WCO Vance Dunbar
http://www.pawco.org/WantToBe/Guardians.htm

Crime Prevention Specialist

National Crime Prevention Council
http://www.ncpc.org

Texas Crime Prevention Association
http://www.tcpa.org

Police and Sheriffs

Charleston Police Department
http://www.charleston-pd.org/

Community Policing Consortium
http://www.communitypolicing.org

Cop Link dot Com
http://www.coplink.com/Home.htm

CopNet
http://www.copnet.org/index.html

Detective Bureau, Palm Springs (CA)
http://www.palm-springs.org/html.detectivebureau.html

Detective Division, Burlington (MA) Police Department
http://www.bpd.org/detect.htm

Detective Division, Des Moines Police Department
http://www.ci.des-moine.ia.us/police/index.htm

Guide to Becoming a Police Officer
http://www.trk9cop.com/copjob.htm

Links site, National Sheriffs' Association
http://www.sheriffs.org/links.html

Metropolitan Nashville Police Department
http://www.nashville.net/~police/index.html

National Troopers Coalition (official Directory of Patrol and State Police Sites)
http://www.sover.net/~tmartin/state.htm

Official Directory of Patrol and State Police Sites
http://www.sover.net/~fmartin/state.htm

Police and Detectives
http://www.exchangenet.com/howto/career/R0418.html

Police Guide
http://www.policeguide.com

Police Officer Quotes
http://www.qni/~nixter/powrd.html

The Police Officer's Internet Directory
http://www.officer.com

Police Operations page
http://emergency.com/policepage.htm

San Jose Police Department, California
http://www.sjpd.org/index2.html

Streetcops
http://shell.acmenet

"10 Reasons Cops Are Different"
http://www.heavybadge.com/10reason.htm

"The New Blue Line: The Making of a Virginia Beach Police Officer," by Mike Mather
http://www.pilotline.com/special/blueline

"Oklahoma sheriffs and Their Duties," by Bill Noland
http://www.geocities.com/CapitolHill/3831/duties.htm

"Who Am I? I Am a Cop," by Sgt. Richard J. Brown
http://shell.acmenet.net/~streetcops/acop.htm

Observer

Air Support Unit, Placer County Sheriff's Department
http://www.iwn.com/pcso/airsppt.htm

Los Angeles County Sheriff's Aero Bureau
http://wwwlasd.org/divisions/index.html

What's Up in Aviation, Riverside Police Department
http://www.pe.net/~rpd/av-lttr.html

"Infrared Tracking and Nightsun Slaving," by Investigator Robert Mulhall
http://ci.pasadena.ca.us/departments/helicopter.html

SWAT Sniper

The Sniper Hootch
http://www.magicnet.net/ocso/swat/snipe.html

Florida SWAT Association
http://www.floridaswat.org

Metro Nashville Police SWAT Team
http://www.nashville.net/~police/citizen/swat.html

Metro SWAT, Special Operations Division, Hancock County (MS) Sheriff's Department
http://www.geocities.com/CapitolHill/Lobby/3681/hcsosniper.html

U.S. Special Operations
http://www.specialoperations.com/sniper.html

ROTORS S.W.A.T. World
http://userdata.acd.net/cantlon.bob/swat.htm

"SWAT School," by Mark K. Anderson
http://fairfieldweekly.com/articles/swatschool.html

PRIVATE INVESTIGATION

"The Guide to Background Investigators"
http://www.usetheguide.com

InfoGuys—Private Investigators and Investigations
http://www.infoguys.com/

Investigator Link Page
http://www.intersurf.com/~lizcabom/links2.html

Investigative Research International
http://www.fatfind.com/fraud.htm

National Association of Background Investigators
http://background.org

North American Investigations
http://www.detectiveworld.com

Private Eye International
http://www.pi-intrntional.com

Private Investigation Short Course
http://www.pimall.com/nais/sc.html

The Private Investigators Mall
http://www.pimall.com/

"How to Become a Private Investigator," by William D. Shelton
http://www.infoguys.com/private_investigators/how_to.html

Arson Investigator

Arson Investigations (Unified Investigators and Sciences Inc.)
http://www.uis.-usa.com/arson.html

California Conference of Arson Investigators
http://www.arson.org

Fire and Arson Investigation Information (Corporate Investigative Services, Ltd.)
http://www.mhv.net/~dfriedman/arson/welcome.html

Fire and Arson Investigation Resource Page
http://home.earthlink.net/~dliske/index.html

International Association of Arson Investigators links
http://www.fire-investigators.org/links.htm

We Tip National Arson Page
http://www.wetip.com/wetip/natarson.htm

"Preserving Evidence: The Responsibility of the Investigator," by Dan McIntyre, Michael Lane, and Thomas Williams
http://www.mhv.net/~dfriedman/arson/spoilait.htm

Financial Investigator

Fighting Fraud and Corruption
http://www.ex.ac.uk/~RDavies/arian/scandals/fight.html

Web Bound—Accounting
http://www.webbound.com/links/accounting.html

"Following the Trail of Financial Statement Fraud," by Jeffrey Johnston
http://www.c-m-d.om/arc5.htm

"What Is Forensic Accounting"
http://www.forensicaccountant.com/one.htm

Insurance Investigator

The Insurance Career Center
http://www.connectyou.com/talent/41160/full_url_serve/grow2.htm

Insurance Claims Investigations Resources
http://www.pimall.com/nais/insrec.html

Legal Investigator

NAIS Private Investigation Web Short Course
http://www.pimall.com/nais/sc.html

"The Legal Investigator Defined" by National Association of Legal Investigators
http://www.nali.com/html/legal_investigator.htm

Personal Protection Specialist

Bodyguard Home Page
http://www.iapps.org

Bodyguards
http://www.bodyguards.com/index3.htm

National Bodyguard Network
http://www.samurai-warrior.com

"Duties of the Bodyguard"
http://www.bikenet.com/bookcase/bodyguard/bg4.htm

Store Detective

Loss Prevention Links
http://www.nettrace.com.au/resource/security/loss.html

Loss Prevention Specialists, Inc.
http://www.lossprevention.com/main.html

Manahan.Net Loss Prevention
http://www.geocities.com/~manahan-net/security.html

National Retail Federation
http://www.nrf.com

Retail Loss Prevention Exchange
http://www.nji.com/u/danno/rlpx.htm

"Retail Loss Prevention and Safety," by James Bruce Hamilton III
http://www.1adventure.com/Law/career/retail.htm

SAFETY

Aviation Safety

Airport News and Training Network
http://www.airportnet.org

Air Transport Association—Airline Handbook
http://www.air-transport.org/handbk

Air Traffic Control Association, Inc.
http://www.atca.org/join.htm

American Association of Airport
  Executives
http://www.airportnet.org

Aviation Home Page
http://www.avhome.com

Aviation Safety Information from the
  Federal Aviation Administration
http://www.faa.gov/asafety.htm

Civil Air Patrol
http://www.cap.af.mil

FAA Aviation Career Series:
  Government Careers
http://www.tc.faa.gov/ZDV/gcd.html

FAA Aviation Education Resource
  Library
*http://www.faa.gov/education/
resource.htm*

Flight Safety Foundation
http://www.flightsafety.org

"Air Traffic Control Specialist: Duties
  and Responsibilities of the Air
  Traffic Controller." Long Beach
  Air Control Traffic Control Tower.
http://www.ghofn.org/~iah-atct/atcs.htm

"Automation of Air Traffic Control
  System Must Account for Air
  Controllers" (National Research
  Council)
http://www.nas.edu/whatsnew/2672.html

"Job Description of the Aircraft
  Dispatcher," by Airline Dispatchers
  Federation
*http://www.dispatcher.org/dispatch/
dispatch.html*

"NAS (National Airspace Systems)
  Concept of Operation: Perspectives
  of NAS Participants," Center for
  Advanced Aviation System
  Development
*http://www.caasd.org/Research/
Arch/Overview/perspec.htm*

Workplace Safety

Industrial Hygiene and Occupational
  Health, San Diego State University
*http://www.rohan.sdsu.edu/dept/gsphsdsu/
web/ih.html*

Environment, Safety, and Health
  Home Page
http://www.if.uidaho.edu/ehs/safety.html

How to Environment/Quality/Safety
  resources
http://www.smartbiz.com/sbs/cats/env.htm

Insurance Career Center: Safety and
  Loss Control
http://connectyou.com/resource/safety.htm

Occupational Safety and Health Net
http://osh.net/index.htm

PERI Risk Institute
http://www.riskinstitute.org

Risk Management Services
http://www.hj.lane.edu/hr/rm/about.html

Safety Online
http://www.safetyonline.net

Safety and Health Professional and
  Standards Organizations
http://osh.net/proorg.htm

"Insurance Careers: What is a Safety
  Career All About?"
*http://www.connectyou.com/resource/
safe1.htm*

"How Loss Control Programs
  Function In and Improve Risk
  Retention Group Profitability"
*http://www.meadowbrookinsgrp.com/
RRR.html*

"What does the future hold for
  Careers In Safety & Health: Tips
  and tactics for getting where you
  want to be," by Dave Johnson,
  Editor, and Adrienne Burke,
  Senior Editor
http://www.metnyaiha.org/aihajob.html

SECURITY

ClearStar Security Network
http://www.clearstar.com

Ken and Linda Schwartz Home Page
  (has fire protection links)
http://www.xnet.om/~kensfire

National Security Association Inc.
http://www.nsai.org

National Security Institute
http://nsi.org

The Online Security Academy
  (security information and links)
http://www.goodnet.com/~ej59217

Security Industry online
http://www.siaonline.org

Security Online
http://www.securityonline.com

Security Resource Net
http://nsi.org

Welcome to Batan Fire Protection
  Classroom
http://www.batan.com/class.htm

Welcome to the Security Resource
  Center
http://www.securityresource.com

Index of F.A.Q. (Locksmithing)
*http://www.premier1.net/~nwlakey/
faqnwls.htm*

"Careers in Security: Security
  Specialty Areas"
*http://www.asisonline.org/
careerspecialty.html*

"What is Security?"
http://www.asisonline.org/careerwhat.html

"Nailing Down Hardware Store
  Security," by James P. Falk, CPP
*http://www.securitymanagement.com/
library/000268.html*

"What Does a Locksmith Do?"
*http://www.aloa.org/about/what
does.html*

APPENDIX X
GLOSSARY

The following is a list of abbreviations, acronymns, and terms that you may find useful as you learn more about the protective sevices industry.

AAFS	American Academy of Forensic Sciences
AAPP	American Association of Police Polygraphists
ACA	American Correctional Association
ACFE	Association of Certified Fraud Examiners
ACM—SIGMOD	Association for Computing Machinery—Special Interest Group on Management of Data
ACP	Associate Computing Professional
ACSR	The Association of Crime Scene Reconstruction
ADF	Airline Dispatchers Federation
ADSA	American Deputy Sheriffs' Association
AFP	American Federation of Police
AFTE	Association of Firearm and Toolmark Examiners
AICPA	American Institute of Certified Public Accountants
AIHA	American Industrial Hygiene Association
AJA	American Jail Association
ALEA	Airborne Law Enforcement Association
ALOA	Associated Locksmiths of America, Inc.
APA	American Polygraph Association
APHA	American Public Health Association
APCO	Association of Public Safety Communication Officials International, Inc.
APPA	American Probation and Parole Association
APWA	American Public Works Association
ARFFWG	Aircraft Rescue & Fire Fighting Working Group
ARC	Certified Arson Reconstructionist
arson	A crime in which a building or property is intentionally set on fire for the purpose of getting insurance money.
ASCLD	American Society of Crime Laboratory Directors
ASCP	American Society of Clinical Pathologists
ASIS	American Society for Industrial Security
ASOSA	American Special Operations Sniper Association
ASQ	American Society for Quality
ASQDE	American Society of Questioned Document Examiners
ASSE	The American Society of Safety Engineers
assets	Money, jewelry, buildings, stocks and bonds, databases, and other property that makes up a person's or group's wealth.
ATF	Alcohol, Tobacco, and Firearms Bureau (a federal agency)
beat	The part of a city, county, state, or region that a law enforcement officer is assigned to patrol.
BOCA	Building Officials and Code Administrators International, Inc.
cadet	A student officer who is in training, particularly at a training academy.
CAI	Certified Arson Investigator
CBI	Certified Background Investigator
CCP	Certified Computing Professional
CDE	Certified Document Examiner
CFE	Certified Fraud Examiner
CHI	Certified Homicide Investigator
CICI	Certified Insurance Claims Investigator
CIH	Certified Industrial Hygienist
CISSP	Certified Information Systems Security Practitioner
CLI	Certified Legal Investigator
CML	Certified Master Locksmith
Emergency communication center	The place where telephone calls from the public for emergency and non-emergency police, fire, rescue, and medical assistance are received and transferred to the appropriate agencies.
compliance inspection	An examination of a home, business, organization, or institution to make sure that government laws and regulations and/or organizational policies and rules are being followed.
computer security	The security measures that are used to safeguard computer hardware, software, and databases from crashes, theft, accidents, natural disasters, and so on.

correctional facility	A jail, prison, or other institution where persons are locked up because they are fulfilling a sentence for breaking a law or are waiting for a court trial.
corrections	The program of treating and rehabilitating criminals that involves custody in a correctional facility, probation, and parole.
CPA	Certified Public Accountant
CPE	Certified Polygraph Examiner
CPL	Certified Professional Locksmith
CPO	Certified Protection Officer
CPP	Certified Protection Professional
CPR	Cardiopulmonary Resuscitation; an emergency life-saving technique to help persons who have stopped breathing.
communication skills	The speaking and listening abilities a worker needs to successfully perform his or her job duties.
crime lab	A laboratory where physical evidence (such as fingerprints, bullets, blood, fiber, and documents) is examined and analyzed.
crime prevention programs	Safety and security programs that are designed to help prevent or lower the risk of crime in a community.
crime scene	The place where a theft, burglary, murder, arson, or other crime has happened.
criminal investigation	An examination of a crime (such as burglary, murder, counterfeiting, terrorism, or rape) to learn who committed the crime and when, where, how, and why it was committed. Evidence is found to link a suspect to the crime so that he or she can be tried in court.
criminalist	An expert who uses scientific techniques to examine and analyze physical evidence.
critical thinking skills	The abilities to examine and analyze a situation and make sensible judgments on how to handle the situation.
CRL	Certified Registered Locksmith
CSP	Certified Safety Professional
CSS	Certified Security Supervisor
data security	The safeguarding of all facts and figures that are stored in a computer system.
DEA	Drug Enforcement Administration
defendant	A person who is being sued in a civil trial or is being accused of having committed a crime.
dispatch	A message for police, firefighting, emergency medical service, or other unit to go a particular location to provide emergency or non-emergency assistance.

EMS	Emergency Medical Services; a network of services that provides immediate aid and medical care to a community.
EMT	Emergency Medical Technician
EOD unit	Explosive Ordinance Disposal unit
evidence	Any type of proof that links a person to a crime.
expert witness	A professional who is recognized as having special skills and knowledge about his or her field such as trace evidence examination, computer forensics, or psychology.
FAA	Federal Aviation Administration
FBI	Federal Bureau of Investigation
felony	A serious crime (such as arson, murder, rape, kidnapping, drug dealing, or counterfeiting) that results in being sentenced to a state or federal prison.
fire protection	The safeguarding of a building or complex with equipment and devices as well as building designs to control or extinguish fires.
FLEOA	Federal Law Enforcement Officers Association
FOP	Fraternal Order of Police
forensic science	The use of scientific methods and procedures to examine and analyze physical evidence in order to link the evidence to a crime, suspect, or crime scene.
HTCIA	High Technology Crime Investigation Association
IAAI	International Association of Arson Investigators
IABTI	International Association of Bomb Technicians and Investigators
IACA	International Association of Crime Analysts
IACIS	The International Association of Computer Investigative Specialists
IACO	International Association of Correctional Officers
IACP	International Association of Chiefs of Police
IAEI	International Association of Electrical Inspectors
IAFCI	International Association of Financial Crimes Investigators
IAFF	International Association of Fire Fighters
IAI	International Association for Identification
IAPMO	International Association of Plumbing and Mechanical Officials
IAPPS	International Association of Personal Protection Specialists
IAPSC	International Association of Professional Security Consultants

IASIU	International Association of Special Investigation Units
IAWP	International Association of Women Police
ICBO	International Conference of Building Officials
IFPO	International Foundation for Protection Officers
IHIA	International Homicide Investigators Association
ILA	Institutional Locksmiths Association
IMSA	International Municipal Signal Association
information system	All computer hardware, software, and databases that belong to an organization.
INFOSEC	Information Systems Security; the safeguarding of all databases that are stored in an organization's computer systems.
INIA	International Narcotics Interdiction Association
INS	Immigration and Naturalization Service
interpersonal skills	The abilities a worker needs to communicate and work well with others on the job.
interrogation	The questioning of a person who is suspected of committing a crime.
IPMBA	International Police Mountain Bike Association
IRECA	International Rescue and Emergency Care Association
IRS	Internal Revenue Service
ISCPP	International Society of Crime Prevention Practitioners
ISSA	Information Systems Security Association
IUPA	International Union of Police Associations
K9	Canine
latent prints	An impression of a set of fingerprints that has been taken from the surface of an object.
LEBA	Law Enforcement Bicycle Association
LETA	Law Enforcement Thermographers' Association
misdemeanor	A crime such as vandalism and disorderly conduct that results in a fine and/or a short sentence in a correctional facility.
MRA	Mountain Rescue Association
NAATS	National Association of Air Traffic Specialists
NADE	National Association of Document Examiners
NAEMT	National Association of Emergency Medical Technicians
NAIS	National Association of Investigative Specialists
NALI	National Association of Legal Investigators

NAME	National Association of Medical Examiners
NAPWDA	North American Police Work Dog Association
NASAR	National Association for Search and Rescue
NATCA	National Air Traffic Controllers Association
NAWEOA	North American Wildlife Enforcement Officers Association
NBFAA	National Burglar and Fire Alarm Association
NDEOA	National Drug Enforcement Officers Association
NEHA	The National Environmental Health Association
NENA	National Emergency Number Association
networking	Making contacts with peers in your profession and with other professionals who may provide you with resources.
NFPA	National Fire Protection Association
NRMET	National Registry of Emergency Medical Technicians
NRPA	National Recreation and Park Association
NSA	National Sheriffs' Association
NSC	National Safety Council
NSPE	National Society of Professional Engineers
NSPII	National Society of Professional Insurance Investigators
NTOA	National Tactical Officers Association
offender	A person who has been committed a crime.
on call	Being available for immediate duty at any time of the day or night.
OPM	U.S. Office of Personnel Management
OSHA	Occupational Safety and Health Administration
personal protection service	Safeguarding an individual who is being threatened, harassed, or in any danger or risk.
plaintiff	A person or group who is suing another person or group.
physical security	The use of security guards, security systems, and security procedures to safeguard people, buildings, and property.
PLEA	Park Law Enforcement Association
private investigation	An examination of an event, person's history, situation, or other problem that private detectives perform for a client.
PRIMA	Public Risk Management Association
problem solving skills	The abilities a worker needs to analyze problems and find ways to solve them.
prosecution	The city, county, or federal government attorneys who are responsible for proving to a jury that a person has committed a crime.

public safety department
A city, county, or state agency that oversees one or more protective services such as law enforcement, fire protection, emergency services, and inspections.

RIMS
Risk and Insurance Management Society, Inc.

RL
Registered Locksmith

SBCCI
Southern Building Code Congress International, Inc.

search and rescue
The operation of looking for and rescuing lost, missing, stranded, or injured persons in urban and wilderness settings as well as in natural or man-made disasters.

security system
The procedures, manpower, and equipment and devices that are used to provide protection for an individual, home, business, organization, or institution.

SFPE
Society of Fire Protection Engineers

SSS
System Safety Society

surveillance
Following, observing, and collecting information about a person because he or she is suspected of committing a crime.

suspect
A person who is believed to have committed a crime.

SWAT
Special Weapons and Tactics

teamwork skills
The abilities a worker needs to work as part of a group on a job or work project.

undercover
Being in disguise so as to spy on a person or group that is suspected of doing criminal activity.

USLA
United States Lifesaving Association

USPCA
United States Police Canine Association

victim
A person against whom a crime has been committed.

warrant
An order issued by a court judge to allow law enforcement officers to search for evidence, arrest a suspect, or perform another specific act.

witness
A person who has personal knowledge of a suspect or a crime.

INDEX